THE IMPACT
OF GLOBAL
AND REGIONAL
INTEGRATION ON
FEDERAL SYSTEMS

THE IMPACT OF GLOBAL AND REGIONAL INTEGRATION ON FEDERAL SYSTEMS

A Comparative Analysis

EDITED BY
HARVEY LAZAR, HAMISH TELFORD
AND RONALD L. WATTS

Published for the Institute of Intergovernmental Relations
School of Policy Studies, Queen's University
by McGill-Queen's University Press
Montreal & Kingston • London • Ithaca

National Library of Canada Cataloguing in Publication

The impact of global and regional integration on federal systems : a comparative analysis / edited by Harvey Lazar, Hamish Telford and Ronald L. Watts.

Includes bibliographical references.
ISBN 1-55339-003-2 (bound).—ISBN 1-55339-002-4 (pbk.)

1. Federal government. 2. Globalization. 3. Regionalism.
I. Lazar, Harvey II. Watts, Ronald L. III. Telford, Hamish, 1964-
IV. Queen's University (Kingston, Ont.). Institute of Intergovernmental Relations.

JC355.I46 2003   321.02   C2003-905456-X

Contents

Preface

The processes of globalization and regionalization of recent decades have spawned a huge literature, both academic and beyond. Some of that literature focuses on whether these processes represent a genuinely new international phenomenon or whether they constitute a return to earlier historical periods. Some of it is devoted to assessing the effects on public policy ("race to the bottom" argument, for instance) or on the quality of our democracies (so-called "democratic deficit" is an illustration).

This volume is motivated by a curiosity about the effects of these internationalizing processes on federal systems of governance. Do the processes of global and regional integration reinforce the kind of political pacts that underlie federal societies and polities or do they jeopardize them? Are they inherently centralizing or decentralizing? How do they affect identities? How would these questions be answered in different federations? Would the answers be different in multilingual and unilingual federations? Would they differ between wealthy and not-so-wealthy polities or between large and small ones?

These are large and important questions that potentially affect the workings of all federal systems. Close to half of the world's population lives in countries with federal systems of governance. And as federal solutions are being mooted as the appropriate answer, or at least part of the answer, for many of the global hot spots (such as Afghanistan, Iraq, and the Philippines), the relevance of these questions is likely to increase.

This volume tackles these questions in respect of eight different federal and federal-type political entities. The authors of the individual chapters are all leading federalism scholars in their own countries. They participated in a conference in December 2000 in Ottawa where early drafts of their papers were presented and discussed. The papers were subsequently revised for publication here.

My co-editors and I have organized the volume by grouping each of the federal or federal-type entities into one of four categories. They are:

centralizing, decentralizing, hour-glassing, and transforming. By its very nature, any typology simplifies a complex reality and each of the political entities examined here no doubt exhibits elements of all four categories. Nonetheless, on balance we consider that we have captured the broad tendencies exhibited in each federation. This does not necessarily mean, however, that global and regional integration — our independent variables in these studies — are responsible for the broad tendencies we have observed. The decentralization in Canada and India, for example, may have been initially motivated by domestic factors, but it is being reinforced by global and or regional integration. And while we have included the United States in the centralizing category, the author of that chapter is of the view that centralization there has been driven mainly, perhaps even exclusively, by domestic factors and not by global and regional integration.

We also chose to adopt a dynamic description (i.e., centraliz*ing*) as opposed a static description (i.e., centraliz*ed*), even though the actual movement in most cases is modest and in some cases the movement may have actually ceased. Switzerland, for example, might not be actively de-centralizing at present, but as a highly decentralized federation it seemed appropriate to include Switzerland in the same category as Canada and India, both of which are decentralizing.

For full information on the larger project within which this volume falls, the reader can go to the following Web site: http://www.iigr.ca/. Support for the project came from several sources including the Government of Canada, the Government of Alberta, the Business Council on National Issues (as it was then known), and the Social Sciences and Humanities Research Council of Canada.

We thank those associated with the publication process in the School of Policy Studies at Queen's University, including Mark Howes, Valerie Jarus, and Marilyn Banting. Their expertise has been crucial to the completion of this volume.

Harvey Lazar
Director
Institute of Intergovernmental Relations
Queen's University
October 2003

1

Divergent Trajectories: The Impact of Global and Regional Integration on Federal Systems

Harvey Lazar,
Hamish Telford and
Ronald L. Watts

Globalization has been a major buzzword since the fall of the Berlin Wall, and various commentators have suggested that it will eventually spell the end for the nation-state model. This fear has perhaps been felt more acutely in federal states, which frequently struggle with questions of unity. This volume considers whether there is good reason for these fears by analyzing the impact of global and regional integration — we prefer these terms to the more generic globalization — through a series of case studies that cover a range of federal and federal-type political systems.

Three main conclusions emerge from the case studies. First, a substantial majority of the federations we have examined have adapted to global and regional integration change pressures without major transformations to their institutions. In most cases, the political actors have been able to modify old institutions for new purposes. This observation is less true, however, of some European political systems. Second, in all but one of the regions covered here, Europe again being the exception, there is little evidence that global and regional integration are fostering new transnational identities between the federal polities we examined and their global and regional partners. At the same time, such integration appears to be modestly exacerbating traditional political cleavages *within* some federations, particularly multinational federations. Third, the impact of global and regional integration is not unidirectional. In any single federation, it will cause effective authority to move upward in some cases and to move downward or outward in others. The net effect is to support greater centralization in some federations and enhanced decentralization in others. That is, the trajectory of its impact is variable. But in no case has recent global and regional integration reversed the pre-existing centralization or decentralization process within a federation. In sum, to date at least, the federal systems of governance we examined have had the flexibility to adapt to international change pressures without undermining the federal bargains that are fundamental to their stability.

GLOBAL AND REGIONAL INTEGRATION IN THEORY AND PRAXIS

There are widely differing views about the ways in which "globalization" and "regionalization" may influence governance in the twenty-first century. At one end of a continuum are those who see the thickening of global and continental networks as heralding the demise or dramatic weakening of the state system as a primary basis for governing the peoples of the world (Ohmae 1990, 1995; Cable 1995; Friedman 1999 and 2000). At the other end are those who suggest that the state is likely to be a dominant institution for a long time to come (Keohane and Nye 2000). In between there are many permutations and combinations of views about the way in which these forces may play out (Keating 2003; Blatter 2001).

Many questions arise from the processes of global and regional integration (GARI). In the case of global integration, how different is its contemporary version relative to previous eras of global connectedness? How should modern globalization itself be governed (Keohane and Nye 2000)? Are globalization and regionalization in competition with one another or are they complementary and mutually reinforcing processes? What are their impacts on domestic governance?

It is a particular subset of the last question that this volume examines, namely, the way in which the forces that are propelling global and regional integration are affecting federal-type systems of governance.[1] What differences are these forces having on the institutions and behaviour of federal systems?

While there is a huge and growing literature about the effects of global and regional integration on democracy (Held 1998), we are not aware of any systematic examination of effects on systems of federal governance. The interest in effects on democracy is hardly surprising given that democratic values and processes are dominant for much of the world. At the same time, there are strong links between federalism and democracy. Federal solutions are frequently used to balance majority and minority interests, and if the constitutional bargains that underlie federal systems are impacted adversely by external forces, then the basic democratic consent of the affected political entities (whether at the level of federation or constituent unit) may be adversely affected. An enquiry into the effects of global and regional integration on federal systems of governance may thus also contribute to the literature on democratic impacts, even if only indirectly.

In tackling these questions, we assumed relatively broad definitions of global and regional integration. In both cases, the thickening of transborder connections and networks is interpreted here to be multidimensional, including growing economic and financial integration, closer ideational ties (including transborder sharing of ideas and values), and an increasing measure of cultural linkage, abetted in part by the emergence of English as a global *lingua franca* and in part by new technologies that allow for instantaneous communication among peoples around the world. Other linkages, for example, those associated with the environment and the spread of disease were also considered to be part of the multidimensional character of these phenomena. And in response to all of this is a growing body of international law, thus enhancing political interdependence across borders.

In some respects regional integration can be seen as a geographically limited subset of global integration, both being driven by similar forces, including the economics and technology referred to above. But regional integration can also be seen and used politically, culturally, and economically as a bulwark against global integration, serving as an instrument for geographically connected states to retain elements of distinctiveness and independence against homogenizing pressures that are global. Thus, in posing our questions, we did not necessarily assume that globally and regionally integrating impacts would be similar.

The initial motivation for this volume arose from a curiosity as to whether the constitutional and political bargains that underlie most federal systems have been, or are likely to be, altered substantively by the processes of global and regional integration. Consider, for example, federations in which the constituent units may have *de jure* sovereignty (law-making power), and have traditionally exercised that sovereignty (*de facto*) for a particular class of issue. Items like public health, regulation of services, or law enforcement might be examples. In the current international environment, with the growing connectedness between economies, societies, cultures, and polities that are spatially separate, there may be pressures for aspects of these once domestic issues to be dealt with at the regional or even global level for functional reasons. In turn, this can result in international agreements (e.g., for controlling the spread of infectious disease or for removing barriers to trade in services). Typically, but not in all cases, only the federal government in the federation will have the constitutional power to negotiate and ratify such agreements. Through the avenue of treaty powers, therefore, federal governments may now be able to influence significantly classes of issues that were previously wholly or mainly within the purview of constituent units, thus upsetting the federal bargain.

An equally plausible case can be made, however, for the opposite conclusion. Constituent units may find that the internationalization of their constitutional responsibilities provides a *de facto* basis for them to enter the world of international diplomacy. In this alternative hypothesis, constituent units acquire an increasing international personality and effectively encroach on what had been the national government's monopoly or near-monopoly in the realm of international relations. There are also other reasons to think that international integration, particularly economic integration, may privilege constituent units. Improved access to regional and global markets may reduce the dependence of states, provinces, cantons, and Länder on federation-wide markets and thus facilitate the economic autonomy of such governments relative to their federal governments, while at the same time creating a strong rationale for them to become internationally involved.

There are other possible impacts as well. As a result of global or regional integration, for example, issues that were once within the domain of federal or constituent units may increasingly be subject to private forms of international governance or expert governance — technical solutions for issues that are at least in part technical, like how best to fight an international epidemic or to assess risk in relation to environmental challenges or genetically modified foods (Coleman and Porter 2000). While such networked governance may have much to commend it, for purposes of this study what is relevant is its potential to weaken the territorial basis of governance and to diminish the effective role for autonomous decision-making by any individual order of government, or decision-making by national and constituent units acting jointly. In so doing, it also has the potential to impact on the nature of the constitutional bargain that underlies federal systems of governance.

In short, a range of plausible arguments can be proffered about the likely effects of global and regional integration. Some suggest that national governments may be privileged whereas others believe that constituent units are emerging relatively stronger. And others still make the case that all orders of government may be ceding effective authority to other actors — be they international organizations, non-governmental organizations (NGOs), or the private sector — as governance becomes more networked. The world of governance is rarely tidy, however, and our "going in" assumption was that all of these impacts may be happening to one degree or other. Part of what this volume is about, therefore, is to assess whether, as a matter of fact, the net impact of all these and other effects is changing the equilibrium point in the federations studied. Is global and regional integration centralizing or decentralizing federal political systems? Is GARI changing the fundamental constitutional bargain that is the bedrock of many federal states? And are the related attachments of the different peoples and regions to their common enterprise (the federal state) becoming stronger or weaker? And whatever the answer to these last two questions, what kinds of adjustment mechanisms are emerging, whether in political institutions or political behaviour, that are associated with these results? Thus, for most purposes, the federal system of governance is our dependent variable while growing regional and global integration are our independent variables.

The internationalization of activities that were once largely domestic is not, of course, a new phenomenon. The blurring of domestic and foreign policy has been with us for a long time. But what could be new is the sheer volume, weight, and speed of new international governance as this process has intensified. That is, more and more of the issues that were once the function of national governments or constituent units can only be effectively dealt with on some sort of international basis, whether global, regional or subregional. In Dani Rodrik's words, the "economic geography" of the world is becoming increasingly disconnected from its "political geography" (Rodrik 1997). David Held argues similarly when he writes that political communities and civilizations can no longer be characterized simply as "discrete worlds"; they are enmeshed and entrenched in complex structures of overlapping forces, relations, and movements (2001).

If, as a matter of fact, Rodrik and Held are right and this disconnect is growing, the equilibrium point in federal systems may indeed be undergoing some kind of fundamental change, either becoming more dominated by their general (federal) governments as a result of their exclusive or overriding role in international relations or, conversely, more dominated by constituent units as their role in international relations expands. Or the equilibrium point could be changing for reasons related to a growth in private or expert governance. To the extent that such a shift is proceeding, this may well signal better governance from a functional perspective. But no system of governance is preoccupied solely with concerns for efficiency and effectiveness. In democratic polities, at least, the expanse of the territory over which a system of governance operates must also have the consent of the people who occupy it. In turn, this raises issues of identity and related symbolism (Blatter 2001). And in federal systems, that territory is variable. For some purposes, the whole of the federation is the relevant territory. For other purposes, the constituent units of the federation (states, provinces, cantons, etc.) and local communities (municipalities) are the relevant territory. In federations, the distribution of powers between orders of government is designed to reflect the desired balance between local and territorial self-rule, on the one hand, and shared rule on the other. And in the ideal case, the constitution will capture and reflect the fine balance between self-rule and shared rule (Elazar 1987; Watts 1998).

Well-established federations will normally have found an equilibrium between the concepts of self-rule and shared rule while newer ones will at least be attempting to do so. What is of interest here is what happens when this equilibrium bumps up against an agent of change, namely, the rapidly growing processes of globalization and/or regionalization. We can thus re-state our above questions in the following terms. Is the balance between self- and shared rule changing? Does this shift have legitimacy in the eyes of the people or are the federations in question experiencing stress as old relationships are eroded by new forces? How are federal systems adapting to global and regional integration? What difference, if any, are the processes of global and regional integration making to federal governance?

The above discussion does not imply that, as a matter of fact, federal systems are being substantively altered. These systems may be relatively stable notwithstanding the change pressures exerted by global and regional integration. This could be the case, for example, if the disconnect between economic geography, or what we shall henceforth refer to as functional or instrumental geography, and political geography is being resolved (more often than not in favour of the existing political geography). Or stated slightly differently, when in competition, state or substate sovereignty may be trumping the functional argument for pooling or ceding such sovereignty to the international or supranational level. There may be "'useful inefficiency'" that leaves room for traditional equilibrium points to be preserved (Keohane and Nye 2000). Of course, not all inefficiency is useful and to the extent that state and substate sovereignty preclude the satisfactory management of serious policy challenges, we might anticipate evidence of a public debate about "policy deficits."

Path dependency may also have an important explanatory role in accounting for stability. To take one example, in some federations, including Australia and the United States, the constitution affords the national government the authority to sign, ratify, and implement international treaties. In others, like Canada and Switzerland, there is no distinctive constitutional authority for the national government to implement international treaties. The authority to implement is determined by which order of government is responsible for the subject matter of the treaty. In this example, therefore, it is easier for Australia's Commonwealth or the US federal government to enter policy domains that would otherwise be within the sphere of their states than it would be for the federal government in Canada or Switzerland to intervene in provincial or cantonal jurisdictions.

There is a third reason why federations may have exhibited stability in the face of global and regional pressures. It is that the impacts of global and regional integration may be varied and effectively counteract one another in relation to the overall balance of the federation. Moreover, there is no demonstrated correlation between shared rule and functional effectiveness, on the one hand, and self-rule and identity, on the other. For some kinds of issues, it may well be the case that functionality argues in favour of large territorial expanses as the appropriate unit of decision-making (e.g., some kinds of environmental issues and some aspects of defence and security). But for others, functionality may argue for local preferences holding the trump card even if the challenge originates outside the territory that is affected. For instance, local authorities may be better able to deal with some types of international terrorism threats than national or international authorities precisely because local authorities are better able to identify non-locals in their midst than more distant officials. And even if environmental pollutants or epidemics come from a distance, they will be experienced in specific locales and part of the response may have to be local for functional reasons. Conversely, while it might appear intuitive that constituent units would normally be the lead actor in preserving and promoting identities, in some situations, this goal may privilege the national government, not the subnational government. This may happen, for example, when the impact of global or regional pressures impacts on that aspect of identity that is more state-wide than regional or local. To take one example, the impact of American cultural products is huge in the mainly English-speaking regions of Canada. People from the English-speaking regions see this as something that is more appropriately dealt with at the federal level even though, for many other purposes, they would often look first to provincial governments on cultural matters.

Thus, while instrumentality and the promotion and protection of identities may be complementary roles of political institutions, it does not follow that functional gains always correlate with decision-making being located in the larger territorial units and identity gains always gain with decision-making being located in the subnational units. A more fine-grained analysis is required.[2]

One final note merits attention from a theoretical viewpoint. As already noted, we have been mainly motivated by a curiosity to understand to what extent and in what ways the forces of global and regional integration have affected federal systems of governance. At the same time, we have also paid attention to the opposite perspective, namely, the ways in which federal systems of governance may have influenced how global and regional integration are experienced in the states studied here. In this alternative view, the federal system is the independent variable and global and regional integration are the dependent variables.

The volume is comparative. It considers the effects of global and regional integration on five developed "federations," two developing countries that are federal or federal-like in structure, and the "federalizing" European Union. The first drafts of the country chapters were prepared before the 2003 Iraq crisis. Were the authors of these chapters to re-write what they have said in the light of the events surrounding Iraq, including the strong disagreements between traditional North Atlantic allies, some might nuance their arguments differently. But their basic analyses remain intact. Indeed, in some respects, they may even be reinforced.

Enquiring about the effects of global and regional integration on federal systems is important. A large share of the world's population lives in federal-type polities. Moreover, in parts of the world that are affected by ethnic conflict (including Afghanistan, Cyprus, Indonesia, Iraq, the Philippines, Sri Lanka, and Sudan, to name but a few), federal solutions are being touted as possible compromises between a unitary state, on the one hand, and state disintegration (separation or civil war), on the other. If federal systems are themselves undergoing, or are about to undergo, fundamental change, this is worth understanding. And if they are not, it is equally important to understand how and why they are able to remain stable in the face of seemingly powerful change agents.

All the authors of the country chapters in this volume begin by outlining the relevant context for their case study. They discuss the history and geography of their federation, key constitutional provisions, and the extent of openness to global and regional integration. They pay attention as well to the unique characteristics of their federations. As a global hegemon, for example, the United States is the source of many of the globalizing forces, political, economic, and cultural. It globalizes more perhaps than it is globalized. Conversely, less populous states like Australia, Canada, and Switzerland, are much more the recipients of globalization. These differences and many others are reflected in the country studies. Nonetheless, the authors tackle a common set of questions that reflect the considerations discussed above. They include:

- Have the institutions or structures of the federation, formal or informal, been altered to manage international relations or for other reasons related to global and regional integration? And, if so, how?
- How extensively have constituent units, including local governments, become involved in external relations? Is the external sovereignty of states being handled differently?
- To what extent has a competitiveness agenda, emerging at least in part from economic globalization/regionalization, come to affect the working of the federation?

- Are the internationally integrating forces affecting the traditional balance between centralization and decentralization in the federation? If so, are there new tensions between the general government and constituent units for this reason?
- Have international institutions or processes emerged at the level of constituent units? In other words, are there new cross-border institutions/processes emerging between constituent units?
- Are these forces affecting identities and loyalties among the citizens of the federation and, if so, how?

Not all of these questions and issues have the same salience in each federation. And not all are dealt with as "stand alone" questions in the chapters that follow. But all these questions were on the radar screens of the authors as they undertook their enquiries.

This comparative analysis is part of a larger analysis about the effects of global and regional integration on federal systems of governance. As part of that larger project, a group of researchers was assembled to devise a set of scenarios for global governance in the year 2015. The country authors of this volume were invited, if they so wished, to include in their chapters a speculative discussion of how these alternative global futures might impact on their federation. Some of the country chapters that follow probe this issue carefully. Others give it less attention. Suffice it here to say that we summarize our scenarios synoptically later in this chapter and the full scenario document is available on-line.[3]

The purpose of the remaining sections of this introductory chapter is to compare the analysis across federations. How similar or different are the answers to the above questions from one federation to another? Are there clusters of federations that provide similar answers to the same questions? In dealing with these questions, we proceed as follows. First, we examine the impact of global and regional integration on institutional arrangements in federal political systems. Second, we explore the impact of GARI on political identity, both the development (or lack thereof) of new transnational identities as well as the impact on traditional political cleavages within federations. Third, we look at the impact of GARI on the political equilibrium in federal political systems. Finally, we speculate about the potential effect of alternative scenarios on the future of these federal systems.

THE IMPACT OF GARI ON FEDERAL
INSTITUTIONAL ARRANGEMENTS

In studying the impact of global and regional integration on federal institutional arrangements, Brian Galligan notes that "we need to keep in mind
the flexibility of institutions and the reflexivity of human agency ... up to
a point," he continues, "human actors can use the same set of institutions
for different purposes as well as different institutions for the same purpose." "Consequently," he concludes, "globalization as the independent
variable does not have a direct causal effect on the structure and processes
of federation as the dependent variable, but an effect that is mediated by
human agency." In almost all the federations we examined, there is evidence of some institutional adjustment as a precondition to effectively
dealing with global and regional economic forces, but on balance the
changes have been modest. Only the EU has experienced massive change,
much of it formal. On a lesser scale, Germany has also undergone some
formal change, almost wholly in response to the deepening of the European Union. In the other cases, political actors have been able to adjust
old institutions or create new institutional processes to complement the
traditional institutions of federalism.

Of all of the federal-type systems examined in this volume, only the
European Union has formally undergone major institutional innovation.
The growth of European institutions is clearly a response to the chal-
lenges of globalization, and especially those that have emerged from the
United States. On this point Hooghe writes boldly:

> European integration accelerated in the mid-1980s, and again in the mid-
> 1990s, and this acceleration was a direct response to problems attributed
> to globalization — augmented national vulnerability to trade and finan-
> cial flows, eroding competitiveness for European firms, structural
> unemployment and labour market rigidities, and increasing immigration
> from its poorer eastern and southern Mediterranean neighbours into the
> European Union. I do not mean to say that globalization determined how
> Europe's institutions, policies, and politics changed. "Domestic politics"—
> national and European leaders' preferences, and societal interests as ex-
> pressed by producer groups and political parties — has mediated these
> changes. Yet I will show that the European Union has become a battle-
> ground for opponents and proponents of globalization. Some want the

European Union to be a bulwark against global pressures, and others want it to accelerate the pace of increasing *global,* as opposed to national or European, interdependence.

To be sure, what has become the EU originated in the postwar *political* dream of ending historic intra-European enmities. But the motivation of much of its subsequent growth rested in a desire to respond to global challenges and opportunities in numerous spheres, with *economic* considerations often a priority, but issues like the environment, social policy, culture, and even military and security issues also finding their way onto its ever-expanding agenda. To the extent that the European Union can now be seen as a distinct polity, formal institution-building has been fundamental to that evolutionary process. In this vein, Hooghe writes, "substantive extension of European integration into all policy areas has gone hand in hand with an institutional transformation from a limited, primarily intergovernmental form of international cooperation to a system of multi-level governance, where autonomous supranational institutions — Commission, European Parliament, European Central Bank, and European Court of Justice — and institutions representing national governments, European Council and Council of Ministers, share authority."

The EU's new and strengthened institutions arguably are about moving from confederal to federal forms of governance, from interstate to intrastate modes of decision-making, and from state sovereignty to various forms of sharing and pooling of sovereignty. More than any other political entity examined in this volume, the European Union has turned to formal institutional innovation and development to bridge the gap between functional and political geography. And more than any other polity covered, it has recognized the need to ensure that these changed institutions deal not only with functional imperatives but also with issues of democratic deficit (a term initially coined to describe some of the EU's growing pains) and identity formation.

In the case of Germany, both global and regional forces have had a strong impact on its form of federalism. According to Rudolf Hrbek, the dynamics stemming from both forms of integration (economic globalization and the establishment of the internal market in the EU) have altered Germany's traditional interlocking and cooperative federalism (and related joint decision trap problems). The global economic pressures have led the richer Länder to seek more autonomy to compete internationally and to limit horizontal equalization payments. The result is a more competitive federalism and there is pressure for this trend to continue. As regards the process of European integration, the massive institutional developments of the EU noted above have had their corollary in the need for institutional adjustment at the national and constituent unit levels. The German system of interlocking federalism has thus been modified as some legislative competencies have moved to the EU level. The resulting multi-level system of governance nonetheless still requires the federal government and Länder to work in an integrated and cooperative way. In other words, German federalism may have become more competitive but cooperation still remains one of its central characteristics.

These dynamics have played out in several ways institutionally. The enhanced powers of the EU include items that were once within the sphere of the Länder (such as culture, the media, and education). When the EU makes decisions in these areas, it is normally the federal government that is at the table of the Council of Ministers. Other things being equal, this would appear to constitute a loss of authority for the Länder. But they have made up for it in other ways. Future transfers of such Land jurisdictions require the approval of two-thirds of both chambers and thus of two-thirds of Land governments. This strengthens the role of Land governments in shaping the constitutional development of the Federal Republic and the EU. To varying degrees, the Länder have also secured the right to participate in EU affairs and be represented in EU bodies. They have as well negotiated the requirement that the federal government take into account, again to varying degrees, Bundesrat opinions (which the Länder control) when deciding on EU matters. The Länder themselves have also reorganized with European sections, EU coordination centres and intergovernmental offices, conferences of minister-presidents, and other innovations. It is also not unusual for them to maintain offices in Brussels to carry out lobbying activities.

Germany has generally been an enthusiastic supporter of a stronger EU. For this reason, it is not particularly useful to question whether and to what extent federal or Land governments have gained or lost authority relative to one another. Both orders of government have, in general, seen a strengthened EU as a good thing notwithstanding occasional political concerns. What is evident is that the combined regional and global change pressures are influencing the character of the German federation. It has become perhaps a model of multi-level governance, with many of the changes being built into its constitutional structure. Finally, in the case of both the EU and its German member state, informal institutions have also been adjusting. For example, political parties and interest groups often organize on a Europe-wide basis as the nature of European politics has altered. In comparison with the European Union and Germany, institutional change among the other federations has been small, although in some cases intriguing.

John Kincaid, perhaps fittingly, titled an early version of his chapter "Atlas Shrugged." We say "perhaps fittingly" because Kincaid's analysis suggests that the effects of global and regional integration on the federal system of the United States are at most modest, certainly smaller than the other federations discussed here. Three mutually reinforcing reasons may help to explain the American case. The first is that as the world's only economic, military, and political hegemon, with powerful global cultural influence as well, the United States is the purveyor of globalization more than a recipient. The second and perhaps more pertinent point to this analysis is that the United States has historically been more sceptical of the benefits of the state as a servant of the public weal than have most of the other polities discussed here. Not surprisingly, therefore, it has also been less enthused about supranational institutions as vehicles for dealing with the growing incongruence between functional and political geography. Third, Kincaid notes that the Government of the United States resists international commitments that would have the effect of encroaching on the sovereignty of state governments under the US Constitution.

While the United States has on balance been a net exporter of globalization, the terrorist attacks on 11 September 2001 suggest that even the world's only remaining superpower is occasionally vulnerable to external shocks and in this case has led to the creation of the Department of Homeland Security. This development marks perhaps the largest reorganization of the American government since the reorganization of the military in 1947. The Homeland Security Strategy devised by the Bush administration entails an unprecedented level of federal-state-local collaboration. The strategy relies largely on central direction with much of the heavy lifting done by police and other emergency agencies at the state and local level. It is still too early to know fully what impact homeland security will have on American federalism.

In the case of Australia, three developments are of note. One is some centralization of power associated with the proliferation of international treaties. Galligan points explicitly to this as the basis under which the Commonwealth government has intervened in what would otherwise be state competencies. The second, however, has been an institutional reaction that has had the effect of softening this centralizing threat to the Commonwealth-state political equilibrium. This shows up in enhanced intergovernmental cooperation aimed at strengthening Australia's economic competitiveness. Galligan writes that the "outcome was a set of new intergovernmental organizations and rules that add up to a major restructuring of Australian federalism at the subconstitutional level." The states work with the Commonwealth in joint national bodies in a variety of areas including the environment, food standards, and road transport where there is provision for a majority of qualified majorities taking decisions. States have also participated with the Commonwealth in the broad area of competition policy, particularly with a view to enhancing the efficiency of government as a provider of services. This commitment to forging a more competitive economy contributed as well to the establishment of the heads of government Council of Australian Governments (COAG) and while COAG's role has since waxed and waned, its *raison d'être* is connected to Australia's need to fashion a coherent national response to global economic competition.

Third is the emergence of a variety of Australian-New Zealand relationships, a kind of regional integration with consequences for the way in which the Australian federation operates. While some of these are traditional bilateral international agreements, others are more unusual. For example, New Zealand participates in some Australian Commonwealth-state ministerial councils and agreements as if it were an Australian state. Another involves joint and shared institutions. Galligan writes: "Increasingly, Australian governance will be a system of complex and diffuse power centres with an intermingling and overlapping of jurisdictional responsibilities and policy activity."

Mahendra Singh's assessment of the transformation of the Indian federation differs markedly from Galligan's account of developments in Australia in the detail but not in overview. Thus, on the economic front Singh cites several examples of the Indian central state lightening the load of regulation, modifying the form of union regulation, and in other ways providing more room for market forces. He explains that the initial pressure for economic liberalization originated in domestic influences, including the fragmentation of federation-wide political parties. But since then, this initial impetus has been reinforced by economic globalization leading to a relative decline in the economic role of the union government. Delhi's policies have also encouraged domestic and foreign investors to focus more on what individual states have to offer, which in the economic development sphere has increased competition among the states. Yet not all of the changes are in the direction of enhanced horizontal competition. While the overall trend has been to privilege state and private bodies relative to the Delhi authorities, in cases where new World Trade Organizations (WTO) commitments have been made, the union government (as in Australia) has acquired *de facto* powers that previously were state competencies.

In both Australia and India, therefore, some informal institutional adjustment has occurred. And while the basic direction of change between federal and subnational governments has been different, centralizing somewhat in Australia and decentralizing in India, in each federation the overall adjustment process has entailed effective authority moving in more than one direction.

The governing African National Congress in South Africa has chosen to work within the neo-liberal economic paradigm that characterizes economic globalization and it has been a leader in various forms of regional integration, both in southern Africa and the larger continent. This has led it to give attention to the efficiency of government operations. Given the limited human resource capacity within that federal-type arrangement, institution-building at the federal level, and to a lesser extent at the local level, has been privileged at the expense of the provincial sphere.

The Canadian constitution was substantially reformed in 1982, and major revisions were proposed in 1987 and 1992, but these were motivated purely by domestic factors: the desire to patriate the constitution from the United Kingdom and to adopt a charter of rights. After a decade of strenuous constitutional debate, the Government of Canada, under the leadership of Jean Chrétien, deliberately pursued a policy of non-constitutional reform (Lazar 1998). For example, the federal government and all the provinces negotiated an agreement to remove barriers to internal trade in the early 1990s. The Agreement on Internal Trade, however, was adopted only after the North American Free Trade Agreement

(NAFTA) negotiations had been completed. Without the example of the regional treaty, the domestic arrangements would have not, in all probability, been implemented.

Given some of our earlier more theoretical discussion, it might be thought that some of the analysis above, particularly in regard to informal institutions, is linked to the way in which treaty-making powers are constitutionally allocated. In four of the federations studied (Australia, India, South Africa, and the United States), the federal government has broad and exclusive or close to exclusive treaty-making authority and extensive authority as well to implement the treaties it has made (either through separate legislation or self-executing provisions). In Canada and Switzerland, the power to negotiate and sign treaties is not paralleled by similarly broad provisions to implement. In these two cases, the constituent units must legislate if treaties affecting their competencies are to be implemented. As for Germany, the Bundesrat ensures that the Länder have a say in implementation with the result that, *de facto*, its situation is similar to that of Canada and Switzerland. (The EU is *sui generis* in relation to this kind of analysis.)

The question considered here is whether these particular constitutional treaty provisions help to explain some of the above analysis. The answer here appears to be a qualified affirmative. The trend toward some centralization of authority in Australia and South Africa has been reinforced by the ease with which the federal governments in these countries can implement what they sign. While we did not detect any large trends in the United States, the self-executing nature of US treaties may strengthen the authorities in Washington. In Canada and Germany, we noted a trend to decentralization and Switzerland remains highly decentralized. These three federations are the ones where constituent units have important implementation powers. The outlier in this analysis is India, where the government in Delhi has strong powers of implementation but where there has been a shift to decentralize. But even in the case of India, notwithstanding the decentralization on economic matters, the centre has maintained firm control on security issues. In short, there appears to at least be a correlation between treaty powers and the broad trends noted above. Of course, it could be that the treaty powers were established to reflect the underlying constitutional deal between the general government and constituent units. If that were the case, the way the treaty powers are assigned would be more of a symptom of the essential character of these different federations than an explanation of recent trends. It is our sense, however, that the truth lies between these two views and that, at the margin, at least, the happenstance of treaty powers may be reinforcing other factors that help to explain the institutional adaptations in the different federations.

In summary then, only the EU has experienced massive change, much of it formal. Germany has also undergone formal change but on a lesser scale than the EU. Australia and India have experienced modest informal change. In almost all the federations, however, there is also evidence of some degree of adjustment in institutional structures and arrangements as a precondition to dealing effectively with global and regional economic forces.

THE IMPACT OF GARI ON POLITICAL IDENTITIES IN FEDERAL SOCIETIES

Citizens of federations enjoy multiple identities. With enhanced global and regional integration, one might expect to see the development of new transnational identities. But, with the important exception of Europe, transnational identities are weak to non-existent between the federations we examined and their global and regional partners. On the other hand, there is some evidence to suggest that relations between regions and communities *within* federations are coming under moderate stress, we emphasize the word *moderate*, from GARI, especially in the more diverse or multinational federations.

In Switzerland, Steiner sees new attachments arising between the French-speaking Swiss and counterparts in France, as well as between Ticino and Italy. Even among German-speaking Swiss, the young professional classes are also more open to Europe. He argues that these new attachments are in opposition to the traditional Swiss identity forged on independence and neutrality. There is thus an emerging cleavage about Swiss identity that has the potential, over time, to put strains on the Swiss Confederation.

The impact of the EU has also been influential in Germany, although in a somewhat different way than in Switzerland. The emergence of transnational politics and organizations has fostered a European identity. With these developments, differences of political opinion are experienced, at least in part, on a Europe-wide level. To date, however, this has not created a major strain within the German federation. The

German people appear to be at ease with the idea of multiple levels of attachment. But the integration of the eastern Länder has been more challenging, which raises questions about how swiftly a common European identity will evolve as the borders of the EU move eastward.

The notion of a European demos is found in Hooghe's tale of the federalizing of the EU, a process that may lead to a full federal state in the coming decades. In her account, the evolution of the EU is a story of political competition between the neo-liberal right and social democratic left. For neo-liberals, an integrated Europe is a free-trade enterprise that should be respectful of traditional national identities. For social democrats, the purpose of economic integration is to regulate capital, but the left also wants the EU to foster a European identity. This kind of right-left and traditional-post-modern political competition is what one would expect in a national polity. This, in and of itself, speaks to the evolution of a European identity, an identity that is reflected concretely in the EU passport. The development of the European identity, however, could be challenged by the rapid expansion of the EU in eastern Europe.

Outside Europe, there is little evidence that transnational identities are forming between the federations we examined and their global and regional partners. In South Asia, the legacy of partition, which segregated the dominant communities, has limited regional integration and prevented the emergence of transnational identities in the subcontinent. And where they do exist (i.e., Kashmir) they tend to be a source of friction. At the global level, the Indian Diaspora has generated a new class of citizen, the non-resident Indian, who connects India to countries around the world and who will likely reinforce India's economic liberalization through huge financial remittances. South Africa similarly displays relatively weak regional integration but, unlike India, South African émigrés are probably too few to have a significant impact on the federal-type constitutional arrangements.

Australia's self-perception appears to have been little changed by the forces of international integration, despite closer economic links with Asia. Australia has long relied on alliances with like-minded and culturally similar countries to protect its territorial integrity. Close ties to the United States in recent decades are in many respects only a replacement for previous linkages to the United Kingdom. And what is true of Australia is even truer in the United States where there is no evidence of any sort of transnational identity emerging (Kincaid, this volume).

The differences between North America and Europe are striking. In the latter, transnational institution-building has purposively impacted identities and helped to create a European identity. Arguably, Canadians and Americans have more in common with one another than do the peoples of Europe, but in North America there has been virtually no transnational institution-building. As such, identities in Canada and the United States have remained more national than they have in Europe. For the foreseeable future, the likelihood of a new North American identity that parallels what is evolving in Europe remains remote.

While Americans have not considered the question of cultural integration in North America, the subject has been intensely debated by the major political parties in Canada, and it has strained the principal linguistic cleavage in the country as well. For Americans, culture tends to be a commodity that properly should be regulated by global and regional trade agreements. For many English-speaking Canadians, culture is a matter that should be protected by national sovereignty. This, in fact, is an article of faith for the liberal-left in English-speaking Canada and even the political-right has historically treaded carefully around this issue.

The people of Quebec, who have in recent decades shaded to the political left in the Canadian political spectrum, tend to be more sanguine about North American integration than left-leaning English-speaking Canadians, believing as they do that American culture does not pose a particular threat to the French language. It is, therefore, not surprising that the Government of Quebec supported the Canada-US Free Trade Agreement and the subsequent NAFTA. A much higher share of Quebec's output is sold outside Canada's borders than was the case 20 years ago. Indeed, Jean-Francois Lisée (2003) suggests that Quebec supported these trade liberalization measures because they promised to reduce Quebec's economic dependence on the rest of Canada. In short, some Quebec nationalists concluded that the cause of independence would be furthered by North American free trade (Meadwell 1989, 1993). It would thus seem that North American integration has served to support Quebec's sense of distinctiveness.

While free trade may realize economic benefits for a federation, constituent units made up of minority nations that are distinct from the dominant linguistic, ethnic, or religious groups nationally may feel emboldened to seek more autonomy, including independence, because they may come to believe that their economic security can be assured through free trade with regional markets as opposed to relying on domestic markets. We may therefore speculate that, over time, the economic liberalization in India might give some succour to the various autonomist movements in states outside the Hindi-speaking heartland.

The interaction of autonomist movements and transnational free trade is evident as well in some countries not covered in this volume. The unrestricted access of Scotland, Flanders, and Catalonia to EU markets has made it easier for the nationalist movements of these regions to demand enhanced autonomy from the larger societies in which they are located (Keating 2001). The United Kingdom, Belgium, and Spain were all highly centralized unitary states only a few decades ago. Today, two are federal-type states and the UK is in the process of substantial devolution. It would thus seem that international economic integration has supported the federalizing processes of these countries. Whether enhanced autonomy will satisfy the subnationalist movements in the rest of Europe or whether they will press for full independence, with all of its limitations in the modern world, remains to be seen (ibid.). Whatever the answer to this question, global and regional integration appears to be a source of strain, at times real and at others only hypothetical, in diverse societies, whether federal or otherwise.

There may be similar tendencies in unilingual federations. In such cases, the motivation may be economic not cultural. Hrbek writes that some Land governments in Germany are seeking to increase their relative role in economic policy in that federation as a result of global and regional integration.

A related impact on intrafederal relations flowing from international economic integration is to put more strain on systems of interregional sharing within federal systems. With ever growing global and regional competition, prosperous constituent units tend to pursue policies that will reduce tax burdens that affect their competitiveness. This is especially the case in relation to those taxes that are redistributed to less prosperous constituent units. Thus, wealthier Länder in Germany, such as Bavaria and Baden-Württemberg, and provinces in Canada, including Alberta and Ontario, have been pressing for less generous systems of either explicit or implicit equalization. In fact, Courchene (1998) has argued that Ontario is developing its own economic strategy, one that is heavily influenced by its need to compete with neighbouring American states. As for the case of India, Singh observes that, starting in 1995, fiscal transfers from the centre began to reward efficiency and performance, perhaps signalling that similar political forces are at work in the subcontinent. The richer states in India have certainly come to resent subsidizing the poorer states, some of which (especially the smaller hill states in the northwest and northeast of the country) rely almost entirely on transfers from the central government. In short, the impact of global and regional integration is not even and it may exacerbate the tensions between rich and poor regions in federal systems, although the impact to date has been relatively modest.

THE IMPACT OF GARI ON THE INTERGOVERNMENTAL BALANCE IN FEDERAL POLITICAL SYSTEMS

The case studies presented here suggest that the impact of global and regional integration is not unidirectional. Federalism is not a static arrangement. Federations go through periods of centralization and decentralization over time. These fluctuations have been referred to as the "federal process" (Friedrich 1968). In each federation, the federal process is motivated by a mix of internal and external variables. If one or more of those variables is increased, the centralization or decentralization processes already underway will in most cases be accentuated. Consistent with these theoretical observations, we have found that, other things being equal, external pressures will lead centralized federations to become even more centralized and vice versa. (Everything is not always equal, of course, and war is likely to lead to centralization in federations, whether they are disposed to be more decentralized or more centralized.) The point of the scenarios exercise in the next section is to try to assess how federations would react with more extreme changes in the global arena (although none of the scenarios involve war).

Canada and Switzerland have long been among the most decentralized federations. Under global and regional pressures, Canada may be becoming more so. While there does not appear to have been a significant change in the intergovernmental balance in Switzerland, the deepening linguistic cleavage observed by Steiner suggests that the Swiss federal society may be modestly fragmenting or decentralizing although economic integration within Switzerland (for example, the way in which large cities serve as a magnet for surrounding cantons) may be a counterbalancing factor. On balance, India has also decentralized since the decline of the Congress Party. Some of the recent changes in India have been associated with a shift away from the state to the market. In this instance, domestic politics were the initial trigger but since then external (especially global) forces have reinforced the twin processes of economic liberalization and political federalization discussed by Singh.

Australia has been a somewhat centralized federation, at least since World War II, and under global pressures it seems to have become more centralized. John Kincaid believes that the United States has experienced "substantial centralization in the twentieth century," but he maintains that this centralization cannot be attributed to global and regional forces.[4] Kincaid acknowledges that globalization has had an impact on American *society*, but he argues that the structure and operation of American *federalism* has been unaffected by recent global forces for a number of reasons. First, he reports that Americans "adapted their federal system to the kinds of challenges associated with globalization" in response to the economic conditions of the early twentieth century and the great wars. He also suggests that the American Constitution was designed to sustain "a great commercial republic," one that was compatible with the project of globalization. And perhaps most importantly is "the absence of fundamental cultural and intellectual contradictions between American federalism and globalization."

In South Africa, global and regional forces appear to be strengthening the central government and local governments at the expense of the state level. Steytler describes this as "hourglass federalism." After the apartheid regime, there was a desire to avoid a splintering of the new polity. Powers were thus allocated to ensure a strong general government, which in turn favoured strong cities over strong provinces.[5] This "pre-existing tendency toward centralization and localization," Steytler argues, "may be reinforced by the pressures of global integration."

The EU is the only political system we examined that is undergoing strong centralization as a result of regional integration, and its federalizing process is both an independent variable, an agent of regionalization, and a dependent variable, impacted by global forces.[6]

Germany is perhaps the most difficult case to assess. Examined in isolation, Germany appears to be decentralizing, with the central government gradually ceding power to the Land governments. In the European context, however, we might conclude that Germany is also experiencing an hourglass process with the powers of the central government shifting up to Brussels and down to the Länder. Regardless of how we characterize Germany, the transformation of Germany is being powerfully shaped by regional integration (i.e., the development of the European Union), which in turn is partly motivated and reinforced by global economic integration.

While the emergence of the EU and the concomitant institutional harmonization in Germany has been profound, we would stress that these developments are the result of deliberate human agency and endorsed by freely democratic processes. The adjustments in the equilibrium of European governance have not been foisted on the unwilling nations or peoples of Europe by the impersonal forces of regional and global integration. To the contrary, Europeans have controlled the processes of regional integration, speeding it up and slowing it down when desired.

Much of what has just been said about the EU is true in a more modest way about Germany. The governance of Germany has been transformed because of the emergence of the EU. There is a large difference in what Germans could once decide on their own acting through their federal and Land governments and the kind of shared and pooled sovereignty that now applies as a result of the large and growing role of the EU, but Germany's decision to join the EU was voluntary. Internal cohesion in Germany thus remains strong (notwithstanding the challenge of integrating the eastern Länder). The German experience is instructive for other polities. It suggests that political integration is not inevitable, it is voluntary. But if transnational political integration is pursued, domestic institutions will almost certainly have to be modified accordingly.

These findings from our case studies can be compared to the so-called "glocalization" thesis. It argues that the traditional nation-state is no longer large enough to deal with some big issues for which the solutions must necessarily be international in scope (e.g., global warming, spread of disease) and too large to handle many other issues where local solutions are more appropriate — a viewpoint that is consistent with our earlier discussion about the growing incongruence between functional and political geography. While this viewpoint may well have some merit, the case studies here do not emphasize that theme. Perhaps it is because nation-states are not powerless in the face of these forces that appear to privilege constituent units and that they are able to take offsetting measures. Perhaps it is because path dependency causes change pressures to be muted or diffused.

Whatever the full explanation, the overriding message that emerges from our case studies is that *apparently* similar change pressures produce divergent outcomes in different federations. It would appear that external change pressures are mediated through the uniqueness of each political entity's domestic reality, as Richard Simeon notes in his chapter on Canada. Since the endogenous conditions differ markedly from one federation to another, it follows that the effects of external forces on domestic governance are experienced differently in each federation.

The divergent responses to global and regional integration may also reflect the different starting points for each federation. It is understandable that a highly centralized federation like India would decentralize somewhat, while a highly decentralized system such as the European Union would find some advantage in centralizing. It would also appear that the long-established federations (those that pre-date World War II) have been influenced relatively lightly by international change pressures, while the more newly established federal polities are more heavily affected. The relatively smaller changes experienced in the developed federations may reflect the fact that their "growing pains" occurred well before the period of modern global and regional integration. To the extent that this point has weight, South Africa might be expected to continue to strengthen its central institutions for a while as it develops. Depending on its success on that front, it might subsequently decentralize somewhat, as happened in India after the decline of the Congress Party.

A final and more speculative observation is that federal systems may find it easier to accommodate global and regional integration than unitary states, at least in some respects. Unlike unitary states, most federal states have experience in multi-level governance at the domestic level. They are used to the unique complexity of shared sovereignty. They are accustomed to intergovernmental processes between federal and regional governments. In short, federalism approximates the complex multi-level reality of the modern world. "Adding a global sphere extends the complexity," Brian Galligan argues, "but in ways that are not so foreign to the already complex system."

In sum, the variable impact of global and regional integration on federal political systems does not lend itself to simple messages, mainly because common external forces are mediated through very different domestic political arrangements. Perhaps the single strongest conclusion to emerge from this analysis, therefore, is that while the forces of international integration are influencing the processes of centralization and decentralization in federal-type systems, to date they have not been powerful enough to alter the basic political equilibrium within the political entities we analyzed in this volume. Put another way, the pre-existing direction of movement has not been reversed in any of the systems we examined.

These general conclusions raise an important question: Are these benign observations falsely reassuring because the nation-states of the world are still in an early phase of global and regional integration? In recent years we have seen what may only be the beginning of the globalization of communication, finance and commerce, terrorism, disease, and other environmental problems. There are many other examples. Regional integration is in some cases proceeding even more quickly. If the issues are tackled 10 or 15 years from now, might we expect to find different answers? This is what we hoped to learn from our scenarios exercise.

LOOKING AHEAD: SOME SCENARIOS FOR THE FUTURE

There is obviously no certain answer to this last question, but we attempt to speculate about the future for our federations with a scenarios exercise that was undertaken in connection with this volume and a wider research project of which it is part. This involved the creation of four different scenarios for global governance in 2015. The process through which these scenarios were created and the details of their content are found elsewhere.[7]

Scenarios are based on the premise that the future is inherently uncertain. This means that a range of future outcomes is possible. Scenarios attempt to capture that uncertainty by developing multiple descriptions of the future. The focus in developing scenarios is to understand the forces driving change and the key uncertainties that lead to different outcomes.

The number of uncertainties affecting global and regional integration is large. From the array of possibilities, we selected two sets of uncertainties and built our scenarios around them. One had to do with whether power in global governance would become more concentrated or more dispersed. The second was whether the world would move toward more extensive regulation or less (more reliance on market forces and individual choice). By combining these two sets of uncertainties, four scenarios were created. Figure 1 and the immediately following summary provide key highlights.

FIGURE 1
Global and Regional Integration, Scenario Matrix

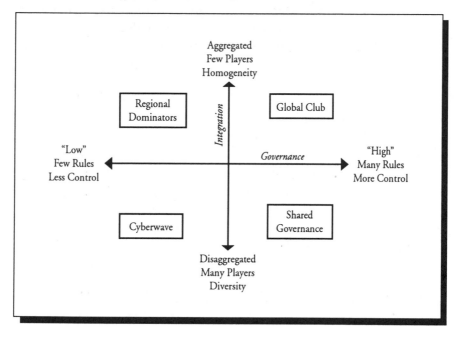

The *global club* scenario is characterized by a concentration of wealth and power in a few hands. Major powers and corporate leaders form a "club" — initially informal and then more formal — to resolve critical issues decisively and effectively. The club creates a highly regulated world with global standards and strict international rules in many fields. A few international institutions oversee these regimes and manage their implementation; and they are controlled by the club. Voices of discontent are discounted. Most national states are marginalized. Their capacity to devise standards or choose the parameters of public policy shrink as international regimes reduce their effective freedom to act. The result is an increasingly integrated global economy governed by a small number of actors committed and willing to use their power to ensure order, stability, and growth.

The *shared governance* scenario is characterized by widely diffused economic and political power exercised within a "balanced" system of global governance. The equality and responsibility of states is recognized. National governments balance sovereignty and independence against the need for growth and international stability. International organizations gain influence. Rules are defined, supported, and enforced. Major powers recognize the need to adhere to the rules and accept compromises in reconciling trade and political disputes. Subnational governments, multinational corporations, and NGOs are all recognized as legitimate players and included in this more networked system of international decision-making.

There is an "egalitarian" push, tempered by self-interest, to accelerate economic growth and social development, including in poor countries. Grass-roots citizen organizations are also increasingly influential, leading to more effective democratic processes and strengthened social programs. Human rights are recognized globally. The result is a complex yet orderly and balanced world in which rules are respected and transparent. Countries adhere to the rules in part because their capacity to act independently is eroded and in part because breaking the rules threatens growth and stability. States recognize their interdependence and the real limits to their economic power in an increasingly integrated global economy.

The cyberwave scenario is characterized by rapid, unpredictable, and continuous technological change that drives business and stimulates growth. It also outstrips the ability of public institutions to stay abreast of change and respond effectively. Individualism and libertarianism are celebrated. There is an ongoing effort to streamline market regulations and increase competition. There are few economies of scale in the new technologies, which are relatively easy and inexpensive to adapt for those with the requisite human capital. Speed and flexibility are more important than size and financial resources. This leads to a proliferation of economic players aggressively exploiting new technology and undermining the dominance of traditional, gigantic international enterprises.

The dynamism of markets and intense competition leads to a wider polarization of well-being within individual countries and exacerbates the north-south income divide. Within the north, there are multiple centres of power and a tendency toward social and political fragmentation. The result is bursts of strong economic growth flowing from markets, an innovative culture and support for individual liberties and initiatives, but it is unclear whether this growth is sustainable (much volatility) given the absence of appropriate regulation of markets. The scope for international governance narrows dramatically.

The regional dominators scenario is characterized by major geopolitical blocs sparring for position and dominance. Blocs are highly integrated internally but externally they jockey for economic and political advantage in aggressive, confrontational neo-mercantilist resurgence. Bloc policies are often designed to support their large and increasingly powerful corporate sectors. Inter-bloc relationships are characterized by conflict rather than cooperation. Multilateral policy coordination across blocs is consciously rejected. Instead, issues are addressed on a bilateral basis between blocs. Bilateral trade restrictions proliferate. International institutions are increasingly irrelevant and largely moribund. Blocs try to access competitors' markets while minimizing concessions. Economic growth is low and uneven. Discrepancies between rich and poor countries are exacerbated.

The question that arises here is whether and how these alternative global futures might affect the federal systems of governance that we examined. The first thing we must acknowledge is that such analysis is necessarily speculative. A second is that the scenarios would impact differentially on the polities studied. For example, in a regional dominators scenario, Germany and the United States could be expected to be lead powers on their continents. The same may be true of South Africa and India. Conversely, Switzerland and Canada would not be in that position. And Australia would be excluded or would be a relatively small power in a bloc with which it might not be geographically contiguous. To provide a second example, the cyberwave scenario would be less of a cultural shock to the United States than it would be for any of the European polities. Given these kind of considerations, what lessons appear to emerge from this exercise?

Consider first the two scenarios that concentrate power (global club and regional dominators). Other things being equal, one might expect them to lead to relatively more centralization of power within the individual federations. This indeed is what our country authors tend to think in cases where the federation is a large one, either in global or regional terms. But for the less powerful federations, the analysis suggests otherwise, with the most likely reaction being for the balance within the federation to remain as it is or to be further accentuated. Thus, for Canada and Switzerland, which begin as relatively non-centralized federations, the authors lean to the view that, under both scenarios, their constituent units are likely to be privileged, in relative terms, while the federal authorities are likely to be weakened. In the relatively centralized Australian federation, the expectation is that the Commonwealth government is more likely to increase its relative stature or at least preserve it.

Consider next the two scenarios that lead to a de-concentration of power (shared governance and cyberwave). In these cases, for most federations, there is a shift of relative power away from the federal government. Other things being equal, this is what we might expect given that these scenarios are inherently decentralizing. And we find assessments for Canada, the EU, India, South Africa, and the United States consistent with that assumption. But the uniqueness of political cultures from one polity to another means that this result is more problematic in other cases. Thus, Galligan speculates that cyberwave would, in relative terms, strengthen the Commonwealth authorities in Australia as the relative weakness of states would make them less well able to function at all in this particular scenario. And Hrbek wonders whether this same scenario might not strengthen the existing cooperative model of German federalism as a necessary response to the threat that cyberwave would pose to German solidarity. Similarly, Hooghe sees a global shared governance model as reinforcing the shared governance that has been evolving in the European Union and thus as potentially reinforcing the federalizing process in that polity, with Brussels growing in relative importance. In other words, in these latter three cases, the scenario serves to reinforce essential features of the polity as it now exists.

This exercise, while speculative, tends to reinforce the analysis earlier in this chapter in a couple of respects. First, when put under stress, there is a tendency for federal systems to accentuate current characteristics. Second and consistent with the first, similar processes of global and regional integration may lead to dissimilar responses from one federation to the next. These forces are mediated by domestic institutions and cultures and they are, of course, variable.

CONCLUSIONS

Federal systems, like all polities, are subject to pressures from within and without. This volume explores the effects of the growing influences from without — the strong recent trends toward regional and global integration — and how they affect federal systems of governance. This study points to the fact that global and regional integration are related but distinct phenomena, and it would seem that most federations are impacted by one more than the other. Canada, Germany, and Switzerland all seem more affected by regional integration, while Australia, the European Union, India, and South Africa are affected more by global integration. As for the United States, it is least affected by these pressures.

Perhaps the single strongest message to come from the chapters here is that federal and federal-like systems have been highly stable in spite of the huge growth of global and regional influences on their polities, economies, and societies. In particular, there is little evidence of external pressures forcing major changes to basic institutional features of the countries studied. In the case of the EU and Germany, there have most certainly been transformative institutional innovations, and they have been influenced by globalizing pressures. But these changes originated in domestic factors, not global forces. In almost all of the other federations, there is evidence of some degree of adjustment in institutional structures and arrangements as a precondition to effectively dealing with global and regional economic forces. But on the whole these changes have been modest.

The effects on identities have been modest. New transnational identities have only been observed with the emergence of the European Union as a distinct entity. Outside Europe, there is little evidence that international integration is having similar effects. While there is reason to believe that global and regional forces are reinforcing traditional cultural and political cleavages within federations, especially the more diverse federations, such as Switzerland, Canada, and India, even in these examples the reinforcement has, at least to date, been modest. Moreover, developments such as the 2003 elections to the Scottish and Quebec assemblies and the ongoing negotiations for a European Union constitution suggests the effects might remain modest.

Our earlier theoretical discussion set out rationales that would support divergent trajectories — trends toward both centralization and decentralization. Indeed, *within* individual federations, we anticipated that the mix of external forces might result in both tendencies operating at the same time, some elements of governance becoming more centrally ruled while others were becoming less so. This is in fact what the evidence shows.

We live in a highly complex world and such a result should not be surprising.

Perhaps a little more surprising to us was that global and regional integration have contributed to divergent trajectories *among* federations. Overall, the net effects of centralizing and decentralizing forces have been to help centralize governance in some federal entities, to help decentralize others, to promote an hourglass phenomenon in at least one setting, while contributing to more transformative effects in two others. The specific situational context of each political entity determines the direction of change.

Federal structures are normally found in societies that include substantial diversity. A question of primordial interest here is whether the federal bargain that underpins each of these societies is being undermined or at least significantly affected by the forces of global and regional integration. We found no support for this idea. To date at least, the forces of global and regional integration have not eroded the political stability that is required to sustain the federal systems we have examined.

A quite separate question is whether this stability is sustainable. The forces that underlie global and regional integration appear to be systemic and possibly cumulative. If that is the case, the gap between functional geography and political geography could reach a tipping point that leads to a new dynamic, one that puts into question the political structures and political equilibrium associated with contemporary systems of federal governance. But we are not there yet.

Notes

1. Not all of the polities we examine in this volume define themselves as "federations." All of them, however, have federal-type features. Hence we use the term "federal-type." To keep things simple, we normally use the word "federation" here to include polities that are self-described federations (including Australia, Canada, Germany, India, Switzerland, and the United States) and two that do not so describe themselves, namely the European Union (which is in reality a confederal-federal hybrid) and South Africa (a federal-unitary hybrid).
2. In this respect, we differ from Blatter (2001, pp. 182-83).
3. Available at <http://www.iigr.ca/publication_detail.php?publication=270>.

4.   This observation relative to the United States is consistent with the chapter by John Kincaid in this volume. That chapter was written before the events of 9/11 and its aftermath.

5.   Even before apartheid was defeated, the South African government was more centralized than is the case today.

6.   Even this analysis understates the complexity of what is happening. We have already observed that India has been decentralizing in relation to economic issues. But regional tensions on matters of security have worked in the opposite direction leading to some centralization.

7.   See <http://www.iigr.ca/publication_detail.php?publication=270>.

References

Blatter, J.K. 2001. "Debordering the World of States: Towards a Multi-Level System in Europe and Multi-Polity System in North America? Insights from Border Regions," *European Journal of International Relations* 7 (2):175-209.

Cable, V. 1995. "The Diminished Nation-State: A Study in the Loss of Economic Power," *Daedalus* 124:23-53.

Coleman, W.D. and T. Porter. 2000. "International Institutions, Globalisation and Democracy: Assessing the Challenges," *Global Society* 14 (3):377-98.

Courchene, T.J. and D.J. Savoie, eds. 2003. *The Art of the State: Governance in a World Without Frontiers*. Montreal: Institute for Research on Public Policy.

Courchene, T.J. with C.R. Telmer. 1998. *From Heartland to North American Region State*. Toronto: Centre for Public Management, Faculty of Management, University of Toronto.

Elazar, D.J. 1987. *Exploring Federalism.* Tuscaloosa, AL: University of Alabama Press.

Friedman, T.L. 1999 and 2000. *The Lexus and the Olive Tree: Understanding Globalization*. New York: Anchor Books.

Friedrich, C.J. 1968. *Trends of Federalism in Theory and Practice*. New York: Praeger.

Held, D. 1998. *Democracy and the Global Order*. Stanford: Stanford University Press.

—— 2001. "The Changing Contours of Political Community," in *Global Democracy: Key Debates*, ed. B. Holden. London and New York: Routledge.

Keating, M. 2001. "Nations without States," in *Minority Nationalism and the Changing International Order*, ed. M. Keating and J. McGarry. Oxford: Oxford University Press.

—— 2003. "The Territorial State: Functional Restructuring and Political Change," in *Governing in a World Without Frontiers*, ed. Courchene and Savoie, pp. 329-52.

Keohane, R.O. and J.S. Nye. 2000. "Introduction," in *Governance in a Globalizing World*, ed. J.S. Nye and J.D. Donahue. Washington: The Brookings Institution, pp. 1-41.

Lazar, H., ed. 1998. *Canada: The State of the Federation 1997: Non-Constitutional Renewal.* Kingston: Institute of Intergovernmental Relations, Queen's University.

Lisée, J.-F. 2003. "Is Quebec a North American Region State? A Preliminary View," in *The Art of the State: Governance in a World Without Frontiers*, ed. Courchene and Savoie, pp. 353-63.

Meadwell, H. 1989. "Cultural and Instrumental Approaches to Ethnic Nationalism," *Ethnic and Racial Studies* 12 (3):309-28.

—— 1993. "The Politics of Quebec Nationalism," *World Politics* 45 (January):203-41.

Ohmae, K. 1990. *Borderless World: Power and Strategy in the Interlinked Economy.* New York: Harper Perennial.

—— 1995. *The End of the Nation State: The Rise of Regional Economies.* New York: The Free Press.

Rodrik, D. 1997. *Has Globalization Gone too Far?* Washington, DC: The Institute for International Economics.

Watts, R.L. 1998. *Comparing Federal Systems*, 2d ed. Montreal and Kingston: McGill-Queen's University Press and the School of Policy Studies, Queen's University, pp. 6-14.

CENTRALIZING SYSTEMS

Globalization and Federalism in the United States: Continuity in Adaptation

John Kincaid

INTRODUCTION

To date, globalization has had no impact on the constitutional design or basic institutional structure of the federal system of the United States of America, nor has it significantly altered domestic intergovernmental relations. Instead, American federalism can be said to have had an impact, though indirectly, on the world insofar as the United States has driven globalization more than it has been driven by globalization. Most of the forces and technologies associated with globalization emanated from the United States. Although many factors account for America's powerful status, one factor has remained virtually constant for 212 years — the US federal system. Despite tremendous change in American society and in domestic conceptualizations and operations of US federalism, including substantial centralization during the twentieth century, no amendments to the US Constitution, significant congressional enactments, or major US Supreme Court interpretations of the Constitution with respect to federalism can yet be attributed to globalization.

This is not to say that globalization has had no impact on American society. There have been many impacts, but this chapter focuses only on the impacts of globalization on American federalism, impacts that have been minimal, in part because intergovernmental responses to globalization have been consistent with intergovernmental responses to other challenges. For example, global competition contributed significantly to the devastation of the steel industry in my area of residence, the Lehigh Valley, Pennsylvania. This devastation produced political rhetoric hostile to globalization, but federal, state, and local responses to the devastation have been forged within long-standing patterns of intergovernmental relations, and the Commonwealth of Pennsylvania and the many local governments in the Lehigh Valley formulated policies to cope with this devastation in much the same manner as they formulate new policies to cope with purely domestic socio-economic challenges. Thus, having identified global economic competition as a new challenge more than 30 years ago, the commonwealth and its localities developed, among other things, programs to increase exports of state products abroad and to attract foreign (and domestic) investment as well as foreign (and domestic) tourists. However, these policies entailed no significant changes in intergovernmental relations or in the distribution of powers among the federal, state, and local governments.

Determining why globalization has thus far had a minimal impact on American federalism, and why American federalism has adapted to and facilitated monumental global change during the past two centuries, is, in the end, a speculative exercise. One can only pose hypotheses.

Part of the answer for today lies in the $9.4 trillion gross domestic product (GDP) and still largely autarkic position of the US economy, which can absorb global economic shocks more easily than most nations and shield the federal system from excessive global turbulence. Despite the near-collapse of the European Exchange Rate Mechanism in 1992–93, the Latin American Tequila Crisis that followed Mexico's peso devaluation in 1994–95, and the Asian financial crisis of 1997–98, the US economy grew by 29 percent from 1992 to 1999, achieving the longest continuous peacetime growth in US history. Likewise, US state economies are huge. In terms of 1998 GDP, California is the world's seventh largest economic power (with Canada ranking 12th, Mexico 14th, India 17th, Australia 20th, and Russia 24th). New York and Texas rank tenth and eleventh, and New York City alone ranks nineteenth. Even the economy of the nation's poorest state, Mississippi, is larger than that of about 120 nations.

Nevertheless, why did this huge economy grow and continue to function within the framework of a federal constitution implemented in 1789? The answer lies partly in the original intent of the American

Constitution, a key purpose of which was to build a great commercial republic. The vision of that republic embedded in the Constitution is expansive, both economically and geographically. In addition, Americans tend to be systemically conservative and operationally liberal, clinging to the structural integrity of their constitutional framework while adapting it to social change. Constitutional change, moreover, is a concurrent federal-state process requiring extraordinary-majority consent in the federal and state arenas.

As a result, when post-World War II globalization first hit hard in the United States with the Arab oil embargo of 1973, Americans — in having responded to late nineteenth-century globalization, World War I, the Great Depression of the 1930s, World War II, and the Cold War — had already adapted their federal system to the kinds of challenges associated with globalization. Massive immigration and economic turbulence associated with the first wave of globalization during the late nineteenth century, which lasted until 1914 (Keynes 1919), contributed to the rise of the Populist and Progressive reform movements, which initiated nationalization of the federal system, obtained federal and state legislation to cope with the nation's new national urban-industrial economy (e.g., federal anti-monopoly laws still used today, as in the Microsoft case), established important new institutions, such as the Federal Reserve System (1913) that figures prominently in today's global economy, and secured two amendments to the Constitution in 1913 (i.e., Amendment XVI, federal authority to tax income, and Amendment XVII, direct election of US senators by state voters), which fostered substantial centralization during the twentieth century. The Great Depression induced a significant centralization of economic regulation in Washington, DC, which produced new federal laws and institutions equipped to cope with later globalization, while, nevertheless, preserving substantial economic and political autonomy for the constituent states (Kincaid 1993), which the states today wish to protect against new global institutions such as the World Trade Organization (WTO).

In turn, discussions of contemporary state and local government involvements in international affairs date back to World War II. The first tangible steps toward such involvement occurred during the 1950s. Republican President Dwight D. Eisenhower (1953–61) encouraged state international activity and helped establish the Pearson Fellowship Program, which funds foreign-service officers to spend a year working with a state or local government. The program is consistent with intergovernmental personnel exchanges that date back to 1803. Under Democrat John F. Kennedy's administration (1961–63), the US Department of Commerce encouraged states to become involved in international economic affairs. Commerce was then headed by Luther Hodges, former Governor of North Carolina, who led one of the states' first trade missions to Europe in 1959 (Kincaid 1999). In short, the United States had substantially prepared its federal system for today's globalization, in part because it responded to the first wave of globalization and, then, to the tragic global crises that resulted, in part, from the collapse of that first wave.

Perhaps more important is the absence of fundamental cultural and intellectual contradictions between American federalism and globalization. The United States is a product of early modernity; globalization is a product of late modernity fostered substantially by the United States. The founders reinvented federalism for modernity in the context of a religious belief system moulded by Reformed Protestantism which, with its covenant or federal theology (Elazar and Kincaid 2000), helped usher in modernity, and in the context of a secular political thought system based on productive tensions between Lockean liberal individualism and Machiavellian civic republicanism. The founders' invention of modern federalism was a theoretically and theologically informed and modernly "scientific" approach to the challenges of creating the world's first continental-size republic and of ensuring both individual and communitarian liberty through mechanisms of anti-imperial political, social, and economic integration. US federalism is based, as well, on what Americans regard as universal truths of nature, such as human equality, natural rights (rather than Natural Right), and individual liberty. Coincidentally, though auspiciously, when Americans promulgated their Declaration of Independence in 1776, Adam Smith published the bible of modern capitalism, *The Wealth of Nations*.

American federalism, therefore, did not emerge from a pre-modern society or in revolt against feudalism, nor was it imposed on a pre-modern society. Furthermore, while the United States is a multinational or multicultural society, it is not a multinational or multicultural federation established to accommodate territorially distinctive linguistic, nationality, or religious states having primordial identities and/or roots in antiquity. The federal union was established to protect individual liberty and the needs that individuals have for local self-government and larger collective action in a continental republic. The original 13 states were simply states, not nationality states; they were collections of individuals living within arbitrarily and imperially determined boundaries that had become political communities by virtue of voluntary political, social, and economic interaction. The existence of the states was constitutionally guaranteed, not to protect ancient communal liberties or primordial identities, but to protect individual liberty and communitarian liberties of local self-government against a tyrannical majority or national imperial centre. This difference between the United States and many other multinational countries is reflected in the international activities of the states. These activities are highly pragmatic and heavily economic, and unconcerned with projecting any nationality or distinctive cultural identity abroad.

The one partial exception to the union's modernity, which jeopardized the union from the outset, was the semi-modern society based on slavery. This society was accommodated at the beginning, but conflict was irrepressible, and the South's slave society was crushed militarily during the Civil War of 1861–65 and buried constitutionally during the civil-rights struggle of the 1960s. Likewise, another partial exception, Mormon Utah, was admitted to the union only after the Mormons were compelled to capitulate to modernity by abandoning polygamy (Gordon 2001).

The Civil War also demonstrated the continuity of American federalism and durability of the Constitution despite the trauma of a bloody war. It also revealed the ferocity with which Americans fight what they regard as righteous wars; it forged new modes and weapons of modern warfare; and it set the United States on the path to twentieth-century superpower status. Equally important for contemporary globalization, the federally imposed Reconstruction of the South that followed the war (1865–77), as well as the federally imposed Mormon theological capitulation of 1896, reflected the aggressiveness of American modernity and its expectation that pre-modernity must capitulate to modernity for the sake of individual liberty. Yet, these events also demonstrated generosity toward defeated combatants and US willingness to reintegrate them (i.e., the South) or integrate them (i.e., the Mormons) on terms of equality and with nostalgia about concluded hostilities.

Generally, American values are also consistent with the values commonly associated with globalization. The free-market values associated with contemporary globalization are consistent with American free-enterprise values, just as protests against globalization — all of which include substantial participation of American citizens — are consistent with historic struggles within the United States over free enterprise versus social justice. Indeed, some US advocates for the poor and low-income workers argue that globalization is little more than an expansion and intensification of historic labour struggles. "The worker strategies constructed in the industrial age have been undermined not because globalization has eviscerated labor power but because it weakened old labor strategies and spurred aggressive new elite strategies with which labor has yet to cope" (Piven and Cloward 2000, p. 414).

American values are also largely consistent with what a recent study of non-governmental organizations (NGOs) worldwide concluded is an emerging world culture displaying "five fundamental cultural themes": universalism, individualism, rational voluntaristic authority, the dialectics of rationalizing progress, and world citizenship (Boli and Thomas 1999). Only "world citizenship" lies outside the zone of comfort for most Americans.

Another factor protecting US federalism is that the United States projects its culture onto the world more broadly and deeply than other nations can project their cultures onto the United States. Even opponents of the United States find it impossible to avoid the ubiquitous products of American culture. During the war against the French in Indochina, Ho Chi Minh smoked American cigarettes. During the war with the United States in Vietnam, he did not switch to French cigarettes; he switched to another American brand (Salems). While many critics view American behaviour as proof that globalization is a project of US hegemony, cultural imperialism, and offensive moralism, American leaders tend to view globalization as a natural, even inevitable, process of modernization and expansion of what Americans regard as the universal principles of their own founding. Repeatedly during US history, one finds proclamations such as that of former President John Quincey Adams on 4 July 1831, "our country and her people have been selected as instruments for preparing and maturing much of the good yet in reserve for the welfare and happiness of the human race" (quoted in Jones 1960, p. 11). Arrogant as this must be to the world, it is the product of the Puritans' "errand into the wilderness" (Miller 1964) in which construction of the American federal polity has been understood as a project undertaken on behalf of humanity primarily, and not merely on behalf of the immigrants from every part of the world who constructed that polity.

SITUATIONAL CONTEXT

Territorially, at 9,666,532 sq. km., the United States is the world's third largest nation (behind Russia and Canada). Occupying the temperate zone in mid-North America, warm climates prevail in the sunbelt states, colder climates blanket the snowbelt states. The east enjoys ample rainfall; the west is arid and, thus, dependent on federally funded water and irrigation projects. The Appalachian Mountains run north-south near the east coast, while the Rocky Mountains run north-south in the west. The country's great heartland river of commerce is the Mississippi, flowing south from the Great Lakes region to the Gulf of Mexico. Historically, the United States has had three great sections: east, south, and west. However, there are many regional classifications, which vary according to the purposes of classification.

As a result of eastern-state cessions of their western land claims pursuant to ratification of the Articles of Confederation in 1781, the US government held original title to all territories acquired outside of the original 13 states. Western land sales were a significant source of revenue for the federal government during its first century of existence. During the nineteenth century, the federal government made massive homestead grants to families to encourage settlement and, then, massive land grants to railroads to facilitate continental integration. The federal government also made large land grants to most of the new states that were admitted to the union. In many states, land grants produced sufficient revenue for four to five decades to minimize state own-source taxation. During the Civil War, the federal government also initiated land grants for all states to establish agricultural research and educational institutions. Today, most of these land-grant institutions are large state universities, some of which are among the world's leading universities.

By the end of the nineteenth century, however, the federal government reduced its land grants substantially, including grants to states entering the union. Consequently, the federal government still owns one-third of the land area of the United States. Nearly all federal land is located in Alaska and eight states of the Rocky Mountain West. Environmental conservation was the principal reason for ending the land grants, and controversies over environmental protection, natural-resource development, and federal land management are continuing flashpoints in relations between the federal government and these states. Globalization has exacerbated these intergovernmental tensions because (i) these states wish to succeed in the global economy; (ii) most are experiencing the country's most rapid population growths; (iii) global tourism, especially to the west's popular sites (e.g., the Grand Canyon in Arizona), is distressing fragile environments; and (iv) environmental advocates now view federal lands as global assets, and they link local environmental problems, such as glacier erosion in Alaska and in Glacier National Park in Montana, to global events, such as global warming. Western growth has also provoked some tension with Canada over American proposals that Canada sell water to the US west.

Canada and the United States share the world's longest unfortified border and have enjoyed peaceful though not always conflict-free relations since the War of 1812. The United States is Canada's dominant trading partner, accounting for about 85 percent of Canada's foreign trade and 42 percent of its GDP. Mexico borders the United States along the southwest. The border has been militarily peaceful since 1917, but politically contentious for decades. Key border issues include illegal migration into the United States, drug trafficking, water rights, environmental protection, and Mexican trucks entering US highways pursuant to the North American Free Trade Agreement (NAFTA). Efforts have been made by governors of the contiguous Mexican and US states to resolve border issues, but key decisions remain to be made in Mexico City and Washington, DC. President Vincente Fox has proposed a deepening of NAFTA into a European Union (EU)-style common market with open borders, expansion of NAFTA's North American Development Bank along the lines of the EU's structural funds, and hemispheric economic union. His proposals have received a cool reception in Washington.

The United States has some 286 million people, approximately 80.3 percent of whom are white, 12.3 percent black (or African American), 12.5 percent Hispanic origin (mostly Mexican American), 3.6 percent Asian and Pacific Islander, and 1 percent Indian, Eskimo, and Aleut. About 9.7 percent of the population is foreign born; 915,900 legal immigrants entered the country in 1996; 1,044,689 persons became US citizens through naturalization in 1996; and some 32 million persons age five and over spoke a language other than English in the home in 1990, including 17.3 million who spoke Spanish; 1.7 million, French; 1.5 million, German; 1.3 million, Italian; and 1.2 million, Chinese. The United States has no official language.

Some demographic factors salient to federalism include the following.

The United States has been predominately Protestant and culturally religious. In 1990, 63 percent of the population belonged to religious institutions: 55 percent Protestant, 38 percent Roman Catholic, 3.8 percent Jewish, and 2.5 percent Orthodox Christian. International opinion polls consistently show the United States being the world's first or second most religious nation in terms of popular beliefs in a Supreme Being, life after death, and the like, as well as participation in religious activities. The Jewish-Christian concept of covenant underlies not only American federalism but also Americans' liberal individualist tradition derived from the civil covenant and compact theories of Thomas Hobbes and John Locke.

The US population is dispersed nationwide. There is no dominant state or metropolitan population centre and, thus, no *de facto* political asymmetry in the federal system. Even the less populated prairie centre of the United States is triangulated by huge metropolitan centres — Chicago, Illinois, to the north, Dallas-Ft. Worth and Houston, Texas, to the south, and Denver, Colorado, to the west, with medium-sized metropolitan centres, such as St. Louis, Missouri, interspersed throughout the region. (In contrast, Ontario comprises nearly 40 percent of Canada's population while the six neighbouring US Great Lakes states account for 18 percent of the US population. Similarly, Ontario produces about 55 percent of Canada's manufacturing output, while the Great Lakes states comprise about 25 percent of US manufacturing.) In turn, the United States has no state like Quebec positioned to be a political or cultural barrier between sections of the nation.

The United States is now a suburban nation; about 55 percent of the population lives in suburbs outside both central cities and rural areas. (Approximately 23.8 percent of the US population is rural.) Although the United States is officially 76.2 percent urban, this figure is misleading because the US Bureau of the Census defines "urban" as any place having 2,500 or more residents. No American regards a town of 2,500 people as "urban" or as a "city." Sprawling low-density settlement in small to medium-sized cities (50,000 people or less) is the overwhelming residential preference. Never in the history of the United States has more than one-third of the population lived in urban places having 100,000 or more residents. Although images of the United States often feature big cities like New York City, fewer than 20 percent of Americans live in such cities. One characteristic of big cities, however, is that they have high proportions of poor and minority people, as well as immigrants.

One federalism consequence of sprawling settlement is a continuing preference for local control of certain public matters and ferocious resistance to consolidations of local governments. Advocates of metropolitan consolidation and regionalism have added globalization to their century-old arguments, maintaining that successful competition in today's global economy requires strong subnational regions or "citistates" (Peirce 1993); yet, voters remain deaf to these arguments. Interlocal cooperation has increased, but it has not been induced by globalization; it has been induced by fiscal pressures arising from voter resistance to tax increases and from a precipitous decline in federal aid to local governments since 1978. Recent research, moreover, suggests that global economic activity has had only weak effects on US metropolitan areas because it is too small in magnitude compared to the domestic economy (Eisinger and Smith 2000). It has been estimated, for example, that the GDP-equivalent of the narrowly defined Los Angeles metropolitan area alone is about the 25th largest in the world. A survey of US mayors in 1996 found overwhelmingly that they regarded their main sources of economic competition to be domestic rather than foreign (Kincaid with Handelsman 1997).

Americans are also mobile; nearly one-fifth of the population changes its county of residence each year. This is an historic pattern, not one induced by globalization. This mobility weakens federalism insofar as it weakens citizen ties to states and localities and erodes sectional and regional subcultures; however, it also strengthens federalism insofar as mobility spurs interstate competition for innovation and efficiency in state and local government. Although critics of competitive federalism argue that it induces "races to the bottom," especially in business regulation, social welfare, and environmental protection, there is, to date, little evidence of negative downslides (e.g., Kenyon and Kincaid 1991).

This mobility also helps to explain a distinctive feature of American federalism, namely, the absence of federal fiscal equalization for the constituent states. Most federations, such as Canada and Germany, engage in fiscal equalization. Given that mobility compels no one to live in a poor state, the US government and wealthy states are not seen as being obligated to supply poor states with revenue to provide services equal to the national average or to a constitutional command for "uniformity of living standards" as in Germany's Basic Law (article 106[3]2). (Per capita income ranged from $38,480 in Connecticut to $19,012 in Mississippi in 1998.) Although, as a practical matter, some states, especially in the northeast, have been long-term fiscal donors while some states in the south and west have been immortal vampires, the historic tendency in Congress has been to treat all states roughly equally or in proportion to population with respect to federal largess. Furthermore, unlike some federations (e.g., Canada and Germany) for which fiscal equalization is a key component of the "social compact," this has never been relevant in the United States. The key component of the American "social compact" is the ability of the federal government and Constitution to deliver individual liberty, economic opportunity, and social welfare, plus national security. As a result, rather than redistribute federal revenues to places via fiscal equalization, revenues are redistributed to persons via welfare programs. Such redistribution is the US government's single largest function, consuming 55–70 percent of the federal budget, depending on how one defines redistribution.

Because business is also mobile, there is competition among the states and their localities for investment. State and local subsidies to attract investment are decried as wasteful by virtually all economists and are under threat from international trade agreements; yet, state and local officials continue to offer subsidies. Political and educational efforts to reduce subsidies and to recover subsidies from failed investments have been somewhat successful, but efforts to eliminate subsidies via federal legislation or interstate compacts have failed. Such subsidies long predate globalization, although exaggerated fears of globalization exacerbated the problem in the 1970s and 1980s as states and localities felt pressed to compete more aggressively for foreign direct investment (FDI).

Citizen and business mobility, coupled with economic growth and governmental reform since World War II, have produced profound changes in most states, particularly economic diversification and party competition. Prior to the war, most states were dominated by one economic factor, such as cotton in many southern states, cattle and then oil in Texas, and copper in Montana. Likewise, most states were dominated by one political party, such as solidly Democratic states in the south and solidly Republican states in the north. Growing economic diversification and rising two-party competition, however, contributed greatly to the late twentieth-century "resurgence of the states" (Bowman and Kearney 1986) as more reformed, efficient, and effective democratic polities. The governmental capacities and abilities of most states now equal or exceed those of the federal government.

A looming demographic problem is the country's aging population, which will increase dramatically after 2010 when the first "baby boomers" (1946–64) reach age 65 and, then, live increasingly longer. As of 1996, life expectancy for women was 79 years; for men, it was 73 years. In 1998, some 63,000 persons were age 100 or more (compared to 37,000 in 1990). Because senior citizens, who make up about 14 percent of the population, have a high voting rate and a strong interest in social welfare, the aging population is likely to further centralize tax revenues and weaken state and local revenue bases. More than 50 percent of the federal budget is already dedicated to entitlement payments to individuals, mostly senior citizens who receive old-age assistance (Social Security), health-care assistance (Medicare), and other assistance. Hence, the United States spends about half, nearly $1 trillion, of its federal budget on 14 percent of its population. Social Security and Medicare, which are federal programs, were two of the leading issues in the 2000 presidential election. The federal Social Security and Medicare taxes, which are already the largest tax bites for the majority of taxpayers (i.e., larger than their federal income-tax payments), could become onerous burdens for non-seniors. At the same time, senior citizens exert downward pressure on state and local revenues because they tend to resist property taxes and extension of the sales tax to services, vote against school bonds and general-obligation bonds for capital investment, and lobby effectively for exemptions from state and local income taxes. In addition, Medicaid, which is an intergovernmental health-care program for the poor partly financed by the states at rates of 50 percent to 21 percent (depending on state per capita income), is now the second largest category of state spending (after K–12 education). Approximately 75 percent of Medicaid spending goes to about 25 percent of Medicaid's beneficiaries, namely, persons in long-term care or nursing homes, most of whom are senior citizens, and many of whom were previously middle-class but became eligible for Medicaid by spending down their assets on late-life health care and/or transferring assets to their children.

As of 1999, 11.8 percent of the US population (32.3 million people) was classified as poor, the lowest poverty rate since 1979. The real level of poverty is lower, however, because the official measure of poverty excludes

non-cash assistance (e.g., housing vouchers and Medicaid) which constitute the bulk of social welfare. In addition, Congress has increasingly
alleviated poverty through tax credits. The federal Earned Income Tax
Credit (EITC) now lifts more people out of poverty than any other single
federal poverty program. Many states have an EITC as well.

Average annual unemployment was 4.2 percent in 1999, the lowest
since 1969; median household income reached a new high, with gross
national product (GNP) per capita purchasing power parity dollars (PPP$)
reaching $28,020 (compared to $21,380 for Canada and $7,660 for
Mexico); and the income disparity between the rich and the poor, which
had widened between 1973 and 1993, has remained unchanged since 1993.
The 1990s marked the longest period of continuous peacetime economic
growth in US history, and the federal budget showed a surplus in 1998
for the first time since 1969. This surplus was a major issue in the 2000
presidential election, with Republican Governor George W. Bush proposing to use part of it for a tax cut and Democratic Vice President Al Gore
proposing to use part of it to reduce the national debt.

How much of this economic growth can be attributed to globalization is difficult to say. US exports as a share of worldwide exports increased
only from 15.7 percent in 1993 to 17.7 percent in 1999, compared to
34.7 percent to 38 percent for the European Union, although the rest of
the world's share of exports declined from 49.6 to 44.3 percent. At the
same time, the United States incurred continual trade deficits during the
1990s, with a record trade deficit of $34.3 billion recorded in September
2000. Most economists, though, attribute these deficits to a robust
economy that has grown faster than the economies of America's trading
partners. During the 1970s and 1980s, US corporations appeared to be
stagnant, bloated, and lagging behind Japan and Germany in innovation
and product quality, but by the 1990s, US corporations had responded to
perceived threats of global competition by restructuring, downsizing, and
improving productivity, especially through the introduction of computer
technology. The US marketplace also became extraordinarily receptive to
entrepreneurial innovation and to foreign entrepreneurs who found it easier
to build a new business in the United States than in their home country.

Perhaps the leading political issue has been whether globalization
favours the rich and powerful, thus accounting for the depression of real-
wage growth for the average American and for the income-disparity growth
that occurred between about 1973 and 1993, in particular because of

declining manufacturing due to low-wage competition and other forms of "unfair" competition (e.g., lax environmental regulation) from abroad. Third-party candidates Ross Perot and Pat Buchanan made much of such issues in the 1994, 1996, and 2000 presidential elections. Each employed inflammatory rhetoric, such as Buchanan's claim that cheap "communist crawfish from China" are undercutting Louisiana's crawfish industry and Perot's 1992 claim that the approval of NAFTA with Canada and Mexico would produce a "giant sucking sound" of US jobs draining into cheap-labour, environmentally decadent Mexico. Although Perot and Buchanan failed to win the White House, one consequence of their concern was congressional refusal to renew "fast-track" negotiating authority on free-trade agreements for President Bill Clinton in 1994 — one year after congressional approval of NAFTA. President Bush is seeking reauthorization of fast-track authority, just as Gore, if elected, would have requested reauthorization, although he would have been constrained by key constituents in his party, especially labour unions.

There are, in reality, two answers to the question of whether globalization has reduced US wages and increased income disparity: empirical and political. The results of empirical research are mixed, but the weight of evidence suggests that real-wage depression and income disparity arose primarily from domestic social and economic factors, especially technological change and the shift toward a service economy, and only secondarily from economic globalization (e.g., Feenstra 2000). Although manufacturing's "current prices" share of GDP declined to 16.4 percent in 1998 (down from 18.7 percent in 1987 and 26.9 percent in 1947), its GDP share in 1996 constant dollars has remained at about 17 percent since 1977; the number of workers on manufacturing payrolls has hovered at about 18.5 million since 1970; America's 380,000 manufacturing firms produced 50 percent more than Japan's firms and one-third more than the combined output of France, Germany, and the United Kingdom during the 1990s; manufacturing productivity increased by 31.6 percent between 1992 and 1999 (50 percent higher than Canada or the UK and one-third higher than Japan); manufacturing accounted for about 80 percent of America's $696 billion of 1999 exports; total hourly compensation for hourly manufacturing employees averaged $23.74 in 1999; for every $1 invested abroad in manufacturing in 1998, US manufacturers invested $7 at home; and while some $147 billion was invested abroad by US manufacturers from 1994 to 1998, foreigners invested some $209 billion in US manufacturing. Furthermore, of some $27 billion US investments in foreign manufacturing in 1998, about 80 percent went to high-wage countries; only 7 percent went to Mexico and China (Siekman 2000). Canadian direct investment in the United States increased by 82 percent from 1994 to 1998, and the United States remains the largest host country for Canadian FDI, while Canada's share of US direct investment abroad declined from 66 percent in 1987 to 52 percent in 1997 (Testa, Oppedahl and Merkel 2000).

The political answer is that so long as the US economy remains robust, Americans will be little concerned about economic globalization. Public approval of free-trade agreements stood at 61 percent in 1997, 59 percent in 1998, 60 percent in 1990, and 57 percent in 2000 (Sarpolus 2000). However, if the current slowing of the economy becomes a recession or worse, protectionist sentiment for tariffs, import restrictions, and export subsidies to boost employment will gain political ground.

This points to a precarious feature of the global economy: the behemothic position of the US economy and US dollar. Although many observers, such as Thomas Friedman (1999), argue that no one is in charge of globalization, this is not exactly true. Alan Greenspan, chairman of the Federal Reserve Board is, *de facto*, in charge. His command position is also due to changes in world monetary policy and to the shift away from fiscal policy and toward monetary policy as the principal mechanism of domestic economic regulation. A failure by the Federal Reserve Board to prevent a US recession would reduce US imports (with Canada and Mexico being the most dependent on these imports), reduce the value of the dollar against other major currencies, pull down stock markets elsewhere, and reduce capital flows, especially into developing economies, thus driving the global economy into recession and sending many developing countries into depression. Given the dependence of the US economy on oil, the one exogenous factor that could trigger a recession would be a sharp increase in oil prices.

If voters respond to recession with demands for protectionism, globalization could give way to balkanization and cause serious political, diplomatic, and military problems. The potential magnitude of the impact of protectionism is highlighted by the fact that Americans already produce 88 percent of what they buy and that some 82 percent of Americans are employed in sectors scarcely involved in global trade, namely, government, non-profits, construction, utilities, and wholesale and retail trade (Lawrence 1997). "The United States is still almost 90% an economy that produces goods and services for its own use" (Krugman 1997, p. 166). Whether the EU and European Monetary Union (EMU) are strong enough to counterbalance a recession is uncertain.

Politically and militarily, the United States is the world's single most powerful national actor, although, like all major powers historically, it does not always get its way. Americans are also ambivalent about their political and military roles in the world. This is largely why, since the end of both the Cold War and the Persian Gulf War in the early 1990s, US foreign policy has lacked consistent, coherent direction. Although Americans generally support globalization, they fear adverse consequences for the United States and are highly suspicious of efforts to strengthen or establish international institutions to govern globalization. They are, in effect, latter-day Anti-federalists, and refuse to rush into international governmental arrangements, especially with 190-some co-equal partners, most of which are undemocratic. Furthermore, given US emphasis on free-market principles in the global economy, Americans are just as reluctant to vest too much regulatory authority in international institutions as they are in their own government institutions.

Historically, isolationism has been a strong tradition, derived partly from George Washington's warning that the nation not become entangled in permanent alliances. Most early leaders preferred neutrality as the policy response to the powerful conflicts in Europe, especially between Great Britain and France, both of which posed military threats to the United States on North American soil and on the oceans. The French Revolution of 1789 had also divided Americans between those who celebrated the revolution and those who were appalled by its terror. Nevertheless, President Thomas Jefferson's naval response to the so-called Barbary Pirates in 1804 and President James Monroe's 1823 declaration that European powers stay out of the Western Hemisphere's internal affairs reflected US willingness to defend its commercial and national interests. For the remainder of the century, however, the United States was preoccupied with nation-building such that, by the mid-1890s, the United States had concluded its Indian wars, consolidated its continental union, and achieved its economic independence.

This isolationist tradition had disastrous consequences for the United States and the world when, after World War I, the nation, despite Democratic President Woodrow Wilson's internationalism, demobilized its military, refused to join the League of Nations, amended the Constitution to impose alcoholic-beverage prohibition nationwide, and then raised tariffs. A period of economic globalization, which had begun in the 1880s and could have been revived after the war, remained moribund.

Arguably, World War II marked the onset of globalization for the United States and its campaign of global modernization. Having learned costly lessons from World War I, the United States pursued an aggressive postwar foreign policy involving, among other things, establishment of the United Nations, creation of security alliances such as the North Atlantic Treaty Organization (NATO), economic reconstruction of Western Europe and Japan, transformation of Germany and Japan into democratic polities, repeated encouragement for Europe to forge a "United States of Europe," development of instruments of international monetary stabilization, promotion of free trade, recognition of Israel, the face-down of the USSR during the Berlin Crisis of 1948, and promulgation of notions of international justice and universal human rights. This was the golden age of US foreign policy. The results were remarkable and unprecedented in history. At the same time, there were significant failures, especially the rise of the Cold War and its nearly 50-year threat of nuclear annihilation. The United States also failed to compel its European allies to liberate all their colonies — a failure that later had costly foreign and domestic consequences for the United States in Vietnam and elsewhere.

Culturally and sociologically, World War II was an important nation-building event in US history. In effect, America entered the war as *these* United States and ended the war as *the* United States. Prior to the war, the average American had had little contact with the federal government outside the Post Office. Furthermore, up until the mid-1930s, state and local governments had accounted for more than two-thirds of all own-source revenues in the federal system, with local governments accounting for more than 50 percent alone. The United States became a world power by the early twentieth century even while its governmental system was financed predominantly by local taxes and secondarily by state taxes, and without the federal government crossing the 50 percent own-source revenue threshold until the enactment of the federal Social Security tax in 1935 and, then, the tax increases needed to finance World War II.

During the war, massive societal mobilization was necessarily led by the federal government; federal regulation of the economy and of consumer behaviour became omnipresent; Americans united behind the war effort as never before; millions of men and women served in the US armed forces under presidential command and were also exposed to foreign cultures, including those of their forebears' homelands; the federal income-tax was expanded to embrace all Americans; and the introduction of tax withholding from wages suddenly gave Americans a weekly reminder of the federal government's existence. Before the war, the army was essentially a federation of state units under presidential command in time of war. The famous Rainbow (42nd) Division formed in World War I of volunteers from all the state units was a precursor of the post-World War II integration of state units into the total force structure of the military under a unified command situated in the Pentagon, though with state army and Air National Guards continuing under gubernatorial command in the absence of wartime call-ups.

The war also engendered social transformations. Black soldiers who had fought for freedom abroad revolted against racial discrimination at home. White-ethnic veterans (e.g., Irish, Italian, and Polish Americans) often revolted against corrupt urban political machines, which were powerful county party organizations. Women who had worked in factories and offices during the war asserted new rights. The two-front (Atlantic and Pacific) war required expansions of military facilities and stimulation of economic development in the south and west, thus opening these regions to massive postwar in-migration. Federal legislation to repay veterans contributed to massive expansion of higher education and massive suburbanization via subsidized home ownership. War-time transportation problems helped stimulate establishment of the massive federal-aid highway program of 1956 — the Dwight D. Eisenhower System of Interstate and Defense Highways — which further aided suburbanization and metropolitanization and gave rise to America's automobile culture and increasing greenhouse gas emissions. Federal support for research and development (R&D) during the war demonstrated the critical importance of R&D not only for the military but for the economy as well. The war also weakened America's limited government tradition, especially limited federal government, by demonstrating government's capacity to deliver public goods at home and abroad. This new vision of government achieved its last great expression in Democratic President Lyndon B. Johnson's Great Society of the mid-1960s and in the Vietnam War, both of which divided Americans into today's limited-government and capacious-government camps. In summary, before World War II, the average American was either a poorly educated rural hick, small-town boob, or not-very-urbane city slicker. The war, however, not only unified the nation of immigrants in a new way sociologically but also propelled the polyglot nation's cultural passage into modernity.

Nevertheless, the basic structure of American federalism and its Constitution remained intact. Compared to the challenges to American federalism of World War I, the Great Depression, World War II, and the Cold War, therefore, contemporary globalization is not yet a serious threat.

CONSTITUTIONAL/FEDERAL FRAMEWORK

The United States was born in revolt against global colonialism rather than against domestic feudalism. The seeds of American identity were planted during the war that Americans call the French and Indian War (1754–63), known also as the Seven Years' War, which raged along the western frontier of eastern North America and embattled regions from Canada to the West Indies and West Africa and from Great Britain and across Europe to India and the Philippines. It was the first world war of the modern era, with Great Britain, Hanover, and Prussia aligned against France, Austria, and Russia. The war achieved nothing but the *status quo ante* for Europe's combatants, but in what is now the United States, it gave George Washington his first military-command experience as a junior officer, as well as knowledge of British military strategy; resulted in Britain's conquest of New France in North America; sounded the death knell of the Iroquois confederacy; forged bonds and a nascent common identity among the American colonists; gave birth to visions of an American "manifest destiny" (i.e., westward conquest); and produced postwar tensions between the American colonists and their mother country with which they had fought and won the war.

Prior to the Declaration of Independence in 1776, the 13 colonies had established a loose alliance under two Continental Congresses. During the Revolutionary War, the newly independent states formalized their relationship under the Articles of Confederation of 1781, which created a "perpetual union." Immediately after the war, leaders in various states, who later called themselves Federalists, advocated a stronger federal union. The confederation government was, in their view, too weak, especially with respect to commerce and national defence. The Constitutional Convention that met in Philadelphia in 1787 produced a constitution for "a more perfect union," which was ratified by 1788 and went into operation in 1789 with the installation of the first Congress, inauguration of George Washington as the first president, and appointment of the first justices to the Supreme Court. The constitutional ratification campaign produced the greatest work of American political theory, *The Federalist Papers*, written by Alexander Hamilton, James Madison, and John Jay under the name Publius.

The framers of the Constitution sought principally to achieve four objectives: (i) establish a free, continental, common market that would enable the new nation to become a great commercial republic; (ii) protect individual and community liberty under a federal republican government of strong but limited, delegated powers; (iii) ensure the defence of the republic against the superpowers of that era — France, Great Britain, Russia, and Spain — all of which had military forces on what is now US soil as well as navies on sea lanes vital to US commerce and defence; and (iv) manage the expansion, pacification, settlement, and admission to the union of vast western lands.

The most singular innovation of the new Constitution, according to Hamilton, was the authority of the new "federal" government, unlike the old federal (i.e., confederal) government, to legislate directly for individuals (i.e., levy direct taxes, regulate individual and corporate entities, and conscript citizens). The Constitution established dual sovereignty and dual citizenship in which the federal government was delegated limited but potentially expansive powers (via the elastic "necessary and proper" clause of article I, section 8) to legislate for citizens nationwide. Within the realm of federal sovereignty, the US Constitution, treaties, and federal statutes are "the supreme Law of the Land" (article VI). Outside that realm, the state constitutions and state statutes are the supreme laws of the nation's constituent lands. The Tenth Amendment (1791) to the Constitution, moreover, explicitly reserves to the states or to the people (who are ultimately sovereign) all "powers not delegated to the United States by the Constitution, nor prohibited by it to the States." Much of the history of US federalism, therefore, is one of friendly debate and vigorous conflict over which constitution and which law should prevail — federal or state.

The Constitution also embodies the separation of legislative, executive, and judicial powers, in which it pioneered the modern idea of a strong, independent judiciary. All 50 state constitutions also embody the separation of powers, more and less sharply than the US Constitution.

The addition of the Bill of Rights (first ten amendments) to the Constitution in 1791 reflected an effort to address Antifederalists' fears that the founders had engineered a *coup d'etat* to consolidate power and suppress liberty. The Bill of Rights was of virtually no consequence for some 150 years, partly because each state constitution has a Declaration of Rights, but since World War II, the federal Bill of Rights has assumed enormous constitutional, political, and social importance.

The powers delegated to the federal government fall into two categories: first, interstate and foreign commerce and second, national defence and foreign affairs. Likewise, most of the Constitution's restrictions on state powers fall into these categories, and are intended to prevent states from erecting barriers to common-market integration (e.g., the "full faith and credit" and the "privileges and immunities" clauses of article IV); to prevent state legislatures from "impairing the Obligation of Contracts" (article I, section 10) — given that contracts are the foundation of a free market and free society; and to ensure that states support but not obstruct national defence. As per the Constitution's roots in modernity, both the federal government and the states are prohibited from granting titles of nobility, and the United States is obligated to "guarantee to every State in this Union a Republican Form of Government" (article IV, section 4).

The limited government tradition in the United States is reflected not only in the limits placed on the federal government, which Alexis de Tocqueville called an "incomplete national government," but also in the language employed by Americans. For example, unlike Europe, the concept of "the state" has never had a place in American popular discourse. What others call "the state," Americans call "the government" (often "the damn guvment"). To an American, the word "state" means New Jersey, Iowa, and the like. Similarly, discourse in the EU refers to allocations of "competences" among levels of government; Americans have customarily used the word "powers," and not even "power" because all power resides in the people, who can choose to parcel out pieces of their power to governments. Traditionally, most Americans never assumed that government is inherently competent or naturally disposed toward competence; instead, government — especially big, distant government — is a necessary evil that wields always potentially dangerous powers. One change that has occurred since World War II, however, is that many Americans, mostly in the Democratic Party, now believe that government is able to exercise comprehensive power competently and benignly. The concept of "the state" has also gained currency among American political scientists, most of whom vote Democratic. The roots of this view lie in the late nineteenth century when the emergence of big corporations and monopolies was seen as a threat to democracy, thus requiring the public power of government, the instrument of the people, to counterbalance private power. The anti-trust case brought against Microsoft was based on federal statutes enacted during that era.

Although the world (and many Americans) might regard the United States as having very big government, all governments in the US federal system remain generally less regulatory and less tax costly than their foreign democratic counterparts. The gigantic size of the United States and its economy also creates misleading perceptions. What looks large outside the United States may be small or insignificant within the United States. For example, while the country maintains the world's most powerful and far-flung military establishment, it does so with less than 10 percent of the federal government's budget and only 3.2 percent of its GDP (down from its last peak of 6.5 percent in the mid-1980s during Republican President Ronald Reagan's military buildup).

Furthermore, the American approach to empowering government to perform more expansive functions is not to load powers into one government but rather to multiply governments to perform more specific functions and to intergovernmentalize the exercise of power. The United States has more than 87,000 local governments, with local special-district governments procreating rapidly. Local government is nowhere mentioned in the US Constitution because it falls within the purview of state constitutional sovereignty. Each state is, strictly speaking, a unitary polity; however, all states accord their general-purpose local governments (i.e., counties, municipalities, and townships) substantial self-governing autonomy, including their own tax, budget, borrowing, and police powers. (There is no federal police force in the United States. The FBI, Secret Service, and other federal agencies having arrest authority perform investigative or protective functions, not general police functions.)

Despite considerable centralization of the federal system during the late twentieth century (Kincaid 1993), the 50 states continue to be significantly sovereign in many respects. In revenue matters, for example, there are only a few inconsequential federal constitutional restrictions on state tax powers (mostly to protect commerce against discriminatory and retaliatory state taxation). Consequently, states levy nearly 40 different taxes, with the income tax and sales tax being the principal sources of state revenue. The property tax is reserved mainly for local governments, although some local governments have been granted modest sales-tax and income-tax powers as well. There are no significant federal restrictions on state and local borrowing, although states impose restrictions on local borrowing. However, the principal mechanisms of fiscal discipline for state and local governments are the bond market and voters (who must approve general-obligation debt, which is paid off with tax money).

Autonomy also allows state and local governments to engage globalization. A key additional factor is that most states are large in their own right; most have larger economies and larger government budgets than most of the world's nation-states. The leading example is California, whose population exceeds Canada's 31 million people. If California were an independent nation, it would have the world's seventh largest economy and one of the world's largest government budgets. The 50 states, moreover, manage and invest nearly $1 trillion in public pension funds plus about $700 billion in annual operating funds. Consequently, the states together, large states such as California and New York alone, and several big cities such as New York City alone can wield substantial financial clout in global markets. For example, threats by a handful of states and New York City to exercise this clout on behalf of Jewish Holocaust victims and their families living in the United States compelled Swiss banks and the government of Switzerland to begin disclosing bank assets seized from Jews during World War II and to pay compensation. Given the increasing domestic social activism of state attorneys general, treasurers, secretaries of state, and others — many of whom are elected executive officials in most states — there will be more such social-conscience forays into international markets by the states.

No amendments to the US Constitution can be attributed to globalization, nor have any amendments altered the basic structure or institutions of the federal system. The most recent amendment (XXVII, 1992), concerning pay increases for members of Congress, was one that had failed ratification in 1791 as part of the Bill of Rights but had no ratification limit. This dormant amendment was discovered by a university student in Texas while writing a term paper. He launched a successful campaign to complete ratification of the 200-year-old proposal.

Three amendments, however, have had profound impacts on the federal system. The Sixteenth Amendment (1913) gave Congress the "power to lay and collect taxes on income, from whatever source derived." This amendment had little domestic consequence until after World War II when the federal income tax became a tremendous fiscal vehicle for regulating the economy, entering policy fields customarily reserved to state and local governments via grants-in-aid, and placing downward competitive pressure on state and local income taxation. The Seventeenth Amendment (1913) provided for the direct election of US senators rather than their selection by the state legislatures. Thus, senators were converted from being ambassadors of their states *qua* states to being direct representatives of the people of their states. These two amendments were products of the Progressive Movement, which advocated a new democratic nationalism, a stronger national government, federal regulation of the economy, the vesting of more power in voters, and redistribution of income from the rich to the poor.

More important is the Fourteenth Amendment, which states, among other things, that no state shall "deprive any person of life, liberty, or property, without due process of law; nor deny to any person within its jurisdiction the equal protection of the laws." This amendment was ratified in 1868 to protect the newly freed blacks in the southern states. The amendment did nothing for blacks for a century, but it did generate two social revolutions. First, the US Supreme Court used it to promote *laissez faire* economic development in the late nineteenth and early twentieth centuries by striking down many state efforts to regulate economic matters (and doing the same to the federal government by defining the interstate commerce clause narrowly). This line of jurisprudence was overturned by the Court itself in 1937 when the Court was under enormous pressure to do so by Democratic President Franklin D. Roosevelt's New Deal forces during the Great Depression. Second, and at the same time, the Supreme Court began to use the Fourteenth Amendment to apply the Bill of Rights to state and local government action. This line of jurisprudence, which has, in its fundamentals, enjoyed popular acceptance, is the legal basis for the civil rights, civil liberties, and equality revolutions that transformed American society during the 1960s and, as noted earlier, finally buried the remains of southern slavery.

This constitutional rights revolution has allowed Americans to reconceptualize and nationalize the federal system in fundamental ways without rewriting the federal Constitution. This judicially induced revolution, coupled with the direct election of senators and the federal individual income-tax power, might have rescued the federal system from possibly strong postwar pressure to amend the Constitution fundamentally. As such, the judicial revolution inadvertently allowed federalism — even the presumed dead notion of dual sovereignty — to be resurrected (controversially) by the Supreme Court during the 1990s.

The United States is in the midst of a significant debate about the nature of its federal democracy, a debate well reflected in the contested 2000 election. Gore and most Democrats believe not only that Gore would have won the election if votes had not been undercounted in Florida but also that he should have won the presidency because he won the national popular vote. Bush believes that he won the presidency because he won in 30 of the 50 states, including Florida, and, hence, won the majority of electoral college votes needed constitutionally to capture the White House. A majority of Americans now oppose the electoral college because it is archaic and undemocratic. The mantra of Gore's post-election campaign was that everyone's vote should count, and count equally.

Abolition of the electoral college would be a significant structural change in the federal system because there has never been a means for the American people as a whole to express a direct majority or plurality will. As Madison argued in *The Federalist*, a principal rationale for the federal system was to rescue democracy from itself and to protect individual liberty by making it impossible for a simple (50 percent + 1), and possibly simple-minded, national majority to rule the country. Hence, the president is not elected by a direct national popular vote but rather by majorities or pluralities within enough states to gain a majority of the electoral college votes. US senators are elected by the people of each state, and US House of Representatives members are elected by the people from districts within each state. US Supreme Court justices and federal judges are nominated by the president and confirmed by the Senate, and they are term-limited only by death, resignation, or impeachment. Amendments to the US Constitution require a two-thirds vote of each house of Congress and ratification by the state legislatures or popularly elected conventions in three-fourths of the states. There are no national referendums, initiatives, or recalls — although mixes of such mechanisms exist in all the states and in most general-purpose local governments.

The current debate reflects a two-century debate over the meaning of the preamble to the Constitution: "We the People of the United States." Does this phrase mean "we the whole people of the whole United States" or "we the people of the several states of these united states?" Nationalists from Hamilton to Gore have emphasized the former; anti-nationalists (and southern secessionists) have emphasized the latter. The anti-nationalists have a slight factual edge because there are no mechanisms for the whole American people to express a majority will, and the federal Constitution itself was ratified by a popularly elected convention in each state. A state rejecting the Constitution would not have joined the union. The nationalists respond, however, that once the people of a state vote to join the union, their decision is irrevocable, as reaffirmed by the union's victory in the Civil War, and they become citizens of the United States and, thus, a part of the whole American people of the whole United States, even while they also remain citizens of the states. The US government, therefore, is a direct expression of the will of the American people. Even so, the preamble does not say, "We the American People."

As Tocqueville predicted, the people's desire for equality, the power of majority opinion, and the complexity of federalism, which is beyond the ken of the average citizen, would likely erode Madison's conception of federal democracy and press the federal system toward a more centralized national democracy. Vast expansion of federal power was the hallmark of twentieth-century US federalism. In a general way, the Democratic Party has come to represent the national democracy view while the Republican Party has come to represent the federal democracy view (although there are important qualifications to this generalization). The battleline between these views was drawn unusually sharply in the 2000 election, though not explicitly, with both sides having roughly equal public support. The Supreme Court's recent federalism jurisprudence is a bellwether indicator of this divisive debate; every one of its state-friendly, dual-federalist decisions, which began to be issued in 1991, has been a five-to-four ruling.

In the debate about the electoral college, which is the most vulnerable structure of US federalism because it can easily be criticized as undemocratic, some critics will employ the rhetoric of globalization. President Clinton stated that the 2000 election was an international embarrassment. However, the electoral college has not been an obstacle to the rise of the United States as a viable federal democracy and world power. It caused no serious problems or constitutional crises for two centuries, while producing a decisive result in 49 (91 percent) of 54 presidential elections. Since popular voting for electors was widely implemented in the 1820s, the popular vote winner has also been the electoral victor in 41 (91 percent) of 45 elections.

From the perspective of globalization, this is perhaps an argument for retaining the electoral college because direct popular election of the president could generate instability and weakened legitimacy by producing plurality-winning presidents or by requiring run-off elections, and by opening the political arena to divisive third-parties, all of which could weaken or complicate America's global role. Arguably, the electoral college also has direct relevance to foreign affairs insofar as it magnifies the voice of certain states and minorities in presidential elections. This is one reason why California, which has the single largest impact on presidential elections, has been able to shield some controversial tax policies affecting international business from federal assault. Neither Reagan nor Clinton wished to risk California's wrath by vigorously opposing its tax policies. Likewise, minority groups, such as blacks and Jews in New York and Mexican-Americans in Texas, can, by voting as blocs, carry a large state for a presidential candidate and, thus, claim a right to influence the administration's policy toward Israel, Africa, or Mexico and Latin America.

REGIONAL AND INTERNATIONAL RELATIONSHIPS

The United States is a member of more than 120 multilateral international organizations, including the United Nations (with a permanent seat on the Security Council and current participation in 16 UN peacekeeping missions), African Development Bank, Asian Development Bank, Inter-American Defense Board (the oldest permanently constituted, international military organization), Inter-American Development Bank, Inter-American Investment Corporation, International Bank for Reconstruction and Development (i.e., the World Bank), International Finance Corporation, International Monetary Fund (IMF), International Organization for Migration, NATO, Organization of American States, OECD, and World Trade Organization (WTO). The United States is also a member of five bilateral organizations: International Boundary Commission with Canada, International Joint Commission with Canada, Permanent Joint Board on Defense with Canada, International Boundary and Water Commission with Mexico, and Joint Mexican-United States Defense Commission (US. Office of the Federal Register 2000).

Although the United States is criticized for refusing to pay its full dues obligation to the United Nations, the United States is often the largest financial and military supporter of international organizations. It is also well-known that the United States devotes a comparatively small portion of its national budget and GDP to foreign aid. However, from a US perspective, American defence costs for Western Europe, Japan, and other countries since 1945 must be added to the calculation. Furthermore, the economic benefits of US security guarantees for other countries' national economies exceed what could be achieved by foreign aid. US defence has also relieved many nations of the need to divert large portions of their GDP to defence for the past 55 years. Additionally, US citizens, foundations, and corporations contribute billions of dollars annually to international governmental and non-governmental organizations and have been the prime movers behind many prominent international NGOs such as Amnesty International, Greenpeace, and the Red Cross. Immigrants to the United States and their descendants send billions of dollars abroad to their families, and some ethnic or religious groups provide enormous support to homelands, such as Jewish support for Israel and Arab support for Middle East countries.

With respect to globalization, several observations might be made about US concerns and approaches. For one, the United States is extremely sensitive about international encroachments upon its constitutional sovereignty. This has been a significant factor in the US Senate's refusal to ratify treaties that might subject the country or its citizens to international legal action (e.g., the International Court for Crimes Against Humanity), a concern heightened by the fact that criminal and civil law are predominantly state powers. Governors and state legislatures are reluctant to surrender their sovereignty as well. Hence, the United States prefers confederal international arrangements in which international institutions lack authority to legislate for individuals, at least within the United States. This attitude might change if democratization spreads and strengthens worldwide, but Americans have also been unwilling to submit to international confederal institutions in which the United States can be outvoted on consequential matters by undemocratic regimes. So long as such institutions remain hortative debating and educational organizations, the United States acquiesces to equal confederate membership. Second, therefore, within consequential institutions, the United States usually insists on a veto power (e.g., the UN Security Council), supreme military command, or weighted voting consistent with what it regards as its economic and military status. Third, this also means that the United States is unlikely to support a transformation of NAFTA into an EU-equivalent. NAFTA is a free-trade area, not an economic union, and it is a trilateral relationship consisting of three bilateral agreements: US-Canada, US-Mexico, and Canada-Mexico. Given the giant size of the US economy in the western hemisphere, any expansion of NAFTA will have to conform to the US preference for the hub-and-spoke model in which each nation concludes a treaty or agreement with the United States and then with each other.

Fourth, consistent with the nation's commercial-republic rationale, Americans believe that economic development is vital for democracy and that economic development and democracy ensure peace. These are among the major reasons why the United States has supported economic development abroad since World War II. It has often done so by extending into the global arena equivalents of its own principles and institutions, such as the promotion of free trade, the support for regional commercial unions such as the EU, the establishment of international institutions such as the IMF (created in 1945) along lines similar to the US Federal Reserve system, the creation of the World Bank in 1945 to provide loans to developing countries, and the provision of grants-in-aid. The United States supported the establishment of the Multilateral Investment Guarantee Agency in 1988 to facilitate private investment in developing member countries by offering long-term political risk insurance against expropriation, currency transfer, and war and civil disturbance.

Such institutions and their policies are often criticized as US efforts to dominate the world. For Americans, they are efforts to apply federal-like principles from their own continental integration to global integration. What others may view as self-serving policies might, in fact, be self-serving; US foreign policy is not driven by pure altruism. But such policies are often viewed in the United States as Tocquevillean "self-interest rightly understood," namely, that world peace and security ensure US peace and security and that by tying nations to international institutions able to foster peace and prosperity, the citizens, if not always the leaders, of nation-states will develop a vested self-interest in maintaining peace. Research supports Tocqueville's theory that democracies are much less likely to wage war against each other than are non-democracies (Hensel, Goertz and Diehl 2000). During the Cold War, the United States had only a secondary self-interest in promoting democracy because its primary interest lay in maintaining friendly regimes and geo-political stability. Now, in the post-Cold War era, the United States has a stronger self-interest in promoting democracy and economic development in order to integrate China and

Russia into a pacific trading regime and to reduce ethnic warfare, which is difficult to prevent diplomatically and to suppress militarily, and for which political support for military intervention is weak at home.

Every country brings its traditions into the global arena; the United States is no exception, but it happens to be the biggest player. American reluctance, for example, to forgive a country's debt is consistent with American domestic tradition. The federal government is not obligated to rescue debt-ridden state or local governments. When New York City teetered on the edge of bankruptcy in 1975, Republican President Gerald R. Ford refused to help the (hugely Democratic) city, prompting a famous *New York Daily News* headline: "Ford to City: Drop Dead." Likewise, state governments are not obligated to bail out municipal governments. Most states monitor municipal budgets to prevent bankruptcy, and a state government will take over a fiscally stressed city, but this is more difficult in the case of fiscally stressed nations. The IMF has been criticized for imposing stringent financial rules on distressed nations similar to those New York State imposed on New York City when it took over the city's financial affairs in 1975.

The United States was also crucial to the establishment of the WTO and remains the principal political decisionmaker on admitting new members, such as China and Russia. The WTO is not, strictly speaking, a *de jure* surrender of national sovereignty because a member nation can refuse to comply with a ruling and, thus, allow itself to be subject to retaliation or, alternately, pay compensation. For the United States, the WTO is not much of a *de facto* surrender of sovereignty either because its economy can absorb retaliation or pay compensation more easily than any other national economy. To date, the WTO has had no adverse impact on the United States. During WTO's first five years (up to 18 April 2000), the United States was a single party in 42 of 187 complaints filed with the WTO. According to the US General Accounting Office:

> As a plaintiff, the United States prevailed in a final WTO dispute settlement ruling in 13 cases, resolved the dispute without a ruling in 10 cases, and did not prevail in 2 cases. As a defendant, the United States prevailed in 1 case, resolved the dispute without a ruling in 10 cases, and lost in 6 cases.
>
> Overall ... the United States has gained more than it has lost in the WTO dispute settlement system to date. WTO cases have resulted in a

substantial number of changes in foreign trade practices, while their effect on US laws and regulations has been minimal (US General Accounting Office 2000).

Fifth, the United States insists that private investment and free markets are the best routes to economic development and to democracy, in part because the voluntary behaviours and individual rights needed to sustain a market economy are also needed to sustain democracy. This dimension of the US approach to globalization has been subject to immense criticism, however, not only outside the United States but also within the country, as reflected in the riotous protests at the WTO meeting in Seattle, Washington, in 1999. Yet, such criticism is also consistent with US tradition, such as the Populist and Progressive movements of the late nineteenth century, the labour union movement of the mid-twentieth century, and the social protest movements of the 1960s. While most of the US corporate sector will campaign for the freest unfettered global trade possible, increasingly assertive citizen organizations will campaign for global labour and human rights, environmental protection, social welfare, and the like. US government policy-making will be whipsawed between these poles.

Sixth, Americans have vigorously projected the third sector of their political economy into the global arena, namely, the non-profit, nongovernmental sector. Because the tradition of voluntary citizen associations (i.e., NGOs) performing public functions and, hence, often substituting for government action, is deeply rooted in US history, this tradition strongly colours how Americans look at globalization and respond to it. Americans and their governments have been significant actors in creating and strengthening NGOs in the international arena and within other countries, especially democratizing countries where the recovery or discovery of civil society is deemed essential (although "civil society" is another term unknown in American popular discourse because there is no "state" in the United States).

Likewise, although the global projection of American culture is well-known and often resented, less recognized is that most of this projection has no relation to government or US foreign policy. It is a product of a free-enterprise economy and free society. This is true, for example, for American religions, especially America's home-grown religion, the Mormon Church, which is believed to have assets of $25–$30 billion and annual revenues of $6 billion. The church owns more than 12,000 meetinghouses worldwide, and has some 11 million members, with 5.1 million in the United States and 157,000 in Canada (Ostling and Ostling 1999). In 1999, the church dispatched 58,600 missionaries across the United States and into 119 other countries. If current worldwide recruitment rates are sustained through this century, by 2100 the Mormon Church will be the second largest Christian denomination (after the Roman Catholic Church) and the first major world faith established since Mohammed founded Islam 1,400 years ago.

Seventh, underlying America's global engagements is the notion of individual rights, a concept that has expanded and deepened enormously within the United States since World War II and, hence, coincidentally with globalization. Although the United States is an easy target for charges of hypocrisy about these matters, individual rights are fundamental to the American psyche. In the final analysis, the American conception of individual rights is the key flashpoint in US relations with the world because this conception is central to America's understanding of modernity and of the struggle between modernity and pre-modernity. The American conception of individual rights, moreover, is primarily negative rather than positive; it prohibits government interference with freedom of speech, press, religion, and the like while giving less weight to government obligations to ensure positive rights, such as provision of food, clothing, and shelter. The US conception of individual rights contradicts pre-modern cultures and rests uneasy with modern democratic cultures, such as those of Europe, which have statist conceptions of government's social welfare obligations. This also distinguishes the United States from Canada and Mexico. Indeed, many Canadians take pride in their social welfare tradition and of not being American in this respect.

This conception of individual rights is a threat to all historic cultures and an anathema to pre-modern cultures because it holds that all persons should be, among other things, free to see, hear, read, and eat whatever they desire. US promotion of women's rights, for example, is a cultural time-bomb because the position of women in society is fundamental to all cultures. Pre-modern cultures and religions are almost uniformly patriarchal, as were modern cultures until recently. The rise of feminism has irrevocably transformed American society. Feminism has also moved American political culture in a stronger social welfare direction, as reflected in the gender gap evident in US elections since 1980 in which women ordinarily vote in larger proportions than men for Democrats, the

nation's social welfare party. Women's support for social welfare and opposition to war are having impacts on US foreign and military policy.
American women also placed feminism on the global agenda, and now,
together with women in other democratic societies who rapidly embraced
feminism, they are not likely to rest until they have rooted patriarchy out
of all cultures. As such, the US women's movement reflects three other
facets of individual rights and modernity, facets rooted in Hobbes' and
Locke's assaults on antiquity: (i) belief that individual rights rather than
culture are natural or God-given and, thus, also universal; (ii) belief, therefore, that culture, like government, is a human artifice constructed to
benefit individuals; and (iii) belief in the inevitable triumph of individual
rights over pre-modernity and its vestiges.

Consequently, Americans are likely to continue pressing for free-
trade agreements that ensure free flows of ideas and information, and to
assault efforts by political, cultural, and religious leaders elsewhere to erect
ideological, technological, and legal defences against their citizens' exposure to American culture. Americans are not hostile to other cultures per
se and are eager to consume them as tourists, but, in the final analysis,
culture is viewed as a product that should be constructed voluntarily and
democratically and should compete for human affection just like other
goods, services, and ideas compete for consumer allegiance. From a US
perspective, the appropriate response to American "cultural imperialism"
is not to impose state protection but to build a better product.

America's social and cultural integration with the world is, for the
most part, the reverse of its economic integration. The United States is a
net exporter rather than importer of intellectual and cultural products. In
turn, no new transnational identities have emerged in the United States
except insofar as many corporations now regard themselves as global citizens and many NGO leaders regard themselves as world citizens having
global responsibilities to promote democracy, economic development,
individual rights, environmental protection, and so on. Old and new
transnational identities are also evident among ethnic groups that maintain ties with their homelands. One change, though, has been increasing
US tolerance for dual citizenship. US citizenship is based on the principle
of *jus soli* with a right of naturalization for the foreign born but no right
of dual citizenship outside dual (federal and state) citizenship within the
United States. This change, however, was due largely to desires of many
American ethnics to hold citizenship and a passport in their country of

origin without renouncing their US citizenship. Meanwhile, federal, state, and local legislative and judicial officials remain mostly inward-looking, in part because the US system of legislative representation, weak non-parliamentary political parties, and single-issue interest groups emphasize accountability to local constituents. Executive officials are somewhat more outward-looking — the president for obvious reasons, and governors and mayors for economic reasons.

IMPACT OF GLOBAL AND REGIONAL INTEGRATION ON INTERGOVERNMENTAL RELATIONS

No changes in the constitutional design or basic institutional structure of US federalism have been made to manage international relations. Global and regional integration have been absorbed into the nation's system of intergovernmental relations rather cooperatively. Issues of global and regional integration have thus far been subject to less intergovernmental and interjurisdictional conflict than domestic issues.

Several factors probably account for this intergovernmental accommodation of global integration. One is that global integration is, in many respects, similar to the country's history of continental integration. Patterns of intergovernmental relations forged during continental integration have been adaptable to regional and global integration. Also, the size of the United States and its economy shields intergovernmental relations from exogenous shocks that might distress intergovernmental relations in other federal systems, while the long-standing openness of the US economy does not expose it to the shocks felt by more closed economies. Likewise, given the size and diversity of most US state economies, globalization is not an overriding concern and does not ordinarily provoke maverick subnational responses. Regional and global integration have also been more shallow for the United States than for some other federal systems such as Germany in the EU. Internally, the twentieth century was marked by the intergovernmentalization of all domestic policy, namely, the involvement of all governments in all policy fields. In turn, globalization has enhanced the intergovernmentalization of foreign policy. State and local governments have always insisted on a voice in matters that affect them; globalization now affects them. All of the states, even while they compete with each other, also have strong economic and political incentives to

cooperate with each other and with the federal government on the fundamentals of globalization just as they have done internally since the founding
of the United States. The governors, moreover, have supported globalization. More than 40 governors lobbied Congress for approval of NAFTA
and the WTO even while some members of Congress from the same states
opposed those agreements.

In addition, although international agreements apply to all governments in federal systems, and national governments are obliged to seek
subnational compliance, national governments are not required to do so
beyond the scope of their constitutional powers. Given the reliance on
law and litigation in the United States as important components of intergovernmental relations, plus the existence of a huge body of federal, state,
and local commercial law developed to integrate the nation's continental
common market, there are ample precedents in law and practice to accommodate global integration.

Furthermore, legal instruments of regional and global integration,
such as NAFTA and the WTO, contain provisions sensitive to subnational
interests in federal systems, including (i) limits (e.g., "carve-outs") on the
scope of trade agreements, (ii) rollback and standstill provisions (e.g.,
"grandfathering") for state laws pre-dating trade agreements, (iii) limits
on who can sue subnational governments, (iv) authorization for member
nations to interpret agreement provisions, (v) general exceptions applicable to all member nation-states, (vi) country-specific exceptions (although
subnational laws usually must be least-trade-restrictive to benefit from
general or specific exceptions), and (vii) provisions in national legislation
about the effects of international agreements on subnational law. NAFTA
includes a number of general exceptions not found in the WTO for such
matters as resource conservation, human and animal health, and protection of public morals. Under the WTO, 13 US states and all local
governments are exempt from its government procurement rules. As such,
international agreements share a characteristic increasingly common in
new as well as some old but changing intranational and international federal-type arrangements, namely, asymmetry. Asymmetrical arrangements
accommodate differences of power, law, and culture among member units.

Constitutionally, the Supreme Court has asserted ultimate federal
supremacy in foreign affairs, but this occurred in the 1930s and 1940s
prior to contemporary globalization. At the same time, the Court has not
excluded the states. This view was reflected even in the Court's June 2000

ruling that struck down an economic sanctions law enacted by Massachusetts against Burma (*Stephen P. Crosby* 2000). *Crosby* makes it difficult, though not impossible, for states to impose economic sanctions on foreign nations. State and local sanctions of various types had gained popularity during the 1980s when they were used to combat apartheid in South Africa. President Reagan opposed these state and local actions but did not attempt to strike them down in court. The Massachusetts Burma sanction was attacked vigorously by US and foreign corporations and by Japan and the European Union. The EU had filed a complaint against the Massachusetts sanction as a violation of the WTO's Agreement on Government Procurement (GPA) — even though the EU Parliament had supported Massachusetts and voted nearly unanimously against the EU's complaint. Massachusetts would likely have asked the United States to defend its sanction as proper legislation under GPA's general exception for laws that protect "public morals and order"; however, the EU dropped its WTO complaint after the Supreme Court struck down the law under US law. This is significant. Although the Court entertained WTO arguments from the EU and Japan, it declined to base its decision on WTO grounds. Instead, it simply ruled that Massachusetts' statute was preempted by a federal Burma-sanctions statute.

For the most part, the federal government has encouraged state and local engagement with the world and responded cooperatively to state and local concerns about globalization, though not always as quickly or fully as desired by state and local officials. Beginning with the administration of Republican Dwight D. Eisenhower, presidents have often encouraged state international activity. Presidents John F. Kennedy, Lyndon B. Johnson, Richard M. Nixon, and Jimmy Carter encouraged states to seek out foreign investment and promote exports. At the request of President Carter, former governor of Georgia, the National Governors' Association formed a standing committee in 1978 on International Trade and Foreign Relations.

New institutions have also been developed within the federal government to facilitate state and local representation in certain aspects of foreign policymaking and to promote intergovernmental cooperation. For example, the US Department of State has an intergovernmental affairs office that endeavors to channel state and local government concerns to appropriate officials and to respond to state and local needs for information, advice, and technical support. An Intergovernmental Policy Advisory Committee to the Office of the US Trade Representative (USTR) was established in 1988 to advise the president on state and local government concerns about international trade and trade agreements. The Department of Commerce has also improved its ability to provide state and local governments with specific data and other information relevant to their international economic concerns. Some states which operate export-financing programs cooperate closely with the US Export-Import Bank and the US Small Business Administration. Relevant federal agencies, such as the USTR, have encouraged governors to establish "single points of contact" in their states to facilitate rapid communication and consultation. Thus, there have been new and cooperative institutionalized responses by the federal government to the institutionalization of international affairs in the states and big cities.

Paralleling these federal intergovernmental responses has been a growing internationalization of federal domestic agencies, some of whose activities intersect with those of state and local governments. The General Accounting Office found that spending on international affairs outside the federal government's 150 account, which funds US embassies and most foreign aid, equaled $7.6 billion for 70 different programs in 1998. Moreover, while "the total number of U.S. personnel posted in U.S. diplomatic missions abroad has changed little over the past 10 years, the portion from domestic agencies has increased by 25 percent, from about 8,000 positions in 1988 to over 10,000 in 1998" (US. General Accounting Office 1998, p. 7). Thus, while the Department of State has reduced staffing since 1988, domestic federal agencies — with which state and local governments have long-standing relations — have increased international staffing. Some of this staffing is intended to help state and local governments promote their global economic interests.

To some extent, globalization has contributed to further centralization of the federal system, though usually more as rhetoric than as substance, although often powerful rhetoric. Since 1969, there has been a tremendous increase in federal pre-emption of state powers (i.e., displacement of state law by federal law under the supremacy clause, article VI of the Constitution). The rhetoric if not always the substance of globalization has played a role in three big areas of pre-emption. First, in civil rights, an argument first made in the 1940s was that failure by the United

States to solve its race problem and to extend equal rights to all citizens crippled the nation's ability to defeat communism and promote democracy and human rights abroad. Second, in environmental protection, environmentalists quickly linked domestic issues to global concerns — think globally, act locally. Third, in the field of commerce, national and multinational corporations have strongly advocated broad federal preemptions to regulate or deregulate sectors of the economy nationwide. The EU also has consistently criticized the United States as a "fragmented market" balkanized by 50 Byzantine state and local tax and regulatory regimes. When Republican President George Bush proposed federal preemption of certain state banking laws in 1991, his secretary of the treasury said that it was absurd that a bank in California could open a branch in Birmingham, England, but not in Birmingham, Alabama (US Advisory Commission on Intergovernmental Relations 1992). Pre-emptions in commerce and environmental protection, however, have been advocated by the National Governors' Association, which believes that a more uniform national marketplace will make the national and state economies more competitive globally. State legislators, more protective of their sovereign legislative prerogatives, have frequently opposed federal pre-emption.

However, the post-1969 pre-emption revolution has had little substantively to do with globalization. Virtually all of it reflects domestic political forces and concerns. Furthermore, much of federal pre-emption, especially in civil rights and environmental protection, is in the form of partial rather than total pre-emption of state powers. That is, the federal government establishes a national standard that is treated as a minimum that can be exceeded by the states. All of the states exceed federal standards in various areas of civil rights and environmental protection, and if state standards equal or exceed federal standards, then states can administer the regulations themselves. Consequently, individual rights protections and environmental protections vary across the states, sometimes substantially, above the federal minimums.

Both NAFTA and the WTO, however, do pose long-run total preemption threats to state and local powers. Negotiations under way on the regulation and procurement of services (GATS) and on chapters of the Free Trade Area of the Americas on services, investment, subsidies, and procurement also invite incursions into state powers. A potentially major extra-constitutional shift of power occurred pursuant to the WTO agreement when Congress vested power in the president to pre-empt state laws held to be in conflict with the WTO. When a federal law is found to be in conflict with the WTO, Congress must vote to repeal or alter the law. The president cannot alter federal law unilaterally. The states fought for the same treatment of state law, namely, that Congress, not the president, should decide whether to pre-empt a WTO-offending state law. How far the president will be able to carry this unprecedented pre-emption power is uncertain, given that Congress has twice nearly refused to appropriate funds to support any federal litigation to enforce WTO rules against state laws.

States anticipate many WTO and NAFTA challenges. The EU, for instance, will likely file WTO complaints against 43 states that have buy-local or buy-American government-purchase preferences, most of which also give preferences to small businesses and to businesses owned by minorities, women, or veterans. Forty-seven states have environmental purchasing preferences. What has restrained the EU is the political embarrassment of appearing to attack women, minorities, and mother nature. Given that the US and the EU are attacking each other's business-subsidy policies under the WTO, it is likely that US state and local governments will be major EU targets because some 84 percent ($32 billion) of US economic development spending is state and local, not federal, money. States also are concerned that US and foreign corporations and investors will use NAFTA and the WTO to accomplish legally under these agreements what they cannot accomplish through domestic legal or democratic political processes. Canadian investors, for instance, are seeking $970 million in compensation under NAFTA for California's clean-air decision to phase out MTBE, a gasoline additive found to be a serious water pollutant. Seven other states are also phasing out MTBE. Through NAFTA, therefore, corporate interests could establish a principle of partial "regulatory taking" requiring compensation, a principle that corporations have not yet been able to entrench in US domestic law.

The dispute-resolution processes under NAFTA and the WTO have proven to be more opaque to state and local officials, and federal officials have not yet devised response processes satisfactory to state and local officials. Given that the government is the buffer between the states and foreign governments in trade-agreement enforcement, and given the president's pre-emption authority under the WTO's domestic enabling legislation, states are pressing for more intergovernmental consultation and more transparency in dispute-resolution processes.

At the same time, there has been little movement among the states to harmonize or coordinate taxation and regulation. In principle, computer technology that enables multinational corporations to manage huge personnel, inventory, and sales databases, as well as data on international and national regulation and taxation, ought to allow them to accommodate subnational data too. The key problems, however, are not interstate differences per se, but differences in state taxation, especially tax bases, and in regulations that produce, intentionally or unintentionally, discriminatory or retaliatory consequences, as well as double taxation, for corporations. The EU argues, for example, that the tax-audit formula employed by many states produces double taxation and *de facto* discrimination against foreign-based firms. The more general problem is that state-local tax systems were designed for an urban manufacturing economy, not for a cybernetic service economy. The principal opposition to reform, though, comes from voters, who have stoutly resisted extensions of state-local taxation into the service sector.

Indeed, voter distaste for taxes has been a significant factor motivating state and local government entry into the global arena. Reluctant to face political death in tax battles, governors and mayors have sought, instead, to increase revenues by expanding their economic bases. Most of their energy has been focused domestically, but promoting foreign exports, recruiting foreign investment, and attracting foreign tourists are important as well. Similar practices were common among states during the nineteenth century when they needed to export goods and raw materials, attract foreign capital, and recruit immigrants. These practices waned when the US economy became strong globally. In the 1950s, however, southern states began to send trade missions abroad. These missions were essentially international extensions of southern domestic strategies. That is, for nearly a century, southern states sought to attract business and capital from the northern states. They succeeded, for example, in denuding New England of its textile industry.

Today, states, and often local governments, can be said to play ten roles in foreign affairs: as junior partners with the federal government in foreign policy development, pressure points in US foreign policy-making, self-governing political communities with substantial tax and regulatory powers, promoters of their own economic and cultural interests abroad, including state and local offices in other countries to foster exports, investment, and tourism, occasional proxies for the nation when overt US government action would be awkward or embarrassing to the United States or a foreign country, parties to agreements with foreign governments, usually subnational governments, such as the many agreements between US states and Canada's provinces, public education and opinion forums about international affairs, problem-solvers on the world scene, patrons of democracy, and practitioners of goodwill (Kincaid 1999). For the most part, state and local governments do not unduly intrude upon or oppose the federal government's foreign-affairs prerogatives, and the federal government's responses to state and local international affairs activities have been tolerant, supportive, and often cooperative.

To date, however, state and local governments have not plunged deeply into the international arena. Their international activities still constitute small portions of their budgets (less than 2 percent) and personnel. A number of factors account for this. One is the huge size of the US economy and most state economies. Second, the United States is an attractive target for foreign investment, thus reducing needs for governments to pursue it. Third, state and local officials still regard domestic economic competition as being more rigorous than global economic competition. Fourth, voters have little understanding of any need for state and local government international activity, in part because they have little understanding of foreign affairs. This lack of understanding, coupled with voter tax sentiment, also makes it difficult to justify state and local government expenditures on international activity. Fifth, the predominate emphasis on economic development in state and local international activity does not require large expenditures on bureaucratic and programmatic activities of an exclusively international nature. Sixth, state and local governments rely heavily on private-sector businesses, non-profit institutions, and civic organizations to help promote and protect state and local interests in global affairs.

In turn, moreover, globalization has not yet eroded state powers or capacities in significant ways. It might be argued, however, that such practices as citizens travelling to Canada and Mexico to purchase cheaper prescription drugs or drugs not available in the United States, or purchasing drugs abroad through the Internet, constitute negative impacts of globalization on federal and state regulatory regimes. This is not so because these activities are products of a free society, not of globalization. They are also products of the technologies of interstate highways and the Internet, which simply make it easier for citizens to do what they have always been free to do. If a citizen is caught bringing illegal drugs or other contraband into the country, however, he or she will face federal and/or state criminal penalties. Regarding the global Internet, states are already engaged in a flurry of debate and policy innovation intended to assert traditional state regulatory powers over this medium while also accommodating, for example, the growing desire of citizens to be able to obtain out-of-state and foreign health-care services via telephone, Internet, and video-conferencing.

In a non-statist society like the United States, the federal and state bills of rights prohibit governments from preventing citizens from obtaining fatal quack treatments on their own via the Internet, but any foreign health-care service channelled through a US-based physician or institution is subject to federal and state regulation — asserted not against the foreign provider (unless there is a treaty) but against the US provider. Likewise, any health-care service emanating from the United States is subject to federal and state regulation. In 2001, for instance, a physician in Maryland was convicted under state law for selling the dangerous fen-phen diet drug to people worldwide via the Internet. The ground for conviction was quite simple: Maryland law requires a physician to personally examine a patient before prescribing medication. In the long run, the United States is likely to support international consumer-protection mechanisms as well as treaties governing domestic prosecution of persons or entities engaged in off-shore criminal activity, but it strongly supports free trade in services and adheres to the principle of *caveat emptor*.

In summary, then, federal, state, and local responses to globalization have, to date, been consistent with previous domestic intergovernmental practices, trends, and responses to socio-economic change, and globalization has not yet altered the federal system or eroded state powers within the federal system in significant ways.

FUTURE SCENARIOS

Given US power, the United States is likely to be a leading, if not *the* leading, force in foreseeable future scenarios.

Under the *global club* scenario, which envisions the United States convening the first meeting of the club in 2003, the United States would presumably be the leader. This scenario would likely occur only if the United States cannot manage anticipated global crises on it own. Such a scenario would have drastic impacts on US federalism, especially severe reductions in state and local government powers, because the scenario envisions an enormous gravitation of now-domestic powers to the global club. It is this aspect of the scenario, however, that makes it unlikely because the strength of democratic federalism in the United States, as well as the separation of powers within the federal government, would pose substantial barriers to US participation in such a club. At the same time, it might be argued that a global club having far less power than that envisioned in the scenario already exists insofar as the United States now engages in informal extra-institutional negotiations and coordination with a few big powers, including the EU, on economic, political, and military matters of major global consequence.

Under the *regional dominators* scenario, the United States would be one of the international hegemons, as well as the hegemon of the North America-Western Hemisphere bloc. The United States is already the hegemon in NAFTA, and will insist on hub-and-spoke development of any hemispheric free-trade area so as not to relinquish its hegemonic position in the hemisphere. This scenario, therefore, would have no significant, independent effect on US federalism. The likelihood of this scenario is probably contingent on two key factors: one, whether the United States, the European Union, and China can resolve their differences sufficiently to sustain globalization without balkanization and two, whether US voters can continue supporting globalization and such global institutions as the WTO during a long-term recession rather than insisting on US withdrawal from the global scene into economic self-reliance. Most US leaders, public and private, support continued worldwide globalization, but many domestic and international factors could frustrate US efforts to sustain such globalization.

Under the *cyberwave* scenario, the United States would not only surf its crest but would also have created the wave. The first movement creating the wave would perhaps be attributed to Congress's current moratorium on state-local taxation of the Internet, a moratorium intended to facilitate Internet growth. The likelihood of certain aspects of this scenario coming into existence is probably high, given the freedom and openness of western democracies; however, the likelihood of cyberspace escaping desired controls by the major democracies is low. This scenario would have little significant, independent effect on US federalism because, to date, there is no evidence that US governments are inherently incapable of regulating cyberspace. Furthermore, governments able to regulate cyberspace will likely try to extend their regulatory reach to help countries unable to do so. Perhaps the greatest Internet threat to the United States is cyber-terrorism in which a single off-shore terrorist could disrupt banking systems and create financial chaos, disrupt electricity transmission as well as oil or gas pipelines, and affect the US defence system in a catastrophic manner. Again, though, federal, state, and local governments and the private sector have begun to respond to such threats in typical intergovernmental and public-private fashions by sharing information, consulting, coordinating, and formulating strategies to prevent and respond to such terrorism. Such intergovernmental action is also needed because of the large roles played by the states in banking, energy, and other potential target policy fields and because state and local governments have the most personnel to respond to terrorism. These intergovernmental responses are slower and less sophisticated than some observers believe necessary, but slowness in confronting new challenges is typical in the absence of a major crisis or catastrophic event.

The *shared governance* scenario, perhaps the most probable scenario, would likely reflect extensions of American-style and EU-style federal principles — self-rule for local purposes and shared rule for collective purposes within a global framework of international, national, and subnational law. This scenario would likely reinforce US federalism because, insofar as it would accommodate semi-autonomous ethnic, Aboriginal, linguistic, and religious local governments worldwide, it would also accommodate state and local autonomy within the United States. Full flowering of this scenario would likely be limited by continuing US refusal to cede sovereignty to international institutions, but insofar as the scenario envisions international commitments that nevertheless recognize national sovereignty, then the United States is likely to continue supporting shared governance arrangements as opposed to substantial government institutions.

CONCLUSION

Given that the United States is perhaps *sui generis* and that all four scenarios envision a dominant or predominant role for the United States, it is difficult to draw specific lessons from the US case for other federal polities. At the risk of oversimplification, there are a number of plausible explanations for this outcome.

For one, the United States was founded by immigrants with a global outlook, namely, a recognition that the newly independent country had to make its own way in the world and that its economic development and national security were vitally contingent on negotiating the perils of superior global forces and two, a missionary zeal derived from the Puritans' notion of New England as a shining "City upon a Hill" and from Republican President Abraham Lincoln's notion of the United States as "the last best hope of mankind," that is, a failure of freedom and democracy in the New World would doom possibilities for freedom and democracy in the Old World.

The federal union implicitly anticipated globalization. The union was established partly to create a great commercial republic and to ensure its diplomatic and military ability to expand across the temperate midsection of North America. Put differently, two of the major reasons for establishing the union were to enhance the economic prosperity and military security of the constituent states. Virtually all of the powers constitutionally delegated to the federal government fall into these two categories, and the prosperity and security incentives for the states to support the federal union have, since the Civil War, far outweighed incentives for dissolution. Hence, the states and their citizens have, for the most part, strongly supported the federal union, even while they have often disagreed about its means and ends. In turn, the United States has sought to create similar global prosperity and security incentives for nation-states to support global peace.

The United States was founded on an idea, not on a nationality or even a federation of nationalities. Americans are the people of the Declaration and the federal Constitution, which brought the American people into existence and sustain their existence. The Constitution nowhere defines an American, nor does it limit its rights protections to citizens. At base, an American is nothing more than a person born or naturalized in the United States willing to swear allegiance to the federal Constitution. All citizens and public officials swear allegiance to the Constitution, not to the United States or to the American people. Likewise, the Constitution nowhere defines the boundaries of the United States. It is a boundless document that provides for the admission of new states, which, in principle, can include a willing territory anywhere in the world. As a practical matter, of course, the founders did not envision a global United States, though many were disappointed when Canada refused to join the union, but nonetheless, the Constitution contemplates no fixed national geographic boundaries and no fixed American cultural, national, ethnic, racial, religious, or linguistic characteristics.

The United States was founded with an openness to the world — a willingness to attract immigrants of different nationalities, religions, and languages such that, today, despite many conflicts, every racial, national, ethnic, linguistic, and religious group present in the world is also present in the American citizenry on essentially equal terms. In turn, Americans embrace ideas and cultural forms from abroad; American culture is dynamic; and the United States has produced a popular culture that has a certain universal appeal because it appeals to the common denominators of its own polyglot diversity. McDonald's food may not be *haute cuisine*, but it is reliably and cheaply accessible to the masses.

The separation of church and state, embedded in the federal Constitution and all state constitutions, has been important, too, in preventing religious zealots from dominating government, balkanizing the union, and blocking modernization and globalization. This separation evolved into a broader philosophy of also confining ethnic, linguistic, and related issues to the private sector, or civil society. Citizens are free to maintain ethnic identities, communal institutions, and native languages voluntarily; they are not permitted to use government power to do so. This means that territorial jurisdictions are neutral; any group that becomes a majority in a local or state jurisdiction gets to elect its own people to office. English, moreover, emerged as the national language much like it is emerging as the international language, not by fiat but as a matter of elite preference and majoritarian convenience in a multilingual immigrant society. As a result, cultural matters of religion, ethnicity, and language are competitive, as Americans believe they should be worldwide, because established religions and cultures are state monopolies that become stagnant, corrupt, and authoritarian like any monopoly.

At the same time, the strongest religious force in the United States, Reformed Protestantism, was not only founded at the outset of modernity but also fostered modernity; consequently, in contrast to Roman Catholics and even Anglicans, who have struggled to reconcile their roots in antiquity with the realities of modernity, American Protestants have struggled more easily with needs to reconcile their theology with modernity. The original covenant or federal theology of Reformed Protestantism also created a culture of federalism and habits of federating that helped give birth to the federal union and its "Presbyterian" Constitution. Thus, as Tocqueville observed, religion in the United States generally supported federal democracy and human equality rather than thwarting these attributes of modernity, as in the Old World. Reformed Protestantism is also evangelically zealous, desiring not only to convert the world but also to modernize it, to fulfill its original mission of liberating people from the Dark Ages (Hutchinson 1992). Consequently, there is only a thin, blurred line in the United States between basic religious and secular beliefs about federal democracy, and American foreign policy is often infused with evangelical moralism.

While the federal Constitution is the nation's sacred lodestone, it is also malleable because Americans interpret their Constitution like Christians interpret the Bible. Vastly different interpretations ultimately accepted by Americans have allowed the Constitution to facilitate and adapt to change without being dislodged from its sacred position or altered in its fundamentals. This flexible approach is due partly to Americans' conceptions of their federal republic as an experiment, to their pragmatic, largely non-theoretical approach to governance, and to the absence of an ancient culture into which they had to sandwich a modern constitution. With respect to federalism, moreover, it became apparent by the late twentieth century that Americans no longer cared much about the constitutional niceties of which government does what, so long as it gets done. One significant change in federalism, therefore, is that all public policy is now intergovernmental.

American federalism is also rooted in productive tensions between liberal individualism and civic republicanism. Liberal individualism emphasizes individual liberty, places limits on government, drives entrepreneurialism, and marketizes everything. Civic republicanism emphasizes civic duty and individual responsibility to community, drives the non-profit, non-governmental sector, encourages philanthropy, employs government to achieve "the public interest" and correct market failures without statism, and seeks to protect individuals and small self-governing communities (i.e., states and localities) from rapacious market forces. In effect, liberal individualism fostered a dynamic private sector that enabled the United States to promote and respond to globalization by restructuring the nation's military and social economy without restructuring its federal system. Civic republicanism fought to preserve the basic structure of the Constitution and to wield its intergovernmental

mechanisms against the excesses of liberal individualism in order to protect the non-market rights of individuals, self-governing state and local
communities, the environment, and other public goods. The battle continues, domestically and globally.

References

Boli, J. and G.M. Thomas, eds. 1999. *Constructing World Culture*. Stanford:
Stanford University Press.

Bowman, A. O'M. and R.C. Kearney. 1986. *The Resurgence of the States*.
Englewood Cliffs, NJ: Prentice-Hall.

Eisinger, P. and C. Smith. 2000. "Globalization and Metropolitan Well-Being in
the United States," *Social Science Quarterly* 81(2):634-44.

Elazar, D.J. and J. Kincaid, eds. 2000. *The Covenant Connection: From Federal
Theology to Modern Federalism*. Lanham, MD: Lexington Books.

Feenstra, R.C., ed. 2000. *The Impact of International Trade on Wages*. Chicago:
University of Chicago Press.

Friedman, T.L. 1999. *The Lexus and the Olive Tree: Understanding Globalization*.
New York: Farrar, Straus, Giroux.

Gordon, S.B. 2001. *The Mormon Question: Polygamy and Constitutional Conflict
in Nineteenth-Century America*. Chapel Hill, NC: University of North
Carolina Press.

Hensel, P.R., G. Goertz and P.F. Diehl. 2000. "The Democratic Peace and Rivalries," *Journal of Politics* 62(4):1173-88.

Hutchinson, W.R. 1992. *The Modernist Impulse in American Protestantism*. Dur-
ham, NC: Duke University Press.

Jones, A. 1960. "Editorial," *Chicago Life*, 2 July, pp. 11-12.

Kenyon, D.A. and J. Kincaid, eds. 1991. *Competition among States and Local
Governments: Efficiency and Equity in American Federalism*. Washington,
DC: Urban Institute Press.

Keynes, J.M. 1919. *Economic Consequences of Peace*. London: Macmillan.

Kincaid, J. 1993. "From Cooperation to Coercion in American Federalism: Housing, Fragmentation, and Preemption, 1780-1992," *Journal of Law and
Politics* 9 (Winter):333-433.

——— 1999. "The International Competence of US States and their Local Governments," *Regional & Federal Studies* 9(1):111-30.

Kincaid, J. with J.L. Handelsman. 1997. *American Cities in the Global Economy:
A Survey of Municipalities on Activities and Attitudes*. Washington, DC:
National League of Cities.

Krugman, P. 1997. "Competitiveness: A Dangerous Obsession," in *The New Shape of World Politics*. New York: W. W. Norton and *Foreign Affairs*.

Lawrence, R.Z. 1997. "Workers and Economists II: Resist the Binge," in *The New Shape of World Politics*. New York: W. W. Norton and *Foreign Affairs*.

Miller, P. 1964. *Errand Into the Wilderness*. New York: Harper Torchbooks.

Ostling, R.N. and J.K. Ostling. 1999. *Mormon America: The Power and the Promise*. New York: HarperCollins.

Peirce, N.R. with C.W. Johnson and J.S. Hall. 1993. *Citistates: How Urban America Can Prosper in a Competitive World*. Washington, DC: Seven Locks Press.

Piven, F.F. and R.A. Cloward. 2000. "Power Repertoires and Globalization," *Politics & Society* 28(3):413-30.

Sarpolus, E. 2000. "Survey Shows Most Americans Still Support International Trade," *Clearinghouse on State International Policies* 10 (Summer): 4.

Siekman, P. 2000. "The Big Myth about U.S. Manufacturing," *Fortune* 142, 2 October, p. 244.

Stephen P. Crosby v. *National Foreign Trade Council*, 147 L Ed 2d 352, 120 S. Ct. 2288 (2000).

Testa, W.A., D.A. Oppedahl and L.S. Merkel. 2000. "The Binational Great Lakes Economy," *Chicago Fed Letter* 153 (May): 2.

United States Advisory Commission on Intergovernmental Relations. 1992. *Federal Statutory Preemption of State and Local Authority: History, Inventory, and Issues*. Washington, DC: ACIR.

United States. 1998. *International Affairs Activities of Domestic Agencies*. Washington, DC: US Government Printing Office.

——— General Accounting Office. 2000. *World Trade Organization: U.S. Experience to Date in Dispute Settlement System*. Washington, DC: US Government Printing Office.

United States. Office of the Federal Register, National Archives and Records Administration. 2000. *United States Government Manual*. Washington, DC: US Government Printing Office.

The Centralizing and Decentralizing Effects of Globalization in Australian Federalism: Toward a New Balance

Brian Galligan

INTRODUCTION

Australia's location in the international political order and global economy is in part the product of its history as a British colonial settler society and its geographic location in the South Pacific adjacent to Asia.[1] Australia has always been a global nation in the sense of being shaped and influenced by international political and economic forces since the first European settlement in 1788. With the demise of the British Empire and Britain's influence in the Asia-Pacific during World War II, Australia formed new strategic alliances based upon the United States. Its trade was diversified to Asian countries with Japan becoming the dominant partner. Since the collapse of the Soviet Union and the end of the Cold War, Australia's need for direct security reliance on the United States has diminished. Nevertheless, Australian foreign policy continues to be dominated by the search for security in the Pacific (Meaney 1985, p. 38).

Australia's economy is heavily dependent on international investment and trade. Even its protective state policies that characterized Australian domestic political economy until the 1980s were a bold attempt at nation-building by boosting manufacturing industries, an industrial workforce, and population (Capling and Galligan 1992). With the floating of the Australian dollar, the deregulation of Australian financial markets, and the phasing out of tariff protection, Australia switched to a market strategy in the 1980s and early 1990s. This was a bold step to take as the challenges of globalization were intensifying. The sea change in national policy was the consequence of adopting neo-liberal strategies of deregulation and competition, whose resurgence has been a global phenomenon (Meredith and Dyster 1999; Goldfinch 2000). Australia's deliberate policy decision to scrap "protection all round" in favour of a deregulated national economy has been instrumental in exposing its domestic political economy to world market forces and influences. The overall benefits of economic advantage and aspects of cosmopolitan citizenship need to be offset against the costs of economic disadvantage to less robust industry sectors and regions, and constraints upon domestic governments in leveraging economic forces. While Australia has always been shaped and influenced by international forces and influences, Australian governments have played a significant role in mediating the impact of global forces.

Although a much contested concept, globalization means essentially an intensification of international linkages in all spheres of human activity, especially those dependent upon communications and market forces. Many see globalization as a modern set of forces that are undermining the sovereign nation and supplanting its governance by transnational regulatory regimes. Others discern a counter movement of power downwards to local governance structures and community associations facilitated by new communication technology. These twin forces of "glocalization"[2] are variously said to be eroding the power of the nation-state on the one hand, and enhancing community and cosmopolitan citizenship on the other. While the impact of globalization on federal systems has received less attention, views are equally divided. Some have contended that federalism based upon historical or regional geographic boundaries is inappropriate for new social movements that are typically issue-orientated and universalist in character (Gibbins 1991). Federalism can be seen more as a complex system of multiple governments with shared sovereignty and over-lapping policy jurisdiction,[3] in which case its compatibility with globalization is more obvious. An additional international level of governance adds another layer of complexity that is appropriate for dealing with international policy issues and spillovers.

The thesis argued here is that globalization is having a profound effect on Australia's political economy and society, but one that is mediated by federal institutions and government policy choices. Partly as a consequence and partly in response, Australia's federal system of government is also being changed in important ways. In mediating global influences, the Commonwealth's domestic powers have increased partly at the expense of the states. But in addition, there has been a streamlining of intergovernmental relations with the states securing their position as key players in the new Council of Australian Governments (COAG) and in national policy-making. Although it has not achieved its full potential, COAG is a significant institutional development of Australian federalism. Other changes due to globalization have been more distorting of Australian federalism. The increased treaty-making role of the Commonwealth has enhanced its role in domestic affairs, especially in the area of human rights and environmental protection, while at the same time increasing the influence of international norms and standards in domestic law and politics.

SITUATIONAL CONTEXT

Today, Australia's security, trade, and political alliances encompass regional arrangements such as the Asia-Pacific Economic Co-operation (APEC) agreement, links between Australia and New Zealand as formalized in the Closer Economic Relations (CER) agreement, which is also linked to the Association of South East Asian Nations (ASEAN) through the ASEAN-CER arrangements; the South Pacific Forum (SPF); and sectoral affiliations, such as the Cairns Group of agricultural exporting nations. Australia is also a member of international economic and political organizations, such as the United Nations (UN), the Organisation for Economic Co-operation and Development (OECD), the World Trade Organization (WTO), and the International Monetary Fund (IMF). Apart from being a signatory to most of the key multilateral agreements on human rights and the environment, many more significant links with individual nations are maintained through a myriad of bilateral agreements. These cover areas as diverse as trade, security, the environment, diplomatic relations, technical mutual assistance and development of standards, financial co-operation, information technology, and scientific and medical research and development. Australia's strategic and trade alliances have undergone enormous change from the middle of the twentieth century to the present.

Strategic Alliances

The Second World War had forced Australia to become more independent from Britain and oriented toward the Asia-Pacific. This process would continue during the postwar decades as Australia's nearest northern neighbours broke the shackles of European colonialism and the United States became the dominant superpower in the region. The relationship with Britain and the Commonwealth would continue to be important for some time, but decreasingly so as Britain declined and retreated into Europe. The geopolitical landscape changed dramatically with the escalating Cold War that had critical security implications for Australia and the region and hampered the effectiveness of the United Nations.

Communism was the new enemy that threatened Asia as well as Europe, and the containment of communism was the main objective of American foreign policy around the world. Australia and New Zealand formed the strategic ANZUS pact with the US in 1951. This tripartite pact effectively disintegrated in the mid-1980s in response to New Zealand's decision to ban US nuclear-armed or powered warships in New Zealand waters. This left Australia in the awkward position of maintaining its links with the United States and New Zealand, neither of whom were cooperating with each other. The Australian-American substitute, AUSMIN, a series of bilateral ministerial talks, has never assumed the prestige and significance of its predecessor (Smith, Cox and Burchill 1996, pp. 75-76). New Zealand's decision in May 2001 to scrap its air force, including a squadron of aging fighter planes based in Australia, has contracted further New Zealand's bilateral capability.

In 1950, Australian troops formed part of the UN force defending South Korea from the communist North in what was really a show of support for the US. Following the French defeat by the communist Viet-Minh in 1954, SEATO (South East Asian Treaty Organisation) was established as a defensive alliance that further linked Australia with the United States, and aimed to stem the domino effect of communism in Asia. Although Australia supported British troops against communist insurgency in Malaya in 1955, its alliance with the United States increasingly dominated Australian foreign policy during the second half of the twentieth century. The Suez Crisis in 1956 and Britain's announcement in 1967 to withdraw its military presence "east of Suez" provided further impetus toward alignment with the US and the military strategy of forward defence. The Menzies government committed Australian troops to fight in Vietnam alongside the US in the 1960s. American defence installations established in Australia, at North West Cape (1967), Pine Gap (1969), and Nurrungar (1970) "tied Australia more closely to American global nuclear strategy" than the ANZUS treaty had done (McDougall 1998, p. 53). While the Whitlam Labor government in the early 1970s attempted a more distinctively Australian foreign policy, Australia and the Asia-Pacific region have remained fundamentally dependent on the US for security since World War II. Australia has been one of the strongest supporters of US military action abroad, providing naval backup forces in the Gulf War in the early 1990s and special forces troops in Afghanistan in 2002. After the 2002 terrorist bombing of a Bali night club that killed more than 60 Australian tourists, the Howard government has closely identified with President George W. Bush's war on terrorism.

Trade

Trade policy is typically more pragmatic and fluid than strategic policy that has crystallized around treaty alliances. That was certainly the case for Australia's trade and economic alliances after World War II. Changes have reflected the shift in Australia's earlier status from British dominion to a more independent nation with a greater focus on the Asia-Pacific region. Australian trade policy shifted toward the Asia-Pacific with Australia signing a special trade agreement with Japan in 1956. Traditional European markets have been supplanted by American and Asian markets. By 1999, 70 percent of Australia's merchandise exports went to APEC nations (Australia. DFAT 1999, p. 10). Even before Britain joined the European Economic Community (EEC) in 1973, its trade with Australia had been surpassed by that of the United States (Higgott 1989, pp. 141-42). By 1970 Japan was Australia's chief export market, taking huge quantities of raw materials for its burgeoning heavy industries. Japan was the market link in Australia's successive mineral and energy resource booms in the 1960s and 1970s that were largely financed by American capital and developed Australian mines for sale of production to Japan (Galligan 1989). These resources booms helped rejuvenate Australian federalism by boosting Queensland and Western Australia, previously "have-not" states, and making them significant players in Australian intergovernmental politics.

Japan remains Australia's leading export market with an overall share of 19 percent; the United States is a distant second with 9 percent, followed by Korea and New Zealand each with 7 percent. Britain still buys 5 percent of Australia's exports, part of the 14 percent of trade that the European Union (EU) takes. Such diversity has helped cushion Australia against the impact of the 1998 Asian financial crisis. Nevertheless, for the first time since the late 1970s Australia recorded a trade deficit with ASEAN, and the first deficit with APEC in a decade. Exports to APEC fell by 4 percent in 1998–99, and by 7 percent to East Asia in the same period. The decline in Asian markets was cushioned by a shift back to the traditional British and American markets. Europe and the Americas remain major sources of Australian imported goods, each supplying 24 percent of Australia's market, with North Asia providing 29 percent (Australia. DFAT 1999, pp. 1-12).

Australia rode on the back of sheep until the 1950s and then on the coal truck through to the 1970s. While still jointly accounting for over half of all exports, the agricultural and mining sectors are being challenged by the services sector that now makes up 22 percent of total exports. Australia's domestic economy has also become increasingly oriented to service industries with large sectors such as tourism and tertiary education being driven in part by international visitors and students. In addition to services, manufactured goods make up the same share of total export returns as rural goods. Once the backbone of Australia's exports, rural goods have declined steadily in relative terms: from two-thirds of Australia's exports in the early 1960s, to 40 percent by 1970, 30 percent in the mid-1980s and less than 20 percent by 2000 (Australian Bureau of Statistics 2000). Despite protective agricultural policies by the United States and the European Union, select Australian agricultural markets are expanding, such as horticultural products for niche markets, and dairying products that are Victoria's largest export.

Australia's traditional political economy of "protection all round" peaked in the 1950s and 1960s under McEwen who was deputy prime minister in the Menzies era and the powerful minister for trade and industry. By 1970 Australia, along with New Zealand, had the highest tariff rates on manufacturing industries in the industrialized world as well as protective schemes for weaker rural industries such as dairying and dried fruits. Although one of the original signatories to the General Agreement on Tariffs and Trade (GATT), established in 1947 to liberalize global trade, Australia refused to take part in any GATT negotiations during the 1950s and 1960s (Capling and Galligan 1992, pp. 106-07). All of that changed with the dismantling of Australia's protective state in the 1980s and its championing of free trade in global forums (Capling 2001). From being an outrider, Australia became a champion of liberal trade orthodoxy and a fervent member of its international organizations. There has been a recent backlash from regional and rural Australia, however, registered in the strong support for Pauline Hanson's reactionary One Nation Party in the 1998 Queensland election and the surprise defeat of the Kennett Liberal Coalition government in Victoria in 1999. Following the well publicized disruption of the World Trade Meeting in Seattle in 1999, the Melbourne 2000 meeting of the World Economic Forum was similarly disrupted.

CONSTITUTIONAL/FEDERAL FRAMEWORK

Australia has a constitutional system that incorporates a parliamentary legislature and a prime ministerial executive (Galligan 1995). In designing the Australian constitution the founders reworked the federal model, copied mainly from the American Constitution. They combined this with the institutions of parliament and responsible government familiar from British and colonial practice, producing a hybrid of parliamentary and federal government.

The federal system adopted by the founders divided government between two spheres, national or "Commonwealth" and subnational or "state." The controlling constitutional document specifies the institutional framework for the Commonwealth and the division of powers between the Commonwealth and the states. Following the American model, the Commonwealth's legislative powers are specified in enumerated heads of power while the residual is guaranteed for the states. Obviously, the extent of powers of each sphere of government depends on how narrowly or broadly the enumerated Commonwealth powers are defined. The High Court has the final say in adjudicating disputes and authoritatively interpreting the extent of such powers. Since the famous *Engineers* case of 1920, the High Court has interpreted Commonwealth powers in a full and plenary way regardless of the effect on state powers. Such an interpretive method inevitably produces a constitutional jurisprudence that favours the expansion of Commonwealth powers, and that has been the dominant pattern in judicial review since 1920 (Galligan 1987).

The Australian constitution embodied something of an institutional mismatch in combining the executive form of parliamentary responsible government which assumes a dominant legislative chamber, the House of Representatives, with bicameralism and a powerful Senate. Despite the misgivings of some that federation would kill responsible government or vice versa, the Australian founders combined both sets of institutions in the constitution. The more prescient argued that the Senate was not properly a federal or states' house, but rather a national chamber that would be mainly concerned with national issues. In fact, disciplined party government became dominant within a decade of federation and transformed both Houses of Parliament into party chambers. The adoption of proportional representation for Senate voting in 1948 has enabled minor parties and independents to control the Senate and further complicated national government. Apart from the constitutional crisis of 1975 when the Senate blocked supply and Governor-General Kerr sacked Prime Minister Whitlam in an unprecedented exercise of the reserve powers, the system has worked quite smoothly.

The Australian constitution was radically democratic for its time, being framed by delegates, who were elected by the people of the various colonies, to a series of constitutional conferences and it was essentially federal in its basic structure. The final draft was endorsed by a popular referendum with the people voting in their respective colonies, before being formally passed by the imperial Westminster Parliament at the request of the Australians. The constitution incorporated a referendum procedure in section 128 that was both thoroughly democratic and federal, with changes to the constitution requiring a double majority of electors overall and in a majority (four out of six) of the states. While only eight of the 44 proposals for constitutional change that have been put to the Australian people have passed, that is more a reflection of the quality of proposals than of popular intransigence. The Commonwealth government, which controls the framing and initiation of proposals, has often sought to expand its own powers or put questions lacking popular support. The most recent example was the 1999 republican referendum to Australianize the head of state. It was roundly defeated. While a majority of Australians favour a republic, most want to elect the head of state rather than have that office filled by someone selected by the prime minister with Parliament's endorsement. This was the proposal put to them and it was rejected (Galligan 2001).

Despite the paucity of change by constitutional referendum, Australian federalism has changed substantially through political initiatives, especially on the part of the Commonwealth and intergovernmental arrangements that have been either uncontested or sanctioned by the High

Court. One of the most significant areas of such development has been fiscal federalism. The original design entailed centralizing customs and excise duties in the Commonwealth in order to create a national customs union, but to leave income tax as a concurrent state and Commonwealth power. The Commonwealth was also given a grants power, under section 96 of the constitution, that enabled it to tie terms and conditions to monies returned to the states from their surrendered customs and excise base. This enabled the centralizing Curtin Labor government during World War II to monopolize income tax. Fiscal centralism was further extended because of the High Court's broad interpretation of "excise duties," an exclusive Commonwealth power, to preclude the states from levying broad-based consumption taxes. The Commonwealth's fiscal centralization has fuelled expansion of its own roles and responsibilities, and allowed it to enter key areas of state jurisdiction, such as education, health, and transport, though tying terms and conditions to state grants. The Commonwealth's fiscal dominance also funds a comprehensive system of fiscal equalization. This compensates states for both revenue and expenditure disabilities and is strongly supported by the smaller states that benefit most.

With the pressure on governments in recent decades to reduce excessive provision of services and rationalize their delivery, fiscal centralism has been under threat. The states were promised some alleviation and a modest share of the income-tax base for cooperating with the Commonwealth in reforming intergovernmental arrangements in the early 1990s. This was jettisoned by Keating when he replaced Hawke as Labor prime minister, and the Special Premiers' Conferences process was derailed as a result. Nevertheless, the imperatives for making Australian federal governance more streamlined in the face of global pressures on the domestic and export sectors did produce the Council of Australian Governments in the mid-1990s. The Howard Liberal National Party government that defeated Keating's Labor government in 1996 was more committed to tax reform than further COAG reforms. However, in a bold step that won state support, it agreed to return all proceeds of the new Goods and Services tax (GST), less collection costs, to the states, distributed according to the equalization formula. Equalization has always been controversial with the larger states whose taxpayers subsidize those in smaller states, so the extension of equalization methodology to the distribution of the GST has met with critical opposition, especially from Victoria. Most states, however, are pleased to have this new tax and the equalization formula seems the fairest way to allocate it among states.

Responding to Current Globalization

Global forces and influences have an impact upon Australia both directly and indirectly, and government plays an important role in mediating their impact and influence. While globalization is not a new phenomenon, the variety and extent of modern global forces and influences are quite unique. Coping with them has led to new developments in Australian government, public policy, and law. This section focuses on the way in which the institutional framework of Australia's constitutional system, especially its federal parts, has developed and been affected in mediating globalization. The focus is upon two of the most important developments. The first is treaty implementation which has involved an enhanced role for the Commonwealth government. The second is rejuvenated intergovernmental arrangements with the establishment of COAG as a new structure of Australian federalism which has increased the significance of the states.

The main institutional means for mediating international influences are the executive and legislative powers of the Commonwealth government over external affairs. At federation, no fetters were placed on the executive power of the Commonwealth government to conduct foreign affairs and enter into treaties, even though it was assumed that the British Imperial government would have sole responsibility for such matters. According to the American-style federal model that the Australian founders followed, of designating particular Commonwealth government powers and guaranteeing the unspecified balance to the states, the Commonwealth was given legislative power over "external affairs" by section 51 (xxix). Despite no explicit mention of treaties, Commonwealth ministers, such as Attorney-General Deakin in 1902, were quick to assert that the power to legislate with respect to treaties was within the scope of the external affairs power. This was used sparingly by the Commonwealth during the first half-century of federation and mainly for routine matters. Diplomacy and security were entrusted to the British Imperial government until World War II when Australia established its own diplomatic service and declared war against Japan in its own right.

In its first case regarding external affairs, *Burgess* in 1936,[4] the High Court upheld the Commonwealth's ability to make laws implementing Australia's international treaty obligations in the new field of aviation. Various judges signalled the potential scope of this power, suggesting that the Commonwealth could make laws over any matter that became the subject of an international treaty. Subsequent cases reinforced the Commonwealth's expansive power to implement international treaties; and during the 1980s and 1990s, the "extreme view" that any subject matter could come within external affairs became dominant in the High Court. According to Mason, one of the prime architects of its extension and chief justice at the time: "the power must be interpreted generously so that Australia is fully equipped to play its part on the international stage (Mason 1988).

Two key policy areas where the external affairs power was used to support Commonwealth expansion into what was otherwise the states' domain were human rights concerning Aboriginal people and the environment. In the *Koowarta* case (1982), the court upheld the validity of the *Commonwealth Racial Discrimination Act*, passed by the Whitlam government in 1975 and implementing the UN Convention on the Elimination of Racial Discrimination.[5] At issue was a discriminatory Queensland law preventing the transfer of pastoral land to an Aboriginal purchaser. In the *Tasmanian Dam* case (1983), the court upheld Commonwealth legislation preventing Tasmania from building a hydro-electric dam on the Gordon-below-Franklin, a wild river in a restricted heritage area listed on the World Heritage List maintained under the UN World Heritage Convention. In his opinion, Mason claimed "there are virtually no limits to the topics which may hereafter become the subject of international co-operation and international treaties or conventions."[6] The dynamics of globalization and such an open-ended Commonwealth power would inevitably change the federal system, expanding the Commonwealth's jurisdiction and eroding that of the states. Brennan affirmed the inevitable consequence: that the power of the Commonwealth had waxed and that of the states had waned (*Commonwealth* v. *Tasmania*, p. 528).

Despite the dire warnings of the dissenting judges that such an open-ended interpretation of the treaty power was "a threat to the basic federal polity of the Constitution," (ibid., p. 517) the expansive interpretation was adopted and consolidated in subsequent environmental and human rights cases.[7] The consequence has not been the demise of Australian federalism, however, but an enhanced role for the Commonwealth and greater reliance on political compromise and intergovernmental relations to work out the respective roles of Commonwealth and state governments. Politics remains the key forum where the Commonwealth has to legitimate any incursions into state jurisdictional areas, with the states remaining vigilant about their interests and politically adept at defending them. To an important extent, the politics of Australian federalism belies the ever-increasing centralism sanctioned by the High Court.

If globalization has allowed the Commonwealth an expanded role as the mediating agent of international affairs and treaties, domestic responses to global economic pressures have favoured more cooperative measures and an enhanced role for the states. To achieve greater economic efficiency and complement the phasing out of tariff protection, Australian governmental arrangements were overhauled as part of a comprehensive drive for microeconomic reform in the early 1990s. This began when Labor Prime Minister Hawke convened a series of Special Premiers' Conferences. The process was driven by the Commonwealth but received the active support of the states. New South Wales under Premier Greiner and subsequently Victoria under Premier Kennett saw national reform as a buttress for state reforms to which they were committed. The states were successful in wresting the mantra of "national" from the Commonwealth's monopoly which had been asserted in the previous decades and in making it a genuine arena for joint decision-making.

The purpose of the 1990s' reforms was to make Australian industry more competitive internationally. It entailed overhauling government regulation and the extensive provision of economic infrastructure that was mainly within the states' jurisdiction, or involved the states as major players. Particular targets were state monopolies in areas such as transport and electricity, state discriminatory regimes, and the patchwork of conflicting standards across multiple states. These were all part of the extensive system of state provision deriving from "colonial socialism." The state in Australia, particularly state governments, had been used as "a vast public utility" to which all sectors of society and the economy were linked through a patchwork of special arrangements and subsidies.

The cooperative process of reform provided strong evidence of the continuing strength of the states and the vitality of Australian federalism (Painter 1998). The outcome was a set of new intergovernmental organizations and rules that add up to a major restructuring of Australian federalism at the subconstitutional level. In areas like competition policy there are strong elements of uniformity to facilitate economic efficiency, but the states are partners in the process and have signed on to a regime monitored by an independent commission. Admittedly, they receive large efficiency dividends from the Commonwealth. The states have contributory roles in joint national bodies that set standards in key areas such as environmental policy, food standards, road transport, and technical training. State diversity is allowed for in various ministerial councils' rules that are based upon majority or qualified majority decision-making, as well as in competition policy and mutual recognition. COAG adds an important peak forum to first ministers' meetings that have become dominated by the Commonwealth government and financial matters. Although they have not achieved full potential, the series of reforms culminating in the streamlining of federal arrangements and the establishment of COAG is a significant re-vitalization of Australian federalism (Brown 1999).

GLOBAL AND REGIONAL INTEGRATION

Australia's ties with Britain were not severed after the Second World War but gradually watered down in the British Commonwealth of Nations. While not bound by any formal legal constitution or framework, the modern Commonwealth operates on the principles of the Singapore Declaration (1971) and the Harare Declaration (1991). These declarations were the outcome of the Commonwealth Heads of Government Meetings (CHOGM), a regular forum in which views are exchanged, agendas set and policy developed and endorsed. The modern Commonwealth actively supports the broader UN objectives of international peace and security, and the promotion of human rights. The Singapore Declaration reinforced the aims of the UN Charter and the UN Declaration of Human Rights by seeking to promote institutions and guarantees for personal freedom under law; to combat racial prejudice and colonialism; and to overcome poverty, ignorance, and disease. The Harare Declaration reaffirmed the pre-eminence of human rights in Commonwealth nations and reaffirmed opposition to apartheid in South Africa. Australia has at times been an active player in the Commonwealth forum and used it effectively for international purposes, as did Prime Minister Malcolm Fraser in his crusade against apartheid in South Africa.

Australia has become a promoter as well as a joiner of international bodies, playing a key role in establishing the regional organization for APEC in 1989, aimed at developing regional free trade and economic cooperation (Ravenhill 1994, p. 88). The Department of Foreign Affairs and Trade bills APEC as the "key component of Australia's regional trade policy" and boasts that the combined output of APEC members accounts for almost half of world exports and more than half of world gross domestic product (GDP). But that also means that APEC is diverse and relatively weak, becoming more an occasional talking-shop for Asia-Pacific leaders than an integrated regional association.

Less ambitious but probably more effective has been the establishment of the Cairns Group, a ginger group of primary-producing nations in world trade forums named for its inaugural meeting in Cairns, Queensland. Australia played a key role in forming the group and getting agriculture included in the Uruguay Round of the GATT in 1986 where some concessions were won. The failure of the Uruguay Round to reach consensus led to the establishment of a new organization, the WTO, in 1995 that now conducts the multilateral negotiations aimed at liberalizing world trade. The WTO has been no more successful with its "Millennium Round" of trade talks. The WTO's 1999 Seattle meeting was disrupted by vigorous protests from anti-globalization campaigners, and the EU remains intransigent against lowering trade barriers, particularly on agricultural products.

Finding a Place in the Modern World

After World War II, and more particularly after the 1970s, Australia had become increasingly independent from Britain and more integrated economically and politically into the new international order. But finding a place and a national role with which Australians are comfortable has proved rather more difficult. Underlying the heightened attention to national identity and the challenges of globalization is a curious blend of uncertainty and exhilaration about the changes that are transforming Australia and its place in the world. There have been both optimistic and pessimistic responses. An energetic internationalist, Gareth Evans, minister for external affairs in the Hawke and Keating Labor governments, saw that Australia could "box above its weight" as a decent middle power in the international arena. While Evans relished the encounters, he often seemed removed from Australian public opinion and sentiment. Keating, Labor prime minister from 1993 to1996, was a brilliant simplifier who cast the options as breaking with Britain and turning to Asia, both of which had mainly occurred. An alternative response is to revive simpler nostrums of old Australia: no coloured immigration or pandering to Aboriginal people, and return to a protective state economy. This was popularized by Pauline Hanson's One Nation Party in the late 1990s and finds support among those marginalized by economic changes.

In a defining White Paper, the Howard government emphasized "practical diplomacy" and a "whole of nation approach" as central to Australian foreign and trade policy (Australia. DFAT 1997, p. iii). Dominant are continuities with previous policies that are central to Australia's strategic and trade concerns: commitment to the Asia-Pacific, sustaining links to key trading partners, such as the United States, Japan, Indonesia, and China, and supporting trade liberalization through forums such as the WTO and APEC. The difference is a preference for bilateral over multilateral relationships as the "basic building block" upon which regional and global foreign and trade policy are to be built (ibid.). This is in reaction to the robust internationalist approach pursued by the previous Labor government and its minister for external affairs, Gareth Evans, who was a firm supporter of the UN and its many specialized agencies (Evans and Grant 1993). The Howard government is more jaundiced about internationalism and sceptical about the United Nations. It has drawn back from the Keating-Evans embrace of Asia, emphasizing Australia's uniqueness as an island continent of primarily European tradition and western culture.

The challenge for Australia is to retain its familiar and historic links to Europe and America while pursuing closer relations with Asia. Being a self-declared middle power has anxieties as well as opportunities. At international forums from Versailles to San Francisco, and in world trade organizations since the Uruguay Round of the GATT, Australian leaders have used middle-power status in advancing their claims. Australia enjoys benefits of credibility, independence, and integrity as a middle power and boasts some notable successes such as promoting freer agricultural trade through the Cairns Group and being broker for a UN peace-keeping force and free elections in Cambodia. APEC is another instance where Australia contributed significantly to the creation of an international body. The downside of middle-power status is the inability to determine outcomes that affect the global economic, political, trade or security agenda.

A middle power might help set the agenda but is unlikely to carry the day; its main contribution to international affairs is facilitating alternative avenues of resolution for superpowers caught in otherwise intransigent positions.[8]

Compared with Canada, there is much more at stake because of Australia's relative isolation from an adjacent powerful friend: "Australia was not protected by a long, open frontier and the Monroe Doctrine," as Hancock observed in 1930. That did not seem to matter while the British Empire was strong and engaged in Asia. Hancock could also observe that "in Australia we are as a rule hardly conscious that we have a foreign policy" (Hancock 1930, pp. 56-57). Australia barely had a foreign policy, having entrusted it to Britain. Nevertheless, distance and isolation were often sobering considerations for those who thought about Australia's geographic and strategic place in the world. For Frederick Eggleston who had an extensive personal knowledge of Asia, Australia in the 1950s was "a small nation in an alien sea," being a "democracy with a way of life and political ideas practically identical with those of the United States or of Britain and other Western democracies (Eggleston 1957, p. 1). From the mid-twentieth century onwards, Australia's challenge has been to integrate its British cultural heritage with its Asia-Pacific geography. With the jettisoning in the 1960s of the White Australia policy that favoured Europeans, Australia's population mix has changed quite markedly with more than a million Asian-born people, mainly from Vietnam, China, and the Philippines, now calling Australia home. As its citizen body becomes more diverse and cosmopolitan, Australia is uniquely poised to capitalize on its enduring links with Europe and the US and its location adjacent to Asia. This has been complicated by the Bali terrorist attack in October 2002, which targeted westerners and killed mainly Australian holiday-makers, and subsequent disclosures of fundamentalist Islamic terrorist cells in Indonesia.

Human Rights and the United Nations

The proliferation of international human rights following the birth of the United Nations (UN) in 1945 has influenced Australian domestic governance, law, and citizenship practices. The way in which this has occurred has been mediated by the Commonwealth government and shaped by Australia's constitutional system, particularly the politics of federalism and the interpretation of the external affairs power by the High Court. The international human rights regime and web of UN agencies challenge traditional notions of the sovereignty of the nation-state. Participation in an international organization that sets norms and standards that affect domestic practice is not novel for Australia because of its history as a colony and dominion within the British Empire. The UN's new world order was rather different from the British Empire, however, and international human rights law and practice markedly different from the common law that Australia traditionally relied upon for human rights protection. Without its own Bill of Rights, Australia has become increasingly dependent upon international rights standards and UN monitoring agencies.

The United Nations General Assembly adopted the Universal Declaration of Human Rights in 1948, and in 1966 the International Covenant on Civil and Political Rights (ICCPR) and the International Covenant on Economic, Social and Cultural Rights (ICESCR). Australia signed the Convention on the Elimination of All Forms of Racial Discrimination in 1966, but it was not ratified until 1975, during the final months of the Whitlam government. The ICCPR was open for signature in 1966, but Australia did not ratify the treaty until 1980, and even then with substantial reservations relating to claimed restrictions of federalism. The strength of "federal reservations," that some have seen as more of a repudiation than an acceptance of the Covenant by Australia, reflected the states' opposition and vigorous defence of their constitutional turf against the Commonwealth (Triggs 1982). Queensland and New South Wales had not agreed to the Commonwealth's proposal at the time of ratification. The states could not agree on a common stance on human rights nor would they cede jurisdiction to the Commonwealth over such issues.

During the 23 years of Liberal Coalition government from 1949 until 1972, Australia remained sentimentally attached to a declining British ethos and lukewarm toward the UN. The Whitlam Labor government elected in 1972 renewed Australia's commitment to human rights and a fuller participation in the UN regime. This was continued by the Fraser Liberal Coalition government, elected in 1975, that took a strong stance on apartheid and finally ratified the ICCPR and the ICESCR. Successive Labor governments of Bob Hawke and Paul Keating stepped up Australia's commitment to the UN.

The current Howard Liberal Coalition government remains strongly committed to the United Nations, although critical of its human rights committees and their procedures. It prides itself on Australia's role in leading the international response to the East Timor crisis that proved highly effective. As Foreign Minister Downer points out: "the involvement of the United Nations had a number of advantages. It placed the action firmly inside the ambit of the Charter and international law" (Downer 2000). But as he also notes, it was a somewhat unique case because of the agreement of the Indonesian government to the intervention, the coalition of countries involved, and the speed with which a decisive mandate for the multinational force led by Australia was granted by the Security Council. This was a happy instance where Australia's interests in securing order in this fledgling next-door neighbour coincided with, and its action could be channelled through, the UN's international organization that provided both legitimacy and support.

In contrast to this supportive UN action, the Australian government is critical of the UN committee system that monitors the compliance with human rights treaty obligations. In contention are the reporting mechanisms set up under such UN human rights treaties as the International Covenant on Civil and Political Rights, the Convention on the Rights of the Child, and the Convention on the Elimination of Racial Discrimination (CERP). The government charges that the CERD Committee's decisions in March and August 1999 and its concluding observations in March 2000 that were critical of the government's recent handling of Aboriginal policy were not well-founded or reasoned. The Geneva-based committee held that mandatory sentencing laws in the Northern Territory were in breach of UN standards and recent federal government adjustments to Aboriginal land rights legislation were discriminatory. According to Attorney-General Williams, the committee failed to "engage seriously with the extensive material put before it by the Government"; it "failed to deliver well-founded criticism, strayed well beyond its mandate and made recommendations of a political nature." In response, the government has announced "a whole of government review of Australia's interaction with the UN Treaty Committee system" to "ensure that such interaction is constructive and worthwhile" (Williams 2000). Reviewing the reviewer and subjecting the process of monitoring to critical scrutiny should help in improving the process, although differences of judgement over whether particular government policies infringe human rights will likely remain. Nor is the Australian government happy about having to defend before the UN Human Rights Committee in Geneva its own domestic policies on Aboriginal native title and the Northern Territory's right to maintain mandatory sentencing laws.

Regional Integration

Asia and APEC

Australia has been active in promoting an inclusive Asia-Pacific regional organization in which it might find a congenial place. Along with Japan, Australia played a leading role in establishing the organization for APEC in 1989, aimed at developing regional free trade and economic cooperation (Garneau and Drysdale 1994; Aggarwal and Morrison 1998; Dutta 1999). While important for Australia because it includes its major trade and strategic partners, APEC is a weak institution of "open regionalism" that has expanded to include Northeast Asia, Southeast Asia, Australasia, and the Americas. APEC achieved a high point of aspiration in the Bogor Declaration signed in November 1994 under the auspices of the ailing Indonesian dictator, General Suharto. APEC leaders committed their countries to the goal of free and open trade and investment in the Asia-Pacific to be achieved by industrialized countries by 2010 and by developing countries by 2020.

This was a "tip-top result" for Australia's Prime Minister Keating who placed great store by his special relationship with Suharto and had worked hard for such an outcome. He boasted to the House of Representatives:

> With Bogor ... Australians can say for the first time that the region around us is truly "our region." We know its shape; we have an agreed institutional structure; we share with its other members a common agenda for change. Just as the Bretton Woods agreements after the Second World War established structures in the IMF and the World Bank, which enabled the world to grow and prosper, so in APEC we have established a model which will serve the interests of the post-Cold War world (quoted in Keating 2000, pp. 116-17).

Subsequent events soon deflated such hopes. US President Clinton did not bother attending the next APEC meeting in Osaka the following year because of domestic political issues. APEC has languished with the Asian countries of the region shaken by the 1997–98 financial crisis and Indonesia weakened in its transition to democracy and strife over East Timor.

APEC has also been partly displaced by Asian rival groupings: ASEAN Plus Three (the three being Japan, China, and Korea); and the Asia-Europe Meeting (ASEM) that first met in Bangkok in 1996. So far Australia has been excluded from these forums due to the opposition of its leading critic, Prime Minister Mahathir of Malaysia, who claims that Australia is not sufficiently Asian. Australia is not part of ASEAN which provides a well-established core for the smaller Asian nations (expanded in the 1990s to ten countries with Vietnam, Cambodia, Laos, and Burma being added to the group that included Indonesia, Thailand, the Philippines, Malaysia, Singapore, and Brunei). But even ASEAN is by no means a tight regional association compared to that between Australia and New Zealand.

New Zealand and CER

Australia means "south land" and Australasia literally "southern Asia." Both names were used by European explorers and dreamers who thought there must be a great south land in the southern Pacific to balance the globe's land masses. New Zealand did not join the Australian federation in 1901, having participated in the first National Australasian Convention of 1891 but not in the subsequent Convention of 1897–98 that produced the Australian constitution. Thereafter, Australia and New Zealand pursued parallel paths of nation-building within the British Empire, cementing a special military association through the ANZACS who fought valiantly with British forces in the disastrous Gallipoli campaign against the Turks in World War I.

With the demise of Britain as a world power and its joining the European Union, Australia and New Zealand have formed a close economic and social relationship. This Australasian association was formalized for economic purposes with the Australia/New Zealand Closer Economic Relations Trade Agreement (CER) in 1983. CER marked a commitment to create a genuine free trade area, and was part of a wider plan to harmonize relations between the two highly similar countries. Perhaps more significant is the extensive "people to people" or social connection between two countries that have few restrictions on movement or settlement. Defence and strategic arrangements are similarly close, with New Zealand becoming more reliant upon Australia after its rift with the United States over banning nuclear ships from New Zealand ports in the 1980s. Currently there are calls for monetary union that would tie New Zealand more closely to Australian economic policy (Grimes, Wevers and Sullivan 2002).

Australia and New Zealand have not formalized their close political association in an overarching treaty. Rather, they are joined by a variety of particular treaties, arrangements, and close cultural and popular ties.

Richard Mulgan and I have described this as "an asymmetric pluralist association" that combines elements of transnational association with traditional forms of intergovernmental relations typical of federalism within a nation-state (Galligan and Mulgan 1999). This Australasian association incorporates a variety of structures involving constitutional relations of three basic kinds. One is relations between nation-states, with New Zealand dealing with Australia like a smaller nation-state deals with a larger one. Another is the more routine federal kind where New Zealand participates in federal-state ministerial councils and agreements, such as mutual recognition of standards, more or less as another state of the Australian Commonwealth. A third involves shared or joint institutions, such as common commercial courts, that make binding rulings applicable for both countries. While the first type of nation-to-nation has been predominant in the past, aspects of the other two federal and joint types are now in place and will likely become more prevalent. Increasingly, Australasian governance will be a system of complex and diffuse power centres with an intermingling and overlapping of jurisdictional responsibilities and policy activity.

IMPACT OF GLOBAL AND REGIONAL INTEGRATION

Because of Australia's situational isolation in the southern Asia-Pacific, it is relatively unaffected by regional integration. Asian regionalism is open and diffuse, with APEC becoming more an economic forum or talking shop than a close-knit regional association. That is hardly surprising since it encompasses the Americas and Russia as well as Asia and Australasia. In contrast to this is Australia's regional association with New Zealand that is based upon a close bilateral association between two countries that share common cultures. In part it is a quasi-federal association in which New Zealand acts like an additional state and slots into Australian intergovernmental arrangements, while in part it is a union of peoples who have free rights of movement and settlement. Because New Zealand is so small, however, the net effect is little impact upon Australian federalism other than expanding it to encompass in part a smaller nation.

Nevertheless, this is probably one of the most innovative developments which might serve as a model for associations between comparable sets of countries. The Australasian experiment shows that novel forms of integrated regionalism are possible through a variety of partial instruments in special circumstances. Variations of this sort of association could conceivably be extended to congenial Asian countries like Singapore. A CER-type free trade association was suggested in a meeting between respective prime ministers at the APEC 2000 meeting, and has been mooted as a possibility with other ASEAN countries. Meanwhile, the Howard government is championing a free trade agreement with the US and has recently opened negotiations with senior US officials.

As mentioned earlier, Australia's political economy response to globalization has been the abandonment of protective state policies and deregulating of its domestic economy. That has entailed winding back tariff protection, dismantling much of "state socialism" consisting of the extensive government provision of infrastructure and utilities, deregulating currency markets and banking, reforming labour markets, and enforcing business competition. The overriding purpose was to make Australia's domestic economy more competitive and export-oriented, forcing Australian business to be more efficient. The complementary set of reforms was to federal arrangements and intergovernmental relations culminating in the new Council of Australian Governments (COAG) discussed above.

COAG

Australians were shaken from their accustomed lethargy in 1986–87 by serious deterioration in the terms of trade and balance of payments. Paul Keating, then treasurer, warned that if national performance did not improve, Australia "was basically done for. We will just end up being a third rate economy ... a banana republic" (Quoted in Carew 1992, pp. 171-73). Part of the Hawke Labor government's response was a push to streamline intergovernmental relations, with the prime minister claiming that there were more obstacles to trade within the Australian federation than within the European Union. Making government more efficient was to be an integral part of microeconomic reform.

The institutional means was a series of Special Premiers' Conferences involving the prime minister and premiers, backed up by extensive officials meetings. While the prime minister and the Commonwealth initiated and drove the process, state premiers such as Nick Greiner from New South Wales played a complementary role. The states were attracted by the promise of fiscal reform to address severe vertical fiscal imbalance (the Commonwealth collecting the lion's share of taxation and the states being dependent for approximately half their revenue on Commonwealth general and specific purpose grants). During a rare period of relatively stable politics in all jurisdictions in the early 1990s, a good deal was achieved that showed the flexibility of Australian federalism in responding to globalization. The array of ad hoc intergovernmental bodies was streamlined and more than halved in the process.

A major area of reform was the adoption of a national competition policy directed at eliminating inefficient government provision of utility services and the privileging of government providers. The new arrangements included the extension of trade practices legislation to state businesses, and establishment of stronger regulatory bodies, the Australian Competition and Consumer Commission (ACCC) and the National Competition Council (NCC). The core principle of competition policy as it applies to government is "competitive neutrality." This prohibition against privileging government providers effectively levels the playing field and ensures that if governments retain state provision, as some states have, that will be subject to competition. Reform of public utilities, including the establishment of a national electricity grid, furthers the process of marketization. Other key reforms include achieving national standards in such areas as food processing and packaging, and adoption of mutual recognition for regulatory provisions for goods and occupations across the various jurisdictions. Sharing in this latter reform was part of New Zealand's motivation in securing quasi-federal status as a contributing state.

The COAG reform process has been extensively documented and critically assessed by Martin Painter and, comparatively with Canadian reforms, by Doug Brown (1999). Brown shows "that Australia has produced a more coherent and innovative set of reforms processes" than Canada (1999, p. 17, 252 ff.), in part because Canada has relied more upon the discipline of free trade with the United States for promoting federal efficiency. The Australian reform of intergovernmental relations was curtailed when Keating ousted Hawke as prime minister, and reasserted Labor's traditional commitment to fiscal centralism. Consequently, Hawke was forced to abandon his pledge to state premiers that the reforms would include some devolution of taxation power. This cooled the ardour of the states for reform, while volatile electoral politics in crucial states like New South Wales and Queensland brought in new players with their own political axes to grind. Nevertheless, despite some backsliding,

Keating, as prime minister, did preside over the formal establishment of COAG to take over the work of the Special Premiers' Conferences. In the process, the states formed a new Leaders' Forum that has continued as a peak body for premiers to address issues of common interest.

The Howard Liberal Coalition government elected in 1996 has been surprisingly unconcerned with federalism, showing little interest in, and giving no leadership to, COAG. Its main policy concern has been with tax reform, and in particular with the introduction of the GST and associated income tax reductions. As with the earlier COAG reforms, this is touted as an efficiency reform to make Australia more internationally competitive. To its credit, the Howard government took the proposal to the people in the general election at the end of 1998 and, against the odds, won (retaining government with a majority of seats, if not a majority of popular votes).

Introduction of the GST has a major impact on federalism since the entire proceeds go to the states, allocated on the standard relativity basis calculated by the Australian Grants Commission in the horizontal fiscal equalization process. Principles for administering the GST were agreed to at a Special Premiers' Conference in November 1998, and an *Intergovernmental Agreement on the Reform of Commonwealth-State Relations* signed at the Premiers' Conference in April 1999. All signed on, even though the Labor premiers had their party opposition to the GST formally registered in the text of the agreement. The agreement set up a Ministerial Council for Commonwealth-State Financial Relations consisting of the various treasurers, and gives the states a role in determining the GST base and future rate. This is currently set at 10 percent and requires the unanimous support of state and territory governments before it can be varied. This elaborate mechanism has gone some way toward alleviating state fears that the GST is yet another dose of fiscal centralism, implemented via Commonwealth legislation, albeit for their benefit.

Expanding the Commonwealth's Role

Besides prompting changes to the institutional machinery and arrangements of intergovernmental relations and taxation, globalization has affected Australian federalism by boosting the role of the Commonwealth in mediating domestic and international affairs. The most contentious aspect has been the Commonwealth's increased use of its external affairs power to invade key domestic policy domains of the states. The Commonwealth has become a major player in domestic environmental policy, protecting rain forests in northern Queensland and blocking a huge pulp mill in Tasmania (Lynch and Galligan 1996). Even more controversially, it has extended Australia's reliance upon international human rights norms and UN monitoring committees. The consequences are that domestic rights issues are increasingly influenced by international practice and domestic controversies are readily escalated to international forums. Ironically, in expanding its policy role vis-à-vis the states, the Commonwealth is making Australia more dependent on policy-making and rule-setting by international bodies.

The *Toonen* case from the mid-1990s was a cameo instance of the practical operation of international human rights norms in trumping discriminatory domestic practice. On behalf of the gay and lesbian reform group in Tasmania, Nicholas Toonen mounted a complaint to the UN Human Rights Committee against Tasmanian criminal law forbidding homosexual conduct between adult males. While Tasmania did not enforce the law, it refused to repeal it. The UN Committee found in favour of Toonen and, when the Tasmanian government refused to act, the Commonwealth government passed legislation overriding aspects of the Tasmanian law.[9] Tasmania first challenged the Commonwealth law in the High Court, but then suspended its challenge and repealed its offending law, replacing it with non-discriminatory provisions. The *Toonen* case shows how determined individuals and groups can now take their human rights grievances to international bodies and use their favourable advisory decisions to leverage political change through the Australian federal system. This alternative is particularly significant for Australia in the absence of a domestic Bill of Rights, as Justice Kirby has noted:

> As we do not have a general constitutional Bill of Rights in Australia and as there is no regional human rights court or commission for Asia or the Pacific, the importance of the ICCPR could not be over-stated. Indeed, the significance of the Toonen decision runs far from Tasmania and Australia ... It brings hope to people in countries where individuals are still oppressed by reason of their sexuality (Kirby 2000, p. 18).

More indirect, but nonetheless significant, is the increasing, indirect influence of international legal norms on Australian common law. Most notable was the *Mabo* decision that overturned two centuries of discriminatory property law based on the doctrine of *terra nullius*, and recognized native title for the first time. In the leading opinion of the High Court, Brennan appealed to international standards:

> The opening up of the international remedies to individuals pursuant to Australia's accession to the Optional Protocol to the International Covenant on Civil and Political Rights brings to bear on the common law the powerful influence of the Covenant and the international standards it imports.... It is contrary both to international standards and to the fundamental values of our common law to entrench a discriminatory rule which, because of supposed position on the scale of social organization of the indigenous inhabitants of a settled colony, denies them a right to occupy traditional lands.[10]

The *Mabo* case revolutionized Australian property law and showed how the line of demarcation between international and domestic law is being blurred through Australian judges transposing international norms into their decision-making.

Also contentious has been the issue of the impact of international law in the absence of domestic legislation implementing it. The basic principle that international treaties do not have effect unless incorporated into domestic law was challenged by the *Teoh* case (1991). The court found that by entering into a treaty the Australian government creates a "legitimate expectation" in administrative law that the executive and its agencies will act in accordance with the terms of the treaty, even when the treaty has not been incorporated into Australian law. The case involved the deportation by the Immigration Department of Mr. Teoh, a non-citizen father of young children convicted of possession and trafficking in heroin. Australia had entered into the United Nations Convention on the Rights of the Child that makes the best interests of the child a primary consideration in cases involving separation from their parents. However, it had not implemented the provisions of the Convention into domestic law, and the Immigration officials had not taken it into account. The High Court's innovative finding was summed up by Mason and Deane:

> [R]atification by Australia of an international instrument is a positive statement by the executive government of this country to the world and the Australian people that the executive government and its agencies will act in accordance with the Convention. That positive statement is an adequate

foundation for a legitimate expectation, absent statutory or executive indications to the contrary, that administrative decision-makers will act in conformity with the Convention.[11]

Both sides of politics were aghast at the decision. The Labor minister for foreign affairs and the attorney-general immediately issued a joint statement denying any such legitimate expectation and promising to introduce legislation to that effect. The court had also made it clear that a legitimate expectation cannot arise where there is a statutory or executive indication to the contrary. Government changed before legislation was passed, and the new Liberal National Coalition government made a similar declaration in 1997. Their proposed legislation also lapsed with the calling of the 1999 election, and a new bill is currently before the Senate. Even if this passes, it is arguable whether the court will accept at face value executive assertion of the determining role of parliament in translating international norms into domestic law.

Despite their reservations with *Teoh*, the Labor government and its forceful minister for Foreign Affairs, Gareth Evans, exploited the untrammelled treaty-making power with little concern for parliamentary scrutiny or public accountability. The practice of bulk tabling of treaties every six months developed and, by the 1990s, between 30 and 50 treaties per year were being tabled in Parliament. In about two-thirds of the cases, Australia had already ratified or acceded to the treaties before tabling and was obliged to comply under international law (Twomey 1995, p. 8). Such contempt for Parliament, combined with concern about the High Court's open-ended interpretation of the external affairs power that favoured the Commonwealth over the states, caused a political backlash. A Senate committee called for greater public scrutiny and public accountability, and its key recommendations were adopted by the incoming Howard Coalition government in 1996 (Australia. Senate Legal and Constitutional References Committee 1995).

The 1996 overhaul of the treaty-making process included: mandatory tabling of treaties 15 sitting days before the government takes action to bring them into force; provision of an accompanying National Interest Analysis explaining the reasons for Australia's becoming a party; scrutiny by a parliamentary Joint Standing Committee on Treaties; establishment of a Treaties Council under the auspices of COAG; and public access to treaty-making information via the Internet. While the COAG Treaties Council has yet to prove itself, other parts of the new policy are operating to give greater scrutiny. Since 1996, the Joint Standing Committee on Treaties has issued 34 reports covering 185 treaty actions (Williams 2000).

Much public discussion has focused on Australia's "loss of sovereignty" because of the recent proliferation of treaties. The Department of Foreign Affairs and Trade estimates that the current Australian Treaty List contains 2,920 entries as at 31 December 1999.[12] The entries break down to 1,669 bilateral and 1,251 multilateral agreements. The figures themselves, however, can be very misleading. For example, although this appears to be an increase of 902 entries since 1989, in fact only 400 entries represent Australia's signature, ratification or acceptance of new treaties. Of the 400 entries generated by new treaties, many are terminations or replacements of existing treaties. Most of the other new entries concern measures for improving the availability of treaty information that are now listed on a Web site.[13] A key point, and one that is often overlooked, however, is that Australia is a member of all the international organizations that oversee the treaties it has ratified. In that way, Australia has, subject to the usual caveats of the disparities of power in international relations, as much or as little influence over the terms, implementation, and enforcement of treaties as any other nation. As a member of all the key international bodies, and particularly in the case of the UN, Australia has historically been highly involved in the long negotiations leading up to the drafting of many major human rights and other treaties. Most importantly, Australia can choose not to support or ratify a particular treaty, and has done so, as the Multilateral Agreement on Investment case shows. Finally, Australia alone can implement treaties domestically. Unlike some other jurisdictions, such as the United States, treaties are not self-executing in Australia: that is, they do not become part of domestic law unless legislation specifically does (subject to the Teoh qualification discussed above).

Numbers aside, Australia is party to a wide range of international instruments touching on almost all areas of domestic policy: environment, health, education, food production, and land use. Many treaties spring from Australia's traditional relations with other nations: bilateral treaties cover diplomacy, medical treatment of another nation's citizens, mutual telecommunications, postal, and other forms of media. Treaties also singly cover novel and modern environmental, military and other security and criminal concerns, many of which have been exacerbated by the global information and technological era. Examples include agreements banning nuclear testing, land mines and chemical testing, as well as those on organized crime and drug smuggling. Treaties that have come into force in the past five years include the 1993 Chemical Weapons Convention, the 1997 Land Mines Convention, and the 1995 Blinding Laser Weapons Protocol. The 1996 Comprehensive Nuclear-Test-Ban Treaty has been concluded but is not yet in force. Environmental standards have also been a focus of international agreements: for example, the 1997 Kyoto Protocol to the Climate Change Convention, and controls over the international movement of hazardous substances incorporated into the 1998 Rotterdam Convention on Prior Informed Consent. On the international crime front, 1990 European Money Laundering Convention and the 1997 OECD Bribery Convention have recently come into force for Australia. Treaties that have drawn particular criticism are in sensitive policy areas of human rights, labour relations, and the environment. Examples include the Convention on the Rights of the Child, the ILO Convention 158 on Termination of Employment, the World Heritage Convention, the Climate Change Convention, the Basel Convention on Hazardous Waste and the Desertification Convention.

A recurring theme has been the states' complaint of lack of consultation in areas they claim to be of vital concern for their jurisdiction. Victoria has put in place its own parliamentary monitoring system of treaties (Federal-State Relations Committee 1997). Key sectoral groups have also criticized the Commonwealth for failing to consult about the domestic implications of treaties in Australia. Examples include mandatory sentencing of juvenile offenders under the CORC; agreements on desertification that have a critical impact on land use and development; and listing sites as World Heritage. It has been claimed that complying with the Climate Change Convention would reduce national output considerably, while compliance with the Hazardous Waste Convention could impact adversely on exports. The COAG Treaties Council is designed to remedy this by providing a regular forum for the prime minister and the premiers and first ministers from the states and territories to meet. As well, states like Victoria have implemented their own state parliamentary scrutiny of treaties that affect them.

FUTURE SCENARIOS

Future scenarios are a tool for selecting and making prominent aspects of the existing order so as to better understand how changes to key parameters of the global might impact upon the domestic. While the future is uncertain, such thought experiments are useful in challenging the usual presumption that the future will resemble the present — it might be quite different as aspects of the present become more dominant. Such an exercise can also help in gaining insight into key variables and linkages in the current complex interaction of global and domestic. This should deepen our understanding of the present and help in preparing for the future.

In assessing the impact of the various global scenarios on Australian federal structure and processes, we need to keep in mind the flexibility of institutions and the reflexivity of human agency. Provided institutional arrangements are reasonably flexible, as are Australian federal ones, they can be used in different ways. Human reflexivity adds a further complication: up to a point, human actors can use the same set of institutions for different purposes as well as different institutions for the same purpose. Globalization as the independent variable does not have a direct causal effect on the structure and processes of federation as the dependent variable, but an effect that is mediated by human agency. Of course, in this instance such human agency is complex and diffuse, and is organized in an existing pattern of federal institutions and arrangements. So, federalism is both a significant intermediate variable, which, because of human agency, is partly reflexive, as well as also being a dependent variable that is shaped and influenced by globalization.

In speculating about how Australia would fare under the various future scenarios, we need to keep in mind a range of key current attributes of its geography, population, culture and political economy, as well as its federal system of government. Australia is relatively small in population and economic terms with a predominantly Anglo-European culture situated adjacent to Southeast Asia. It has a highly developed and stable liberal, democratic political system, an educated citizenry and a relatively open economy that is closely linked to diffuse world markets. While it is destined to be a "taker" rather than a "maker" in terms of global influence, it has both the domestic institutions and global connections to mediate global challenges. Recent changes, ranging from economic deregulation to streamlining of intergovernmental arrangements and increased Asian migration, have enhanced Australia's ability to cope and even prosper in a more globalized world. But clearly some future scenarios are more favourable than others.

The worst-case scenario for Australia is that of *regional dominators* where orderly trade is internalized within powerful blocs and there is predatory competition between blocs. This would be a threat to Australia if it were not part of any regional bloc and were left out in the cold. Currently,

Australia's trade is spread between Asia, the United States, and Europe and that has helped insulate it from regional downturns such as the Asian economic crisis in 1997–98. If trade were internalized within regional blocs and Australia remained outside, its economy would be jeopardized. In such a scenario the Commonwealth would become more dominant in having to take desperate initiatives to make representation to bloc leaders and salvage national interests. A likely by-product would be New Zealand's merging more fully with Australia, but a united Australasia would be too small to change much in this scenario.

The development of an Asian regional bloc comparable to the EU or the North American Free Trade Agreement (NAFTA) seems unlikely at this point, and Australia's becoming an integral part of such an Asian bloc even less likely. If both did eventuate, however, Australia might do very well indeed since it would have an insider advantage in the areas of specialization that it shares in common with Europe and America. If, with the globalization of communications and the shrinking of distances, blocs became less regional geographically, Australasia might join NAFTA and become part of the American bloc. This alternative is already being pursued by the Howard government. If Australia were part of a strong "regional" bloc, then the significance of the Commonwealth government would be reduced as its role was supplanted by bloc decision-making. The states might become more significant as the governments of the domestic regions with closer links to the people and productive activity.

The best-case scenario for Australia and for Australian federalism is that of *shared governance*. A stable international order governed by the rule of law and the principles of fair trade is ideally suited for Australia because of its relatively advanced and stable political economy, diffuse trading ties, and deregulated economy. Australia would benefit from an orderly world market with fair trading standards because of its efficient primary export industries, agriculture, and mining. Moreover, such an order would complement Australia's modern national polices of an open and competitive economy. Some Australian economists have argued that the country is better off deregulating its economy even if others do not. But such unilateral adoption of economic orthodoxy is fraught unless there is some approximation of the world order to that of shared governance where trade is fair and markets can actually operate.

In such a global order, domestic federal governance should also thrive because there is less need or opportunity for the Commonwealth to take a dominant role in mediating global access and managing predicaments. Indeed, once the global regime was implemented, the role of the national government would shrink. The consequence would be a re-balancing of domestic federalism, even if both spheres of domestic government had more constrained roles as global governance became more pervasive.

The *global club* scenario where a few major powers control international affairs and create an orderly global system is probably more attractive than the chaotic scramble of *cyberwave*. It depends on who the global oligarchs are and how scrupulously they enforce an orderly system. Such a system of world governance by the powerful few, if in fact decent and orderly, is not so far removed from what middle powers face in the real world of today. In such a scenario, there would still be ample scope for domestic governance without the need for the national government to take an enhanced role in mediating globalization. Hence, in Australia's case, there should be no need for Commonwealth hyper-activity that would skew the federal system in its favour.

The opposite would likely be the case for cyberwave because of the demands upon national government to deal with the fluid dynamism of rampant global markets and rapid technological change. In moving away from protective state policies, Australia has not adopted adequate strategies and arrangements for domestic compensation. Consequently, the differential impact of global forces is producing disgruntled losers as well as satisfied winners, and these are concentrated in certain sectors and regions — the losers predominantly in rural and regional Australia from whence there is a current political backlash. Within the limited role for governments associated with this scenario, cyberwave globalization would result in the Commonwealth government taking a dominant role meeting global challenges and helping to mediate their effects. Such a response would be consistent with Australia's tendency to privilege the central government during periods of stress. At the same time, state governments might well be implicated in such compensation arrangements as were made available in a more closely integrated federal process.

CONCLUSION

Whatever the global future, Australia's current position in the world order has both advantages and disadvantages. It is well positioned to take advantage of global opportunities, but because of its size and location it is vulnerable to risks from larger players dominating the world system for their advantage. Not being part of a regional bloc, Australia will have to live by its wits if it is to prosper and meet the challenges of global change. Australia's best option is an orderly and decent world system and it has the limited resources of a smallish middle power to assist in putting that in place. Its federal system is an advantage and has shown itself sufficiently flexible for the job. Perhaps we can go further and say that federalism is in fact more suited to a world where sovereign nationhood is undermined and replaced by global regimes of rule-making and standard-setting. Because of federalism, Australian governments are not sovereign and policy-making in most key areas involves a complex interplay between multiple governments that have local, regional, and national bases. Adding a global sphere extends the complexity, but in ways that are not so foreign to the already complex system.

In the above account of how Australian federalism has responded to globalization, there are two powerful trends that run in opposite directions. Despite its classic federal structure that is encapsulated in the constitutional system, Australian federalism has become relatively centralized in its domestic arrangements. This is most evident in fiscal federalism where the Commonwealth has asserted a near monopoly over taxation for half a century. It has been evident in the Commonwealth's expanded role in recent decades due to its superiority in matters to do with foreign affairs and treaties. If this were all, one might conclude that Australia's response to globalization has been in keeping with its established centralist mode of operation, and that the effect of globalization in Australia has been to extend and consolidate Commonwealth dominance. There is a contrary tendency, however, that favours federalism and an enhanced role for the states that was apparent in the reform of intergovernmental arrangements in the 1990s and resulted in COAG. Meeting the economic challenges of globalization has entailed reforms to governance and federal arrangements that require state participation and have reaffirmed the states' role in national policy-making and regulatory regimes. On balance, the latter tendencies have countered the former. Despite some immediate advantage for the Commonwealth government in mediating international affairs, an increasingly globalized world will likely see a reduction in the role of national government. This should continue to favour federalism and the states, which has been the other part of Australia's recent experience.

Notes

1. This chapter draws extensively upon a joint research project and recent book, Galligan, Roberts and Trifiletti (2001).
2. The term "glocalization" was coined by Tom Courchene (1993).
3. See Dan Elazar's suggestion of a matrix conceptualization (Elazar 1987).
4. *R. v. Burgess; Ex parte Henry* (1936) 55 CLR 608.
5. *Koowarta v. Bjelke-Peterson* (1982) 153 CLR 168.
6. *Commonwealth v. Tasmania* (1983) 158 CLR 1, at p. 486.
7. For an environmental example, see *Richardson v. Forestry Commission* (1988) 164 CLR 261; *Queensland v. Commonwealth* (1989), 167 CLR 232. The human rights case is *Polyukhovich v. Commonwealth* (1991) 175 CLR 501; *Horta v. Commonwealth* (1994) 123 ALR 1.
8. For a comparison of Australia and Canada, see Cooper, Higgott and Nossal (1993).
9. *Nicholas Toonen and Australia*, United Nations Human Rights Committee, Communication No. 688/1992, Doc: CCPR/C/50/D/488/1992 (4 April 1994). See also Tenbensel (1995).
10. *Mabo v. Queensland (No. 2)* (1992) 175 CLR 42. See Kirby (1995).
11. *Minister of State for Immigration and Ethnic Affairs v. Teoh* (1995) 183 CLR 291.
12. Communication from DFAT officer, 6 April 2000.
13. The Australian Treaties Library is a Web site containing Australian treaties from 1901 at <http://www.austlii.edu./au/other/dfat/>.

References

Aggarwal, V. and C. Morrison, eds. 1998. *Asia-Pacific Crossroads: Regime Creation and the Future of APEC.* New York: St. Martin's Press.

Australia. Department of Foreign Affairs and Trade (DFAT). 1997. *In the National Interest: Australia's Foreign and Trade Policy White Paper.* Canberra: Government Printers.

—— 1999. *Composition of Australian Trade, 1998-1999.* Canberra: Government Printer.

Australia. Parliament of Victoria. Federal-State Relations Committee. 1997. *Report on International Treaty Making and the Role of the States.* Melbourne: Government Printer.

Australia. Senate Legal and Constitutional References Committee. 1995. *Trick or Treaty? Commonwealth Power to Make and Implement Treaties.* Parliament of the Commonwealth of Australia.

Australian Bureau of Statistics. 2000. "Developments in Australian Exports: A Longer Term Perspective," *Australia Now: A Statistical Profile, International Accounts and Trade, Year Book Australia, 1999.*

Brown, D. 1999. "Market Rules: Economic Union Reform and Intergovernmental Policy-Making in Australia and Canada." PhD thesis, University of Melbourne.

Capling, A. 2001. *Australia and the Global Trade System: From Havana to Seattle.* Cambridge: Cambridge University Press.

Capling, A. and B. Galligan. 1992. *Beyond the Protective State.* Cambridge: Cambridge University Press

Carew, E. 1992. *Paul Keating: Prime Minister.* Sydney: Allen & Unwin.

Cooper, A., R. Higgott and K. Nossal. 1993. *Relocating Middle Powers: Australia and Canada in a Changing World Order.* Vancouver: UBC Press.

Courchene, T. 1993. "Glocalisation, Institutional Evolution and the Australian Federation," in *Federalism and the Economy: International, National and State Issues*, ed. B. Galligan. Canberra: Federalism Research Centre, Australian National University.

Downer, A. 2000. "Upholding the 'Sword of Justice': International Law and the Maintenance of International Peace and Security." Speech to Joint Meeting of the Australian and New Zealand Society of International Law (ANZSIL) and the American Society of International Law (ASIL), Canberra, 28 June.

Dutta, M. 1999. *Economic Regionalization in the Asia-Pacific: Challenges to Economic Cooperation.* Chelternham, UK: Edward Elgar.

Eggleston, F.W. 1957. *Reflections on Australian Foreign Policy.* Melbourne: F.W. Cheshire.

Elazar, D. 1987. *Exploring Federalism.* Tuscaloosa: University of Alabama Press.

Evans, G. and B. Grant. 1993. *Australia's Foreign Relations in the World of the 1990s*, 2d ed. Melbourne: Melbourne University Press.

Galligan, B. 1987. *Politics of the High Court.* St. Lucia: University of Queensland Press.

—— 1989. *Utah and Queensland Coal.* St. Lucia: University of Queensland Press.

—— 1995. *A Federal Republic: Australia's Constitutional System of Government.* Cambridge: Cambridge University Press.

—— 2001. "Amending Constitutions through the Referendum Device," in *Referendum Democracy: Citizens, Elites, and Deliberation in Referendum Campaigns*, ed. M. Mendelsohn and A. Parkin. New York: Palgrave.

Galligan, B. and R. Mulgan. 1999. "Asymmetric Political Association: The Australasian Experiment," in *Accommodating Diversity: Asymmetry in Federal States*, ed. R. Agranoff. Baden-Baden: Nomos Verlagsgesellschaft.

Galligan, B., W. Roberts and G. Trifiletti. 2001. *Australians and Globalisation: The Experience of Two Centuries.* Cambridge: Cambridge University Press.

Garneau, R. and P. Drysdale, eds. 1994. *Asia-Pacific Regionalism.* Sydney: Harper Educational Publishers.

Gibbins, R. 1991. "Ideological Change as a Federal Solvent: Impact of the New Political Agenda on Continental Integration," in *The Nation-State versus Continental Integration: Canada-North American-Germany-Europe*, ed A.L. Pal and R.-O. Schultze. Bochum: Universitätsverlag Dr N. Brockmeyer.

Goldfinch, S. 2000. *Remaking New Zealand and Australian Economic Policy.* Wellington, NZ: Victoria University Press.

Grimes, A., L. Wevers and G. Sullivan, eds. 2002. *States of Mind: Australia and New Zealand 1901-2001.* Wellington, NZ: Institute of Policy Studies, Victoria University of Wellington.

Hancock, W.K. 1930. *Australia.* London: Benn.

Higgott, R. 1989. "The Ascendancy of the Economic Dimension in Australian-American Relations," in *No Longer an American Lake?* ed. J. Ravenhill. Sydney: Allen & Unwin.

Keating, P. 2000. *Awakening: Australia Faces the Asia-Pacific.* Sydney: Macmillan.

Kirby, M. 1995. "The Role of International Standards in Australian Courts," in *Treaty-Making and Australia: Globalisation versus Sovereignty?* ed. P. Alston and M. Chiam. Annandale: Federation Press.

—— 2000. "International Law: Down in the Engineroom." Paper presented to the ANZSIL and ASIL joint conference, Sydney, 26 June.

Lynch, G. and B. Galligan. 1996. "Environmental Policymaking in Australia: The Role of the Courts," in *Federalism and the Environment*, ed. K. Holland, F.L. Morton and B. Galligan. Westport, CT: Greenwood Press.

Mason, A. 1988. "The Australian Constitution 1901-1988," *Australian Law Journal* 62: 755.

McDougall, D. 1998. *Australian Foreign Relations: Contemporary Perspectives.* South Melbourne: Longman.

Meaney, N. 1985. *Australia and the World: A Documentary History from the 1870s to the 1970s.* Melbourne: Longman Cheshire.

Meredith, D. and B. Dyster. 1999. *Australia in the Global Economy.* Cambridge: Cambridge University Press.

Painter, M. 1998. *Collaborative Federalism: Economic Reform in Australia in the 1990s.* Cambridge: Cambridge University Press.

Ravenhill, J. 1994. "Australia and the Global Economy," in *State, Economy and Public Policy*, ed. S. Bell and B. Head. Melbourne: Oxford University Press.

Smith, G., D. Cox and S. Burchill. 1996. *Australia in the World: An Introduction to Australian Foreign Policy.* Melbourne: Oxford University Press.

Tenbensel, T. 1996. "International Human Rights Conventions and Australian Political Debates: Issues Raised by the Toonen Case," *Australian Journal of Political Science* 31(1):7-23.

Triggs, G. 1982. "Australia's Ratification of the International Covenant on Civil and Political Rights: Endorsement or Repudiation?" *International and Comparative Law Quarterly* 31:278.

Twomey, A. 1995. 1995. "Procedure and Practice of Entering and Implementing Treaties." Parliamentary Research Service Background Paper, No. 27, Canberra: Department of Parliamentary Library.

Williams, D. 2000. "International Law and Responsible Engagement," ANZSIL-ASIL Conference Keynote Address, Canberra, 29 June.

DECENTRALIZING SYSTEMS

Important? Yes. Transformative? No. North American Integration and Canadian Federalism

Richard Simeon

INTRODUCTION

Globalization is not a new phenomenon in Canada. Indeed throughout its history Canadian economic and social development has been profoundly shaped by external forces. From the early fisheries to the fur trade, the forestry, and wheat economies, to the more recent focus on other resources, and its recent embrace of North American free trade, it is the needs of foreigners that have driven Canada's economic development. Canada's politics have been shaped by its historic relationship to three great empires — the French, the British, and now the American. Canada's social makeup has been formed through its role as a settler society — first the French, then the British, then Ukrainians and many others from southern and eastern Europe; and most recently from Asia, Africa, the Caribbean, and Latin America. Canada has always been heavily dependent on foreign trade and foreign investment — in fact, Canada's integration with the United States is today just reaching the levels that occurred in the late nineteenth century (Bourne 1999, p. 57). The "brain drain" that has occurred recently is actually far less today than it was throughout the long period when there were no US restrictions on movements across the border. So it is worth asking "What is new?" about the contemporary form of globalization, and whether it will have very different effects on Canada than earlier experiences.

In contemporary Canada, one external relationship dominates all the others. That, of course, is integration with the United States. It is hard to think of any other two sovereign countries so closely intertwined. As one author recently stated, in Canada "80 percent of globalization is Americanization" (quoted in Hoberg 2000, p. S36) The relationship is at once economic (85 percent of all Canadian exports go to the United States), cultural, and political. It is also profoundly asymmetrical, as Pierre Trudeau famously put it, it is the relationship of an elephant and a mouse. Dramatic as their impacts are, the Canada-US Free Trade Agreement (FTA) and the subsequent North American Free Trade Agreement (NAFTA) were only the latest steps in a long period of deepening integration since World War Two.

For many writers, these developments signal the virtual end of Canada as a distinctive, autonomous society. American cultural influence would steadily chip away at any distinctive Canadian identity. North-south trade would supplant the east-west trade nurtured by the National Policy of the 1870s, exacerbating regional competition and reducing the significance of all the other links that go along with trade. This, along with the constraints imposed by mobile capital seeking cheap labour and low taxes and regulation would decimate Canadian industry and make it more and more difficult to sustain Canada's somewhat more generous and redistributive social policies (Clarkson and Lewis 1999; Drache 1996). As Thomas Courchene put it, it would become harder and harder to sustain the east-west social railway in the face of north-south economic linkages (Courchene 1992, pp. 98-99). My own first attempt to explore this issue · reflected this perspective. Writing in 1990, I argued that "to put it bluntly, global and North American integration promotes Canadian disintegration" (Simeon 1991, p. 51).

I am now much less certain about such a conclusion. My own shift reflects the larger literature on the impact of globalization generally. Recent writings suggest that rather than the hollowing out or virtual disappearance of the state, we are witnessing instead a shift in the role of the state: while some functions may be diminished, others, such as promoting competitiveness and mediating and cushioning the impact of globalization on the domestic society, have increased (Skogstad 2000; Hoberg 2000, 2001; Banting, Simeon and Hoberg 1997). It also shows that the trend toward convergence or harmonization of public policies is less than previously expected: national differences in policy choices and the size and role of government have remained marked (Cameron and Stein 2000; Wolfish and Smith 2000). Domestic institutions, policy legacies, and political forces remain critical determinants of both policy and political practice. Indeed, while it is true that globalization is a set of factors to which all countries must respond, it does not have a single inherent logic or imperative. There are many ways to respond to it, and these will largely be shaped by domestic factors.

Work by Keith Banting, George Hoberg and myself suggests this is true even for a relationship as close as that between the United States and Canada (Banting, Hoberg and Simeon 1997). We found both convergence and divergence across a range of policy areas. Convergence was as much explained by the countries' similar response to common problems as it was by direct cross-border influence. US influences were strong, but they were a "constraint, not a wall." Political institutions and processes were the most resistant to tendencies to convergence.

With these perspectives in mind, the thrust of this chapter is that the effects of North American integration and globalization on the politics and practices of Canadian federalism have been relatively limited. I thus question (while not completely abandoning) some of the more sweeping generalizations and predictions that have been made by writers such as Tom Courchene. This is not to argue that globalization is unimportant. Indeed it is, in a thousand ways. But it is to question how much the dynamics of contemporary federalism and intergovernmental relations in Canada today can be seen as a response to and result of globalization, rather than of the dynamics of domestic politics. Globalization affects the economic constitution much more than it does the political constitution.

The chapter proceeds as follows. First, I provide a brief analysis of Canada's economic, social, and political links with the United States and the rest of the world. Second, I will explore the implications of these developments for a number of different dimensions of Canadian federalism. In particular, I will focus on an assessment of the "glocalization" thesis, most associated in Canada with the work of Courchene. The glocalization thesis generates a number of predictions.

- With respect to *identity* this thesis predicts a diminution or weakening of national identities and a strengthening of provincial/local identities.
- With respect to *regional conflict*, it predicts an intensification of federal-provincial and interregional conflict for jobs, investment and markets,

and a decline in the idea of Canada as a "sharing community," with its strong commitments to regional redistribution and equalization.

- With respect to the French-English, Quebec-Canada division, it predicts a stronger commitment to autonomy for Quebec; and a diminished set of costs for secession.

- With respect to *centralization/decentralization* or the balance of power between federal and provincial governments, it predicts a decline in federal influence and a relative growth in provincial power, along with a potential for further devolution to a number of strong city-regions.

- With respect to the *policy agenda* confronting federal and provincial governments, it predicts a heightened emphasis on policies to promote productivity and competitiveness, increased flexibility and diversity in social programs, continued reduction in internal barriers to trade, and better federal-provincial coordination in such areas as the environment and external trade policy.

- And finally, with respect to the *institutions and practices of intergovernmental relations,* it predicts a movement toward a more collaborative mode of decision-making, and one that is more likely to approach a confederal pattern, with national standards set more by provinces and territories acting together than through the leadership of the federal government.

I will also consider a quite different set of predictions that suggest that the long-run implications of globalization are to undermine the autonomy of provinces and strengthen the federal government as the chief exponent of Canada's interests in the global environment.

I conclude that both sets of arguments overstate the impact of globalization on federalism in Canada. The greatest impact of globalization has been on the policy agendas that Canadian governments at all levels face. The effects on national and provincial identities, and on regional and linguistic conflict, while potentially great, have not yet manifested themselves in important ways; globalization is moderately associated with a decentralist trend, but not unambiguously so; and the impacts on the institutions and practices of intergovernmental relations have been minimal. What is puzzling perhaps is how little the forces of globalization have forced change in Canadian federalism.

Taken together, these observations suggest a further conclusion — that the impact of external forces may serve to reinforce and exaggerate tendencies already present in domestic societies and politics, rather than fundamentally to change and reorient them. This is suggested by Brian Galligan's analysis of Australia in this volume. Starting with a much more centralized federation than Canada, he concludes that the impact of globalization there is moderately centralizing. I, starting with a more regionally divided and decentralized federation, conclude that the effects here are moderately decentralizing.

Any such conclusions must be highly tentative. Partly this is because globalization is such a multi-faceted phenomenon, whose influence may push in different ways in different areas. Partly it is because it is so difficult to sort out the effects of globalization itself from all the other forces at work, such as the recent preoccupation with debts and deficits, recent ideological trends toward "neo-liberalism," and the increased social diversity of modern society. Are these separate phenomena, or differing aspects of a single phenomenon? I prefer the strategy of clarifying the distinctions rather than lumping them all together. There is also a more subjective judgement to be made: Is one most impressed with the evidence for change, or with the evidence for continuity? In this chapter I emphasize the latter.

I conclude with a cautiously optimistic assessment of the capacity of Canadian federalism and its characteristic pattern of intergovernmental relations to adapt and respond to the undeniable challenges that globalization poses for Canadians, just as it adapted to the postwar agenda of building the Keynesian welfare state.

CANADA, NORTH AMERICA AND GLOBALIZATION

Historical Background

The very creation of the Canadian federation in 1867 flew in the face of the global and North American economic and political trends of the time. The British North American colonies were economically vulnerable, especially after the withdrawal of British preferences: one of the drivers of Confederation was the greater economic security and the ability to raise capital that union would provide. Union would also provide some political security against an expansionist United States following its Civil War. The new Dominion then set out to create an east-west economy extending from the Atlantic to the Pacific. The 1867 constitution provided the new central government the primary tools for this nation-building project. The blueprint for achieving this was the National Policy, 1875, comprised of three major elements: construction of the Pacific railway, high tariffs to provide revenue and to stimulate domestic manufacturing, and settlement of the prairie west in order to promote agricultural exports. The resulting political economy helped shape Canadian politics: a financial and manufacturing "heartland" in Central Canada, enjoying a protected market for its products in the agricultural and resource producing west and Atlantic Canada, whose workers sold their wheat, timber, and fish in the international economy. This model was very much a political construction, led by a strong central government.

In the early years of the twentieth century the rise of a new set of export industries — timber, mining, and hydro power — promoted a provincial challenge to federal dominance, in part because under the constitution, resources and public lands were owned and controlled by provincial governments (except for the prairie provinces which did not win ownership rights until the 1930s). In addition, western politics was shaped by resistance to the implications of the National Policy, which made them dependent on protected eastern Canadian suppliers for their equipment, while exposing them to the vagaries of the international market for their products. The conflicts generated by these issues undermined federal power, and by the 1920s Canadian federalism was considerably more decentralized than it had been in its early years. Moreover, the debates in that period — free trade versus protectionism; which level of government was to play the primary role in economic development — were very reminiscent of the contemporary period.

In the 1930s, as elsewhere, protectionist impulses dominated Canadian economic policy, with a last ditch effort to maintain Canada's privileged access to the British market through imperial preferences. World War II, however, signalled the end of the imperial dream, and underlined the fundamental fact that Canada's most important economic relationship was to be with the United States. The National Policy was to be gradually dismantled.

Under the National Policy, Canada had developed a "branch plant" manufacturing economy, by which foreign, mainly US, companies would establish facilities in Canada to serve the Canadian market. The fundamental shift from this pattern came in the Auto Pact of 1965 by which a single North American market in automobiles and related parts was created. Instantly, a large chunk of Ontario's manufacturing was reoriented from east-west to north-south. Canada's dependence on the US market, its reliance on US investment, and its openness to US cultural influences became a major political issue in the 1970s, with a number of related policy responses — a Foreign Investment Review Board, various subsidies for Canadian cultural industries, and so on. But the logic of North American integration prevailed. In 1988, after an impassioned internal debate about the future of Canadian sovereignty, culture, and social programs, Canada signed the Canada-US Free Trade Agreement, which soon added Mexico, to form the North American Free Trade Agreement.

The bitterly fought 1988 federal election was in many respects a referendum on free trade. A majority of Canadians voted for parties opposed to the agreement, but the Conservatives, led by Brian Mulroney, nonetheless won a decisive majority. Support was divided on both class and regional lines, with Ontario voters most strongly opposed. The federal Liberals, returned to power in the 1993 election, had campaigned against the FTA but once in office quickly embraced it.

The NAFTA is fundamentally aimed at reducing barriers to trade and investment among its members. It does not include free movement of people across borders. More importantly, it does not have the broad political purpose of unification that underpins the treaties of the European Union. It is much more limited in scope. It has no provisions for common policies on economic matters, nor does it create a network of joint decision-making institutions, such as the European Commission, Council of Ministers and Parliament. It does include a dispute settlement mechanism, and two parallel bodies (on the environment and labour standards) which have little impact. Despite the impassioned debate prior to the agreement, and differing views about its continuing effects, free trade is now an accomplished fact; no major Canadian political party calls for its renegotiation or repudiation. A survey done by the Centre for Research and Information in Canada in 2001 found that two-thirds of Canadians support the general idea of Canada negotiating new free trade agreements, including specifically a Free Trade Area of the Americas (FTAA). Remarkably, in light of the strong regional divisions highlighted by the original free trade debate, there are today only small regional differences. Support for an FTAA ranges from 57 percent in BC to 70 percent in Quebec (CRIC 2001, pp. 6, 7).

NAFTA, of course, is not the only multinational institution in which Canada participates. It is also a member of the World Trade Organization

(WTO), the G8, and a host of other agencies, based on its sense of itself as a "middle power," and as a country that can use multinational bodies as something of a counterweight to its dependence on the United States. Arguably, rulings of the WTO have had as much, if not more, influence on Canadian economic practices than has NAFTA.

Canada today is the most trade-dependent member of the G7 group of countries. Exports as a share of gross domestic product (GDP) have risen dramatically in recent years — from 24 percent of GDP at the start of the 1990s to 37 percent by 1995. Exports and imports combined (a measure of exposure to international competitive pressures) rose from 41 to 62 percent in the same period (Hoberg 2000).

Canada's trading links are overwhelmingly, and increasingly, with the United States. Between 1975 and 1995, the US share of Canadian exports rose from 25 to 75 percent, and is now over 85 percent. Despite sporadic efforts to increase trade with other regions such as the Pacific Rim and Europe, the proportion of trade with these areas is stable or declining. In the first seven years after NAFTA came into force, Canadian exports to the US and Mexico rose 129 percent; those to the rest of the world by 29 percent. Exports to the EU, Canada's second largest trading destination, declined from 14 percent to 6 percent between 1975 and 1995. The US is also much the largest foreign investor in the Canadian economy, although the share of other regions such as Europe and Japan has increased.

In all provinces, except Nova Scotia and Prince Edward Island, international exports by 1986 had exceeded interprovincial exports as a share of provincial GDP. In Ontario, the share of GDP devoted to exports — driven especially by the automobile trade — rose from 33 to 43 percent. Reliance on trade with other provinces declined to 20 percent of GDP. In the same decade, international trade increased for all provinces; and in all but one, interprovincial exports declined marginally. Overall, then, the pattern is one of stable, or slightly rising volumes of internal trade, and dramatically rising levels of international trade. Through the early 1990s, exports were growing by 11 percent per year; while those to other provinces were growing at 3 percent (Cited in Brodie and Smith 1998, p. 82; Page 2002).

These trends suggest that the model of Canada's economy embodied in the nineteenth-century National Policy has been decisively broken. The image of Ontario as the manufacturing and financial "heartland" of the Canadian economy has shifted as it integrates more deeply with the

American economy, and in particular with the neighbouring US. As Courchene has stated: "Globalization and the geo-economics of NAFTA are forcing a profound rethinking of the politics and geography in the upper half of North America" (1998, p. 81). For Courchene and others, the fundamental axis of the Canadian economy has shifted from east-west to north-south. Canada's railways, once the most potent symbol of east-west nation building, are now reorienting their tracks in a north-south direction; the logo for the legendary Canadian Pacific Railway now includes both American and Canadian flags; Others have questioned how profound the change is. Helliwell and McCallum agree that the FTA has substantially reduced the "border effect," but argue that internal linkages within Canada remain many orders of magnitude greater than Canada's integration with the United States (Helliwell 1996, 1999; McCallum 1995). Taking into account distance and size of markets, and the effect of the FTA, Helliwell concludes that east-west trades in merchandise is about 12 times that of north-south trade, and that the gap is much larger in trade in services (1999, p. 93). "The economic fabric of Canada and other nation-states has a much tighter weave than previously thought" (ibid., p. 95).

The American cultural embrace is also potent. American television, films, and magazines dominate their Canadian counterparts. Many commentators suggest that these trends erode Canadian identity and cultural distinctiveness, and hence erode Canadians' ability to construct an overarching unifying national identity. Despite the globalization, or "North Americanization," of culture and despite limits on the ability of Canadian governments to regulate and promote culture, it is also the case, as Harvey Lazar points out "there is more 'Canada' in both pop and high culture, both domestically and internationally than ever before" (Lazar and McIntosh 1999, p. 18).

Indeed, a plethora of recent data have confirmed Lazar's observation. In his *Fire and Ice: The United States, Canada and the Myth of Converging Values*, Michael Adams documents large and growing divergence between Canadians and Americans across a broad spectrum of values and attitudes. "At the most basic level — the level of our values, the feelings and beliefs that inform our understanding of and interaction with the world around us — Canadians and Americans are remarkably different, and are becoming more so" (2003, p. 4).

Globalization and North American integration, then, have indeed led to some fundamental changes in the Canadian political economy. The puzzle is why they have not generated greater change in the structure and operation of the Canadian federal system.

THE INSTITUTIONAL LEGACY

Canada's original federal design, embodied in the *Constitution Act, 1867*, seemed to suggest a highly centralized model of federalism. The federal government was given the most important powers necessary to engage in the Canadian nation-building project. These included interprovincial trade and commerce, currency, banking, and the then most important sources of revenue, notably the tariff. Moreover, the national government was given important powers to constrain the provinces. These included a sweeping "disallowance" power by which the federal government could set aside any provincial legislation; federal appointments of provincial lieutenants-governor, who also had the power to "reserve" provincial legislation for consideration by the national government; and continued federal control (until 1930) of natural resources in the prairie provinces created in 1905. More generally, section 91 gave Ottawa what appeared to be a plenary power to "make laws for the peace, order and good government of Canada," and it was widely assumed at the time that the enumerated powers that followed were illustrative, rather than exhaustive. In addition, there was an implied, though not explicitly stated, "spending power," by which Ottawa could spend public revenues for any purpose, including on matters assigned to the provinces in section 92. This became the primary instrument through which the federal government became deeply involved in the design and financing of the Canadian welfare state. It is at once one of the chief instruments of flexibility in the Canadian federal system; and in recent years, one of the most contentious. Provincial powers in the original constitution were focused primarily on social and cultural matters, though there was a second implied reserve power, in the assignment of "property and civil rights" to the provinces. The former became much more important in the middle of the twentieth century, since they included jurisdiction over health, education, and welfare, the chief pillars of the welfare state; the latter gave the provinces important powers in the regulation of business, labour, financial institutions, and the environment. In addition (with the exception of the prairie provinces noted above) the provinces' role in economic development was strengthened by their ownership of public lands, and by their ownership and control of natural resources including hydro power, oil and gas, and forestry, all of which are vital components of Canada's international trade.

This "quasi-federal" centralized model was not to last. The reasons were partly political and partly economic. From the early years provinces, especially Ontario and Quebec, challenged federal dominance and articulated a "compact" view of federalism that saw Ottawa as the creation of the provinces. The courts (until 1949, and reflecting the legacy of Canada's colonial past, the Judicial Committee of the United Kingdom Privy Council [JCPC] also played a critical role in transforming the operating constitution. Some new policy areas, related to what we now call globalization, were deemed to be within federal jurisdiction. These included air transport and telecommunications. But in some other areas directly related to our topic, the courts leaned in a distinctly provincialist direction. For example — and directly in contrast to the Australian case — the federal power to make treaties was interpreted in a way that denied Ottawa the power to implement their provisions in areas of provincial jurisdiction. Even when it ventured into foreign waters, the JCPC ordained, the Canadian ship of state must maintain its watertight compartments. Second, and this time in sharp distinction from the American Supreme Court, the trade and commerce power was interpreted not as sweeping power over all economic activity in the Canadian economic union, but rather in a way that left considerable room for intraprovincial trade subject to provincial regulation and not subject to federal regulation. The broad "peace, order and good government" (POGG) clause, in turn, was narrowly interpreted as an emergency power. The disallowance and reservation powers remain in force, but have come to be considered constitutional dead letters.

Since the Supreme Court of Canada became the country's final court of appeal in 1949, its decisions have modestly strengthened federal power in some areas, but in general it has been highly sensitive to federalist values, and has been careful not to interpret the broad federal powers in such a way that Ottawa could push the provinces aside (Baier 2002). Nor has the court aggressively pushed Ottawa to broaden its powers to regulate the economy.

As federal tariffs have been virtually eliminated as a tool of trade policy, and as international agreements increasingly focus on non-tariff barriers found in public expenditures and regulation, the erosion of federal dominance is accentuated, since such policies are, as Grace Skogstad puts it, "as likely to be provincial as national policies" (2002, p. 160). Ottawa needs to keep the provinces onside if it is to succeed in international forums; provinces need federal support for their objectives. Hence the requirement for a high degree of cooperative federalism, not only in domestic policy but also in international relations. Indeed, in a global era, the federal character of Canada is projected beyond its borders; and international forces reach deep down to affect provinces, regions, and cities.

The result is that if one thinks of the policy sectors and policy instruments that might potentially be used to enhance Canadian competitiveness in a globalized world, or to respond to global pressures, both orders of government are deeply engaged. Both have many levers at their disposal. In a great many areas, they are highly interdependent. Neither level alone can fully address the problem. With respect to trade in forest products, for example, federal dominance in international and interprovincial trade interacts with provincial ownership of the resources and their management of forest activities. With respect to the environment, the policy instruments are shared, with Ottawa responsible for cross-border pollution and other matters, and the provinces for regulating waste disposal and the emissions performance of most corporations. With respect to current speculation about a North American energy policy, provincial ownership of the resources is a crucial bargaining chip. Hence, the imperative for coordination in all these areas.

Both orders of government also have a high level of fiscal autonomy. Ottawa is able to raise revenues by any means; provinces are limited to direct taxes, but these encompass most of the major sources of taxation, including personal and corporate income taxes. The long-term trend has been toward increasing provincial shares of both revenues and expenditures, and toward diminishing federal control over tax policy. There are no constitutional limits on the ability of provinces to borrow, either on domestic or international markets.

The decentralized model is complicated by another central feature of the Canadian federal design: in sharp contrast to the integrated model of Germany, with its high level of concurrency in the division of powers, state implementation of national laws, a highly integrated fiscal system, and powerful state representation in the national legislature, Canada is more accurately described as a separated or dualist system. Despite the high degree of *de facto* shared responsibilities, the model is one of separate lists of federal and provincial powers, watertight compartments; of separate financial systems, and so on. This separation extends to national institutions: the Canadian Senate plays no role in bringing the provinces into national decision-making, and very little in representing provincial interests at the centre. Two other aspects of Canada's parliamentary system are also important: a first-past-the-post electoral system whose effect is to radically exaggerate regional differences in party support, and, more important, to facilitate the concentration of power in single party prime ministerial governments at both levels, with very strict party discipline. Taken together these can mean that in most periods significant provinces or regions can feel excluded from exercising influence at the centre, thus exacerbating regional grievances, and leading protest to be expressed through assertive provincial governments. Canada's parliamentary federalism also strongly influences the practice of intergovernmental relations in Canada. It takes place in the interactions of federal and provincial ministers and officials — executive federalism — with little role played by legislators or political parties.

The result is a federal system in which the interactions among the constituent governments can often look like the relations between states in international relations (federal-provincial diplomacy), which is often competitive and adversarial, and in which the institutional interests of governments — for power, status, blame avoidance, and credit-winning — play a central role; and in which territorial interests and conflicts are deeply entrenched.

GLOBALIZATION AND CANADIAN FEDERALISM

Globalization, as we have seen, exerts powerful influences on the Canadian economy and society. Its effects are mediated through a relatively decentralized, divided, and competitive federal system. We now turn to the central question for this volume: Whether and how global and North American forces are changing the practice of Canadian federalism. We look at each dimension in turn.

Globalization and Regional Conflict

There are some grounds for believing that these external forces may exacerbate regional conflicts and divisions in an already divided society.

First, the important differences in provinces' resources and economic structure mean that they are differentially integrated into the global and North American economies. Their interests in trade policy and other areas are thus likely to diverge. In an ever more regionalized economy it becomes harder and harder to envision Canada as a single national economy, and hence harder to think that a single national economic policy will serve all their needs. Global shocks, such as the 1970s energy crisis, will often impact differently on different provinces. In that case, the battle over prices and revenues pitted oil and gas producing provinces against consuming provinces in something close to a zero-sum game. As the country now considers how to meet international commitments to reduce the output of greenhouse gasses, the Alberta government argues that the costs will fall disproportionately on its industries, and seeks either to slow down the changes or to arrange for some compensation. Provinces will continue to seek their own way in the world, independently of the national government, and of the other provinces.

Second, a globalization-induced diminution of economic linkages across the country may weaken other linkages as well. Once auto workers in Oshawa and Windsor are manufacturing cars to sell in the United States, rather than to other Canadians, then, in principle, Ontario auto workers might be less concerned with the economic well-being of the other regions. No longer would their ability to sell cars depend on it. The idea of Canada as a giant mutual insurance company, as Saskatchewan Premier Allan Blakeney once put it, would erode.

Third, the competitive pressures of globalization may lead not only to greater competition among nations, but also among regions within nations for investment, trade, and the like. Each region or province is more likely to look out for its own interests.

In particular, there may be a diminished interest in Canada as a "sharing community," committed to reducing regional disparities through equalization and other transfers. Equalization takes on different political implications when an equalizing dollar moves from, say, Toronto, to Ottawa, to Fredericton, New Brunswick, and then back to Ontario in the form of purchases of goods and services, than it does when that same dollar goes from Toronto, to Ottawa, to Fredericton, to, say, Chicago. The first dollar could be seen as an "integrative" dollar; not so the second.

The idea of Ontario as a region-state, with interests increasingly diverging from those of other provinces, builds on these ideas. No longer, Courchene argues, in *From Heartland to North American Region-State,* is Ontario so dependent on the Canadian economic market; its future lies in North American integration. As a result, Ontario may be less willing to subordinate its interests to those of other provinces, and be less willing to support equalizing policies. Moreover, when once Ontario's interest in the health of the national economy was intimately linked to federal policy, there may now be increasing divergence between Ontario's interests in

North America and the continuing federal obligation to be concerned with the welfare of all regions.

All these suggestions are plausible, but a number of caveats need to be entered. First, the divergence of regional economic interests is not new, it has been a recurring feature of Canadian federal politics. Regional cleavages are certainly less prevalent today than they were during the 1970s, when globally induced rising energy prices sharply divided the interests of the producing provinces — Alberta, BC, and Saskatchewan — from those of the consuming provinces. More generally, as provinces diversify internally, the regional differences themselves are declining. Helliwell concludes that far from being a regionally fragmented economy, the national economy in Canada "operates as a fairly seamless web of intersecting regional markets for goods, services, capital, and migration.... The degree of segmentation is tiny compared with that between nations, even in post-FTA North America" (1999, pp. 97-98).

In terms of the commitment to regional equalization, it is true that the Ontario government and other wealthier provinces have argued strenuously that redistribution policy should be confined to the explicitly labelled Equalization program, rather than be built into other federal transfer programs and regional development. And Ontario governments, both left and right, have vociferously argued for its "fair shares" of federal funding, primarily in reaction to a federally imposed cap on the Canada Assistance program in the 1980s, at a time when Ontario itself was entering a severe recession. The cap has now been removed, and equal per capita funding in the Canada Health and Social Transfer (CHST) has been restored. Ontario decisionmakers have been very frustrated by the failure of Ontario citizens to respond to its position on issues such as fair shares or limitations on the federal spending power.

Disputes over the Equalization program itself have intensified in recent years. Poorer provinces seek to include more revenue sources, to abolish the five-province standard that excludes the wealthiest provinces from the calculation of entitlements, and, in the case of Nova Scotia and Newfoundland, to end or reduce the claw back by which, as their oil and gas revenues increase, their equalization payments are automatically reduced (Brown 2001).

But no province has mounted a direct attack on the principle of equalization itself. Moreover, Ontario citizens have continued to elect overwhelming numbers of Liberal MPs at the federal level, despite the Liberals' commitment to equalization and regional development programs.

Canada's provinces do compete with each other and neighbouring jurisdictions for jobs and investment, especially in tax policies. But there has been no evidence of the kind of outright bidding for specific corporations to locate in a particular province, as is common in the United States, and no sign of the damaging "fiscal wars" that plague Brazilian federalism (Simeon 2001). As Grace Skogstad notes, the existing rivalries have not prevented cooperation on many other economic development fronts, perhaps best exemplified in the numerous Team Canada trade promotion tours, in which the prime minister and the premiers descend on foreign countries brandishing contracts to sign (Skogstad 2002, p. 161; see also Bird and Vaillancourt 2001; Simeon 2001).

In some respects, North American integration might *reduce* regional conflict in the future. Recall that the National Policy of the nineteenth century was itself divisive: leaving western farmers to the vagaries of global markets, while forcing them to buy more expensive equipment and supplies from tariff protected central Canada. The National Policy fuelled a long line of western protest parties and movements. The removal of tariffs under free trade thus removes an important source of regional grievance. More recently, one of the most divisive national government policies in Canadian history was the National Energy Program (NEP) (1981) by which the national government held Canadian energy prices below world levels and appropriated a larger share of the associated revenues. Bumper stickers in Alberta proclaimed "Let the eastern bastards freeze in the dark"; while those in Ontario complained about the "Blue-eyed Sheiks of Alberta." In the present global climate, it appears unthinkable that any Canadian government would attempt to impose such a policy in the future. When the Progressive Conservatives won office in 1983, the NEP was quickly dismantled; and when energy prices peaked in 2000–2001, again driving Alberta revenues far above the national average, there were virtually no calls for a revived NEP.[1]

Some writers (Courchene; Jacobs 1984) argue that another emerging trend with implications for Canadian federalism and regional conflict is the emergence of powerful city-regions such as Toronto, Montreal, and Vancouver. The futures of these cities, it is argued, are increasingly linked not so much to their own provincial hinterlands, but to global markets and to other large cities around the world. Centre and periphery should now be seen less as central Canada versus the east or the west, but rather as a network of large cities strung along the border, with resource-based and agricultural regions across the country as the periphery. In this view, Vancouver, Toronto, and Halifax have more in common with each other than Vancouver has with Prince George, Toronto with Kapuskasing, or Halifax with Yarmouth. Moreover, it is in these large cities that Canadian cultural diversity is manifested most strongly, as recent immigrants have concentrated there. Hence, the interests and aspirations of the metropolitan areas are likely to diverge more and more from those of provincial governments, setting up strong divisions within provinces. In Toronto, a group of activists has produced a Toronto Charter, mapping substantial independence and autonomy for the city-region; while the mayors of Canada's five largest cities met in 2001 to explore ways of enhancing their roles. Again, however, these developments remain potential rather than real. Cities remain firmly under the constitutional and financial thumbs of provincial governments; and Ottawa has few levers through which to influence local government (Sancton 2002). They have not developed the strong party systems that might lead to a more coherent and organized thrust for a greater role. One of the continuing anomalies of Canadian federalism is that in terms of the relationship between central government and the provinces it is one of the world's most decentralized federations; but in terms of the relationship between provinces and local government, it is one of the world's most centralized. Andrew Sancton recognizes the dilemma: "Given many of the standard claims about how globalization enhances the role of cities, we might reasonably expect the municipal governments of Canadian cities to become more important, both as partners in Canadian federalism and as key actors in enhancing Canada's global competitiveness. Most of the rest of this chapter is devoted to refuting such claims" (2002, p. 261).

Finally, there have been some suggestions that regions that cut across the Canada-US boundary may become more important. There are enormous similarities in the economies and societies of British Columbia and the Pacific Northwest of the US, of the prairie provinces and the contiguous states, and especially of Ontario and its neighbours who share the Great Lakes basin. As a result, they share many common interests and concerns both economic and environmental. A wide variety of province-state agreements on a host of questions have been developed. State governors and provincial premiers meet regularly on a regional basis: western premiers with their US counterparts and eastern premiers with the New England Governors' Conference. In May 2000, western premiers and governors endorsed a framework for ongoing cooperation; in July, the New England governors and eastern Canadian premiers agreed to establish a Standing Committee on Trade and Globalization; and in August 2001, they agreed on an ambitious joint plan to reduce greenhouse gasses (New England Governors and Eastern Canadian Premiers 2001). On the west coast, the idea of a "Cascadia" tying together British Columbia, Washington, Oregon, and perhaps Alberta has received some attention, especially from business interests. A North America of distinct regions spanning the national border is plausible, especially in economic terms, but it flies in the face of political realities. Moreover, similarity of interests does not necessarily breed cooperation, as the bitter dispute over softwood lumber between BC, Oregon, and Washington well demonstrates.

Some writers on both sides of the border have argued for a closer and deeper North American Union, including a common currency, a full customs union, free movement across borders, a common policy with respect to immigration, and common policy-making in such areas as the environment (Pastor 2001). Such developments would prove enormously controversial in all three countries, and would have major implications for their domestic politics, including their federal systems.

Globalization, we may conclude, has relatively little impact on regional divisions in Canada, but the shifting issues raised by globalization have major effects on the salience of underlying divisions and the policy areas around which they crystallize.

Globalization and Canadian Identity

An associated argument is that the effect of globalization is to weaken national identities, to strengthen local attachments on the one hand, and build commitments to transnational communities on the other. Again, the "glocalization" thesis is plausible. If national governments are no longer able to act effectively in response to citizens' interests, then they are likely to turn on the one hand to international arenas where the real decisions are made, and, on the other, to local communities which can provide a greater sense of security and an affirmation of traditional loyalties in an insecure world. To this can be added in the Canadian context, the potentially corrosive effects on national identity of exposure to US cultural influences.

The plausible prediction then is one of declining attachments to Canada and a strengthening of attachments to local and provincial communities.

A weak and fragmented Canadian identity, along with the salience of provincial identities, have long preoccupied Canadians. But the most thorough analysis of recent trends, by Frank Graves and his associates, confounds the prediction (1999). Canadians are indeed strongly attached both to their provinces and their localities. But the proportion expressing strong attachments to Canada (81 percent) is second only to attachment to the family and considerably larger than the proportion expressing attachment to their province (71 percent) and locality (74 percent). Between 1991 and 1998, the proportion of those who say they belong "first of all" to Canada remained unchanged at 40 percent; as did those who feel belonging first to the province (19–20 percent). Primary attachment to locality or town actually declined from 42 to 21 percent (Graves *et al.* 1999, p. 315). Graves *et al.* conclude that the sense of attachment to Canada is high, and is not declining. "Comparatively, Canada has the highest levels of belonging to country of all areas tested in the World Values Survey." They also argue that "longer term (30 year) trends show national attachment strengthening, local attachment declining, and cosmopolitan attachment rising but still clearly subordinate to national attachment" (ibid., p. 335). Another recent study, conducted for the then Council on Canadian Unity, found that in 2000, 81 percent of Canadians from outside Quebec "strongly agreed" to a "profound attachment to Canada," compared with 59 percent feeling the same way about their province.

Ontario, firmly placed at the centre of Canada, and assured of carrying powerful weight in Ottawa has always demonstrated the highest levels of attachment to the country, and the lowest levels of identification with the province. Yet Courchene's Ontario as a region-state thesis clearly implies that Ontarians will be inclined to lose faith in Ottawa and to look to their provincial identity in the future. That may be, but there is little if any evidence for such a shift. In fact, Graves *et al.* conclude that "Ontarians' sense of attachment to province has declined significantly since 1995" (1999, p. 316). As Nelson Wiseman puts it, "Fed-bashing falls flat in Ontario. It does so because of the stronger attitudinal attachment of Ontarians to their national government than their provincial government" (2000, p. 8). He concludes that "the notion of Ontario as a conscious and self-interested region-state is shaky and problematic" (ibid., p. 10).

Globalization, then, has not, or at least not yet, fundamentally altered the distribution of loyalties and identities that underpin Canadian federalism. We have no way of knowing whether this will continue to be true. Two factors suggest the possibility of change. First, Graves *et al.* find that younger Canadians are significantly less attached to Canada than older Canadians, leading them to conclude that this brings "to question the idea that nationalism will persist indefinitely without state intervention" (1999, pp. 300, 331). Moreover, there is some evidence that Canadian national pride and identity are strongly linked to a small number of distinctive Canadian social programs, notably the "sacred trust" of medicare. To the extent that globalization potentially undermines the Canadian capacity to sustain such distinctive programs — or to support Canadian cultural industries — further erosion of national identity is possible.

In terms of the possibility of cultural assimilation into the United States, a slight majority of Canadians believe that over the last ten years, Canada has become more like the United States, but only 11 percent of those outside Quebec, and 17 percent of Quebecers, would like to see Canada become more like its neighbour in the future. None of this is to deny the salience of regional politics in Canada, manifested most recently in the 2000 federal election results. Again, however, this has been a persistent thread throughout Canadian history, ebbing and flowing depending on the prevailing political issues. But regionalism is neither created nor exacerbated by globalization per se.

There are thus no clear patterns in the association of globalization and shifting Canadian identities.

Globalization and Quebec

If globalization has yet to show any effects on the balance of national and provincial loyalties in English Canada, can the same be said of Quebec and its loyalties? Perhaps not. It is significant that while the Ontario government vigorously opposed the original Free Trade Agreement, with the apparent support of the bulk of its population, most Quebec opinion appeared to be strongly in favour. There are several possible reasons for this difference between the two most industrialized provinces. First, the historic source of grievance in Quebec has been not so much the dominance of English-speaking capital, but of *Canadian* English-speaking capital. Thus, a closer association with the United States could be seen as a way to escape the historical pattern. Second, the vigorous attempt to use the Quebec state to promote a Quebec-based capitalist class, Quebec Inc., created a number of industries (Quebec Hydro, Bombardier, and the like) with a strong outward export orientation that would be served by free trade. Third, at the cultural level, francophone Quebecers, unlike their English-speaking fellow citizens, possess a strong bulwark against assimilation: their language. American cultural "imperialism" therefore has never been seen to be as much of a threat in Quebec as it has been in the rest of Canada.

In a broader sense, global forces have perhaps contributed to the legitimacy and self-confidence of the Quebec independence movement. The rhetoric of Quebec nationalism has been strongly associated with movements for independence, liberation from colonial rule, and self-determination throughout the world.

North American free trade may do so as well. Quebec nationalists also argue that the weaker the economic linkages between Quebec and Canada become relative to those with the US, the smaller the costs attendant on a secession. The more Canada disengages economically, the easier it will be to do so politically. Moreover, membership in NAFTA is seen as a powerful counterweight permitting Quebec both to maintain the advantages of economic union with Canada, and with the rest of North America. This helps explain the strong support for NAFTA expressed by the present Quebec government. There are, of course, weaknesses in this argument. Helliwell's data on the continuing strength of the "border effect" applies to Quebec as well as other provinces; indeed it is more dependent on the Ontario market than Ontario is on it. Nor would it be a foregone conclusion that in a post-secession negotiation Quebec would automatically become a member of NAFTA. Both Canada and the US would have something to say about that. Moreover, it could well be the case that a Quebec in NAFTA would have to abandon or radically change many of the economic development policies that allowed Quebec Inc. to be formed in the first place.

In any case, it appears that the ebb and flow of support for independence in Quebec has little to do with global or North American developments. It has much more to do with domestic developments — support for secession rising after the failure to win support for recognition as a distinct society within Canada and slowly declining after these episodes have passed.

In the event that secession were to occur, we can expect that the United States would play an important role either in facilitating or blocking it, but with its primary goal being the maintenance of its economic interests and social order. Moreover, my observations above with respect to the continuing viability of an independent Canadian nationality would have to be rethought. Following the psychological blow of the breakup, and the enormous domination of Ontario in the rump federation, there would clearly be a fundamental rethinking of Canada, including, perhaps, a decision by all or parts of the country to join the United States (Cairns 1999).

Globalization and Centralization/ Decentralization

Here the familiar thesis is that under globalization, power flows three ways: upwards to supranational institutions and corporations, downwards to provincial and local governments, and outwards to citizens and consumers. Globalization, it is argued, places more constraints on national governments than on provincial or state governments. For example, the tariff, long one of the most powerful instruments of federal economic policy, is no longer available to the federal government. Fiscal and monetary policies, also primarily in federal hands, are highly constrained in a globalized world. On the other hand, it is argued that it is provinces that have primary jurisdiction in many of the policy areas that have come to play a larger role in economic success — labour market policies, infrastructure, education, land-use planning, and other areas that affect the "quality of life." Thus, the balance is said to shift from the federal government as the primary guarantor of economic and social policy to the provinces.

Measuring something as multi-faceted as centralization and decentralization is extremely difficult, but there is some evidence that at least in some policy areas the balance has shifted to the provinces. The provincial/municipal share of revenues and spending has been rising relative to the federal share. There has been significant downloading of responsibility for social policies, both from Ottawa to the provinces and from the provinces to local governments. For example, federal transfers in support of health, welfare, and postsecondary education were combined into a single block grant, the CHST, in 1995. The system included fewer federal conditions than previous grant programs and disconnected the level of federal payments from actual provincial program spending. No longer was Ottawa obligated to share the burden when social costs escalated, as they did dramatically in Ontario in the early 1990s. Beginning in 1995, the federal government made dramatic cuts in social transfers to the provinces, further reducing its presence in the social policy area. For example, the federal contribution to health, once pegged at 50 percent, has declined to about 14 percent.[2]

The decline in federal transfers to the provinces, from 24 percent of provincial revenues in 1961 to 13 percent in 1999 is dramatic, but it happened in even steps from decade to decade. "Fiscal decentralization," Boadway argues, "has been the operative policy in the 1990s world of fiscal discipline and government retrenchment" (Boadway 2000, p. 72). The reduction in federal transfers means that provinces are now raising a greater proportion of their spending on their own. In turn, this places strain on the system of tax-collection agreements by which Ottawa collects income taxes on behalf of the provinces (except Quebec). Provinces have won the successive battles over their freedom to set rates, provide credits, and free their own tax revenues from federal decisions by moving from a "tax on tax" (with provincial income tax rates expressed as a proportion of the federal tax) to a "tax on base." This is what makes it possible for Alberta, for example, to introduce a flat-rate income tax on its own. Indeed some observers worry that Canada is losing the benefits of a harmonized tax system; but the point here is that the progressive fiscal decentralization did not originate in globalization.

An active labour market policy was a central part of the Liberal government's design for a globally competitive policy in 1993. Between 1993 and 2000, however, federal spending in these areas declined, despite such much-touted expenditures as the Millennium Scholarship Fund. More importantly, much of the responsibility for administering funds for these programs was devolved to the provinces (Bakvis 2002). Between 1997 and 2000, labour-market-related federal support to the provinces increased marginally to $1.85 billion; funds disbursed directly by the federal government were cut almost in half, to $863 million (Haddow 1998). Labour market training agreements, now signed with all provinces except Ontario, also devolve responsibility to the provinces. (The story is well told in Bakvis 2002.) Similarly, Ottawa has devolved much of its enforcement of environmental regulation to the provinces, and is now engaged in negotiating national standards for toxic substances, instead of developing unilateral federal standards. New federal funding to the provinces concerning the well-being of children (the National Child Benefit) involves virtually no federal strings or policy leverage.

A major exercise to rationalize federal and provincial roles in social policy resulted in the Social Union Framework Agreement (SUFA) in 1998. Started as a provincial initiative, the agreement concluded by reaffirming the power of the federal government to spend in areas of provincial jurisdiction, while subjecting it to some provincial constraints. Thus, it was neither centralizing nor decentralizing. Nor has it fully institutionalized the image of a collaborative partnership that inspired it (Boismenu and Jenson 1998).

Thus, the overall trend is clear: a less interventionist federal government, some devolution of program and fiscal responsibilities to the province, and more emphasis on intergovernmental agreement, rather than unilateral action by Ottawa in many areas. But for our purposes, we must ask the question: Are these trends a consequence or product of globalization? Two very important caveats must be made.

First, the proximate cause of many of the recent changes was the fiscal crisis: the rise of unmanageable government deficits and levels of indebtedness. As Courchene put it, "the reality of the last few years is that the federal deficit and debt burden is driving Canada into unprecedented decentralization" (1992, p. 53). Only if one can, as seems unlikely, attribute the fiscal crisis itself to globalization can one use it to explain much of the devolution that has occurred. Now that governments have slain the deficit (but not the debt) dragon it will be interesting to note whether the federal government reverses itself and begins to play a more activist role both in domestic and external policy.

More importantly, trends toward fiscal decentralization began long before the recent preoccupation with globalization. It was in about 1960 that provincial spending first exceeded federal spending in the postwar period. Since then, the provincial-municipal share of total taxing and spending has steadily increased (Treff and Perry 2001, Appendix A). The federal share of total government spending dropped sharply in the 1960s, and then declined much less slowly in the last three decades. The provincial-local share similarly rose quickly between 1960 and 1980, but has altered only marginally since (Lazar 2000, pp. 11-12). The provincial share of all revenues raised by governments from their own sources peaked in 1980. There has been little change since then.

In a series of agreements beginning at the end of World War II, federal control over the income tax steadily declined; we moved from tax rentals, to tax sharing, and then to independent taxation, with fewer and fewer federal controls over provincial actions. The big jump in provincial and corporate income taxes as a fraction of the total came between 1955 and 1975 (from 11 to 43 percent of the personal income tax and 4.5 to 27 percent of the corporate income tax), rather than between 1975 and 1995 (when provincial shares rose another 11 percent and 4 percent respectively). The same is true for intergovernmental transfers. We moved from conditional grants with relatively detailed federal conditions, to Established Programs Financing (EPF) to the CHST. Each step of the way, federal conditions were relaxed. Only in the *Canada Health Act*, which funds health care, do there remain clear federal conditions, but these too are broad, vague, and much contested. Canadian fiscal federalism has thus experienced considerable decentralization. But the major shifts occurred before globalization became our great preoccupation.

Several factors other then globalization drove the postwar pattern of decentralization. First, most of the areas of rapid growth in the period of expanding government lay in spheres of provincial jurisdiction. Only a few elements of the welfare state were constitutionally shifted to Ottawa (pensions and unemployment insurance). Even with conditional grants, it was provincial bureaucracies that grew to implement the new social policies. This, in turn, increased the size, competence, and self-confidence of provincial governments. Less and less were they willing to defer to a superior federal government. Provincial assertiveness was also driven by other factors. The energy crisis drove citizens to embrace a strong provincial government to challenge Ottawa in several provinces. Successive federal governments in which the governing Liberals were largely frozen out of regions like the west compounded this. Thus, provincial status and influence were growing for very domestic reasons. Similarly, there is little new in calls for Ontario to look to its own interests and undertake its own economic development strategies as a region-state (Courchene 1998; Wolfe 1997). This is simply a contemporary version of province-building, especially in provinces like British Columbia, Alberta, Saskatchewan, and Newfoundland that attracted much attention in the 1970s. In an era of global and North American integration, province-building strategies take on different forms and deploy new policy instruments. The phenomenon itself is not primarily a product of globalization.

Nowhere, of course, was this more true than in Quebec. Its Quiet Revolution embraced the Quebec state as the primary political instrument for the provincial society. In the 1960s, the federal government responded to its claim to be *maîtres chez nous* with a number of concessions. These included a major shift of income tax revenues to the provinces; the right of Quebec to opt-out of a number of existing shared-cost programs and the negotiation of a separate Quebec Pension Plan. One of Pierre Trudeau's primary goals when he came to power in 1968 was to stop what he saw as an inevitable slide down a slippery slope from "special status" to eventual independence. Henceforth, Quebec was to be treated as any other province. The implication of this logic was that federal involvement in areas of provincial jurisdiction would be constrained by what was politically saleable in Quebec. One result was the EPF program that, among other things, increased federal funding for postsecondary education, but without buying any policy leverage in the area. Again, it was domestic political forces, not globalization that were driving decentralization, and the big changes occurred earlier rather than later in the contemporary period.

Thus, the argument that globalization and decentralization are causally linked remains at best unproven. Indeed, Ian Robinson has made a strong case for the reverse argument: that globalization is centralizing and fundamentally diminishes provincial autonomy and capacity. "The net impact of the FCA's [Free Capital Agreements, a term he prefers to free trade agreements] is likely to be centralizing." Broader definitions of investor rights, stricter control of procurement, tighter technical standards, and the extension of trade agreements to include a broader array of services all have major implications for provincial powers even in areas central to their role such as education and health care. Moreover, he argues, this movement is led by a national government that has promised to "take all necessary measures" to ensure compliance by lower level governments. While he agrees that Ottawa has not yet invoked the Trade and Commerce or POGG clauses to force provincial action, he suggests that the potential remains, and that this in itself leads provinces to act in a compliant manner. Moreover, provinces are more vulnerable to pressures from mobile capital, since "it is easier for TNC's to play off the 91 state and provincial jurisdictions against each other than it is to whipsaw three national governments" (1993, p. 200). He adds that any decentralization associated with cuts in federal transfers is not associated with any increase in real provincial powers. It is odd indeed to suggest that the restructuring engineered by national governments through trade agreements constitutes an enhancement of provincial power" (ibid., p. 206). In a later article, Robinson (2002) assessed the evidence of five years of experience, and came to a more modest conclusion. He noted that few challenges have been brought against the provinces; Ottawa has been threatened much more by sanctions under the FTA and WTO. Thus, whether the FCA's are centralizing or decentralizing must remain an open question. Nor has the greatly intensified federal-provincial conflict he had expected materialized. Nevertheless, Robinson remains convinced that the long-run effect of making an economic constitution through the federal spending power will eventually lead Canada to a limited form of "residual federalism," with the provinces in a clearly subordinate position.

Robinson's analysis involves some of the same problems as do Courchene's. Globalization, fiscal crisis and neo-liberalism are conflated; many of the changes he notes were well underway before globalization came to the fore and the causal arrows are unclear.

In these assessments of the alleged decentralizing implications of globalization, it is also important to note that elements of *is* and *ought* tend to be intertwined. For Courchene, both globalization and decentralization are "good things" because they constrain the federal government — indeed all governments — from doing "bad" things. Decentralized government will mean less government. Robinson opposes globalization and centralization, since he looks to at least some provinces as potential arenas for progressive politics. Courchene and Robinson make different empirical predictions, one for decentralization, the other for centralization. Both prefer a measure of decentralization, but for very different reasons. Many other critics on the left agree with Courchene's predictions about the inevitability of decentralization but come to a very different normative judgement than he does, arguing that in a decentralized Canada, with provinces even more vulnerable to capital mobility and intergovernmental competition, then the national government's commitments to equalization, redistributive policies, and regulation in areas like the environment and its capacity to achieve them will decline. This leads to a line of argument that suggests that more, not less, centralization is what is necessary in a world of global competition.

This might be so for two reasons. First, it can be argued that a strong central government is necessary to ensure equity in the face of the disruptive and regionally differentiated effects of globalization (Boadway 2000). Second, it is argued that in order for Canada to succeed in the global arena, especially in negotiations in international decision-making forums, such as the WTO, or in negotiations with the United States on issues such as softwood lumber, then it becomes all the more important that the country be able to speak with a single voice. A divided Canada will be less effective, as its opponents will be able to employ tactics of divide and rule, and as Canadian negotiators will be less confident of their ability to deliver on their international commitments once made. Such perspectives would argue that the Canadian government would need to increase its capacity for redistribution, would need stronger powers to police the Canadian economic union and would need a greater ability to enforce international agreements once made. As we have seen, however, the domestic politics of Canadian federalism make any such centralizing agenda politically impossible. Equally impossible is the alternative model of radical decentralization. Instead, the reality is one of two sets of competing governments, each jealous of its own powers, but at the same time each highly dependent for its success on the actions of the other. If the domestic dynamics of Canadian federalism mean that neither drastic centralization nor decentralization is on the cards, then the lesson for managing interdependence must be on improved mechanisms of intergovernmental coordination and cooperation.

Globalization and the Processes of Intergovernmental Relations

Given the demonstrated impossibility of agreement on any fundamental constitutional restructuring of powers and responsibilities, and given the realization that effective responses to global pressures require a coordinated response if Canada is to succeed, most observers of Canadian federalism stress the need for improved machinery for the conduct of intergovernmental relations. So far we have treated federalism and intergovernmental relations as the dependent variables, asking how globalization is shaping them. Here we turn the question around, asking how well federalism as practised in Canada works to shape the country's role on the world stage.

In the Canadian system, combining parliamentary government and federalism, intergovernmental relations, as in Australia, are characterized by negotiations among first ministers, ministers and senior officials of the federal government, the ten provinces, and, recently, the leaders of the three northern territories — all of which is collectively referred to as executive federalism. In recent times, about one hundred meetings of ministers or deputy ministers have been held each year, with a myriad of other planning and coordinating meetings of officials to back them up. There is no parliamentary or legislative involvement in this process (Cameron and Simeon 2000; Simeon and Cameron 2002).

A number of intergovernmental ministerial councils have been established to coordinate actions within major policy areas. Typically, these are jointly chaired by federal and provincial ministers. These mechanisms involve both meetings of three orders of government (federal-provincial-territorial, FPT), and of the provinces and territories acting together (PT). The centrepiece of the latter is the Annual Premiers' Conference (APC), convened since the 1960s, which plays a major role in coordinating provincial responses to federal actions. The rotating chair of the APC acts as the primary spokesperson for provincial interests during the year. In addition, western and Atlantic premiers have their own regional conferences.

The implicit model of policy-making here is that governance in Canada is a joint and shared responsibility of both orders of government acting together as equal partners. Neither is subordinate to the other. Major national policies will emerge from intergovernmental agreements, in which governments collaborate to set major policy directions, to clarify each of their responsibilities and to minimize the costs of implementation. Much of the new rhetoric of intergovernmental relations also draws on ideas related to New Public Management — with an emphasis on agreement on performance standards, transparency, accountability, and the like.

A number of recent agreements reflect this approach. The Agreement on Internal Trade (AIT), 1994, was directly related to the challenge of globalization. How could Canada continue to experience a wide range of federally and provincially originated barriers to its internal common market when trade barriers throughout the world were falling? Canadian economic efficiency must be based on a full economic union.

The political dynamics of federalism made two obvious responses impossible. One would have been to strengthen federal powers over interprovincial trade and commerce by broadening its existing constitutional powers. The other would have been to strengthen the ability of the courts to police the Canadian common market. Both were unacceptable to the provinces. The upshot was an intergovernmental agreement, the AIT, by which all governments pledged to reduce barriers and to establish a dispute settlement mechanism modelled on that of the FTA. In one sense this was a demonstrated success of the intergovernmental model; on the other hand, critics contend that the agreement remains highly permissive of barriers and provides few opportunities for non-governmental actors to influence the process. Like other intergovernmental agreements in Canada, it is not judicially enforceable.

A second major intergovernmental accord is the Social Union Framework Agreement (SUFA). Its focus is on the future of social policy. It began as a provincial initiative driven by provincial concerns over unilateral federal cuts in funding for social programs, and their sense of the need to rein in the federal spending power. In the end, the agreement reaffirmed the federal spending power in areas of provincial jurisdiction, subject to prior provincial agreement for new programs, prior notification of funding changes, and collective discussion of program standards. In September 2000, a similar agreement promising future collaboration in health care and support for children was reached.

Many other such agreements have been reached in areas such as labour force training, environmental management, and the like. These are important, and much debated, developments in Canadian intergovernmental relations. They suggest a closer and more cooperative relationship across a wide range of policy sectors, and they constitute a significant institutionalization of the intergovernmental relationship.

However, in many respects these arrangements remain ad hoc and underinstitutionalized. No legislation establishes the intergovernmental machinery. Intergovernmental agreements do not have any statutory base. There are no institutionalized, regular arrangements for First Ministers' Conferences backed by administrative support, instead meetings are called sporadically, in response to the political pressures of the moment. There are no formal voting procedures in intergovernmental meetings. There is no routine involvement of Parliament or legislatures in intergovernmental processes. And so on.

But how well does this process work in managing Canadian involvement in a globalized world? The answer varies across different policy areas.

Trade Negotiations
With respect to Canada's participation in international trade negotiations, some adjustments have been made to intergovernmental processes. Before 1973, trade negotiations were mainly about tariffs, unequivocally a

federal jurisdiction. Provinces did get involved in major cross-border issues like the debate over dams on the Columbia River.[3] But even on a matter as fundamental to Ontario's interests as the Canada-US Autopact, provincial officials were not involved.

By the Tokyo Round of multilateral trade negotiations a wide variety of non-tariff barriers, including subsidies, procurement, and the like were on the table. Many of these were within the provincial jurisdiction, or had important implications for their interests. By 1975, a federal-provincial committee of deputy ministers was in place; and in 1977 the office of Canadian Coordinator for Trade Negotiations was established to channel provincial and industry views to federal negotiators. All the larger provinces sent observers to the negotiations, though they were not part of the official Canadian delegation. Thus, provinces were developing greater expertise in external matters; and Ottawa was learning that it increasingly needed to keep the provinces onside (Brown 1990, p. 93).

The Canada-US Free Trade Agreement had potentially even greater implications for the provinces. At a First Ministers' Conference in November 1985, it was agreed that there would be "full provincial participation" in the negotiations. Shortly afterwards, provinces called for joint federal-provincial oversight of the chief negotiator, full information-sharing, full participation in development of the negotiating strategy, and provincial representation on the negotiating team itself (ibid., p. 94). This was too much for Ottawa, but eventually it was agreed that first ministers would meet every three months as the discussions progressed, that designated ministers would meet more frequently, that Ottawa would establish the mandate of the chief negotiator after consultation with the provinces, and that Ottawa would seek the views of provinces before endorsing any final agreement (ibid., pp. 94-95). Despite the inevitable tensions, it seems clear that provinces had ample opportunity to shape the federal negotiating position. Ontario and Manitoba remained opposed to the FTA in principle, but all the other provinces generally endorsed the agreement. One result of this provincial participation is that despite a strong federal state clause in the final agreement, the FTA left existing provincial practices largely unscathed. In the final approval of the FTA the support of most provinces was an important asset of the federal government, though they were not asked to formally ratify it. Thus, federalism did not block the FTA, and arguably helped open the process to wider debate.

The pattern established in the Canada-US free trade negotiations has continued (Skogstad 2002, p. 164). The principle of "provincial consultation and briefing" has remained in effect. Federal and provincial officials meet regularly, provinces are fully briefed, and information is exchanged over a protected Web site. "The current pattern of intergovernmental relations in international trade constitutes a partnership of *de facto* concurrent jurisdiction" (ibid.). As Skogstad suggests, the federal government has a number of options when international trade negotiations impinge on the provinces: to seek prior provincial concurrence; to conclude agreements only when they fall within federal authority; to make agreements affecting the provinces but leave it to them to implement them; or to invoke its (potential) overriding powers in Trade and Commerce and POGG. So far, at least, it has scrupulously avoided the last (ibid., p. 163) Her conclusion is that federal-provincial cooperation has not acted as a barrier to effective Canadian participation in international trade negotiations. Trust and effective communications have developed between federal and provincial officials. "Executive federalism facilitates, rather than undermines, effective pursuit of trade goals as mutually defined by federal and provincial governments.... The substantive outcomes of executive federalism are generally consistent with Canada's position as a trade dependent country" (ibid., pp. 172-73) .

Nevertheless, specific issues can cause strains in the relationship. Three current issues illustrate the difficulties. First, Canada has been embroiled in a recurrent battle with US timber interests which have sought punitive taxes on imports of Canadian lumber based on the contention that Canadian provinces as the owners of forest land make timber available to Canadian producers at below market prices, thus constituting a subsidy. While various international tribunals have supported the Canadian position, American interests have continued the struggle. In formulating a Canadian strategy, the federal negotiating position must be worked out with the provinces and the industry, and differing provincial interests have to be reconciled. American interests have a strong incentive to exploit these differences. Summarizing an earlier round in this dispute, in the 1980s, Douglas Brown argues that Ottawa was unable to dictate terms to the provinces; nor was it able to manufacture consensus. Interprovincial divisions and threats of independent action by some provinces weakened the overall Canadian case, and the need for intergovernmental agreement pushed industry interests aside. In the end, however, "a domestic solution to a very difficult trading problem was found" (Brown 1990, pp. 104-05).

Second, the possible movement toward an integrated continental energy strategy was placed on the Canada-US agenda after the election of George Bush in 2000. Provinces, we have noted, are the owners, regulators, and major financial beneficiaries of all forms of energy — oil, gas, and hydro power (except for those in the Canada lands north of the 60th parallel). Producing provinces have made it clear that they are to be at the table in any discussions, and Alberta Premier Ralph Klein has independently touted his province's willingness to proceed in Washington. At their meeting in August 2001, the premiers called for an agreement to ensure full federal/provincial/territorial participation in Canada's international energy discussions and negotiations (CICS 2001). Another press release called for Ottawa to ensure provincial representation at future ministerial meetings in the context of the WTO, FTAA and other trade negotiation forums. As *The Economist* (2001) observed, "Jean Chrétien's federal government finds itself running to keep up." Again, Canada is involved in a two (or more) level game, negotiating with itself even as it negotiates with an external partner.

Third, as discussed below, similar issues arise with respect to Canada's international commitments to combat global warming through the Kyoto Agreement. Regional issues are deeply engaged and Ottawa cannot deliver on its promises without provincial cooperation.

The Internal Market

By most standards, Canada is a fully functioning, open economic union. Yet in the 1980s, there was increasing concern that a wide variety of provincial policies, including government procurement, the practices of provincial liquor control boards, and various regulatory policies, constituted important non-tariff barriers to internal trade within the country. "Powers over the economy" became an important item in Canadian constitutional negotiations. In part this was driven by the belief that such barriers meant that Canadian industries would be smaller and less efficient, and hence less able to compete in the global economy. In part it was driven by quite different factors, including a desire of the federal government to put its own nationalizing agenda on the constitutional negotiating table. The economic union gave its name to a major Royal Commission, the Royal Commission on the Economic Union and Canada's Development Prospects, appointed by Ottawa in 1982.[4] The commission found a long list of provincial (and federal) barriers to internal trade, but also concluded that their aggregate impact on Canadian economic growth was small.[5] Following the failure of constitutional discussions either to strengthen the federal role in managing the economic union, or to strengthen constitutional protection of the freedom of movement of goods, services, capital, and people, governments sought to negotiate a code of conduct. This was the AIT, which itself was modelled in many ways on the FTA (MacDonald 2002, p. 141). The agreement seeks to prevent the erection of new barriers, to reduce existing ones, and to set in motion continuing efforts to enhance the economic union. It also includes a dispute-settlement mechanism. However, it is careful to preserve or grandfather many existing provincial practices, and to avoid turning enforcement power over to either the courts or the federal government. For some, the agreement achieves little; it is merely window dressing (de Mestral 1995); for others it is a major step that deals comprehensively with most important internal trade issues (Trebilcock and Behboodi 1995); for yet others it is a useful if limited first step (Trebilcock and Schwanen 1995). The World Bank's assessment is that progress since the AIT came into effect has been slow: open-ended commitments in such areas as procurement, labour market policies, and energy have not been met, and many loopholes and gaps remain. In general, as Mark MacDonald suggests, the AIT provides a "useful example of the trade-offs between the economic union and federalism"; and between interprovincial cooperation and competition. Nevertheless, despite the lack of central control over the economic union, and the strong potential in the structure of Canadian federalism for destructive levels of competition, the experience is that mutually destructive competition for investment and jobs has not been a problem in Canada (Bird and Vaillancourt 2001; Bird and Tassonyi 2001).

Financial Institutions
Few policy areas are as influenced by globalization as those of financial institutions, banking, and the like. Historically, there has been a division of labour between the federal government, constitutionally responsible for banking and the provinces, primarily responsible for regulation of trust companies, credit unions, and financial markets. The resulting separate

tiers have been overtaken by globalization and the integration of various financial institutions. As William Coleman points out, "both these market developments — expanding territorial reach of financial services firms — and these political changes — institutionalized intergovernmental collaboration at the global level — have favoured the centralization and rationalization of the regulation of the financial services sector" in Canada. Despite this, and the "market players own self-regulatory" centralization, governmental authority in the sector remains fragmented (Coleman 2002, p. 191).

Yet there is little suggestion that the federal division of powers has acted as a major barrier to Canadian adaptation to globalization. Provincial Securities Commissions remain formally separate, but have developed a "strong working relationship and approach to rule-making through their common organization, the Canadian Securities Administrators" (ibid., p. 191). The creation of the federal Office of the Superintendent of Financial Institutions strengthened the federal hand. But meanwhile, Quebec has moved to establish its own regulatory regime focused on the Caisse populaires Desjardins and the Caisse de dépot et de placement. The result, suggests William Coleman is a movement toward two "single regulator regimes" in Canada and Quebec — an asymmetric model, but one in which the two "appear to co-operate closely with one another" (ibid., p. 184). Canada is the only country to be represented on the International Organization of Securities Commission by two provincial bodies: the Quebec Securities Commission and the Ontario Securities Commission. As Coleman suggests, the efficacy of policy-making in this area is more dependent on the capacity of national governments to work together in international forums than it is on the division of responsibilities in the domestic environment (ibid., p. 192).

Labour Market Policies

Most discussion of adaptation to increased global competition places heavy emphasis on developing flexible labour markets and policies to ensure a highly trained labour force. Historically, this too has been an area in which provinces have had primary jurisdiction. Except in industries directly under federal supervision, such as transport, provinces are responsible for regulating most aspects of commerce; and their jurisdiction over education at all levels is fundamental to training. Beginning in the 1960s, however, Ottawa became deeply involved in this area through shared-cost programs and the funding of training that takes place in provincial institutions, in addition to its control of the unemployment insurance program. Provinces have always been jealous of their jurisdiction in this area and in Quebec, government, business, and labour are united in their defence of exclusive provincial control.

Recent trends in this area, unlike financial services, have been in a decentralizing direction. In 1996, the federal government offered to withdraw from its purchase of training and involvement in apprenticeship programs and the like. It also offered to delegate to the provinces related services such as employment counselling and labour market placement (Bakvis 2002, p. 205). Moreover, when the provinces took on these roles, Ottawa was prepared to transfer the federal public servants running them to the provincial public services. The only condition was that provinces agreed to an unspecified "results based accountability framework" (ibid., p. 206).

Two models were on offer. One was a "co-management model" in which programs would be jointly administered; the other, full devolution, in which provinces would take full responsibility for active labour market policies. Five provinces, and one territory opted for co-management; five provinces and two territories opted for full devolution. Negotiating an agreement with Quebec, in the aftermath of the 1995 referendum, was a major political accomplishment. Ontario was the only province that did not complete an agreement, partly because the large phalanx of Liberal MPs from Ontario was unwilling to see training placed fully in the hands of the arch-enemy, Mike Harris' provincial Conservatives. Once again, change in the federal system was driven by domestic politics rather than global imperatives, and the result is an increasingly checkerboard federalism (Bakvis 2002, p. 214). The implications of these changes on the ability to develop national policies to meet global challenges are unclear; much will depend on the ability of governments to work together, their ability to exploit their own comparative advantages, and Ottawa's capacity to deploy its own remaining powers, both in the Employment Insurance program and in measures to support research and the education of postsecondary students.

The Environment

Environmentalists call for strong, enforceable standards at the national level, and for a strong united Canadian voice in international forums on issues such as global warming. They too see a centralist imperative; and they also have been confounded by recent developments in intergovernmental relations. Devolution of responsibilities to the provinces and an emphasis on consensus and harmonization have set the pattern (Winfield 2002). As with labour market policy, the federal desire for accommodation with Quebec and the other provinces tended to drive the process, despite federal environmental activism in the early 1990s (ibid., p. 127). In January 1998, all governments except Quebec signed the "Canada-wide Accord on Environmental Harmonization" and sub-arrangements on standards, inspections, and environmental assessments. The Accord emphasizes the primacy of intergovernmental consensus and can be amended only by unanimous consent. It calls for one-window delivery of environmental services, by the "best-situated" governments (normally the provinces) (ibid., p. 129). Standards are to be developed collectively by governments, and Ottawa is to consult the provinces on virtually all proposals for action under recent amendments to the *Canadian Environmental Protection Act* (ibid., pp. 130-31). The most contentious recent environmental issue is Canada's response to the *Kyoto Agreement* and efforts to limit greenhouse gas emissions. The costs of implementation will fall differentially on different provinces; and the provinces hold many of the levers that might be used to give effect to the agreement. Again, in the absence of a plenary federal power over the environment, cooperation is essential. The public appears to support this view: in a 2001 survey, 54 percent of respondents said that provinces should be at the negotiating table along with the federal government; another 35 percent said Ottawa should consult the provinces; and only 6 percent said the provinces should not be involved at all (CRIC 2001, p. 9).

It is impossible to judge whether federal-provincial arrangements in these and other fields seriously hamper concerted national action in the face of global challenges. On the one hand, as I have discussed, there are those who see the global imperative as a centralizing imperative and would wish for wider federal powers to manage Canada's interaction with the world. On the other hand, are those who see value in the flexibility, innovation, and variability of local and provincial responses to these same pressures. Yet others see the complex interaction of decentralization and collaboration as a second best — while in some ideal world Canada would speak with one voice, the realities of regionalism and federalism make that simply impossible. Hence, the desire to clarify responsibilities where possible and to further develop an intergovernmental process that is open, accountable, and responsive to a wide variety of interests. Moreover, both orders of government are highly sensitive to global pressures and challenges; whatever their political differences at home, they have a common interest in keeping conflicts under control and in resolving their differences.

This brief survey suggests that, yes, federalism does complicate Canada's ability to construct domestic policies that will enhance Canadian competitiveness, and yes, it makes the conduct of Canada's international relationships more difficult to manage. Yet there is little evidence that these arrangements are a fundamental impediment, and no sense that global imperatives are driving a fundamental reform of the institutions and practices of federalism and intergovernmental relations. Even if Canada were a unitary state, regional differences would loom large in Canadian policy-making. Federalism, then, is neither a boon to Canada's participation in a globalized world, nor a great hindrance. It is, as Donald Smiley put it many years ago, a "condition" that citizens and politicians work with, around, and through.

Globalization, then, has not engendered major change in the ways Canadian governments manage their relationships. The modest changes that have occurred have been much more a response to domestic factors: the failure of constitutional reshaping of the federation, the concern with debts and deficits, the desire to prove to Canadians that federalism works, and the like. Global pressures lurk well in the background.

CONCLUSION

This analysis does not deny the fundamental impact of globalization on many aspects of Canadian economy and society. Nor does it deny that the agenda for federal-provincial relations is deeply affected by these changes. Many of the predictions of the glocalization thesis are highly plausible. The puzzle, perhaps, is why they have not had a greater impact. I argue that the reason is that the central dynamics of federalism and intergovernmental relations are primarily driven by domestic factors — by the institutional structures, historic legacies, and the immediate concerns of contemporary political actors.

I have concentrated here on federalism as the dependent variable: how has it changed in response to global pressures? The answer is, as I have suggested, surprisingly little. Many of the possibilities postulated by writers remain just that — possibilities, not yet realities. But we can also turn the question around: Does the pattern of Canadian federalism inhibit Canada's ability to respond effectively to the challenges posed by globalization? Two sets of answers are possible. One is that the fragmented, divided, adversarial Canadian federalism does get in the way. It might also be argued that the decentralized jurisdiction over areas such as education and labour market policy — essential to global competitiveness — inhibits the possibility of developing coherent national strategies. There is also likely to be increased scrutiny by international agencies not only of federal, but also of provincial law and practice, and hence increasing pressure to harmonize their policies. Indeed, the more decentralized the federation becomes the more provinces will be responsible for implementing international obligations. As the Trends report put it, "Canadian governments must enhance interdepartmental and federal-provincial coordination so as to minimize possible disparities between international and Canadian standards."

On the other hand, it could be argued that the decentralized character of Canadian federalism permits a flexible, varied response to global pressures. In a regionally diverse economy like Canada, Canadian federalism permits responses attuned to local needs and concerns. Where coordination among governments is necessary, the machinery of intergovernmental relations, however creaky, does work effectively.

The first answer implies that effective Canadian responses to globalization would require more centralization: a strengthening of the federal treaty power, along Australian lines, to ensure that Canadian commitments abroad can be implemented and enforced in Canada; a strengthening of federal powers with respect to management of the Canadian economic union; a greater role for the federal government in areas like training, labour relations, and postsecondary education. Whatever the abstract merits of this approach, we have seen that such a centralizing agenda is not likely in Canada. It would take a massive external threat to generate effective centralizing pressures in a federation with such strong provinces and regional differences.

The alternative is to worry less about the capacity of Canada as a single entity to respond to globalization, and to argue that in a regionalized country, in which Ottawa has already lost many of the tools of economic management, that provinces should play the critical role in managing their own economic development and relations with the world. This would imply that provinces would play a larger role in Canada's international relations — consulted more frequently, and perhaps joining the Canadian delegations; or that provinces themselves would become more active international actors in their own right. We have seen some tentative steps in this direction, but the federal government continues, through its jurisdiction over interprovincial and international trade, through its spending power, and through its role in many other areas, to exercise important powers, and to have considerable influence on the economic well-being of every province. It would also imply that to the extent the provinces share common interests, they could be achieved through interprovincial cooperation where necessary.

The reality is that Canadian responses to globalization will remain a combination of the individual actions of each order of government — federal and provincial — where possible, and governments acting together in areas of common interest and shared jurisdiction. It is common to suggest that external challenges require fundamental institutional change. Canadians have found many times that such changes are impossible to achieve. The task, therefore, is to build on collaborative federalism, through a strengthened, more rule-driven and more transparent intergovernmental process.

Finally, what of the impact of the four scenarios postulated in this volume for the future political economy of Canadian federalism?

Regional dominators. Geography, history, and resources have combined to cast Canada's economic future ineluctably as a member of a North American political economy, in which Canada will be tightly integrated economically with the United States, not only in terms of trade, but also in terms of investment flows, corporate ownership, and population movements. In this relationship, Canada (along with Mexico) will be economically subordinate to the size and dynamism of the neighbouring American economy. Relationships between the larger and smaller economies will be shaped by NAFTA, but its influence will be limited by the continued pre-eminence of US trade law, and by the lack of joint decision-making institutions. Canadian debates will continue to be shaped by the competing ideas of greater integration in the North American economy (such as through a common currency, and a common North American "perimeter" against the rest of the world) against the desire to maintain Canadian distinctiveness. The relationship with the dominant partner will often be contentious, and the specific issues that arise (wheat, steel, softwood lumber, beef, oil and gas, water) will produce different regional and intergovernmental tensions within Canada. Provinces will be active participants in this model — demanding a strong voice in bilateral negotiations, building relationships with contiguous states, and actively lobbying in Washington (as Alberta's Ralph Klein did in June 2003 over BSE in one cow) when they feel Ottawa is not defending their interests aggressively enough. The overwhelming recent evidence, however, is that economic integration does not produce integration in terms of values, attitudes, identities, or policy preferences. In all of these, Canada remains distinctive within the North American context.

Global club. As a leading economic power, a member of the G7, Canada is a charter member of the global club. It has been a strong supporter of the WTO, World Bank, and other institutions of this association. It is true that Canada is a secondary player in a global club, dominated by the US, the European Union, and perhaps soon by China. Its status as a relatively "small, open, price-taking economy" is not easily challenged. Nevertheless, its role as an accepted member of the club is a significant counterweight to its subordinate position in the North American region. Rule-based international regimes are preferred to the vagaries of US congressional politics, as can alliances with similarly situated countries, such as Australia. While there is in Canada, as elsewhere, a vigorous debate about participation in global institutions, this debate is not one that mobilizes interprovincial or intergovernmental tensions. Provinces, however, do demand a greater voice in the negotiation, ratification, and implementation of any international treaties that trench on provincial constitutional powers, or have a differential impact on the regional economies. The institutions of the global club, however, tend to be based on the participation of unitary nation-states, and hence are unsympathetic to subnational claims or participation. Provinces, in this scenario, must therefore concentrate on influencing the Canadian government's positions, not on acting directly.

Shared governance. Canadian political rhetoric strongly supports the image of widely diffused power and influence in global affairs, and the integration of developed and developing worlds in global governance. But the gap between the rhetoric and performance is large. (Canada talks the talk on foreign aid and international peace-making, but the recent record suggests it is increasingly uninterested in walking the walk.) This broad debate about Canada's role in the world has little impact on domestic politics or the practice of Canadian federalism. But in a larger view of shared governance, the traditional nation-state plays a smaller role. Other actors — cities, provinces, and non-governmental — come to the fore. Thus a shared governance model is likely to increase the role of the provinces and other subnational actors in the broader arena. Federal assertion of its monopoly over the expression of Canada's interest abroad is likely to be undermined.

Cyberwave. Canada may well be exceptionally well-placed to find its way in the fluid, dynamic, unpredictable cyberwave scenario. This may follow from the country's multicultural and diverse character, and from its defining culture of the accommodation of difference. In addition, Canada has been a leading adapter of Internet technologies. Federalism and intergovernmental relations has little if anything to do with this adaptive capacity of Canadians; but nor does it create major barriers and blockages.

The cyberwave model might be expected to exacerbate interregional differences and to further undermine the federal government's capacity to shape the system. This in turn might shift attention to the innovative capacities of provincial, and especially local governments.

In reality, we are likely to see some indeterminate combination of these scenarios. Any combination will pose new challenges to Canadians and their governments. But their responses will be shaped by the institutional and attitudinal legacies of the past more than by any presumed external "imperatives" of the present. The conclusion is that federalism is indeed both a dependent and an independent variable. Dependent, in the sense that any history of the Canadian political economy, or of tensions within its federal system, must pay considerable attention to external influences. As I have argued earlier, following Innis, from furs, to fisheries, to wheat, to oil and gas resources, canadian economic and political development has been shaped by the country's relationship to the external world. This is not likely to change.

On the other hand, federalism — both constitutionally and in terms of regionalism in a federal "society" — is a powerful independent variable. *Whether* Canada will respond is a result of exogenous variables, *how* it will respond is shaped by an endogenous variable.

Notes

1. When Prime Minister Chrétien mused in an Edmonton speech in August 2001 that Alberta's runaway oil and gas revenues were posing problems for neighbouring provinces, and that there may be need for Alberta to share the wealth, it immediately revived memories of the hated NEP, and outraged reactions from Albertans; the prime minister quickly denied any intention of reviving the NEP.

2. Calculating the actual federal contribution to health care is a highly contentious issue among federal and provincial governments. For a careful evaluation see Institute of Intergovernmental Relations (2002, pp. 18-22).

3. A cartoon of the time shows US President Lyndon Johnson, Prime Minister Lester Pearson, and BC Premier W. A. C. Bennett riding in the back of an open car. Johnson and Bennett are occupying most of the back seat as they discuss the dam; Pearson, left out of the conversation, is scrunched into a corner.

4. Its central recommendation was for a Canada-US Free Trade Agreement, initiating the events that led to signing of the FTA.

5. Estimates of the economic impact range from 1 to 1.5 percent of GDP (Trebilcock and Behboodi 1995).

References

Adams, M. 2003. *Fire and Ice: The United States, Canada and the Myth of Converging Values*. Toronto: Penguin Canada.

Armstrong, C. 1981. *The Politics of Federalism: Ontario's Relations with the Federal Government, 1867-1942*. Toronto: University of Toronto Press.

Baier, G. 2002. "Judicial Review and Canadian Federalism," in *Canadian Federalism*, ed. Bakvis and Skogstad, pp. 24-39.

Bakvis, H. 2002. "Checkerboard Federalism? Labour Market Development Policy in Canada," in *Canadian Federalism*, ed. Bakvis and Skogstad, pp. 197-219.

Bakvis, H. and G. Skogstad, eds. 2002, *Canadian Federalism: Performance, Effectiveness and Legitimacy*. Don Mills: Oxford University Press.

Banting, K., G. Hoberg and R. Simeon. 1997. *Degrees of Freedom: Canada and the United States in a Changing World*. Montreal and Kingston: McGill-Queen's University Press.

Bird, R. and A. Tassonyi. 2001. "Constraints on Provincial-Municipal Borrowing in Canada: Markets, Rules and Norms," *Canadian Public Administration* 44:84-109.

Bird, R. and F. Vaillancourt. 2001. "Fiscal Arrangements for Maintaining an Effective State in Canada," *Environment and Planning C: Government and Policy* 19:193-97.

Boadway, R. 2000. "Recent Developments in the Economics of Federalism," in *Toward a New Mission Statement for Canadian Fiscal Federalism: Canada: The State of the Federation 1999/2000*, ed. H. Lazar. Montreal and Kingston: McGill-Queen's University Press for Institute of Intergovernmental Relations, pp. 41-78.

Boismenu, G. and J. Jenson. 1998. "A Social Union or a Federal State?: Competing Visions of Intergovernmental Relations ion the New Liberal Era," in *Balancing Act: The Post-Deficit Mandate, How Ottawa Spends 1998-1999*, ed. L. Pal. Toronto: Oxford University Press, pp. 57-79.

Bourne, L. 1999. "Is Ontario a Region? A Commentary on 'Ontario as a Region State,'" in *Ontario: Exploring the Region-State Hypothesis*. Colloquium proceedings. Toronto: University of Toronto, pp. 55-58.

Brodie, J. and M. Smith. 1998. "Regulating the Economic Union," in *Balancing Act: The Post-Deficit Mandate, How Ottawa Spends, 1998-1999*, ed. L. Pal. Toronto: Oxford University Press, pp. 81-98.

Brown, D.M. 1990. "The Evolving Role of the Provinces in Canadian Trade Policy," in *Canadian Federalism*, ed. Brown and Smith, pp. 81-128.

—— ed. 2001. *Tax Competition and the Fiscal Union in Canada*. Kingston: Institute of Intergovernmental Relations, Queen's University.

Brown, D.M. and M. Smith, eds. 1990. *Canadian Federalism: Meeting Global Economic Challenges?* Kingston and Montreal: Institute of Intergovernmental Relations and Institute for Research on Public Policy.

Cairns, A.C. 1999. "Looking into the Abyss: The Need for a Plan C," in *The Referendum Papers: Essays on Secession and National Unity*, ed. D. Cameron. Toronto: University of Toronto Press, pp. 199-243.

Cameron, D.M. and J. Stein. 2000. "Globalization, Culture and Society: The State as a Place Amidst Shifting Spaces," *Canadian Public Policy/Analyse de Politiques* 26 (Supplement 2):S15-35.

Cameron, D.M. and R. Simeon. 2000. "Intergovernmental Relations and Democratic Citizenship," in *Governance in the Twenty-first Century: Revitalizing Public Service*, ed. B.G. Peters and D.J. Savoie. Montreal and Kingston: McGill-Queen's University Press, pp. 58-118.

Canadian Intergovernmental Conference Secretariat (CICS). 2001. News Release Ref: 850-083/014, 42nd Annual Premiers' Conference, 1-3 August.

Cashore, B. 1998. "An Examination of Why a Long Term Resolution of the Canada-U.S. Softwood Lumber Dispute Eludes Policymakers," Working Paper No. 98-02. Victoria: Pacific Forestry Centre, Canada Forest Service.

Centre for Research and Information on Canada (CRIC). 2001. *Trade, Globalization and Canadian Values*, CRIC papers. Montreal: CRIC.

Clarkson, S. 2001. "The Multicentred State: Canadian Government under Globalizing Pressures," in *Who's Afraid of the State?* ed. G. Smith. Toronto: University of Toronto Press, pp. 232-37.

Clarkson, S. and T. Lewis. 1999. "The Contested State: Canada in the Post-Cold War, Posy-Keynesian, Post-Fordist, Post-National Era," in *How Ottawa Spends: 2000*, ed. L. Pal. Toronto: Oxford University Press.

Coleman, W.D. 2000. "The Trends Project," *Canadian Public Policy/Analyse de Politiques*, 26 (Special Supplement 2, August).

—— 2002. "Federalism and Financial Services," in *Canadian Federalism*, ed. Bakvis and Skogstad, pp.178-96.

Courchene, T.J. 1992. *Rearrangements: The Courchene Papers.* Oakville: Mosaic Press.

—— 1995. "Glocalization: The Regional/International Interface," *Canadian Journal of Regional Science* 18(1):1-20.

Courchene, T.J. with C.R. Telmer. 1998. *From Heartland to North American Region State.* University of Toronto: Centre for Public Management, Faculty of Management.

de Mestral, A. 1995. "A Comment," in *Getting There: Assessment of the Agreement on Internal Trade*, ed. Trebilcock and Schwanen.

Doern, G.B. and B.W. Tomlin. 1991. *Faith and Fear: The Free Trade Story.* Toronto: Stoddart.

Doern, G.B. and M. MacDonald. 1999. *Free Trade Federalism: Negotiating the Canadian Agreement on Internal Trade.* Toronto: University of Toronto Press.

Drache, D. 1996. *States Against Markets: The Limits of Globalization.* London: Routledge.

The Economist. 2001. "Sandstorms: Energy Policy in Canada," 25 August, p. 33.

Fafard, P.C. and K. Harrison, eds. 1997. *Managing the Environmental Union: Intergovernmental Relations and Environmental Policy in Canada.* Montreal and Kingston: McGill-Queen's University Press and the School of Policy Studies, Queen's University.

Graves, F.L. with Tim Dugas and Patrick Beauchamp. 1999. "Identity and National Attachments in Contemporary Canada," in *How Canadians Connect, Canada: The State of the Federation 1998/99*, ed. Lazar and McIntosh, pp. 307-56.

Haddow, R. 1998. "How Ottawa Shrivels: Ottawa's Declining Role in Labour Market Policy," in *Balancing Act: The Post-Deficit Mandate*, ed. L. Pal. Toronto: Oxford University Press, pp. 99-126.

Helliwell, J. 1996. "Do National Borders Matter for Quebec Trade," *Canadian Journal of Economics* 29:507-22.

—— 1999. "Canada's National Economy: There's More to it than you Thought," in *How Canadians Connect, Canada: The State of the Federation 1998/99*, ed. H. Lazar and T. McIntosh. Kingston: Institute of Intergovernmental Relations, pp. 87-100.

Hoberg, G. 2000. "Capacity for Choice: Canada in a New North America," *Canadian Public Policy/Analyse de Politiques* 26 (Supplement 2):S35-50.

—— 2001. *Capacity for Choice: Canada in a New North America.* Toronto: University of Toronto Press.

Jacobs, J. 1984. *Cities and the Wealth of Nations.* New York: Random House.

Keating, M. 1999. "Challenges to Federalism: Territory, Function and Power in a Globalizing World," in *Stretching the Federation: The Art of the State in Canada*, ed. R. Young. Kingston: Institute of Intergovernmental Relations, pp. 8-127.

Lazar, H. 2000. "In Search of a New Mission Statement for Canadian Fiscal Federalism," in *Toward a New Mission Statement for Canadian Fiscal Federalism: Canada: The State of the Federation 1999/2000.* Montreal and Kingston: McGill-Queen's University Press and the Institute of Intergovernmental Relations, Queen's University, pp. 3-41.

Lazar, H. and T. McIntosh. 1999. "How Canadians Connect: State, Economy, Citizenship and Society," in *How Canadians Connect: Canada: The State of the Federation 1998/99*, ed. H. Lazar and T. McIntosh. Kingston and Montreal: Institute of Intergovernmental Relations and McGill-Queen's University Press.

MacDonald, M.R. 2002. "The Agreement on Internal Trade: Trade-offs for Economic Union and Federalism," in *Canadian Federalism*, ed. Bakvis and Skogstad.

McCallum, J. 1995. "National Borders Matter: Canada-US Regional Trade Patterns," *American Economic Review* 85 (June):621-23.

New England Governors and Eastern Canadian Premiers. 2001. Canadian Intergovernmental Conference Secretariat. *26th Annual Conference of the New England Governors and Eastern Canadian Premiers, August 26-8, 2001. Resolution 26-4.*

Page, M. 2002. "Provincial Trade Patterns," Agriculture and Rural Working Papers Series, Working Paper No. 58. Ottawa: Statistics Canada.

Pastor, R. 2001. *Towards a North American Community: Lessons from the Old World for the New.* Washington: Institute for International Economics.

Ritchie, G. 1997. *Wrestling with the Elephant: The Inside Story of the Canada-U.S. Trade Wars.* Toronto: Macfarlane, Walter and Ross.

Robinson, I. 1993. "The NAFTA, the Side Deals and Canadian Federalism: Constitutional Reform by other Means?" in *Canada: The State of the Federation 1993*, ed. R.L. Watts and D.M. Brown. Kingston: Institute of Intergovernmental Relations.

—— 2002. "Neoliberal Trade Policy, Globalization, and the Future of Canadian Federalism Revisited," in *New Trends in Canadian Federalism*, ed. M. Smith and F. Rocher, 2d ed. Peterborough: Broadview Press.

Sancton, A. 2002. "Municipalities, Cities and Globalization: Implications for Canadian Federalism," in *Canadian Federalism*, ed. Bakvis and Skogstad, pp. 261-77.

Simeon, R. 1991. "Globalization and the Canadian Nation-State," in *Canada at Risk? Canadian Public Policy in the 1990s*, ed. G.B. Doern and B.B. Purchase. Toronto: C.D. Howe Institute.

—— 2001. "Making Federalism Work: Intergovernmental Coordination and Institutional Capacity." Paper presented at Working Session on Alternatives to Tax Wars: Sustainable Economic Development. Sao Paulo, Brazil. At <http://www.ciff.on.ca/reference/documents/docm10>.

Simeon, R. and D. Cameron. 2002. "Intergovernmental Relations and Democracy: An Oxymoron if Ever There Was One?" in *Canadian Federalism*, ed. Bakvis and Skogstad, pp. 278-95.

Skogstad, G. 1995. "Warring over Wheat: Managing Bilateral Trading Tensions," in *How Ottawa Spends 1995-96,* ed. S. Phillips. Ottawa: Carleton University Press.

—— 1998. "Canadian Federalism, Internationalization and Quebec Agriculture: Dis-engagement, Reintegration?" *Canadian Public Policy/Analyse de Politiques* 24 (1):27-48.

—— 2000. "Globalization and Public Policy: Situating Canadian Analyses," *Canadian Journal of Political Science* 33:805-28.

—— 2002. "International Trade Policy and Canadian Federalism: A Constructive Tension?" in *Canadian Federalism*, ed. Bakvis and Skogstad, pp. 159-77.

Stevenson, G. 1988. "Canadian Regionalism in Continental Perspective," reprinted in *Perspectives on Canadian Federalism*, ed. R.D. Olling and M.W. Westmacott. Scarborough: Prentice-Hall Canada, pp. 122-35.

Trebilcock, M. and D. Schwanen, eds. 1995. *Getting There: Assessment of the Agreement on Internal Trade.* Toronto: C.D. Howe Institute.

Trebilcock, M. and R. Behboodi. 1995. "The Canadian Agreement on Internal Trade: Retrospect and Prospects," in *Getting There*, ed. Trebilcock and Schwanen.

Treff, K. and D.B. Perry. 2001. *Finances of the Nation: A Review of the Expenditures and Revenues of the Federal, Provincial and Local Governments of Canada.* Toronto: Canadian Tax Foundation.

Winfield, M.S. 2002. "Environmental Policy and Federalism," in *Canadian Federalism*, ed. Bakvis and Skogstad, pp. 124-37.

Wiseman, N. 2000. "Political Culture, Economics and Public Policy," in *Exploring the Region-State Hypothesis*. Proceedings of a Colloquium, University of Toronto, 26 March, pp. 7-14.

Wolfe, D. 1997. "The Emergence of the Region-State," in *The Nation State in a Global/Information Era: Policy Challenges,* ed. T.J. Courchene. Kingston: The John Deutsch Institute for the Study of Economic Policy, Queen's University.

Wolfish, D. and G. Smith. 2000. "Governance and Policy in a Multicentric World," *Canadian Public Policy/Analyse de Politiques* 26 (Supplement 2):S51-72.

Continental Integration and Swiss Federalism: A New Openness to Europe?

Jürg Steiner

INTRODUCTION

Over the centuries the Swiss have developed a firm national identity, at the core of which is the notion that Switzerland is a special case (*Sonderfall*) among the countries of the world. Many people believe that Switzerland is special because it united within its borders some of the major European cultures and religions, and, in the interest of European stability, it had to practise a foreign policy of neutrality. With increased globalization and European integration the internal consensus on this view of Switzerland has broken down. A severe cleavage has developed over how to define Swiss identity in a rapidly changing world. There are those who want to stay with the old identity of Switzerland as a special case in the world community, whereas others see Switzerland as just another small European country. Under the scenarios of a global club and regional dominators, this cleavage over the nature of Swiss identity would further increase, whereas the scenarios of shared governance and cyberwave are likely to decrease the salience of the cleavage.

CONTEXT: THE HISTORICAL DEVELOPMENT OF THE LANGUAGE ISSUE

The current cleavage over how to define Swiss identity is closely linked with the language issue. Switzerland has four official languages, as shown on the Swiss currency: 63.7 percent speak German, 19.2 percent French, 7.6 percent Italian, and 0.6 percent Romansch, and the remaining 8.9 percent speak a variety of non-official languages. It is important to note that at the beginning of Swiss history, language was not an issue since at that time Switzerland was linguistically homogeneous. The three mountain cantons in central Switzerland — Uri, Schwyz, and Unterwalden — that founded the Swiss Confederation in the thirteenth century were all German-speaking. Over the next three centuries they were joined by ten other cantons, eight of which were exclusively German-speaking, while two — Bern and Freiburg — were predominantly German-speaking but with a French-speaking minority.

Although linguistically largely homogeneous, the Old Swiss Confederation was not religiously homogeneous. On the contrary, with the Reformation it was severely split between Catholics and Protestants. Most cantons were either Catholic or Protestant: Lucerne, for example, was Catholic, while Zurich was Protestant. Tensions between the two groups became so severe that from the sixteenth to the eighteenth centuries, Switzerland had four religious wars with neither side winning a decisive victory. This confederation of the 13 "old" cantons endured until the invasion by Napoleon in 1798. It was an extremely loose political system; perhaps we should not even call it a political system but a system of alliances. There were no central authorities except a Diet where the delegates appointed by the cantons met. Decisions of the Diet had to be unanimous and concerned mainly foreign policy and military matters. With the split into Catholic and Protestant cantons, there were often separate Diets for each religious group.

When the armies of Napoleon invaded Switzerland, the old regime abruptly broke apart, and France imposed a centralized regime based on the ideas of the French Revolution. It was only at that time that Switzerland really became multilingual. French-speaking Vaud, for example, which formerly belonged to Bern, became a canton of its own. Geneva, which before had only a loose alliance with the Swiss Confederation, joined as a full canton. The Italian-speaking Ticino canton and the trilingual canton of Graubünden (German, Italian, and Romansch) also joined Switzerland at this time. At the Congress of Vienna in 1815, the old order with largely autonomous cantons was re-established to a large extent in Switzerland. So once again language was no longer a big issue since the most important decisions were made in the individual cantons, which were nearly all linguistically homogeneous. It was only in 1848 that language became an issue in Switzerland. In the previous year, the progressive cantons had won a short civil war against the conservative cantons. The victorious progressive forces established a modern constitution with federal institutions, in particular a federal parliament, a federal cabinet, and a federal court. So for the first time in their history, the Swiss had to prove whether they were able to live peacefully together in a multilingual country with central political authorities.

In the last 150 years, there have been many conflicts among the language groups, but, generally speaking, these conflicts have been managed quite smoothly (Steiner 1974). The greatest potential conflict was between those of the German and French language. Tensions between these two language groups were particularly high during World War I, when the French-speakers sided with France and the German-speakers with Germany. At the time, one spoke of a trench (*Graben*) dividing Switzerland. The most severe language problem arose not at the national level but within the bilingual Bern canton which is predominantly German-speaking but has a French-speaking minority in the Jura. So why were historical language relations relatively harmonious? Much had to do with the institutional framework that Switzerland was able to establish. In the next section we turn to this framework.

THE INSTITUTIONAL FRAMEWORK

When the victorious progressive forces wrote the constitution of modern Switzerland in 1848, they did not push centralization very far, but rather kept a large measure of autonomy for the cantons. This was a conciliatory gesture toward the conservative forces. The spirit of compromise was visible in the previous year when the military commander of the progressive forces made a successful effort to minimize the losses on the other side, so that the war was very short and with few casualties. It must also be noted, however, that the progressive forces were not altogether selfless in keeping autonomy for the cantons since they were not really interested in too much centralization. After all, most progressive cantons had a strong sense of cantonal identity. Whatever the exact motives of the writers of the constitution, the important fact is that the constitution of modern Switzerland gave the cantons a significant degree of autonomy.

The crucial feature in the relationship between the cantons and the Confederation was that all tasks that were not explicitly assigned to the Confederation remained with the cantons. The Confederation was mainly responsible for foreign affairs, national defence, the currency, customs, and the postal and railway services. Over time, new tasks were assigned such as telecommunications, aviation, nuclear energy, and old age pensions. For the language situation, it was important that educational matters remained under the domain of the cantons. To be sure, the Confederation received the right to create a federal university, and it used this power to establish the Federal Polytechnical University in Zurich. But all other universities remained in the hands of the cantons. For the lower educational levels, the dominance of the cantons was even stronger. Such educational autonomy allowed the cantons to handle language questions however they wished. This meant, in particular, that classes had to be taught in the language of the canton. In the four linguistically mixed cantons, the language in the school was determined according to the territorial principle.

The degree of cantonal autonomy becomes impressive if we look at how many of the public expenditures occur at the federal level. Even today, only about a third of all public monies are spent at the federal level (Linder 1998, p. 51). The other two-thirds are spent either at the cantonal or the communal level. Each of the three levels has the right to raise its own taxes. In his comparison of 36 democracies, Arend Lijphart found that in Switzerland the central government's tax share is by far the lowest (1999, p. 193). It is also an important aspect of Swiss federalism that cantons often work together to address common problems. This may happen informally, as well as in an institutional framework. Thus, there is a Conference of the Cantons of Central Switzerland. An example of an intercantonal institution is the Conference of the Cantonal Ministers of Education. Thus, many tasks are handled without the participation of the Confederation, either within the individual cantons, or as intercantonal cooperation.

A final aspect of Swiss federalism is that the cantons are important actors at the federal level. Switzerland has a bicameral parliament. In the National Council the cantons are represented according to their population. In the Council of States, each full canton has two seats, the half-cantons one.[1] For legislation, both chambers have exactly the same weight since all bills must pass both chambers. The chambers rotate the first reading of a bill. For the election of the seven-member executive Federal Council and the members of the Supreme Court, the two chambers assemble in a joint session. Here, however, the National Council with its 200 members has more weight than the Council of States with its 46 members. It is also the president of the National Council who presides over the joint sessions.

Bills are prepared by the Federal Council, which relies heavily on a process of consultation *(Vernehmlassungsverfahren)*, and it is here where the cantons play once again an important role. They are always included in this process of consultation, together with the political parties and the relevant interest groups. Although this process of consultation goes back to the beginning of modern Switzerland, it was greatly expanded after World War II. When a bill is passed by the federal parliament, implementation is most often left to the cantons. The federal administration has no regional offices in the cantons as the United States federal administration has in the states. Federal taxes are collected by the cantonal authorities. For social security payments, a federal program, citizens have to deal with the cantonal and the communal authorities. Cantons, finally, have a say in any changes to the constitution which must be submitted to a mandatory referendum. For such referenda to pass, they need a majority of all Swiss voters as well as a majority of the cantons. Here again, the half-cantons have only half the weight of the full cantons. Since there are 20 full cantons and six half-cantons, there are 23 cantonal votes. A majority of the cantons means therefore that at least 12 cantons must support a constitutional amendment. It has happened eight times in modern Swiss history that a constitutional amendment has received a majority of the voters but not a majority of the cantons and therefore failed (Linder 1998, p. 74). In 1994, for example, a constitutional amendment concerning cultural policy received the support of 51 percent of all Swiss voters, but only ten cantons voted in favour. The amendment failed.

To what extent can the institutional framework account for the relatively high degree of linguistic harmony in Swiss history? Let us take the counterfactual situation that the constitution of 1848 would have established a centralized political system. Then the situation with regard to linguistic issues may have become as tense as in Belgium, which was until recently a very centralized country. In Switzerland, federalism allowed the linguistic minorities to keep their identities by managing many of their own affairs, especially with regard to education, which is always sensitive for linguistic groups. With regard to being important players at the federal level, the Federal Council of 1848 had two French-speakers and one Italian-speaker among its seven members. Given that the linguistic minorities were only about 30 percent of the population, they were even slightly overrepresented in the Council. Ever since, the linguistic minorities have always had at least two representatives on the Federal Council.

In recent years, however, language has become an ever more important issue in Swiss politics. That the language cleavage is currently of high salience was revealed in an investigation of 51 recent federal referenda (Linder, Riedwyl and Steiner 2000). We captured the importance of the cleavage between German- and French-speakers with a variable obtained when we divided the number of German-speakers by the number of French-speakers for each district. This ratio turned out to be the most important variable in our investigation, being statistically significant for 35 of the 51 referenda. We captured the importance of Italian in looking at the percentage of Italian-speakers per district. This variable is significant for 27 of the 51 referenda, ranking third after social class.

GLOBAL AND REGIONAL INTEGRATION

That the language issue has become more important in Switzerland has much to do with European integration and globalization. I will argue this in the next section. But first I describe to what extent Switzerland participates in global and regional integration. For a very long time, neutrality was the key maxim for Swiss relations with the outside world. When modern Switzerland was created in 1848, this maxim was already so well established that it was written into the new constitution as the guiding principle for foreign policy. At the beginning of the Old Swiss Confederation in medieval times, however, neutrality was not yet seen as the maxim of how the Swiss cantons should deal with the outside world. Some of the cantons even pursued an aggressive foreign policy, such as advancing into Northern Italy. It was there that the Swiss lost a key battle in Marignano against the French. The retreat from Marignano is described in many history books as the beginning of Swiss neutrality. Although at the time this appeared to be a minor turning point, it is important that in the myths about Swiss history, Marignano received a prominent place giving the idea of neutrality deep roots in history and thus legitimacy.

During the European religious war of 1618 to 1648 the Swiss cantons were at great risk of becoming involved, with the Protestant and the Catholic cantons at opposite ends of the warring factions. There was no conscious decision to pursue a policy of neutrality and to stay out of the war. It was more a lucky circumstance that the war did not spread to the Swiss cantons. But after the awful destruction of this war, many Swiss began to realize that staying out of wars had great benefits, and the concept of neutrality began to take shape as a foreign policy device. At the Congress of Vienna in 1815, the Swiss neutrality was formally recognized by the large powers, and, in the context of the Treaty of Versailles, a document was signed in 1920 stating that Swiss neutrality was in the interest of world peace. By this meant that it was in the interest of an equilibrium among the large European powers: none of them controlled the strategically important mountain passages at the centre of Europe.

In World War II, Swiss neutrality was put to a severe test when the country was surrounded by the Nazi forces. In order to survive, Switzerland made many concessions to the Nazis, in particular with regard to the transport of war material through Switzerland, a harsh refugee policy, bank dealings with the Nazis, and the delivering of war material. In recent years, Switzerland has rightly been criticized for the fact that many of these concessions went too far. But immediately after World War II, the view prevailed among the Swiss people that it was thanks to their heroic military efforts that Hitler did not dare to invade the country. Thus, the legitimacy of neutrality as a foreign policy device was further strengthened, and great emphasis was put on the necessity of being militarily strong if neutrality was to be respected by the international community. During the Cold War, the notion could still be kept up that a militarily defended neutrality was the optimal foreign policy for Switzerland. The "brown" danger of Hitler was substituted with the "red" danger in the minds of most Swiss, and public opinion polls continued to show overwhelming support for the concept of neutrality.

After the end of the Cold War, the situation dramatically changed for the justification of Swiss neutrality. Between what foreign forces should Switzerland be neutral? Against whom should the Swiss army be ready to fight? It was not only the end of the Cold War but also European integration that made Swiss neutrality problematic. With all its neighbours being members of the European Union, it became difficult to argue why Swiss neutrality was in the interest of European peace and stability. There were increasing suggestions that Switzerland should join the European Union and the United Nations.

Historically speaking, neutrality meant that Switzerland did not join any military alliance. Thus, until very recently, membership in the North Atlantic Treaty Organization (NATO) was completely out of the question. Even now it is not politically a serious option, and probably not for some time to come. Switzerland has become, however, a member of the Partnership for Peace, which gives it some connection with NATO. Switzerland also found ways to send some troops to Bosnia and Kosovo.

The way Switzerland interprets its neutrality, the barriers to joining political organizations, are still very high, although somewhat lower than for military alliances. In 1920 Switzerland joined the League of Nations, hoping that the League would gain a universal character. This hope was not realized and in 1938 Switzerland returned from what it called differentiated to integral neutrality, no longer participating in any sanctions of the League of Nations. The disappointment with the experience of the League was so great that after World War II Switzerland decided to stay out of the United Nations, although it joined specialized agencies of the UN such as UNESCO and the World Health Organization (WHO). In 2002, finally, after a previously unsuccessful referendum, the Swiss voters accepted that Switzerland should become a full member of the United Nations. This ended the bizarre situation of Switzerland being the only European country, besides the Vatican, not being a regular member of the UN.

Economically, Switzerland was always accessible to the world and stressed the necessity of a free world market. As the Swiss Federal Statistical Office notes, Switzerland is among the countries of the world most involved in international trade.[2] In 1999, Switzerland had exports of US$15,018 per inhabitant. For the 15 countries of the European Union the corresponding figure is only US$6,887. Large countries have, of course, usually lower figures since they can sell more within their own national borders. Therefore, the most relevant comparison is with other smaller European countries. Here, the importance of exports for Switzerland becomes very clear. Neighbouring Austria exports only US$11,588 per inhabitant. Even for the traditionally export-oriented Netherlands the corresponding figure is only US$13,715 dollars. What are Switzerland's main exports? The stereotypical expectation is cheese, chocolate, and watches.

Although these products have some importance, they pale in comparison with chemical products and machines. The former is 30 percent of all exports, the latter is 29 percent. Thus, Switzerland has, technologically, a very modern economy. Its main export countries are Germany with 27 percent of all exports, the United States (13 percent), France (11 percent), Italy (9 percent) and the United Kingdom (6 percent). The high international economic involvement of Switzerland can also be seen by the number of resident aliens: 19.3 percent of the population.[3] For the European Union (EU) the corresponding figure is 4.7 percent. A relatively high number of resident aliens live in Austria (9.3 percent) and Germany (8.8), but even these figures are much lower than in Switzerland.

As a consequence of the heavy economic involvement of Switzerland with the world, neutrality was never considered an obstacle to joining purely economically oriented international organizations such as the Organisation for Economic Co-operation and Development (OECD). Switzerland is also a member of the World Bank, the International Monetary Fund (IMF) and the World Trade Organization (WTO). With regard to European integration, Switzerland was always ambivalent. If integration could be seen only in economic terms, the country did not hesitate to join, but it feared the political aspect of European integration. Initially, Switzerland had hoped to find a solution by joining the European Free Trade Association (EFTA), whose most important member was Great Britain. But after Britain and most other EFTA members changed to the European Union, EFTA lost most of its importance with Switzerland, Norway, Ireland and Lichtenstein left as the only members. Switzerland now tries to reach special arrangements with the EU short of full membership. The first attempt failed in 1992 when membership in the European Economic Area was defeated by the Swiss voters in a referendum. In 2000, however, the Swiss voters accepted a bilateral treaty with the EU which regulates important matters such as labour market, transportation, and research. The Federal Council, the executive cabinet of Switzerland, sees full membership in the EU as the strategic goal of Swiss foreign policy. For the time being, parliament has refused to make such a commitment. And the voters do not seem to be ready to accept full EU membership any time soon; although it does not seem impossible to get a majority of the voters. But as we saw earlier, for important matters such as EU membership a majority of the cantons is also required and here a positive decision is out of reach for the time being.

IMPACT OF GLOBAL AND REGIONAL
INTEGRATION ON SWISS POLITICS

Earlier in the chapter, I argued that language has become an ever more important issue in Swiss politics and that this has much to do with European integration and globalization. This argument does not deny that other factors contribute to the increased salience of the language issue. One of these factors is the decreased importance of religion in Swiss politics. Religious and language cleavages used to crosscut each other. Such crosscutting cleavages helped to stabilize the country, because for some political issues French-speaking Catholics, for example, had more in common with German-speaking Catholics than with other French-speakers. With the vanishing of the religious cleavage, the language groups are more pitted against each other. Language has become more important in Swiss politics as cantonal borders have become less important. This is particularly true for the French-speaking cantons. The two largest French-speaking cantons, Geneva and Vaud, traditionally had their own special identities, and there was much rivalry between these two proud cantons. Now there is talk of merging the universities of the two cantons and even of merging the cantons altogether. Although a merger of the two cantons may never happen, the mere talk of it indicates that cantonal borders in the French-speaking region have become less important, which contributes further to the perception of a common French-speaking identity. Still another factor contributing to increased linguistic segmentation has to do with the increased importance of television for political discourse. The three major language groups all have their own programs. Efforts to broadcast trilingual programs have failed as the public did not watch them. The political discourse in Switzerland always takes place to a large extent within the individual language groups; and with the increased importance of television this has become even more so.

Although other factors also play a role in the increased salience of the language issue, European integration and globalization must be considered of crucial importance. The risk of European integration and globalization is not that Switzerland will suddenly break apart along linguistic lines, but that the language groups will drift apart. The French-speaking Swiss tend to see Switzerland as part of Europe and the world, whereas many among the German-speaking Swiss see the outside world as a constant danger. The more the French-speakers want to integrate into

Europe and the world, the greater the fears of many German-speakers that Switzerland is falling apart. That the German-speakers are particularly fearful that Switzerland is falling apart is related to their much longer roots in Swiss history. As noted earlier, the Swiss Confederation was founded in the thirteenth century in German-speaking Switzerland, whereas the other language groups, for the main part, joined around 1800. Many German-speakers fear that the French-speakers never really understood the *idea* of Switzerland and are therefore willing to abandon it. According to the traditional view, Switzerland was always threatened by external enemies — the Hapsburgs, Napoleon, Hitler, and many others. Given these permanent threats, Switzerland has had to fight to keep its independence. The best way to stay independent was to fortify the mountains and to remain neutral in international affairs. This myth of Swiss history is strongest in German-speaking Switzerland, especially in the mountain valleys where Switzerland was initially founded.

A charismatic politician from Zurich, Christoph Blocher, founded an organization "Action for a Neutral and Independent Switzerland," based on this historical myth of Switzerland. Its supporters are mainly from German-speaking Switzerland. The mission of the organization is that this time the danger for Swiss neutrality and independence comes from Brussels and the United Nations. There are even parallels drawn to the Nazis. As Switzerland had to defend itself against the Nazis, today it has to defend itself against the bureaucrats and the judges of the European Union. The threat of being ruled by foreign judges goes back to the foundation of the Swiss Confederation when the Hapsburg judges were expelled from Swiss territory. Therefore, it hits at the core of the Swiss historical myth when Christoph Blocher exclaims that Switzerland will never allow itself to be ruled by foreign judges. Politically, the Action for a Neutral and Independent Switzerland is similar to the Swiss People's Party; and here again, it is important to note that this party has its main support in German-speaking Switzerland.

What we see then is a clash between two perceptions of the place of Switzerland in Europe and the world. One perception is that Switzerland is a typical small European country and that it should take its place in the European Union and the United Nations like other small countries. The other perception builds on the historical myth of Switzerland that the Swiss people were always a special case (*Sonderfall*) in the sense that their very existence was constantly endangered and that therefore they must continue to be vigilant against potential threats to their neutrality and independence. They further believe that they have to defend their federalist structure and direct democracy with extensive citizen participation in referenda.

The conflict over Swiss membership in the European Union and the United Nations will most likely have the consequence that the French-speakers will drift further apart. There will be increasing cooperation among the French-speaking cantons who will try more and more to resolve political problems on their own. They will also increasingly exploit all the constitutional opportunities that they have to cooperate with France. When the Swiss constitution was written in 1848, the cantons received a fair amount of authority to deal with other countries, in particular in matters involving border issues. The French-speaking cantons have already begun to use this authority. In the region between the canton Neuchâtel and France, for example, some hospitals are run on a common basis across the border. In the region of Geneva, there is an even more intensive cross-border cooperation on a large number of issues. Many people work in Geneva but live across the border in France, which means that many issues such as taxes, social security, and health insurance have to be resolved between the two countries.

Italian-speaking Switzerland in the canton of Ticino and in the southern valleys of the canton Graubünden are also likely to drift further away. Economically speaking, Italian-speaking Switzerland is to some extent part of the greater Milano region. The newly created first university in Italian-speaking Switzerland is likely to reinforce the drifting apart of this language region. When Italian-speaking Switzerland had no university of its own, its students had to study either in German- or French-speaking Switzerland, which bonded them to the rest of the country. This kind of bonding will continue to some extent because the newly founded university does not encompass all the faculties. On the other hand, it will attract students from Italy, which will reinforce the orientation of Italian-speaking Switzerland toward Italy.

In German-speaking Switzerland, there is also increasing cross-border cooperation. This is particularly true in the region of Basel, where France, Germany, and Switzerland come together. This cross-border cooperation in the region of Basel is institutionalized in the form of the *Regio Basiliensis*. The agglomeration of Basel extends to France and Germany such that it is hardly visible in everyday life where one country ends and another begins. The airport is in France, and Germany has its railway station on Swiss territory.

Do all these developments mean that Switzerland will slowly cease to exist as a nation-state? When in 1991, the 700th birthday of the Swiss Confederation was celebrated, some artists and intellectuals only half-jokingly coined the motto "700 years are enough" (*700 Jahre sind genug*). Shortly afterwards, at the world exposition in Sevilla, the official Swiss booth had the theme "Switzerland does not exist" (*La Suisse n'existe pas*). And recently, a federal councillor speculated that some day Switzerland may indeed cease to exist. It has been suggested that Geneva should separate from Switzerland and, analogous to Monaco, become its own country. All these ideas were said and written in order to provoke and should therefore not be taken too seriously. But it is nevertheless noteworthy that the very existence of Switzerland has become a theme for public discourse. In the initial thirteenth-century treaty which laid the foundation for the Swiss Confederation, it was solemnly stated that the treaty shall be eternally valid. In the current political culture of Switzerland it has become difficult in the minds of many people, especially the young, highly educated, and urban dwelling, to see the existence of Switzerland in terms of eternity. Old songs and poems glorifying the eternal existence of Switzerland are shrugged off by many.

For all practical purposes, however, Switzerland will most likely continue to exist for a long time to come. There will be a Swiss national soccer team, and the Swiss social security system will still pay benefits. But if the cleavage over the identity of the Swiss deepens, this will put severe strains on the country. This cleavage is particularly troublesome because it is to a large extent superimposed on the language cleavage between German- and French-speakers. Over the centuries, Switzerland has developed an accommodative or consociational style of conflict management across the various cleavage lines (Steiner 1974). The challenge for the future is to keep this consociational decision-making style for issues involving the cleavage over what the Swiss identity should be (Steiner 2002). Accommodating the two divergent views of Swiss identity is a big task for Swiss politics. Traditional patterns of consociationalism do not seem to work. One major difficulty is that the groups with different identities of Switzerland cannot easily be identified. To some extent it is a cleavage between French- and German-speakers. But there are many

German-speakers, especially the young, the highly educated and urban dwellers, who support the concept of an open Switzerland. On the other hand, the traditional view of Switzerland has also some support in French-speaking Switzerland. If the conflicting groups cannot easily be identified, consociationalism is difficult to achieve because it remains unclear between exactly what groups accommodation should take place. Conflicts over one's national identity are also particularly difficult to accommodate because it is difficult to find a middle ground. Where is the middle ground between a backward and a forward looking view of Swiss identity? But consociationalism presupposes that a middle ground can somehow be found.

FUTURE SCENARIOS

It is an interesting challenge to speculate on how the salience of the Swiss identity cleavage will develop under the four future scenarios: (i) regional dominators, (ii) a global club, (iii) shared governance, and (iv) cyberwave. I expect that under the first two, the cleavage over Swiss identity will further increase, whereas the second two are likely to decrease the salience of the cleavage.

Under *regional dominators*, the supporters of the old Swiss identity will make the argument that the outside world remains dangerous with powerful blocs confronting each other and that Switzerland is better off staying out of such confrontations and staying neutral and independent with a strong army. On the other hand, there will be those who argue that Switzerland, like other smaller European countries, has no choice but to integrate into the European bloc and to defend its national interests within this bloc. As a consequence, the cleavage over Swiss identity will become stronger. The French-speakers will further drift away and will seek special arrangements with the European Union in specific issue areas. The same will happen for the region of Basel and the Italian-speakers. Overall, the federal ties within Switzerland will weaken. The cantons will become more important. Groups of cantons will increasingly tackle common problems. Cross-national regions will increase in importance.

Under the conditions of the *global club*, Switzerland as a small country is marginalized. The supporters of the traditional Swiss identity argue that under these conditions it is pointless to try to play a role in world affairs and that the reasonable thing to do is to rely on the maxim of defended neutrality. Those opposed to this identity are also not happy with the conditions of the global club, but they declare that the concept of defended neutrality is a myth if a few powerful actors dominate world affairs. Thus, the cleavage over Swiss identity grows with one side arguing that neutrality is still a valuable concept and the other side dismissing the concept as lacking any basis in reality. No great changes will occur in the federal structure of Switzerland, but the country will feel increasingly powerless and frustrated not knowing in what direction to turn. There will be many deadlocks and stalemates in the federalist system. Referendum outcomes will be increasingly negative since the two identities block each other.

If, under the conditions of *shared governance*, economic and political power in the world are exercised within a balanced system of global government and the equality and responsibility of the individual states are recognized, the supporters of the old identity of Switzerland will have increasing difficulties making the case that Switzerland should stay neutral. The concept of neutrality will continue to lose its credibility. Thus, the cleavage over the nature of Swiss identity will slowly lose salience. Most Swiss will turn to the notion that their country is just a regular small European democracy. The country finds its role in the world. Domestically, it is easier to have a well-functioning federalism since the question of the correct Swiss identity vanishes from the political agenda. Relations between the federal level and the cantons are quite smooth with both levels showing signs of great vitality. Referenda outcomes will rarely lead to a blockage of the system.

Under the *cyberwave* scenario, individualism and libertarianism are celebrated, and anarchic forces lead to a diminished ability and role for governments to govern. Under these conditions, it becomes also very difficult for the supporters of the old Swiss identity to make the case that Switzerland should stay independent and neutral. Independent of what and neutral between whom? Given the difficulty of answering these questions in a credible way, the cleavage over Swiss identity will weaken since the traditional identity will lose more and more ground. But it also becomes less important to be Swiss at all. Cantons often act on their own, seeking their own niches in the dynamic world economy. Depending on the situation, they collaborate as easily with regions outside Switzerland as with other Swiss cantons. Big cities such as Zurich and Geneva become quite independent actors on the international economic scene.

NORMATIVE CONCLUSIONS

In my conclusions I want to take a normative stance and tackle the question about which of the four scenarios is best for Switzerland, as well as for Europe. My normative position is based on an ethics of discourse (see Steiner 1996).[4] As Melissa Orlie puts it, people should attempt to imagine other views and be willing "to deliberate, to listen and respond to others' claim about our effects and possibly to modify them" (1994, p. 693). Agreeing with Kristen Renwick Monroe, I reject "the view of human nature as exclusively self-interested, acquisitive, aggressive, and individualistic"(Monroe 1991, p. 396). Politics should be more, in the words of Orlie, than the "thoughtless assertion of power." As an ideal to strive for, politics in a democracy should be an arena where citizens are willing to listen to each other and to consider the interests of others. Of course, citizens never quite know what the interests of others are because they can never *transcend* their own self; but people can make an effort to understand the interests of others and to *transfigure* their way of life in the sense that they consider not only their own interests but also the interests of others. Habermas calls such a way of governing a deliberative democracy (Habermas 1992).

The classical nation-state as it developed in the last 400 years in Europe is not hospitable to such ethics of discourse across national borders. The classical nation-state is characterized by the imposition of political, economic, military, and cultural boundaries. As a consequence, the national boundaries are firmly set and do not allow easy exit.[5] Either one is British or French, Italian or Spanish, and so on. The interests of one's nation-state tend to be seen in conflict with the interests of other nation-states. If the others win, we lose. Living in such a political environment makes it hard to consider the interests of people outside one's own nation-state. As we know from European history of the last four centuries, an international system based on the classical nation-state easily leads to war. People outside the boundaries of one's own state are easily seen as enemies and not as other human beings whose interests one should also consider. Recent tragic events on the Balkan once again remind us in a sad way of this danger.

In my view, a multilayered political system with fluid borders is more hospitable to an ethics of discourse at the international level. In such a political environment people activate different identities at the local, regional, national, and European levels. There are also identities that reach across national borders. Such multiple identities should help people to imagine identities outside the set of their own. To imagine other identities does not necessarily mean that one is willing to consider the interests of the people with these other particularities, but the chances are better that one would do so. Considering the interests of other groups may lead to a learning process whereby it becomes a *habit* to imagine other identities and to consider the interests of the people holding these.

There are, however, also severe risks if a country takes this path. As Stefano Bartolini shows, fluid boundaries with easy possibilities to exit weaken domestic political structures, which, in turn, may lead to feelings of insecurity among many citizens (Bartolini 1997). They feel at a loss and long for the well-established order of the classical nation-state with its firmly set boundaries. It is precisely such a backlash that currently happens in Switzerland with the strengthening of the Swiss People's Party and the prominent role of such organizations as the Action for a Neutral and Independent Switzerland. From the perspective of ethics I am concerned about this backlash, and it is not easy to know what to do about it. Writing this chapter gave me hope that there may be some world scenarios that decrease the importance of the old nationalistic identity of Switzerland and that strengthen an identity more open to Europe and the world. The most promising scenarios in this respect are the scenarios of shared governance and cyberwave, or, even better in my view, a combination of the two. Under these conditions, Switzerland may serve as a useful model for Europe. European citizens will still have a certain identity within their nation, but no longer in a nationalistic sense. In addition to their national identities, they have local and regional identities, and some of these do cross national borders. These multiple identities will mean that politics in Europe will no longer be dominated by nation-states, but that regions and supranational institutions will play an important role. Such a model would be particularly helpful in reducing tensions in Eastern Europe. The model has the potential of being applied to the world at large.

Notes

1. In the course of history three cantons have split into half-cantons.
2. For this statement and the figures quoted below, see <www.statistik. admin.ch>.

3.   Although it is quite difficult to become a Swiss citizen, Switzerland depends to a large extent on foreign workers.
4.   For a current research project using this normative approach and applying it to empirical data see the Web site <www. ipw.unibe.ch/discourse>.
5.   See, on the question of boundaries and exit options in the classical nation-state, Bartolini (1997).

References

Bartolini, S. 1997. "Exit Options, Boundary Building, Political Structuring." Florence: European University Institute.Unpublished paper.

Habermas, J. 1992. *Faktizität und Geltung: Beiträge zur Diskurstheorie des Rechts und des demokratischen Rechtsstaats*. Frankfurt a. M.: Suhrkamp.

Lijphart, A. 1999. *Patterns of Democracy: Government Forms and Performance in Thirty-Six Countries*. New Haven: Yale University Press.

Linder, W. 1998. *Swiss Democracy: Possible Solutions to Conflict in Multicultural Societies*, 2d ed. London: Macmillan.

Linder, W., H. Riedwyl and J. Steiner. 2000. "Konkordanztheorie und Abstimmungsdaten: eine explorative Aggregatsanalyse auf Bezirksebene," *Swiss Political Science Review* 6(2):27-56.

Mesmer, B. 1998. "Reformbedarf im Innern – Druck von aussen. Die Helvetik im historischen Kontext," *Neue Zürcher Zeitung*, 21./22. Februar, S.67.

Monroe, K.R. 1991. "John Donne's People: Explaining Differences between Rational Actors and Altruists through Cognitive Frameworks," *Journal of Politics* 53(May):394-433.

Orlie, M.A. 1994. "Thoughtless Assertion and Political Deliberation," *American Political Science Review* 88(September):684-95.

Steiner, J. 1974. *Amicable Agreement versus Majority Rule: Conflict Resolution in Switzerland*. Chapel Hill, NC: University of North Carolina Press.

—— 1996. *Conscience in Politics: An Empirical Investigation of Swiss Decision Cases*. New York: Garland Publishing.

—— 2002. "The Consociational Theory and Switzerland Revisited," *Acta Politica* 37 (Spring/Summer):104-120.

Steiner, J., A. Bächtiger, M. Spörndli and Marco Steenbergen. 2004. *Deliberative Politics in Action. A Cross-National Study of Parliamentary Debates*. Cambridge: Cambridge University Press.

Economic Liberalization and Political Federalization in India: Mutually Reinforcing Responses to Global Integration

Mahendra Prasad Singh

INTRODUCTION

India in 1950 adopted a parliamentary federal constitution that bore a striking resemblance to the Canadian constitution; this can be attributed to the British colonial heritage in both countries. The dominance of one party, the Indian National Congress, with which India began its independent existence as a nation, further reinforced the parliamentary tenor of its politics, and this overshadowed its federal aspects. In the economic sphere, India, soon after independence, adopted a strategy of development with a planning commission and the state as the major agent of change and growth. The 1990s, however, witnessed a significant transformation in the Indian polity, including a decline in the Government of India's role. The two most notable dimensions of this change are political federalization and economic liberalization.

India has moved cautiously away from a planned economy, controlled largely by the government according to the principles of democratic socialism. At the same time as Delhi's control over the economy has relaxed, some states of the Indian Union have seized the opportunity to encourage the private sector.

Economic liberalization was preceded by a degree of political federalization. The two factors subsequently reinforced each other. The decline of Delhi's control over the economy was prefigured by the decline of the national party system. One-party majority governments, the norm until 1989, were replaced by federal coalition governments in which regional parties play an important role. This has strained the parliamentary system originally designed for a more centralized federation according to the principles of parliamentary supremacy.

There have also been signs of global and regional integration, but India is perhaps exceptional in being relatively unaffected by these trends. If anything, India has experienced economic liberalization (in the sense of deregulation and partial privatization) more than globalization. Also, its trade has been relatively more inclined toward globalization (with the United States and the European Union especially) than integration within the region of South Asia.

Both globalization and regionalization are highly contested terms, depending on which side of the exchange the protagonist is speaking from. My approach here is not to proceed from theories but to move empirically from praxis by sketching out the emerging scenario in which India finds itself today. I begin therefore with the rather open-ended definitions of the term:

> Globalization might be defined as the rapid intensification of social, economic, and political transactions, necessitated by the emergence of issues that transcend international boundaries and facilitated by technological developments (especially in telecommunications and transportation). Regional integration would be characterized by the same processes, but in a smaller geographical area (e.g. Western Europe or North America) (Institute of Intergovernmental Relations 2000, p. 1).

Inevitably, nationalism, regionalism, and globalism would be dialectically interrelated with contradictions and complementarities.

This chapter is organized into seven sections. The next section shows how India's economic growth has arguably improved since 1990. It also situates India in its regional and global contexts. India is a middle-level regional power rather low on economic development, but with great potential. With neo-liberal economic reforms currently under way, India is gradually integrating itself into the larger regional and global economies, but because of both internal and external impeding factors the pace has been rather slow. The third section outlines the structure of the parliamentary federal constitution and the aggregate governments in India with

a focus on their historical origin, evolution, and contemporary developments. Section four explores the extent of India's global and regional
integration in economic, technological, and cultural terms. Section five
analyzes the impact of global and regional integrations on the Indian federal system, while section six sketches the probable future scenarios. Finally,
the last section presents the conclusions.

INDIA IN CONTEXT

India, a developing economy in its South Asian regional and global economic
contexts, is a bundle of paradoxes. Lloyd and Susanne Rudolph (1987, p. 1)
aptly characterize it as "a rich-poor nation with a weak-strong state." The end
of British colonial rule in 1947 and partition of the country left it with a
mixed legacy of problems and possibilities. Independence found India facing
an uncertain yet not entirely bleak political and economic future. British rule
had accelerated the transition of the Indian economy from feudalism into
capitalism, though in a colonial setting. The initial impact of independence
on the regional and global integration of the Indian economy was rather negative. India under British rule was both regionally and globally more integrated
than it was to be immediately after independence. Partition sowed the seeds
of perpetual regional discord and conflict. The colonial experience prompted
India to look for national, economic self-reliance to get out of the "near stagnation" of the Indian economy whose "growth of aggregate real output during
the first half of the twentieth century [was] estimated at less than 2 percent a
year, and per capita output by half a percent a year or less. There was hardly
any change in the structure of production or in productivity levels. The growth
of modern manufacturing was probably neutralized by the displacement of
traditional crafts, and in any case was too small to make a difference to the
overall picture" (Vaidyanathan 1982, reprint 1984, p. 947).

The post-independence patterns of economic development displayed
at least three different trends. First, from the 1950s to the end of the
1970s India followed a strategy of economic development that aimed at
heavy industrialization together with import-substituting national self-
reliance. The result was a mixed economy with the state sector seeking to
scale "the commanding heights of the economy," but leaving some scope
for the private sector. Domestic industries were protected from global competition. These objectives were to be achieved through centralized (though
democratic) planning and a state-regulated economy. There was a modest

improvement over the rate of economic growth registered during the British Raj. The total gross domestic product (GDP) growth rate in the first three decades between 1950–51 and 1980–81 declined, however, from 4.1 to 3.3 percent, from 6.3 percent to 4.8 percent in the industrial sector, and from 3 percent to 2.1 percent in the agricultural sector (Ahluwalia 1999, p. 9).

Second, liberalization of the public sector began in a somewhat limited way in the 1980s, and it resulted in acceleration of GDP growth to 5.6 percent per annum. This was better than the performance of developing economies as a whole (ibid., p. 2). But the better performance of the economy in the 1980s could not be sustained. It was hampered by the populist policies of the governments. This required huge subsidies. Another obstacle was the rent-seeking propensity of the political and bureaucratic elites. There was also a lack of development on the export front. The balance-of-payment problems arising in the mismatch of exports and imports assumed the proportions of a crisis in 1990–91.

Third, this finally necessitated the acceleration of economic reforms beginning in July 1991. The economic reforms included deregulation of the economy from state controls, disinvestment of government shares in the public sector, opening up of the economy to foreign trade/investment/ and technology, and financial sector reforms aimed at increased productivity. Economic reforms gradually inched GDP growth between 1993–94 to 1996–97 forward to 6 to 7.5 percent, the average for the period being 6.8 percent (ibid., p. 9). But these rates tended to decline somewhat thereafter. The overall growth in 2001–2002 was 5.4 percent, "supported by a growth rate of 5.7 percent in agriculture and allied sectors, 3.3 percent in industry, and 6.5 percent in services (Government of India 2002, p. 2).

Its large population and land surface area makes India the dominant economy with the fastest growth rate in South Asia. Its GNP was $442.2 billion in 1999 and the average annual growth rate was 6.9 percent in 1998–99.

However, major South Asian countries did not differ substantially in GNP per capita in 1999. Sri Lanka's GNP per capita with $3,056 is higher than India's. Moreover, with a growth rate of 5 and 4.6 percent, Bangladesh and Nepal were ahead of Pakistan and Sri Lanka. Pakistan's and Sri Lanka's growth rates were the lowest in the region: 3.6 and 3.8 percentage points respectively (World Bank 2001, pp. 274-75, Table 1).

Table 1 gives some additional information about the economic profile of the South Asian region. India led the region with the highest values

TABLE 1
Economic Growth in South Asia

Country	Average Annual % Growth					
	GDP 1990–99	Agricultural Value Added 1990–99	Industrial Value Added 1990–99	Services Value Added 1990–99	Exports of Goods and Services 1990–99	Gross Domestic Investments 1990–99
India	6.1	3.8	6.7	7.7	11.3	7.4
Pakistan	4.0	4.3	4.9	4.6	2.7	2.1
Sri Lanka	5.3	1.5	7.4	5.6	8.4	6.2
Bangladesh	4.8	2.3	3.9	6.3	13.2	7.0
Nepal	4.8	2.3	7.0	6.0	14.3	5.7
Bhutan	-	-	-	-	-	-
Maldives	-	-	-	-	-	-

Source: *World Development Report 2000/2001*, compiled from World Bank (2001, pp. 294-95, Table 11).

of average annual growth rate in GDP in 1990–91 (6.1 percent), services value-added (7.7 percent), and gross domestic investments (7.4 percent). However, Pakistan was marginally ahead of India in agricultural value-added (4.3 percent), Sri Lanka in industrial value-added (7.4 percent), and Nepal and Bangladesh in export of goods and services (14.3 and 13.2 percent respectively).

PARLIAMENTARY FEDERAL STRUCTURE AND PRACTICE

The Structure

The constitution of India is parliamentary and yet in some respects federal. The Parliament, with overriding powers over state legislatures, is supreme, subject only to judicial review premised on fundamental rights of citizens and centre-state division of powers and revenues. Some of these regular powers of Parliament can be further augmented with the sanction of the federal second chamber, the Rajya Sabha, whereby Parliament can legislate in the national interest on subjects within the exclusive jurisdiction of the states. Also, during constitutionally contemplated emergencies — national, regional, fiscal — the parliamentary federal structure of the government for all intents and purposes becomes unitary (Part XVIII of the Constitution of India).

The head of state at the centre, the president of India, is elected by an intergovernmental electoral college consisting of the elected members of both Houses of Parliament and elected members of the Legislative Assemblies of the states. The head of the provincial state, the governor, is appointed by the government at the centre and functions as the link between the two levels of government. The heads of the governments at the two levels are the prime minister and the chief ministers respectively, who, advised by their respective Cabinets, exercise the real governmental authority. The president and the governor use discretionary powers in the formation of the government and the dissolution of the popular chamber in the event of the party system failing to produce a clear legislative majority. The governor can reserve a bill passed by the state legislature for consideration by the president (which means the Union Cabinet) who may disallow it (article 201).

An issue of great federal relevance here is the nature of the treaty-making power of the Union. As in Australia, but in contrast to Canada, the power to make and implement treaties lies solely with the central government. The Indian constitution does not *expressly* make treaty-making an executive power. In terms of explicit provisions (Seventh Schedule, entries 10 to 16 of the Union List) it is within the jurisdiction of the Parliament of India. However, since the executive power of the Union is normally coterminus with its legislative jurisdiction, the federal executive can make treaties by implication on behalf of Parliament. The implied executive power is construed by the Supreme Court as the residue of functions of government, which are not legislative or judicial (*Madhav Rao* v. *Union of India*, 1971).[1] The Supreme Court has further ruled that in conformity with the constitution or law the executive power may be exercised without prior legislative sanction (*Maganbhai Ishwarbhai Patel* v. *Union of India*, 1969, and *Ram Jawaya* v. *Union of India*, 1955).[2] Article 253 of the constitution empowers Parliament "to make any law for the whole or any part of the territory of India for implementing any treaty." There are two cases — *State of Tamil Nadu* v. *Union of India* and *State of*

Punjab v. *Union of India* — pending before the Supreme Court which argue that states should also have a say in signing international treaties like the World Trade Organization (WTO) that affect areas within their exclusive jurisdiction, for example, agriculture.

The Rajya Sabha, the federal second chamber of Parliament, consists of 238 members elected by the members of the Legislative Assemblies of the states through a system of proportional representation by means of the single transferable vote. Twelve additional members are nominated by the president based on their standing in the areas of literature, science, art, and social service (article 80). Representation is given to the states on the basis of proportionality of the population rather than equality of states as federating units. The Rajya Sabha is subordinate to the Lok Sabha in terms of collective responsibility of the Cabinet. It is further subordinated by limitations on its ability to originate money bills. It is also hampered by being less than half the size of the Lok Sabha when disagreements between the two houses are resolved in joint settings (article 108). In his classic study of the Indian Parliament in the 1950s, Morris-Jones (1957, p. 256) found that the workings of the Rajya were more amenable to a *parliamentary* rather than *federal* interpretation of its role.

However, the decline of the Congress Party's dominance and regionalization of the party system in the 1980s at the state level and after 1989 at the Union level has invested the Rajya Sabha with a greater federal relevance. A differential party configuration in the two Houses, which has been typical in the post-Congress dominance phase, enables the Rajya Sabha to block the intentions of a Union government to legislate in national interest in an area of exclusive state jurisdiction, and to create a new All-India Services (articles 249 and 312).

The 26-member Supreme Court is appointed by the Union executive in consultation with such judges of the Supreme Court and High Courts in the states as the president may consider necessary (in the case of the chief justice) and mandatory consultation with the chief justice (in the case of other judges) (article 124). In terms of the Supreme Court judgement in the *S.C. Advocates-on-Record Association* v. *the Union of India* (1982) the president of India is bound to appoint the most senior judge of the Supreme Court as the chief justice and follow his or her advice in appointing other court judges. Judges of the Supreme Court shall not be removed from office except by presidential order after a decision in each House of Parliament by a majority of the membership and two-thirds majority of those present and voting (article 124, clause 4). Their privileges and allowances shall not be varied to their disadvantage after their appointment (article 125, clause 2).

The judiciary in India is thus an integrated rather than bifurcated structure. But it may, and has, encouraged federalization and weakened parliamentary supremacy (centralization) by buttressing judicial review and state rights.

Union-State Division of Powers and Revenues

Legislative subjects are divided between Parliament and the state legislatures according to three lists: Union, State, and Concurrent (Seventh Schedule). Consisting of 96 entries, the exclusive Union List includes defence, foreign affairs, banking, insurance, currency and coinage, citizenship, railways and airways, interstate trade and commerce, census, All-India Services, audit and accounts of the Union and the states, taxes on income other than agricultural income, customs and export duties, corporation tax, Union excise duties, any other matter not enumerated in other lists, etc. The exclusive State List consists of 61 entries, including public order and police, local government, public health and sanitation, agriculture, fisheries, land revenue and agricultural income tax, state excise duties and sales taxes, etc. The Concurrent List contains 47 entries including criminal law and procedure, civil procedure, marriage, contracts, torts, trusts, labour, planning, education, etc. Both the Union and state legislatures can legislate on these items, with Union law prevailing in cases of conflict (article 246 and the Seventh Schedule).

Intergovernmental Agencies

Article 263 of the constitution provides for the establishment of an Inter-State Council (ISC) to address issues of common concern or disputes between or among states and the centre. It may be taken as an indicator of the centralized nature of the Indian federal system during the Congress Raj up to the 1980s, that the centre managed to go without setting up a constitutional intergovernmental council. The Inter-State Council was implemented eventually in 1990. This coincided with the transformation of the one-party dominance under the Indian National Congress into a multi-party system in the Lok Sabha election in 1989 and the onset of a coalition/minority government by the National Front led by Janata Dal. The council consists of the executive heads of governments of the centre, state, and Union territories plus six central ministers named by the prime minister. It is chaired by the prime minister and makes decisions by consensus, not by majority. The decision of the chairman as to consensus is final (Inter-State Council Order 1990, notified on 28 May 1990, Ministry of Home Affairs, Government of India).

The delayed implementation of the Inter-State Council under the constitution can partly be explained by the preference of Congress governments in the past to deal with intergovernmental matters in less comprehensive forums than an Inter-State Council or in ad hoc bodies outside the framework of the constitutional provision. For example, the government, under article 263 of the constitution, set up the Central Council of Health in 1952, the Central Council for Local Government and Urban Development in 1954, and the Council for Sales Tax and State Excise Duties in 1968. All these bodies are partially intergovernmental in scope. Then, the government established the National Development Council (NDC) for intergovernmental consultation and decision-making in the area of planned economic development in 1952 with its secretariat in the Planning Commission in New Delhi (Resolutions Constituting the National Development Council dated 6 August 1952 and Reconstituting it dated 7 October 1967, Cabinet Secretariat, Government of India). Both the NDC, representing the executive heads of the two levels of government, and the Planning Commission, consisting of experts and politicians named unilaterally by the Union government, were set up by Cabinet resolutions outside article 263 of the constitution. Intergovernmental matters are also regularly sorted out at ad hoc conferences of civil servants and ministers of concerned departments in New Delhi and state capitals. For example, the Union Ministry of Health and Family Welfare (HFW) convenes two annual meetings of Union secretaries and state ministries for formulation and implementation of intergovernmental policies and schemes (interview with A.R. Nanda, I.A.S., Union HFW Secretary, winter 2001). Another example was the convening in 1998 of a conference of education ministers and secretaries of states in New Delhi to discuss a new national education policy emphasizing Hindutva values.

NDC and ISC are two major intergovernmental agencies. The former was set up by Cabinet resolution by the Nehru government in 1952 as a matter of convention and the latter by a presidential order under article 263 of the constitution during the National Front government in 1990. Neither of these two bodies is entrenched in the constitution in the sense of being written into the text itself by constitutional amendment. Thus, their operation is optional for the government of the day.

During the era of Congress dominance, the NDC was eclipsed by the Congress Party's parliamentary board overseeing the work of Congress governments at both the centre and in the states. Even during a multi-party system and coalition/minority governments since 1989, the NDC and ISC have not really come into their own, since parties in power in the states, including major regional parties, are partners in the federal coalition governments. With direct representation in the government, regional parties holding the reins of power in the states and their chief ministers, do not have much incentive to empower the intergovernmental forums. They use, through remote control, their representatives in the Union Cabinet instead to make their points in matters under exclusive federal or concurrent jurisdictions. This weakens the authority of the prime minister and the collective responsibility of the Cabinet, but the new breed of regional satraps stand to gain.

Additional reasons why the NDC and ISC have failed to emerge as the grand federal councils of "executive federalism" are that the bulk of fiscal Union-state arrangements are written into the constitution itself, supplemented by a five-year constitutional finance commission to recommend on the patterns of revenue-sharing; and central or national councils of health, local governments and urban development, water resources, sales tax and state excise duties, population, etc. are in place to deal with intergovernmental affairs in these policy areas. These bodies include Union and state ministers and officials who can commit their governments to the decisions made therein (Singh 2002*a*). Moreover, the *Inter-State River Water Disputes Act*, 1956, provides that disputes of this nature be referred to a tribunal on receipt of an application from a state and on satisfaction of the Union government that the dispute "cannot be settled by negotiations." The Union government has so far set up the Narmada Tribunal, the Krishna Tribunal, the Godavari Tribunal, the Kaveri Tribunal, and the Satluj-Jamuna Canal Tribunal. This mode of dispute settlement has generally been effective, except for the last two which have proved to be rather sticky. Finally, other forums such as the Zonal Councils and the North-Eastern Councils of intergovernmental scope have worked with some degree of regularity and usefulness at the regional level. Additionally, on complex national issues, some prime ministers, notably Indira Gandhi and P.V. Narasimha Rao, have tended to convene the National Integration Council (NIC) founded by Prime Minister Nehru in 1962 in the wake of the Chinese aggression. The NIC is intergovernmental in scope as well as being representative of various aspects of civic life and business. Also, recourse is often made to all-party conferences on controversial issues of wide concern.[3]

There has recently been a new trend of growing interface between the private sector and state governments alongside the more regular interface of this nature between Union ministers and business groups. For example, the Punjab-Haryana-Delhi Chamber of Commerce and Industries (PHDCCI) organized the "Dynamic North: Vision and Action Conference" on 12 November 1999 in Delhi, which was attended by representatives of eight northern state governments. The conference underlined the point that states have to play an important role in the second phase of economic reforms and that the centre would not always be able to cover state deficits. States must manage their finances efficiently and attract private sector investment by improving the infrastructural facilities and services. In sum, contrary to some analyses (Sáez 2002, ch. 4), intergovernmental institutes are alive and well in India.

Union Agencies

The constitution makes provision for strong federal agencies, armed with considerable autonomy from governments at the centre and in the states. Among them are constitutionally entrenched agencies of the Comptroller and Auditor General of India, the Election Commission of India, and the Union and state public service commissions. All these agencies have responsibilities relating to the accounts, elections, and highest levels of civil services of both the Union and state governments. The incumbents of these offices have been guaranteed special constitutional protection as to their removal and emoluments. Their performance has generally been of a very high order, although the Bihar, Punjab, and Maharashtra Public Service Commissions have recently received bad press due to large-scale, corrupt practices in rigged examinations and venal public employments.

The Union Public Service Commission is responsible for the All-India Services (AISs). AISs are perhaps a unique feature of Indian federalism. They are federally recruited and trained by autonomous Union agencies and allocated to the states and the Union (on deputation). Their antecedence goes back to the British Indian Civil Service, which in turn may be traced back, in terms of being the highest echelons of bureaucracy, to the Mughal *mansabdari* system and the Maurya *mahamatta* system. The decision to create the first two All-India Services — the Indian Administrative Service (IAS) and the Indian Police Service (IPS) — was taken at a conference between the Union home minister, Sardar Ballabhabhai Patel, and provincial premiers in October 1946 called by the interim Government of India. Under article 309 of the constitution, the Parliament enacted the *All-India Services Act*, 1951, empowering the Union government to make rules in consultation with state governments for the regulation of All-India Services. Article 312 (2) makes the services, IAS and IPS, "deemed to be services created by Parliament." In consultation with the state governments, the Union government created a new All-India Service — Indian Forest Service — in 1966.

The tradition of having autonomous federal agencies established under the constitution prepared the way for autonomous statutory regulatory agencies when the market economy began in 1991.

Over the years there has been a tremendous proliferation of central agencies created by the Union government which have a significant impact upon centre-state relations, for example, the Reserve Bank of India (RBI), National Human Rights Commission (NHRC), National Minorities Commission (NMC), Central Vigilance Commission (CVC), Central Bureau of Investigation (CBI), and a number of central paramilitary forces such as the Central Reserve Police Force (CRPF), Central Industrial Security Force (CISF), Railway Protection Force (RPF), National Security Guard (NSG), Border Security Force (BSF), Assam Rifles, and Indo-Tibbetan Border Police (ITBP). Some of these agencies are created by Cabinet resolution, and some by parliamentary statutes.

In the backdrop of growing incidence of corruption and political vendetta, the judiciary in a recent historic judgement has intervened to lend greater autonomy from the Union executive's control to the CVC and CBI. (*Frontline*, 9 January 1998, p. 26).

Law and order being a state subject, state governments in the past have complained about deployment of central paramilitary forces in the states without their consent. But with the growing costs of maintaining law and order, the state governments are now demanding more and more deployment of central police forces within their jurisdictions.

Panchayats and Municipalities

Local political systems in India, after a "promising start," had been functioning unevenly in different units of the Indian federation. In 1993 local bodies were elevated from the statutory to the constitutional level. This was done by the seventy-third and seventy-fourth constitutional amendments (1992) relating to panchayats and municipalities respectively with a model legislation making it mandatory for the states to pass matching laws and holding regular elections under improved institutional and financial frameworks. A strong grassroots base would hopefully lead to a greater democratization and federalization of India. Panchayat Raj institutions have evoked a high degree of electoral participation. The seventy-third amendment is a pioneer in that it reserves one-third of the seats in the Panchayats for women (including the number of seats reserved for women belonging to the Scheduled Castes/Tribes), beginning a "silent revolution" (Mathew 1994). However, a qualitative transformation of local bodies into instruments of participatory and developmental agencies is yet to come. Nonetheless, it is more probable now than ever. In due course the Indian federal structure may become effectively one of three tiers of government.

Constitutional Amendments

The constitutional amendment procedure in India includes a flexible and centrally dominated process for territorial reorganization and incorporation, befitting a federation with previous internal boundaries dictated more by accidents of history than culture and geography. However, the core federal features of the constitution can only be amended by concomitant ratification by state legislatures. Judicial interventions and regionalization of the party system — both in Parliament and state legislatures — have further made constitutional amendments more difficult.

The federal provisions of the constitution may be amended by the following three procedures:

1. where it affects the admission or establishment of new states it can be done by simple legislative process by Parliament (article 2);
2. where it relates to the formation of new states and alteration of areas, boundaries or names of existing states it can be done by Parliament by the usual process of legislation but only after referring

the proposed bill to the affected state legislatures for expressing their views thereon (article 3); and

3. where it concerns the institutions of Union and state governments and division of powers and revenue resources between them, it can be done by Parliament by majority of the membership plus two-thirds majority of those present and voting in each House of Parliament and its ratification by the legislatures of at least half of the states (article 368).

The Indian constitution has been frequently amended but the changes have been rather marginal. In the judgements of the *Keshavananda Bharati* (1973) and *Minerva Mills* (1980) delivered by the Supreme Court of India, the amending power of the Parliament and/or aggregate legislatures have been forbidden to alter the "basic structure" of the constitution. The *Minerva Mills* judgement illustratively enumerates, among others, parliamentary federal features and judicial review as parts of the basic structure of the constitution.[4]

A "Federalarchy"?

Wheare (1964) pointed out an interesting contrast between the Canadian and Indian federations in the early 1960s by saying that although the constitution of Canada was quasi-federal, its governance had become federal in practice. However, in his assessment, both the constitution and government in India were quasi-federal. In my assessment, India by the 1990s had become more federal, as discussed below, despite its constitution, and the direction of this change continues into the new century. This change in federal functioning is largely attributable to two crucial factors, namely, the transformation of the Congress Party's dominance to a multi-party system of political pluralism with internal regional segmentation following the 1989 Lok Sabha election, and a new reorientation in judicial behaviour favouring an activist construction of judicial power supportive of the autonomy of states and human rights.

This federalization, however, has been reinforced by the economic liberalization in the 1990s and India's escalating integration into the global economy. With increasing deregulation and partial or full privatization of sectors of the economy, the administrative federal state is changing into a regulatory federal state, a theme to which we return in a subsequent section. Independent regulatory authorities under Union and state statutes are being created in sectors such as electricity, telecom, finance, etc., giving rise to a phenomenon called "sectoral federalism."[5]

Institutions of federal relevance like the president and the governors, intergovernmental agencies like the National Development Council and Inter-State Council (Saxena 2001), and Union agencies such as the Election Commission of India are much more autonomous and federally oriented in their role today than ever before (Mitra 1998, ch. 5). Moreover, the prime minister and his Cabinet colleagues, indeed the Parliament itself, today function in a more amicably federal configuration with significant participation of regional parties in state governments and Union coalition and/or minority governments (Singh 2001). Even the parliamentary component of the government is generally more receptive to federal sensibilities and interests, which is evident in the differentiated party configuration in the popular and federal chambers of Parliament. These effects are reinforced by the coalitional and/or minority nature of the governments in India since 1989, although the federal coalition governments got off to a very unstable and bumpy start under the Janata Dal-led National Front government, which consisted of regional parties in the Cabinet coalition supported by the Communist parties and the Hindu Right BJP.

One particularly telling indicator of the increased federalization in the 1990s is a definite decline in the incidence of president's rule in states during the decade (Singh 2002*a*). And this is despite the pressures on the governments in New Delhi by coalition partners to dismiss the governments of their adversaries in the states to settle political scores.[6] The manipulation of president's rule in states by the party or parties in power at the centre is made particularly difficult now. In the prevailing long tradition of gross misuse of this power by Union governments, irrespective of parties in power, the court has ruled that while the "satisfaction" of the president regarding the "breakdown of constitutional machinery" in a state contemplated in article 356 is "subjective in nature" to be exercised on Cabinet advice, it is a "conditional" rather than "absolute" power exercisable on the basis of some "relevant material."[7]

The process of federalization has been caused as well as conditioned by a phenomenal increase in the power of the judiciary in India. This trend is also reinforced by evident inactivity on the parts of the executive and legislative branches of governments. The court's power, of course, predates the federal thrust in the 1980s, especially since 1990. It was first in the late 1960s, when judicial activism on fundamental rights was initially seen, that a mild and brief wave of federalization was triggered by the defeat of the dominant Congress Party in the north Indian states in 1967. The judgement in *Golak Nath* v. *State of Punjab* (*AIR*, Supreme Court 1967, p. 1643) was delivered within days of the electoral result. Judicial activism receded during Indira Gandhi's authoritarian emergency regime, especially after the habeas corpus decision (1976), which conceded an unqualified power of the executive over life and liberty. The end of the emergency regime in 1980 "allowed the court to invite and collaborate with, especially, a complex of social movements, social activists, socially committed academics and investigative journalists in constructing its constituency" (Ramanathan 2002, p. 30). In the 1990s the court's activism expanded to target corruption in public life and to articulate environmental concerns in cities and elsewhere. However, confronted with conflicting interests, the court was faced with the dilemma of deciding which interests should be allowed to prevail. Evidently the court is liable to get drawn into political controversies, especially since there has been a tendency to become converted into "a gigantic clearinghouse of all [kinds] of major political questions."

It is an indicator of the temper of the times that the recommendations of the Sarkaria Commission Report on Centre-State Relations (1987–88)[8] for a more federally informed role on the part of the government functionaries has, after gathering dust for a period now returned to the forefront. Party system transformation, judicial intervention, federal empowerment of the constitutional functionaries, plus parliamentary empowerment of the speaker(s) has brought this miracle about.

In the period since the 1989 Lok Sabha election there has been a string of seven coalition/minority Union governments, more often both, punctuated by three mid-term elections (1991, 1998, and 1999) and one regular one (in 1996). These elections witnessed frequent electoral swings and realignments and shifting inter-party coalitions ranging from left-of-centre to right-of-centre. All these coalition governments have been minority dispensations, except the second Vajpayee government which is a majority, coalition arrangement. The number of parties participating in these coalitions have been as follows: National Front (1989–91), five; United Front (1996–98), ten; National Democratic Alliance (1998–99), 13; National Democratic Alliance (1999-to-date), 24. The NF and UF may be characterized as left-of-centre and NDA, right-of-centre. It is difficult to neatly characterize the Rao Congress regime (1991–96) as in the past the party was broadly left-of-centre, but it pioneered in initiating neo-conservative economic liberalization reforms in 1991 as a minority dispensation in the midst of a serious balance-of-payments crisis. Under successive coalition governments economic reforms have continued, with a slower pace by the UF (whose Cabinet or parliamentary allies included Communist parties adhering to economic nationalism), and faster by the NDA (in spite of BJP's professed commitment to protectionist *swadeshi* — Indian industries first).

All these federal, coalition governments have included regional or state parties alongside national ones. Major regional parties ruling in some states have kept their top leaders in state politics as chief ministers (e.g., J. Jayalalitha, M. Karunanidhi, N. Chandrababu Naidu, Prafulla Kumar Mahanta, Prakash Singh Badal, Farooq Abdullah, Naveen Patnaik) and sent second-rung leaders to join the Union governments whom they could attempt to control from the state capitals. This has often weakened the Union prime minister and the collective responsibility of the Cabinet to the Lok Sabha, particularly at a time (1990–2002) when the presidents happened to be leaders with a Congress past elected as multi-party consensus candidates, and the Rajya Sabha has been dominated by parties (mainly Congress) sitting on opposition side in the Lok Sabha. This has provided an exceptionally federalized matrix in Parliament and the state legislatures, and Union and state executives. Combined with an activist judiciary, this setting has made it possible for a regime that can only be described by a neo-logism, namely, "federalarchy."

Fiscal Federalism

Under the constitutional provisions and the processes of planning introduced in the early 1950s, fiscal federalism in India has been a highly centralized affair. Fiscal transfers from the centre to the states are made by the centre on the recommendations of the Finance Commission appointed every five years by the president of India (under article 280 of the constitution) and of the Planning Commission (a non-statutory central agency set up by Cabinet resolution in 1950). By and large, constitutionally sanctioned plan and non-plan transfers, are made on the recommendation of the Finance Commission, whereas other substantial transfers, often called discretionary, are made by the Planning Commission. The discretionary transfers include grants for state plans, allocation of finances from public financial institutions set up under the *Companies Act*, 1956, like the Life Insurance Corporation, General Insurance Corporation, and Unit Trust of India; loans and grants, and disaster reliefs; and grants from the Central Road Fund for maintenance of national highways.

Finance Commissions have enjoyed a considerable degree of legitimacy in federal relations as a constitutional body with mixed membership consisting of retired politicians, experts, and bureaucrats, more so than the Planning Commission, which is mainly a body of bureaucrats and politicians. The role of the Planning Commission has become partly diluted under the accelerating economic liberalization since 1991, but it has managed to survive these reforms as a government think-tank and an agency coordinating the relationship between the governments and the private sector: domestic and global. With the decline in public investment in economic liberalization at Union and state levels and gradual deregulation and privatization, there is less for the Planning Commission to plan. According to an official of the Commission, it does one-third of what it used to do.[9] "During the heyday of planning, [the government] attempted to implement the Plan objectives, but since 1991 the budget has been the main forum for articulating the strategy of [economic] transition" (M.G. Rao 2002, p. 10).

Despite its wider legitimacy, even the Finance Commission reports appear to reflect changes in electoral equations and party system transformations. For example, beginning with the fourth Finance Commission Report (1965) there was a trend of increasing the net proceeds of non-corporate income tax distributed to the states: from 60 to 75 percent (Rao and Chelliah 1996a, Annexure I). This happened around the 1967 general elections in which the hitherto dominant Congress Party lost in half of the then 16 states. Furthermore, in the distribution of the states' share in the net yield from Union excise duties, the percentage of the states' share jumped from 20 to 45 in the seventh Finance Commission Report (1978) (Rao and Chelliah 1996a, Annexure II). This happened after the Congress Party suffered its first electoral defeat in the 1977 Lok Sabha election. Thus, the pattern of devolution of the two major taxes — the only ones shared between the centre and the states before the eightieth amendment to the constitution in 2000 — subtly reflected the new political realities of the transformed party systems in the states and in the Union under federal coalition governments with strong regional representation. After the constitution's (eightieth) amendment (2000) the Union's entire tax revenue receipt became shareable with the states. The eleventh Finance Commission (2000–05) fixed the aggregate share of the states in the centre's divisible pool at 29.5 percent.[10]

The transfer of fiscal resources by the centre to the states had been heavily weighted in favour of more populous and economically backward states. Beginning with the tenth Finance Commission (1995–2000) the formula for transfer has been revised to a limited extent to reward efficiency and performance by the states. But the more developed states clamour for more revision. Economic liberalization and federalization have been reducing the capacity of the centre to curb regional economic disparities, which may be aggravated further in the years ahead.

Moreover, the eleventh Finance Commission also recommended the transfer of Rs. 1,600 crores and Rs. 400 crores for panchayatas and municipalities respectively to the states from the centre (Report of the eleventh Finance Commission for 2000–2005, paras. 6.16 and 8.27). This was the first occasion that a Finance Commission devoted a full chapter in its report to the problem of fiscal transfers to the local bodies. The seventy-third and seventy-fourth constitutional amendments since 1993 also require each state government to appoint a state Finance Commission to consider and make recommendations on the financing of local self-governing institutions.

INDIA'S GLOBAL AND REGIONAL INTEGRATION

For historical and contemporary reasons India's global and regional integration has been limited. Earlier committed to the policy of national self-reliance, even today India is a cautiously and gradually globalizing country. Indeed, the East Asian financial meltdown (1997), which affected India less severely, has reinforced its cautious approach. Because of regional tensions and the fear by South Asian countries of India's dominance in the region — which does not, however, result in an anti-India action — even regional integration of India via the South Asian Association for Regional Cooperation (SAARC) is limited. Nevertheless, being centrally placed, India shares land or sea borders with all its South Asian neighbours, which, in turn, generally do not have common borders.

India's global trade data are presented in Table 2. Computing percentages on the raw statistics, we find that India's largest exports in 1998 (the year for which complete figures are available) were with the industrial countries: 56.56 percent. Its largest imports were from developing countries: 51.36 percent.

As a region, South Asia is comparatively more integrated in global than in regional terms. Even though the entire region has a common Indian civilizational heritage and a common British hegemony in the late nineteenth and first half of the twentieth centuries, South Asia today is more pulled apart than pulled together. Early efforts by the British Commonwealth of Nations to promote regional cooperation among South and Southeast Asian nations in the 1950s in the form of the Colombo Plan soon petered out (Mendis 1991, pp. 1-2). Another major move in this direction was late in coming. SAARC was organized in 1985. Although it has survived so far and made some progress both in terms of institutionalization — it has now a common secretariat located in Kathmandu — and trade relations, it is constantly plagued by bilateral issues of conflict, especially between India and Pakistan and mostly over Kashmir. It has so far held nine summits marked by considerable enthusiasm and rhetoric. But the summit for 2000 was postponed because of the Kargil war between India and Pakistan and the subsequent military coup in Pakistan.

Security concerns in South Asia are festering thorns in the regional flesh. While India has been inclined to keep external powers out of the region, some South Asian countries are receptive to them as counterpoise to India's dominance in the region (Mendis 1991). Under President Clinton, the United States shifted its South Asia Policy toward India, recognizing India's preponderance in the region to block Islamic fundamentalism and China in Asia and the world at large, although the United States was forced to work closely with Pakistan in its post-9/11 anti-terrorism policy.

Intra-SAARC trade has been limited and to an extent was even declining until 1989 (Chisti 1994, p. 231). However, there was a major breakthrough in trade relations among the SAARC members with the signing of the South Asian Preferential Trade Agreement (SAPTA) at the seventh SAARC summit in Dhaka in 1993. With all the member countries having ratified the agreement, SAPTA went into effect on 7 December 1995, the date marking the completion of the first decade of SAARC's existence. India's total, as well as preferential, trade with Sri Lanka, Bangladesh, and Pakistan in 1996–97 were

TABLE 2

India's Global Exports and Imports, 1998 and 1999
(millions of US dollars)

	Exports		Imports	
	1998	1999	1998	1999[1]
World Total				
IFS Data[2]	33,626	26,829	42,742	32,806
DOTS Data[3]	36,674 [y]	28,704 [y]	43,409 [y]	33,303 [y]
Industrial Countries	20,742 [y]	16,733 [y]	20,922 [y]	15,394 [y]
Major Partners				
United States	7,682 [T]	6,539 [v]	3,968 [T]	3,045 [v]
Canada	574 [T]	523 [v]	240 [T]	212 [v]
Australia	415 [T]	316 [v]	1,526 [T]	817 [v]
Japan	1,888 [T]	1,518 [v]	2,659 [T]	1,949 [v]
Belgium	1,223 [T]	993 [v]	2,827 [T]	2,631 [v]
France	1,002 [T]	817 [y]	857 [T]	692
Germany	2,118 [T]	1,579 [v]	2,411 [T]	1,630 [v]
Italy	1,244 [T]	940 [y]	1,202 [T]	948 [y]
Netherlands	689 [T]	560 [vy]	472 [T]	420 [v]
United Kingdom	2,090 [T]	1,585 [v]	2,397 [T]	1,940 [v]
Developing Countries	15,226 [y]	11,508 [y]	22,296 [y]	17,737 [y]
Major Partners and South Asia				
Nigeria	197 [T]	133 [y]	1,115 [T]	834 [y]
Bangladesh	1,038 [T]	852 [vy]	65 [T]	44 [v]
China PR: Mainland	858 [T]	554	1,192 [T]	846 [vy]
China PR: Hongkong	1,703 [T]	1,507 [v]	690 [T]	855 [v]
Indonesia	543 [T]	402 [y]	740 [T]	566 [y]
Korea	522 [T]	379 [y]	1,793 [T]	1,323 [y]
Malaysia	399 [T]	339 [vy]	2,059 [T]	1,299 [v]
Nepal	324 [T]	238 [y]	147 [T]	103 [y]
Pakistan	137 [T]	104 [vy]	217 [T]	159 [vy]
Singapore	553 [T]	480 [v]	2,496 [T]	2,042 [v]
Sri Lanka	534 [T]	378 [y]	45 [T]	37 [y]
Europe	1,445 [y]	1,066 [y]	1,214 [y]	1,265 [y]
Russia	633 [T]	409 [v]	693 [T]	803 [v]
Middle East	3,583 [y]	2,558 [y]	6,898 [y]	5,046 [y]
Western Hemisphere -Latin America	767 [y]	536 [y]	727 [y]	803 [y]
Oil Exporting Countries	3,506 [y]	2,493 [y]	7,384 [y]	5,493 [y]
Non-Oil Developing Countries	11,719 [y]	9,015 [y]	14,912 [y]	12,245 [y]

Notes: 1. Data available for the first three-quarters of the year.
2. Data published in *International Financial Statistics*.
3. Data published in *Direction of Trade Statistics*.
[y]Consolidated data estimated by other methods, sometimes including the use of partner records; also used in world and area totals.
[T]One to five months of reported data and 7–11 months of estimates.
[v]Consolidated data derived solely from partner records.

Source: IMF (2000, Intro. and pp. 121-22).

balanced in the sense of exports paying for the imports, except for a deficit (Rs. –555.75 millions) in preferential trade with Bangladesh.

There is considerable contact and movement of people across the borders in South Asia despite cross-border terrorism from Pakistan against Indian and Tamil separatist activities in Sri Lanka. India is indeed afflicted with illegal migrants, especially from Bangladesh, Nepal, and Pakistan. There is a regular bus service between India, Nepal, Bhutan, and Bangladesh. Pakistan has train service, now supplemented by bus. This service opened with much fanfare and the Indian prime minister, Atal Behari Vajpayee, travelled to Lahore in the spring of 1999. This goodwill has subsequently been threatened by the Kargil war in the same year and by the strained relations following the allegedly Pakistan-supported terrorist attacks on the Assembly in Srinagar and Parliament in New Delhi in the winter and spring of 2002. Well-meaning Indians and Pakistanis believe that the cold war between the two governments can be contained by Track-II Diplomacy at the personal level. Furthermore, after its war in Afghanistan, the US has attempted to reduce the influence of militant Islamic groups in Pakistan, including groups fighting against India in Kashmir.

The extent of global trade links in South Asian countries is evident from Table 3. India, due to its sheer size, naturally accounts for the largest global exports and imports in gross terms, both in merchandise and commercial services. However, when we consider the figures for the export of the percentage of total manufactured goods, all South Asian countries represented here are ahead of India. In view of the large domestic market in India, this is to be expected.

THE IMPACT OF GLOBAL AND REGIONAL INTEGRATION

State and Market

Since economic reforms in India were necessitated by a severe balance-of-payment crisis in 1991, we may start our discussion here with the impact of these reforms on this aspect of Indian economy. Although the country's exports expanded in the 1990s — from $23,028 million (7.13 percent of GDP) in 1990 to $47,419 million (10.31 percent of GDP) in 1998 — its imports expanded more rapidly — from $31,485 million (9.75 percent of

TABLE 3
Global Trade Links in South Asia

Country	Merchandise		Merchandise		Merchandise Trade Balance	Export of Commercial Services Millions of $	Import of Commercial Services Millions of $	Trade Balance in Commercial Services
	Millions of $	Mfg. % of Total	Millions of $	Mfg. % of Total				
India	33,626	74	42,742	55	-9,116	11,067	14,1902	-3,125
Pakistan	8,594	84	9,415	55	-821	1,473	2,468	-995
Sri Lanka	4,735	*	5,917	**	-1,182	888	1,325	-437
Bangladesh	3,831	91	6,974	69	-3,143	252	1,180	-928
Nepal	474	90	1,245	42	-771	433	189	244

Notes: 1. Data about Bhutan and Maldives are not available in the source.
2. Data regarding Mfg. of total merchandise exports and imports in relation to Sri Lanka are not available for 1998. However, the missing values here for 1990 were 54 and 65 respectively.
3. Trade balance computed from data available in the source.

Source: World Bank (2001, pp. 312-13, Table 20).

GDP) to $59,138 million (12.90 percent of GDP) in the same period (World Bank 2001, Table 15, p. 302). Thus, the adverse trade balance worsened from $–8,457 million in 1990 to $–11,719 million in 1998. But India's gross international reserves position considerably improved from $5,637 million in 1990 to $32,667 million in 1999 (World Bank 2001, p. 302).

There was an increase in India's GDP from $322,737 million in 1990 to $459,765 million in 1995. The structure of output in the economy has also been changing. The share of agriculture in the GDP declined from 31 to 28 percent, but so have the shares of industries and manufacturing — from 27 to 25 percent and 17 to 16 percent respectively. The service sector (including freight, insurance, travel, transport, communications, and financial services) is now the largest component of the economy: 42 percent in 1990 and 46 percent in 1999 (World Bank 2001, pp. 296-97, Table 12).

The impact of economic liberalization is also evident on the Indian economy in the growing share of private investment in the gross domestic fixed investment (up from 56.7 percent in 1990 to 70.1 percent in 1997), higher stock market capitalization (up from $38,567 million in 1990 to $184,605 million in 1999), a jump in the number of listed domestic companies (from 2,435 in 1990 to 5,863 in 1998), and a hike in foreign direct investment (from $162 million in 1990 to $2,635 million in 1997). The state subsidies as a percentage of the total expenditure have also registered a modest decline from 43 percent in 1990 to 40 percent in 1999 (ibid., pp. 304-07).

India's global as well as its regional integration has still been rather limited. Its failure to globalize may be largely explained in terms of its inability to control the fiscal deficit (–7.5 percent in 1990 and –5.2 percent in 1998) (World Bank 2001, Table 14) and break the stagnation of the economy, and secondly, its failure to bring about conditions of sustainable economic growth reflected in a very slow change in the composition of its export and low and declining rate of foreign direct investment (FDI). In 1990–91, the year before the acceleration of economic reforms in 1991, India's exports were dominated by agricultural goods (24 percent) and light manufacturing products (54.2 percent); sophisticated manufactures formed 21.8 percent. By 1999–2000 the share of agriculture declined to 17 percent, light manufacturing remained at 54.2 percent, while sophisticated manufactured commodities had registered only a modest increase, moving up to 29.8 percent. FDI inflows also were very tardy. Between 1991 and 1998, they actually reached only 21.7 percent of the $55 billion of FDI approvals. Except for some investments in telecommunications and the final failure of Enron's Dabhol power project, the bulk of this inflow stopped short of establishing new enterprises exporting to global markets. Instead, the inflows were used to gain a majority share in existing foreign enterprises still hooked onto the huge Indian market (Jha 2002, p. 16). India failed to attract foreign investment despite its low labour costs because it could not supplement this advantage "by creating the infrastructure and institutions of advanced capitalism in the country as a whole," nor has it "tried to do so in the limited area of special economic zones either" (ibid.). Besides opening up a decade earlier than India, China was assisted by its diaspora with expatriate investment which pioneered export-led growth in labour-intensive manufacturing in Taiwan, Hong Kong, and Singapore. Later, when wages rose steeply in these locations, industries moved into China bringing huge amounts of foreign investment. This Chinese experience was not replicated in India — neither in terms of phase nor volume (Srinivasan 2002, review in *The Hindu*, 30 April 2002, p. 17).

India's integration within the region is limited due to inter-state rivalries and backward national economies in a backward region. Barring limited enclaves of affluence, mass poverty is considerable in all South Asian countries. The percentage of the population below the national poverty line is quite sizeable. Due to this degree of mass poverty as well as low productivity South Asia Preferential Trade Agreement (SAPTA) has not really picked up. Despite reducing preferential tariffs by India at a rate faster than its regional partners, there is no surge in imports "partly due to inelasticity of supplies in exporting countries" (Mukherji 2001, p. 306). Kewal *et al.* point out why South Asian Free Trade Agreement (SATA), which is to follow SAPTA, may not be a big deal. For the exports of almost all the economies of the region largely consist of the same kind of products, for example, agricultural commodities and basic manufactures. So there is little scope of mutual trade, trade complementarity, and intra-trade linkages.

Federal Institutional Innovations

There has been a greater impact of global than regional integration on the Indian federal system. The effects of economic reforms and transnationalization are evident in areas such as industrial delicensing; financial sector reforms in banking, the stock market, and the insurance sector; telecommunications; electricity; mass media; etc.

Moreover, through a more open communications policy — the open skies of the 1990s in the field of electronic mass media — globalization has simultaneously affected cultural identities in favour of global and local cultures and weakened the national culture with its centralizing overtones. Until the 1980s the official electronic media played a strong centralizing role in India. Though their regional stations in the states catered to local languages, there was considerable national content in their news. Now the field is wide open to national as well as international private TV channels as well as direct-to-home telecasts (DHT). Book printing has opened up in India, though newspapers and magazines are excluded from foreign ownership by a 1955 Cabinet resolution of the Nehru government. Debates have often been triggered by the central government's intention to liberalize the print mass media as well, but it continues to be restricted.[11]

An analysis of the impact of economic reforms on federalism must take into account the Seventh Schedule of the constitution dealing with the division of powers and revenue resources between the centre and the states. For example, industries figure in Union, State, as well as Concurrent Lists. Entries seven and 52 of the exclusive Union List include industries declared by the laws of Parliament as "necessary for the purpose of defence or for the prosecution of war" and "expedient in public interest" to be under the control of the central government. Subject to the above limitations, industries are on the exclusive State List, entry 24. However, factories are on the Concurrent List under entry 36. Economic and social planning is entry 20 of the Concurrent List. In the era of centralized development planning, industry was heavily under the control of the Government of India. Gradual deregulation of industrial licensing has provided a new opening to the state governments which now compete with each other to invite industrialists, both Indian and foreign, to invest in their states. The capitals of more developed states are now frequent destinations for visiting foreign dignitaries, including former US President Bill Clinton and World Bank President James D. Wolfensohn, along with many industrialists. Even the backward states offer incentives of expeditious land acquisitions, tax holidays, and "congenial" labour relations to those willing to locate their industries there. A few years ago, the

Government of Maharashtra hosted a conference of Australian entrepreneurs in Mumbai. In 1996 the United Front finance minister, P. Chidambaram, goaded by Telugu Desam Chief Minister Chandrababu Naidu, decided to have the World Bank focus directly on the states with the centre only playing the role of facilitator. In November 2000 Wolfensohn, during his visit to India, spent more time in the states than in New Delhi! Jenkins (1999, pp. 134-35) cites the fierce competition between the relatively developed states of Tamil Nadu and Maharashtra to induce the location of the Ford Fiesta assembly plant in their respective territories with Tamil Nadu finally winning in 1996. The estimated sales tax concessions offered to that multinational alone were placed at Rs. 2.9 billion. Deregulation in this area has notionally increased the autonomy of the states and reduced the centre's relative powers. But the competitive disadvantage suffered in this area by backward states is likely to worsen regional economic disparities even more than at present.

India's integration within has not produced any great impact on its federal institutions, except for some consultative role for the states in external matters of direct concern to them. Examples are Kerala in relation to the coffee trade, West Bengal in relation to the jute trade and the sharing of international river waters with Bangladesh, Bihar in relation to Nepal, and to Tamil Nadu in relation to Sri Lanka.

Globalization has had a mixed impact on the process of federalization in India. On the one hand, economic liberalization increases the autonomy of not only the private sector but also the state governments in the area of economic activities. On the other, when the central government signed the international trade agreement at the conclusion of the Uruguay Round of global trade negotiations and joined the World Trade Organization (WTO) in 1995 it bound the states in the Indian Union as well to the treaty obligations thus entailed. True, international trade is a Union jurisdiction, but some international multilateral treaty obligations such as the reduction of subsidies in agriculture, a state subject, also circumscribe the policy options of state governments. For the states cannot institute divergent policy regimes even in their exclusive jurisdictions functionally intermeshed with concurrent and Union subjects. Two cases — one each from the states of Tamil Nadu and Punjab — are pending before the Supreme Court precisely on the point of treaty-making power of the Union in the wake of the WTO regime.[12]

Since telecommunications, the stock market, insurance, and electronic mass media are Union areas, institutional innovations like the Telecom Regulatory Authority of India (TRAI), the Insurance Regulatory Development Authority (IRDA), and the Security and Exchange Board of India (SEBI) created under Acts of Parliament in the 1990s are central agencies with considerable autonomy from the government. The state governments have no role in them, but the entire economy is affected by these regulatory authorities. TRAI and IRDA regulate the pace of privatization as well as arbitrate conflicting interests of governments, the private sector, and consumers either themselves or through appellate tribunals set up under the Acts, subject to judicial review.

Another similar institutional innovation was introduced by the *Information Technology Act*, 2000, in response to the "need for legal changes" required by "the new communication systems" such as electronic commerce that "eliminate the need for paper-based transactions" "which should bear signatures" (Introduction to the Act, p. 1). The Act confers legal recognition on digital signatures and electronic records. As a signatory to the Model Law on Electronic Commerce adopted by the United Nations Commission on International Trade Law in 1996, India has now fulfilled its obligation to make suitable changes in its trade laws. The Act empowers the central government to frame rules and regulations in regard to e-commerce which would become effective after publication in the *Official Gazette* or *Electronic Gazette*. It also provides for the appointment of a Cyber Regulations Advisory Committee by the central government.

The *Information Technology Act* does not create an independent regulatory authority like, say, TRAI. The central government itself has reserved the authority to make regulations that are required to be placed before Parliament for approval, without, however, jeopardizing the validity of anything previously done under that regulation. However, the Act provides for the setting up of the Cyber Regulations Appellate Tribunal (CRAT) with considerable autonomy. The awards of the tribunal are subject to judicial review. Article 90 of the *Information Technology Act* prompts the state governments to make rules to carry out the provisions of the Act which are subject to approval by the state legislatures.

Proposals to create central regulatory authorities are being worked out for oil and gas as well as for coal. Political economists are already sounding warnings to avoid conflict between regulatory authorities in closely interlinked sectors of the economy. The report of the competition committee, appointed to study the anti-competitive behaviour of firms, has recently proposed a new competition regulatory commission, whose jurisdiction must avoid inherent conflict with other regulatory commissions. In the opinion of one observer: "The correct thing would have been to make them part of one regulatory commission. But the bifrucation of ministries in the Union government will prevent this obvious correction." This analyst goes on to lament "a continuing lack of clarity about the respective roles of the Comptroller and Auditor General (CAG) and the industry regulators created for the purpose of regulating tariffs" (S.L. Rao 2002, p. 6).

The most interesting developments involving the centre and the states alike have occurred in the era of economic liberalization in the power sector. Electricity is included in the Concurrent List, while taxes on the consumption or sale of electricity are part of the State List in the Seventh Schedule of the constitution. Economic reforms have brought power sector reforms onto the active agendas of governments and business. The central government convened two conferences of chief ministers on this issue. The consensus arrived at in these meetings led to the adoption of the Common Minimum National Action Plan for the power sector. This plan considered it "necessary to create a regulatory commission as a step to arrest deteriorating conditions of the State Electricity Boards and to make plans for the future developments" (Introduction, *Electricity Regulatory Commissions Act* 1998) (ERC Act).

The electricity sector in India was developed until recently as a government monopoly. Over the decades it has run into a serious crisis situation. The Statement of Objects and Reasons to the first major parliamentary enactment, the ERC Act (1998) mentioned above, listed the following as the "fundamental issues" relating to the power sector: "the lack of rational retail tariffs, the high level of cross-subsidies, poor planning and operation, inadequate capacity, the neglect of the consumer, the limited involvement of private sector skills and resources and the absence of independent regulatory authority." As the first step in institutional reform, the Act set up the Central Electricity Regulatory Commission (CERC) as a corporate body consisting of a chairperson and three other members appointed by the central government on the recommendation of an independent selection committee. The incumbents of CERC are required to be persons with knowledge and experience and capability in the fields of engineering, law, economics, commerce, finance or management. The chairperson is to be appointed from amongst persons who are or have been judges of the Supreme Court or Chief Justices of a high court. All appointments to the commission are to be made only after consultation with the Chief Justice of India. The Act takes care to ensure the independence and autonomy of the chairman and members of the commission by guaranteeing them security of service and emoluments.

The CERC is empowered by the Act to regulate the tariffs of electricity-generating companies in the central government sector, including those that are part of composite schemes for generation and sale of electricity in more than one state. It also regulates inter-state transmission of energy. In the new climate of experimentation with disinvestment and privatization the CERC is expected "to promote competition, efficiency and economy in the activities of the electricity industry" (clause 13, section d of the Act). The Act also provides for a 31-member central advisory committee giving representation to the interests of commerce, industry, transport, agriculture, labour, consumers, non-governmental organizations, and academic and research organizations in the field. Appeals against the decisions of the commission to the high court is permissible. The Act also enabled the state governments to set up State Electricity Regulatory Commissions to ensure their integrity and autonomy to depoliticize the pricing and distribution of power.

Following the establishment of CERC in 1998, several states also set up SERCs. The process is still under way. After a series of formal and informal consultations the central government convened a meeting of power ministers in February 2000. The centre's proposal for federal legislation ensuring uniform patterns and standards was resisted by several states. Yet there was some consensus in favour of the centre's recommendation for "unbundling" and trifurcation of the State Electricity Boards (SEBs) mired in the populist politics of ruling parties in states and resulting in huge subsidies, heavy theft and loss of electricity in transmission, and predatory trade unionism among the employees. Trifurcation aims at entrusting generation, transmission, and distribution of electricity to separate corporations, some private and some public.

Citing the lack of public funds for investment in the power sector, privatization is parroted by governments as the solution. But there are few who are interested in privatization. There is not only an economic but also a political dimension to the problem involved. This is illustrated by the classic case of the Dabhol power project in Maharashtra undertaken by the US company Enron. The power sector in Maharashtra is one of the most advanced utility suppliers in the country. But even there Enron started operating only after getting a counter guarantee from the Government of India as well as from the state government. The Enron project, although sanctioned by a Congress government in the state, was cancelled by the Shiv Sena-BJP government that was subsequently voted to power. However, the successor government finally renegotiated the deal with some changes. Enron went into operation, but the Maharashtra government wanted another review as the company's electricity was very expensive, nearly double the prevalent rate in India. Enron withdrew, and later went out of business for reasons not exclusively related to its Indian venture.

There is an interesting success story of a domestic private sector company, but with a smaller scale of operation. Tata Power has been generating, transmitting, and distributing electricity in metropolitan Mumbai since 1910. In 2001 it made a hefty 11.6 percent margin on sales of Rs. 3,361 crores. Incidentally, Tata Power, far from stampeding to leave India's power sector, is one of the bidders for the beleaguered Dabhol Power Company promoted by Enron Corporation.

Some hastily crafted independent power producers (IPP) programs in some sates have been self-defeating for the State Electricity Boards "because in a situation where *basic* reform [curbing political interference and pilferage] was not pursued, private parties have successfully shifted nearly all risks on to the state sector." This kind of half-hearted privatization can be neither sustainable nor exhaustive of its full potentiality (Morris 2000, p. 1915).

Beginning with Orissa, several states have already set up independent regulatory authorities in the power sector. With some variations, most SERCs are designed to perform the basic function of determining the retail or distribution tariffs (Sankar and Ramachandra 2000, p. 1827). An analysis of the early tariff orders of SERCs suggests that tariff fixation has been mostly based on the following principles: (i) the cost of service methodology is the most appropriate for the determination of tariffs; (ii) efficiency gains can neutralize the need for realignment of tariffs to efficient levels; (iii) the developer must share the burden of adjustment under the reform process; and (iv) the burden of subsidies on public finance can decrease through reforms (Ahluwalia 2000, p. 3407). The study, however, questions the validity of the above assumptions, especially in

India. Its conclusion is: "The need of the hour is to forge partnerships across countries, states, agencies and institutions. In the end tariff reform has to ensure stability, continuity, efficiency and equity." It also advocates "an inclusive, participative, transparent and forward looking policy process" (ibid., p. 3419).

To sum up, the recent economic reforms in India are marked more by the replacement of bureaucratic regulation by autonomous regulatory authorities and partial privatization than by globalization of trade and investment. To the extent that decontrol and privatization reduce the intervention of the federal state in the affairs of industry, business, and state governments, the forces of federalization (in contrast to parliamentary executive centralization) have been reinforced. Another notable development in the era of new economic reforms has been the creation of semi-judicial regulatory authorities at Union and state levels under legislative enactments in sectors such as electricity, telecommunications, etc. These agencies have replaced direct bureaucratic control by government departments in functionally intermeshed Union and state jurisdictions in certain sectors. Since this emerging centrist sectoral federalism tends to move away from the kind of "cooperative federalism" that has existed in the domain of political federalism for so long, it is imperative to curb jurisdictional conflicts. In Sáez's (2000) assessment India's federal relations are in for a change "from cooperative federalism to interjurisdictional competition." In view of the deepening cultural conflicts, this apprehension may not be too exaggerated. But India has a way of living in crisis.

FEDERAL AND CONFEDERAL CONCENTRIC CIRCLES

This section analyzes and speculates about the trends and prospects of India's supranational federal integration in regional and global economic, security, and political networks. India finds itself enmeshed in four orders of layered relations: (i) internal federal relations among states and nationalities constituting India's multicultural federal nation, (ii) associational South Asian regional orders of bilateral and multilateral integration, (iii) competing or complementary linkages between India and South Asian countries and powers external to the region, and (iv) India's United Nations connection.

In each of these relational segments India has adopted variable but complementary strategies of ordering its domestic and foreign policies. In the segment designated as internal federalism the objective has been the consolidation of the multi-ethnic Indian nation-state premised on parliamentary federal constitutionalism. Excessive centralization under the Indira Gandhi regime at least partly aggravated militancy in Jammu and Kashmir and Punjab and engendered milder protests elsewhere. These dysfunctionalities brought forth the systemic response of federalization and decentralization of the 1990s that still continues.

In the confederal relational segment India has pursued the double-pronged strategy of bilateral as well as multilateral relations in the South Asia and Asia-Pacific regions. India's multilateral relations in Asia have especially burgeoned since Prime Minister P.V. Narasimha Rao's Look East Policy (Wadhva 1999, pp. 40-54). Besides playing a leading yet constrained role in SAARC, India is now also a member of the ASEAN Regional Forum and a dialogue partner with observer status in Asia-Pacific Economic Cooperation (APEC).[13]

In the competing global relations segment the most important powers with particular relevance to South Asia are the United States, Russia, and China. With the recent shift in the US policy toward India, especially since the mutual visits of former President Bill Clinton and the Indian Prime Minister Atal Behari Vajpayee in the spring and autumn of 2000, and the revival of India-Russia "strategic" ties during the Russian President Vladimir Putin's trip to New Delhi later the same year, Pakistan could seek elusive security in drawing still closer to Islamic fundamentalism and China. As it happened, Pakistan reverted to the past pattern of closer ties with the US and other global powers in flushing out the Taliban regime in Afghanistan. In the changed scenario the United States as well as the major global and Eurasian powers appear keen to take a more balanced and legal stance in their relations with India and Pakistan.

That India is not an expansionist power is evident from the fact that it has routinely returned the lands captured from Pakistan in the 1960s, and did not stay in Bangladesh, Sri Lanka, and Malle after its legitimate interventions, by provocation in the first instance and the latter two by invitation (in 1971, 1987, and 1988 respectively). It also fought to remove the Pakistani intrusions in the Kargil sector in 1999 on its land without crossing the Line of Control in Jammu and Kashmir at any point, a restraint for which it received diplomatic acclaim worldwide. The spectre of a war, at a time when India and Pakistan have both become nuclear power states since May 1998, still haunts the region. The developed world would do well to support democracy and development in South Asia in the interest of regional and global peace. Only sustained peace would create conditions for greater regional and global economic integration in South Asia.

Although the United Nations and its initiatives for the UN Conference on Trade and Development (UNCTAD) and New International Economic Order (NIEO) have been marginalized by a globalization led by the highly industrialized nations of the world in the WTO, India still continues to attach due importance to the UN world body as an agency for peace and security and multilateral cooperation for tackling common global goals like disarmament, human rights, ecology, and control of narco-terrorism. India's candidature for a permanent seat on the UN Security Council has been supported by the US and Russia, among others.

THE EFFECT OF ALTERNATIVE SCENARIOS OF GLOBAL GOVERNANCE ON INDIAN FEDERALISM

The history of India is a story of endurance. It is an epic empire that has survived over 5,000 years. It will undoubtedly be just fine in 15 years, regardless of what happens to the rest of the world. As a civilization unto itself, India can live in peaceful cooperation with other nations, or it can survive happily on its own. The question we deal with next is how Indian federalism might be affected by the four scenarios for global governance outlined in chapter 1. To do this, the text immediately below speculates (tells a hypothetical story) about how each global scenario might be experienced in India looking out to the year 2015 and how that experience in turn might influence Indian federalism.

We begin with the *shared governance* scenario. It entails a regulated world but with power widely dispersed. Looking backward from 2015, India's preferred foreign policy orientation, *Pansheel Raj*, can be seen as the real foundation of the shared governance scenario. The five principles of *pansheel* are mutual respect for territorial integrity and sovereignty, non-aggression, non-interference, equality and mutual benefit, and peaceful coexistence. India promoted these principles selflessly after the Bandung Afro-Asian conference in 1955. It just took 60 years for the West to accept these basic principles of international governance.

With the global acceptance of *pansheel raj*, India was finally able to convince the other great powers that it was in their interests to accept an elimination of nuclear weapons, and other weapons of mass destruction. India consequently endorsed the Non-Proliferation Treaty and the Comprehensive Test Ban Treaty and dismantled its nuclear arsenal. (Pakistan was forced to sign the respective treaties and dismantle its nuclear weapons, in exchange for a massive IMF bailout in 2006.) India contributed greatly to the development of international shared governance with its steadfast opposition to Islamic fundamentalism and terrorism in the first decade of the new century.

The stable regional and global environment created by international shared governance allowed India to complete and consolidate the dramatic federalization process that began in the 1990s. With a more stable global and regional environment, the centre grew less suspicious of state autonomy movements, while at the same time the states came to trust the central government as truly representative of India in international forums. The states also recognized that it was simply more efficacious to have one government representing all of India in these organizations. In short, the emergence of shared governance internationally facilitated the development of shared governance domestically in India. Sixty-eight years after independence, India finally obtained the optimal federal and constitutional arrangements envisioned by Nehru and Ambedkar in 1950.

The *global club* scenario entails extensive regulation with power highly concentrated. Again looking back from 2015, it has become quite clear that India blasted its way into the global club in May 1998, when it detonated five nuclear devices. Although the United States and other nations protested the Indian action, President Clinton's visit to India in 1999 actually signalled India's entry into the global club. While American Republicans historically tended to denigrate India, they came to realize in the early years of the twenty-first century that they needed a reliable partner to balance the role of China in Asia. The 11 September 2001 (9/11) terrorist attacks against the United States demonstrated to sceptical Americans that India was an important bulwark against Islamic fundamentalism in Asia. Furthermore, many Americans discovered that the Indians were actually much better capitalists than the Chinese, and they spoke better English.

India has envisioned itself as a global club member since independence; its entry into the club at the turn of the century was the realization of a national dream. India's global club status has had a mixed impact on centre-state relations. On the one hand, Delhi has become a much stronger player internationally and this strengthened its position vis-à-vis the states, especially in relation to international treaties and their implementation in India. On the other hand, the improved security context for India as a whole and Delhi's new found confidence caused it to be less suspicious of the more autonomist state governments.

India has actually lived in the *regional dominators* scenario (concentrated power but not heavy global regulation) since 1971 when it decisively defeated West Pakistan and liberated Bangladesh. This event was significant for two reasons. First, Pakistan finally realized that it could never defeat India militarily. Second, the other states in South Asia discovered that India had no intention of conquering the region. Regional dominators is the status quo scenario for India.

The 9/11 terrorist attacks confirmed India's long-maintained position that Islamic fundamentalism in Pakistan and Afghanistan was a grave international security threat. By 2001, the centre had waged war against Islamic terrorism for 12 years in Kashmir, and this conflict followed on the heels of unrest in Punjab. The government of India was certain that both these conflicts had been aided and abetted by the Government of Pakistan and, at least indirectly, the Government of China. As such, the Government of India has felt compelled to maintain a vigorous position against regional competitors, as well as troublesome states within the Indian federation. While there have been no major wars on India's borders over the past 15 years, and no other states have overtly pursued secession, the Government of India has had no choice but to maintain, and employ when necessary, the emergency provisions of the constitution, which essentially subvert the federal character of the constitution. With the uncertain regional context, and with the fear that India's external enemies may seek to exploit regional animosities in India, the centre will continue to forestall the federalization of the country for the foreseeable future.

The fourth scenario examined is *cyberwave*. India in the 1990s was not dissimilar to this scenario (little regulation and dispersed power) and it demonstrated not only the ability to survive but to thrive in this environment. India has endured the assassination of prime ministers and former prime ministers; the imprisonment of former prime ministers; insurgencies and criminal gangs, and the complete fractionalization of both federal and state party systems. It is well practised in the politics of uncertainty, and consequently it had a considerable comparative advantage over other countries as the world descended into this chaotic scenario.

India has succeeded in this world of uncertainty because of its extremely strong computer and space sectors. India's ability to produce, launch, and protect its own satellites has proven invaluable. As well, the huge non-resident Indian community around the world, which tends to dominate the computer industry in many other nations, has also proven very beneficial. The non-resident Indians in the computer sector, especially in the United States, channelled considerable intelligence to India, keeping India's computer sector one step ahead of the world. Indeed, its advanced software development capabilities, and its lower labour costs, put much more of a dent into the failing fortunes of Microsoft than the American anti-trust case against that company.

When Narashima Rao was imprisoned for corruption in 2000, it was a source of national shame in India. No one ever imagined that corrupt and wily politicians would be the key to India's success in the world. But working closely with Bombay crime syndicates, India's politicians were provided with some of the best intelligence available to any world leaders; this political-crime nexus also allowed India to capitalize on international financial transactions, and it ensured a ready supply of precious commodities: supercomputers, enriched uranium, and other critical technologies.

As this scenario is really just an extension of the 1990s, at least as far as India is concerned, it will have very little impact on centre-state relations in India. India's federal system has demonstrated a capacity to handle this sort of strain. While there may be a decentralizing thrust in this scenario, the federal government will continue to have significant constitutional powers to slow or reverse intolerable decentralization. This is the great virtue of the Sarkaria approach. In the 1980s, when the dangers of centralization were all too apparent and many people were demanding significant constitutional reforms to limit the power of the central government, Justice R.S. Sarkaria and S.R. Sen, a member of the commission chaired by Saarkaria, recommended in their mammoth report on *Centre-State Relations* that India did not require significant constitutional changes; they suggested only that India needed to adopt a federal political culture. It took more than ten years, and the collapse of the Congress Party system, for this culture to take root, but when it did these recommendations became self-implementing. Centralizing constitutional provisions nonetheless still exist in the constitution, which gives the central government considerable leverage if the fissiparous tendencies in the country suddenly become too dominant. In the event of a global cyberwave, India will be well-served by Sarkaria's foresight and wise recommendations. Another 11-member constitutional commission, chaired by Justice M.N. Venkatachaliah and appointed in 2000 (it reported in 2002) to review the entire gamut of constitutional review and reforms, broadly reiterated the Sarkaria approach with minor constitutional amendments to consolidate case laws and positive conventions relating to federal relations.

The four scenarios accentuate current trends in global politics and, to the extent that the trends are divergent, they would have somewhat different impacts. The shared governance and cyberwave scenarios would support the current federalization of India, the latter more than the former. The global club scenario, which would strengthen the centre but also relax it, would likely consolidate the federalization process at its current levels of decentralization. On the other hand, the regional dominator scenario, which envisions a worsening of India's regional security situation, would reverse the federalization process in India and return the country to the more quasi-federal situation that pertained in the tumultuous years following independence. But resilience is perhaps the best description of the Indian character. India has survived all sorts of tragedies and calamities in its 5,000-year history, and India can endure all of these short-range scenarios without much change to the lives of ordinary citizens.

CONCLUSIONS

In summary, India, since the 1990s, has become considerably more federalized than before. This is evident in the increased political autonomy and revenue of state governments vis-à-vis the Union government; growing manoeuvrability of the constitutional heads of states — president and governors; growing salience of Union constitutional agencies like the Election Commission of India and intergovernmental agencies like the ISC and NDC; decline in the role of centralized planning; creation of a series of independent regulatory agencies and appellate tribunals under parliamentary statutes in such vital sectors of the economy as communications, electricity, insurance, finance, stock exchange, etc.; greater visibility of the Human Rights Commission, Minorities Commission, Scheduled

Castes and Tribes Commission appointed either under the constitution or a parliamentary statute; and the revival and constitutional entrenchment of local self-governing institutions of Panchayat and Nagar Raj, etc. This remarkable transformation is due mainly to factors such as (i) the change in the party system of Congress dominance to one of a multi-party system of federal segmentation resulting in unstable federal coalition/ minority governments, (ii) judicial interpretation supporting the autonomy of states, (iii) more economic liberalization and globalization, rather than to formal constitutional amendments. Federalization has been strongly reinforced by economic liberalization and also to some extent by globalization. The federal state and its centralized role have been considerably reduced under pressure from above and below. The centralized federal state that relied on direct administrative mechanisms of control and the state-owned public sector is transforming itself into a regulatory state with semi-judicial autonomous statutory agencies and partially or fully disinvesting/privatizing public sector undertakings. Lloyd and Susanne Rudolpf (2001) hypothesize that economic reforms in India since 1991 have created a "federal market economy" that facilitates a wider "sharing of sovereignty" within the state and the market.

The foregoing trends are supplemented by the creation or revival of institutions of civil society in two broad forms: first, proliferation of non-governmental organizations (NGOs) in the voluntary sector funded nationally and globally, and second, emergence of *new* social movements with a non-partisan temper centring around single issues on regional lines. The latter have often been in contrast to the old peasant and worker movements based on issues of production and distribution and politico-economic corruption and organized on macro-regional or national scales, for example, ecological and environmental protection, gender justice, bonded or child labour, victims of mega-developmental projects like big dams, grants of seed marketing and coastal fishing to multinational corporations affecting agricultural and fishing communities, etc. (Wignaraja 1993; Singh and Roy (1998, chs. 15, 16, 24). Calling these two major aspects of the civil society organization "Action Groups in the New Politics," Sethi (1993, p. 239) records their major contributions in terms of greater responsiveness to local situations and neglected sections of the population, along with an extension of politics and mass democratic methods to certain spheres of life traditionally considered non-political.

India's global and regional integration are still rather limited. Yet their impact on the federal system is evident in an expanded process of policy-making in political and economic matters in which state governments and a variety of national and regional parties in federal coalition government(s) have enjoyed greater access in the new atmosphere engendered by political federalization and economic liberalization. Even though state governments under the Indian constitution, or in practice, do not have any formal power to establish contact with foreign governments and join Indian delegations going abroad, except as observers by the courtesy of the Union government, state chief ministers have started going abroad in search of foreign investments, especially in countries containing sizeable Indian diaspora with heavy Gujarati, Maharashtrian, Punjabi, Bengali, Tamil, Andhra, Malayali, Karnataki, and Hindi concentrations. Also, states having borders with Nepal, Bangladesh, Sri Lanka, etc., have usually been involved with the Union government to some extent in an advisory capacity in bilateral issues with those countries relating to trade, river waters, infiltrators, migrants, and refugees.

The preamble to the Indian constitution proclaims India "a Sovereign Socialist Secular Democratic Republic" committed "to secure to all its citizens: Justice, social, economic and political; Liberty of thought, expression, belief, faith and worship; Equality of status and of opportunity; and to promote among them all Fraternity assuring the dignity of the individual and the unity and integrity of the Nation." The chapters on fundamental rights and directive principles of state policy guarantee legal civil, and political rights and promissory economic rights and social security in the future. Given this constitutionally entrenched political and economic constitutionalism, coupled with cumulative economic inequalities and regional disparities, it is difficult not to feel that there are important implications. In opting for an appropriate model of the role of the state in the regulation of the market economy, India can settle only for a state-market diarchy in which the state cannot be excluded from influencing economic development. But market mechanisms may have to have a balanced dualist role under compulsions of state failure attributable to an overspending populist and parasitic political class, overstaffed bureaucracy and public sector undertakings, and overstrained security apparatus. Historical traditions, state apparatus, and economic structure after more than a decade of economic reforms in India buttress the probability of continuing with the emerging model of state-market-civil society triarchy.

Economic reforms have proved to be irreversible, though with varying pace, under shifting coalition/minority governments, left-of-centre (United Front) as well as right-of-centre (Rao-Manmohan Singh Congress regime, National Democratic Alliance). In the post-anti-terror Afghan war scenario, which seems to herald the arrival of a mix between a global club and regional dominators in the world at large as well as in South Asia in the security domain, India can probably shed its paranoia and look forward to an era of greater global and regional integration in economic terms as well.

Admittedly, it would not be very easy. All South Asian countries, at least formally democratic excepting Pakistan since 1999, have minorities living on their borders as well as deep within. "Ethnic affinities are stronger than national identities ... [and] can be easily channelled into dissent and insurrection against the State or violence against other ethnic groups" (Chari 2001, p. 168). The temptation to aggravate these tensions with ulterior motives by all concerned is often too frequent to resist, especially in a culture of poverty, criminalization, and inter-state rivalries in a region with a feudal past and contemporary trends of militarization. Security in such a situation is primarily conceptualized in statist and elitist terms rather than in human and welfare terms. Yet South Asia must exit from this vicious circle of underdevelopment and militarization.

Ringed by patched pockets of affluence in Australia-Pacific, Central Asia, China, and the Persian Gulf, India holds out the double possibility of either growing into a zone of democratic development or into an "area of darkness," a land of "a million mutinies," or a "wounded civilization," in terms of the fictional trilogy of Nobel laureate Sir V.S. Naipaul. The land of Buddha, Gandhi, Nehru, and Ambedkar is haunted by the spectre of Talibanese terror from without and post-Mughal disintegration from within. India began its post-colonial multicultural federal nation-building experiment following the British Raj in the 1950s as an alternative model to authoritarian-communist China. Over half a century later, India must still stand out as a beacon of democracy and development with justice and equity. As Cohen aptly observes: "India's elites have ... demonstrated a flexibility that has been absent in other complex, multi-ethnic, multinational states such as Pakistan, Yugoslavia, and the former Soviet Union. Like a ship with many watertight compartments, India is relatively immune to the kinds of large-scale, or extremist, or totalitarian movements that have afflicted other states" (2001, pp. 299-300).

Notes

A version of this paper was presented at the international seminar on comparative federalism with the above focus in Ottawa under the auspices of the Institute of Intergovernmental Relations, Queen's University, Kingston, Canada, on 8-9 December 2000. My thanks go to Harvey Lazar, Douglas Verney, and Hamish Telford for their comments on the earlier drafts of this paper which were helpful in making revisions.

1.   *Madhav Rao* v. *Union of India, All India Reporter (AIR)*, Supreme Court (SC): 530.

2.   *Maganbhai Ishwarbhai Patel* v. *Union of India, AIR*, Supreme Court, 1969: 783; *Ram Jawaya* v. *State of Punjab, Supreme Court Report (SCR)*, 1955: 225.

3.   These aspects are not yet fully explored by research. On inter-state river water disputes, see Sondhi (1993). On NIC, see A.K. Singh (1997).

4.   *Keshavananda Bharati* v. *State of Kerala, All India Reporter (AIR)*, 1973, Supreme Court (SC). *Minerva Mills Ltd.* v. *Union of India, AIR*, 1980, SC.

5.   Reeta Chaudhary-Tremblay used the term "sectoral federalism" when she discussed my paper at the IIGR Conference in Ottawa (2000) on which this chapter is based. Indeed, there was and still is a regular exercise in sectoral federalism in the Union secretaries — comparable to deputy ministers (civil servants despite their political sounding designation) — who virtually become captains of state secretaries of respective government departments and sectors of the economy in their charge for official-level intergovernmental relations. Comment by Vijay Kapur, Lt. Governor of Delhi, in an international conference on Intergovernmental Relations in Federal Systems jointly organized by the Forum of Federations, Ottawa, and the Institute of Social Sciences in New Delhi, 22 April 2002.

6.   In the BJP-led coalition government between 1998–99, "Jayalalita-Mamata-Samata" allies of the Union government pressured it to dismiss the governments of DMK, Left Front, and Rashtriya Janata Dal in Tamil Nadu, West Bengal, and Bihar respectively.

7.   *Supreme Court of India, S.R. Bommai* v. *Union of India*, 1994.

8.   Government of India (1987–88), Two Parts. The first part contains the recommendations of the Sarkaria Commission and the second, the submissions and memoranda to the commission by state governments and political parties.

9.   Interview with Rajiv Malhotra, New Delhi, Autumn 2001.

10.   It is notable, however, that in real terms even though the states' and Union territories' share in the total divisible pool has nearly doubled in figure from Rs. 20,593 crores in 1992–93 to Rs. 40,253 crores in 1997–98, in

percentage terms there is a marginal decline: 27.6 to 26.2 (Sáez 2002, p. 202).

11.	See, for example, *The Economic Times* (New Delhi), 31 October 2000, p. 13. On an earlier occasion a similar debate took place during the time of the Rao Congress government, and disallowed again in November 2000 by the NDA government. In March 2002 during the NDA regime a parliamentary committee report again recommended against foreign equity in the print media on the grounds that it might destroy cultural life and disorient the Indian mind (*The Times of India*, New Delhi, 23 March 2002, p. 11). The NDA Cabinet, however, has since allowed 26 percent foreign equity in this sector, with editorial and managerial incumbency remaining with Indian nationals (*The Economic Times*, New Delhi, 22 November 2002, p. 8).

12.	See also NCRWC (nd).

13.	For a perceptive analysis of the first decade of South Asian regionalism, see Khatri (1992). Prime Minister Rajiv Gandhi of India aptly observed at the second SAARC summit in November 1986: "Like embroidery, regional cooperation will have to be fashioned patiently, stitch by stitch" (SAARC 1990, p. 9).

References

Ahluwalia, I.J. 1999. "Indian Economy: Looking Ahead," in *Contemporary India*, ed. V.A. Pai Panandiker and A. Nandy. New Delhi: Tata McGraw-Hill Publishing Company Limited.

Ahluwalia, S.S. 2000. "Power Tariff Reform in India," *Economic and Political Weekly* 35(38):3407-19.

Baxi, U. 2002. "Situating Arundhati Amidst Ayodhya," *The Hindu* (New Delhi), 27 March.

Chari, P.R., ed. 2001. *Security and Governance in South Asia*. Colombo: Regional Centre for Strategic Studies and New Delhi: Manohar.

Chisti, S. 1994. "Regionalism and Globalization in South Asian Countries," in *Understanding South Asia* (*Essays in the Memory of the Late Professor Urmila Phadnis*), ed. S.D. Muni. New Delhi: South Asian Publishers.

Cohen, S.P. 2001. *India: Emerging Power?* Delhi: Oxford University Press.

The Economic Times. 2002. "ET 500: The Changing Face of India Inc.," March.

Elazar, D. 1987. *Exploring Federalism*. Tuscaloosa: University of Alabama Press.

Finance Commission of India. n.d. *Report of the Eleventh Finance Commission (for 2000-2005)*. New Delhi: Ministry of Finance, Government of India.

Government of India. 1987-88. *Commission on Centre-State Relations, Report*, 2 Vols. Nasik, Maharashtra: Government of India Press.

—— 1999. *The Constitution of India*. New Delhi: Ministry of Law, Justice and Company Affairs.

—— 2002. *Economic Survey, 2001-2002*. New Delhi: Ministry of Finance.

Institute of Intergovernmental Relations. 2000. "The Impact of Global and Regional Integration on Federal Systems: Discussion of the Working Template." Kingston, ON: Queen's University.

International Monetary Fund (IMF). 2000. *Direction of Trade Statistics*. New York: IMF.

Jenkins, R. 1999. *Democratic Politics and Economic Reforms in India*. Cambridge: Cambridge University Press.

Jha, P.S. 2002. "Why India's Globalization Has Failed," *The Hindu* (New Delhi), 27 March.

Khatri, S.K. 1992. "A Decade of South Asian Regionalism: Retrospect and Prospect," *Contemporary South Asia* 1(1):5-23.

Mathew, G. 1994. *Panchayati Raj: From Legislation to Movement*. New Delhi: Concept.

Mendis, V.L.B. 1991. *SAARC: Origins, Organization and Prospects*, Monograph No. 3. Perth, Western Australia: Indian Ocean Centre for Peace Studies.

Mitra, C. 1998. *The Corrupt Society: The Criminalization of India from Independence to 1990s*. New Delhi: Penguin India.

Morris, S. 2000. "Regulatory Strategy and Restructuring: Model for Gujarat Power Sector," *Economic and Political Weekly* 35(23):1915-36.

Morris-Jones, W.H. 1957. *Parliament in India*. London: Longmans Green.

Mukherji, I.N. 2001. "Role of the Private Corporate Sector in India for Strengthening Regional Cooperation in South Asia," *South Asian Survey* 8(2):277-314.

National Commission to Review the Working of the Constitution (NCRWC). nd. *Treaty-Making Power Under Our Constitution: A Consultation Paper*. New Delhi.

Parliament of India. 2000a. *The Electricity Regulatory Commissions Act, 1998* (Bare Act with Short Notes). Delhi: Universal Law Publishing Co. Pvt. Ltd.

—— 2000b. *The Information Technology Act, 2000* (Bare Act with Short Notes). Delhi: Universal Law Publishing Co. Pvt. Ltd.

Ramanathan, U. 2002. "Of Judicial Power," *Frontline*, 29 March.

Rao, M.G. 2002. "A Balancing Act," *The Hindu* (New Delhi), 9 March.

Rao, M.G. and R.J. Chellia. 1996a. *Fiscal Federalism in India*. New Delhi: Indian Council of Social Science Research.

—— 1996b. *Fiscal Federalism in India: Theory and Practice*. Delhi: Macmillan India Ltd.

Rao, S.L. 2002. "Avoid Conflict Between Regulators," *The Economic Times*. New Delhi, 25 March.

Rudolph, L. and S. Rudolph. 1987. *In Pursuit of Lakshmi: The Political Economy of the Indian State.* New Delhi: Orient Longman.

—— 2001. "Iconisation of Chandrababu: Sharing Sovereignty in India's Federal Market Economy," *Economic and Political Weekly* 36 (18):1541-52.

Sáez, L. 2000. "Economic Liberalization and Federalism: The Case of India," in *Handbook of Global Economic Policy*, ed. S.S. Nagel. New York: Marcel Dekker, Inc.

—— 2002. *Federalism Without a Centre: The Impact of Political and Economic Reform on India's Federal System.* New Delhi: Sage Publications.

Sankar, T.L. and U. Ramachandra. 2000. "Electricity Tariffs Regulators: The Orissa Experience," *Economic and Political Weekly* 35(20 and 21):1825-1834.

Saxena, R. 2001. "Intergovernmental Agencies in Parliamentary Federal Systems in Canada and India," PhD dissertation, Department of Political Science, University of Delhi.

Sethi, H. 1993. "Action Groups in the New Politics," in *New Social Movements in the South: Empowering the People*, ed. P. Wignaraja. London and New Jersey: Zed Books.

Sheth, D.L. 1998. "Micro-Movements and Future of Politics," in *Indian Political System: Structure, Policies, Development*, ed. M.P. Singh and H. Roy. New Delhi: Jnanda Prakashan.

Singh, A.K. 1997. "Evaluation of the Role and Working of National Integration Council," in *Pluralism, Minorities, National Integration*, ed. A.P. Vijapur *et al.* New Delhi: South Asian Publishers.

Singh, M.P. 2001. "India's National Front and United Front Coalition Governments: A Phase in Federalized Governance," *Asian Survey* 41(2):328-50.

—— 2002*a*. "Towards a More Federalized Parliamentary System in India: Explaining Functional Change," *Pacific Affairs* (Winter):553-68.

—— 2002*b*. *Party Systems in Parliamentary Federal Canada and India*, Shastri Faculty Research Fellowship Report 2001. Delhi: Shastri Indo-Canadian Institute.

Singh, M.P. and H. Roy, eds. 1998. *Indian Political System: Structure, Policies, Development*, 2d ed. New Delhi: Jnanda.

Singh, M.P. and R. Saxena. 2002. *India at Polls: Parliamentary Elections in the Federal Phase.* New Delhi: Orient Longman.

Sondhi, D.K. 1993. "River Water Disputes and Indian Federalism," PhD dissertation, Department of Political Science, University of Delhi.

South Asian Association for Regional Cooperation (SAARC). 1990. *SAARC Summits (1985-1988).* Kathmandu: SAARC Secretariat.

Srinivasan, T.N., ed. 2002. *Trade, Finance and Investment in South Asia.* New Delhi: Social Science Press for South Asia Network of Economic Research Institutes. Reviewed by C.R. Reddy in *The Hindu* (New Delhi), 30 April.

Supreme Court of India. 1967. *Golak Nath* v. *State of Punjab*, *All India Reporter*, Supreme Court Section.

—— 1980. *Minerva Mills* v. *Union of India* (1980). *All India Reporter*, Supreme Court Section.

—— 1993. *S.C. Advocates on Record Association* v. *Union of India* (1993). Supreme Court Cases.

—— 1994. *S.R. Bommai* v. *Union of India* (1994). *All India Reporter*, Supreme Court Section.

Vaidyanathan, A. 1982 "The Indian Economy Since Independence (1947-70)," in *The Cambridge Economic History of India, Vol. 2: c. 1757- c. 1970*, ed. D. Kumar and M. Desai. New Delhi: Orient Longman in Association with Cambridge University Press. (Reprinted in 1984.)

Venkatarangaiya, M. and M. Shivaih. 1975. *Indian Federalism*. New Delhi: Arnold-Heinemann Publishers [India].

Wadhva, C.D. 1999. "Geoeconomic Positioning of India's Trade and Allied Relations: Perspectives on India's Experiences with Regional Integration," in *Contemporary India*, ed. V.A.P. Panandiker and A. Nandy. New Delhi: Tata McGraw Hill Publishing Company.

Watts, R.L. 1999. *Comparing Federal Systems*, 2d ed. Montreal and Kingston: McGill-Queen's University Press.

Wheare, K.C. 1964. *Federal Government*, 4th ed. New York: Oxford University Press.

Wignaraja, P., ed. 1993. *New Social Movements in the South: Empowering the People*. London and New Jersey: Zed Books.

World Bank. 2001. *World Development Report 2000/2001: Attacking Poverty*. New York: Oxford University Press.

HOUR GLASSING SYSTEMS

The Impact of Global and Regional Integration on Decentralization in South Africa

Nico Steytler

INTRODUCTION

Emerging from the dark abyss of apartheid, the new democratic South Africa embarked on a process of decentralization domestically while, at the same time, it enthusiastically entered the international community that had played a significant role in the apartheid regime's demise. The question to be addressed in this chapter is how these two processes — decentralization domestically and global and regional integration — have interacted. More particularly, how do the processes of globalization and regionalization impact on the nature, direction, and operation of South Africa's system of decentralized government?

Globalization is associated in South Africa, and even more so in less-developed countries in Africa, with the shrinking of state sovereignty, particularly in the area of economic policy (Mills 2000a, p. 12). There are "laws" of the global economy which, like domestic laws, must be obeyed as there is no escape from the long arm of the international market. Global integration has also intensified the need for regional integration, for in numbers (be it countries, people, or finances) strength is sought. For South Africa's neighbours the drive toward political and economic integration of the region will compound their loss of sovereignty. Yet regional integration is accepted as an inevitable consequence of globalization and a bulwark against marginalization.

The impact of global governance, both formal and informal, is experienced acutely by developing countries, because their growth strategies have been linked to, and often made dependent upon, external intervention by the market and international institutions. In South Africa the global "laws" of the marketplace have penetrated domestic policy, which now reflects the need for fiscal discipline and good governance requiring efficient and lean government.

In this chapter it will be argued that South Africa's system of decentralization with its strong centralist features, is still in an evolutionary stage. With political ambivalence about the future of the middle-level institutions of government — the provinces — the demands of fiscal discipline and good government may give direction to their eventual fate. At the same time, the newly established strong local government structures, including mega-cities, dovetail with the second wave of good governance demands that see localization as the path to effective and efficient development. The result may be an hourglass federation — the provinces are squeezed between national and local government, with their width determined by the nature and direction of the process of globalization itself.

SITUATIONAL CONTEXT

Located on the southern tip of the continent, South Africa's geographical context ties its fortune to that of Africa. Whereas the apartheid regime sought to keep South Africa euro-centred, the new government places South Africa in the world through Africa (Pahad 2000, p. 48). Its key foreign policy, called the African Renaissance, aims at continentwide growth, development, and security. South Africa, then, as one of Africa's dominant players, has consciously sought to play a leadership role to this end.

Bordered by the Atlantic and Indian Oceans, the horizons to the east and the west of South Africa are also hazy. To the east, there are the rudimentary beginnings of cooperation around the Indian Ocean Rim. To the west, linkages with South American markets are in the offing. Facing north, and reaching both east and west, South Africa's "butterfly strategy" seeks south-south cooperation and integration (Mills 2000a, p. 331). While geographic location becomes less significant for global economic integration, South Africa's strategic position offers a challenging prospect for political and economic manoeuvring. Success, however, will depend on how it manages a number of crucial domestic cleavages.

South Africa is a multilingual, multicultural society. With 11 official languages, there are linguistic/ethnic divisions and in seven of the nine provinces there are linguistic majorities.[1] More importantly, President Thabo Mbeki describes South Africa as a country of two nations — white and black — divided by income, political persuasion, and identity. Coinciding with the black/white divide (but increasingly within the black group as well) are vast disparities in income, with 45 percent of the population living below the national poverty line; 61 percent of Africans are poor as compared to 1 percent of whites (UNDP 2000, pp. 55-56). And this divide is expanding due to the growth in the skilled service sector and increased use of technology.[2] The inequality divide further overlaps with a new division drawn by HIV/AIDS (see Karrim 2000). South Africa has one of the highest infection rates in the world, and the latest calculation is that the pandemic, if it remains unchecked, will claim the lives of between five and seven million people in the next ten years (UNDP 1999, p. 23).[3] By 2003, AIDS deaths will outnumber all other deaths combined (Shell 2000, p. 22). Life expectancy will drop from 63.4 years in 1998 to 48 in 2010. With 26 percent of the economically active population becoming infected, needless to say, the pandemic will have a devastating effect on economic growth and prosperity (Quattek 2000) while accelerating crime (Schonteich 2000). The devastation caused by AIDS will also pose a major challenge to peace and stability in sub-Sahara Africa (Mills 2000b).

The cleavages along ethnic, linguistic, racial, and economic lines may well be heightened by external economic pressures when global economic forces leave South Africa marginalized in the global competition for wealth. This in turn could stimulate centrifugal forces for geographically based ethnic self-rule.

With a gross national product (GNP) per capita of $3,160, South Africa is classified as an upper-middle income economy.[4] The GNP for 1999 was $131.1 billion with a growth rate fluctuating below 3 percent.[5] The years of apartheid rule bankrupted South Africa and its indebtedness to international and local banks means that 20 percent of its current budget is devoted to debt-servicing. Growth is premised on the inflow of foreign direct investment (FDI) and the development of the South African export market. However, both internationally and internally, there is a lack of confidence in the economy. Foreign direct investment, after an initial spurt, has not been forthcoming in the last few years. As an emerging market, in competition with other developing countries (particularly the new economies of Southeast Asia), South Africa's economy is characterized by high levels of labour costs and low levels of skills and productivity. Domestic investment is at an all-time low and there is a continual drain of skills and finances. It was reported that for every dollar that came in during 2000, $24 flowed out of the country.[6]

South Africa has made Africa the geographical centrepiece of its foreign policy and the creation of wealth and security its overriding goals (Mills 2000a, p. 28). Success on the world stage will greatly depend on regenerating Africa, the very goal of the African renaissance policy, and the reform of international governance. In participating in the major international institutions such as the United Nations and its organs, the World Trade Organization (WTO), the World Bank, and the International Monetary Fund (IMF), South Africa's objective has been the reform of those institutions to reflect a better deal for the developing world. To this end South Africa has sought to mobilize the south through institutions as diverse as the Non-Aligned Movement (NAM) and the Commonwealth.

As a major power on the African continent, international expectations are that South Africa will increasingly play a policing role. Thus far South Africa has been hesitant. Under the new government the defence budget was slashed from its peak of 17.7 percent of the national budget in 1988–89 to less than 5.2 percent in 1998–99 (Mills 2000a, p. 239). After a poorly executed military expedition into Lesotho in 1998, under the banner of the Southern African Development Community (SADC) and on a request by a beleaguered government, South Africa has been reluctant to venture further afield. While its neighbours, Zimbabwe and Namibia, sent forces to prop up the government of the Democratic Republic of the Congo, South Africa confined itself to committing a small contingent of 90 technical personnel to a UN peacekeeping force (Chigara 2000).

Some of these features of the South African landscape were ingredients in the constitutional negotiations of 1992–96 that produced the contours of its decentralized form of government.

CONSTITUTIONAL CONTEXT

The Union of South Africa that emerged in 1910 from four British colonies established a strong centralized state.[7] Unlike the federal models in the British Empire in Canada (1867) and Australia (1901), the arguments for federalism were firmly rejected by the white polity in the National

Convention of 1909; a strong union was necessary to promote nation-building between the two British colonies (Cape and Natal) and the former Boer republics (Transvaal and Orange Free State) which had been engaged in war a decade before. As a sop to federal sentiments, an upper house, the Senate, was instituted to represent provincial interests (Welsh 1994, p. 243). Provincial legislatures and executives were created but had no original powers (see Boulle, Harris and Hoexter 1988, pp. 123-24).

In contrast to the sentiments underlying the 1909 National Convention, apartheid's constitutional design was to separate and remove Africans from the white polity. Under the guise of ethnic self-determination, the grand apartheid design of "divide and rule," institutionalized inequality. While there was a high degree of devolution of power to "homelands," the system remained highly centralized with the purse remaining in Pretoria. In contrast, the 1983 tricameral Parliament sought to bring the coloureds and Indians into an alliance with whites; while each group had competence over "own affairs," all three had to deliberate jointly over "general affairs." This led to the disappearance of the provinces as a feature in the political life of whites; the Senate and the provincial legislatures were abolished while limited provincial executive authority was retained.

With the normalization of politics in 1990, federalism was one of the dominant issues in the constitutional negotiations between the outgoing government, represented by the National Party (NP) and the African National Congress (ANC). From the NP's perspective, with its support base dispersed across the country, decentralization was not necessarily linked to the protection of territorially based interest groups (although it had concentrated power bases in the provinces of the Western Cape and Northern Cape). Rather, it was seen as a brake on a strong central government.

The ANC saw federalism as a method of thwarting majority rule; creating strong federal units could simply be a method of legitimating the homelands and creating a separate white *volkstaat* (see Welsh 1994, p. 244). Moreover, a strong central state authority had to be created to effect the restructuring of the South African society. While the ANC softened its stance on decentralization largely due to the influence of the German model of cooperative government, the Zulu ethnic party, Inkatha Freedom Party (IFP), campaigned for a very loose form of confederalism, including the right of secession (Ellman 1993).

The interim constitution that was negotiated during 1993 did not establish a fully-fledged federation, but the state structure nevertheless contained important federal elements.[8] In an effort at peacemaking, constitutional amendments were effected shortly before the April 1994 elections, which enshrined the right to self-determination for the white right-wingers and greater provincial constitution-making powers as a sop to the ethnic sentiments of the IFP (see Steytler and Mettler 1998).

The interim constitution divided the country into nine provinces by carving the Cape Province into three and the Transvaal into four, in addition to Natal and the Orange Free State. Provincial legislatures had concurrent legislative competence with the national Parliament in respect of a number of listed areas. A second chamber, the Senate, was indirectly elected by provincial legislatures to cater to provincial interests.

While the 1993 constitution was a negotiated interim compact, the next constitution had to be the product of the democratic will. The democratically elected Parliament doubled up as the Constitutional Assembly, but was bound by the Constitutional Principles negotiated in the 1993 constitution which required, among other things, "legitimate provincial autonomy" (see Steytler 1995).

The 1996 constitution established three "spheres of government" — national, provincial, and local — with legislative and executive competences divided between them. Provincial legislatures have only those competences specifically listed in the constitution (Schedules 4 and 5). The national Parliament has plenary power over all other matters, but also enjoys concurrency with respect to almost all of the provincial competences (Steytler 2000b). Provinces have "concurrent" jurisdiction with the national government over a list of matters, and "exclusive" jurisdiction over a much shorter list. These exclusive competences are not, however, beyond the reach of the national Parliament, and legislation is possible in these functional areas of broadly defined grounds related to national security, economic unity, national standards, and prejudicial provincial action.

Local government has executive and legislative powers in matters listed in both the concurrent and exclusive areas of provincial competence. Where there is a conflict between a national or provincial law and a municipal bylaw, the former will prevail as long as it does "not compromise or impede a municipality's ability or right to exercise its powers or perform its functions" (section 151(4) of constitution).

In contrast to their substantive legislative powers, the provinces' powers to raise revenues are severely circumscribed and must be regulated by national legislation. With no enabling legislation as yet in place, the provinces' main source of income is intergovernmental transfers; each is entitled to an "equitable share" of revenue raised nationally.

As a counterweight to the division of the state power into spheres of government is the obligation of cooperative government, a concept borrowed from the German *Bundestraue*. At the legislative level the provinces are drawn into the national legislative process, through the National Council of Provinces (NCOP). The power of NCOP is limited to provincial issues; where a matter falls within the area of concurrent or exclusive competency, the will of NCOP can be overridden only by a two- thirds majority in the National Assembly. NCOP also has an important reviewing function when the national government intervenes in the affairs of a province, or a province in a municipality. With regard to the ratification of international treaties, NCOP is, ironically, in its strongest position — it is co-determinous with the National Assembly. An international agreement, bar those of a technical, administrative or executive nature, binds the country only after it has been ratified by both the National Assembly and NCOP. While international affairs are excluded from the provincial competence, this provision is a quirky leftover from the 1994 Senate (Levy *et al.* 1999, p. 123).

At the executive level there is a statutory Budget Council, comprised of the minister of finance and provincial counterparts, which advises on the allocation of revenue raised nationally. Most intergovernmental structures are, however, informal and deal with the sectoral interests such as local government, health, education, welfare, tourism, and economic development.

The "federal practice" that is emerging is shaped largely by the dominance of one political party, the ANC, which received 66.5 percent of the vote in the 1999 election and governs seven of the nine provinces with large majorities. Although its percentage of the vote in the December 2000 municipal elections dropped to 62 percent, it captured five of the six megacities. The ANC's reluctant compromise on the provinces in 1993 has not turned into an embrace of the institution. Its initial ambivalence about their value has been strengthened by increasing party factionalism caused, among other things, by what it referred to as "creeping provincialism." As a result, all ANC candidates for premiers of provinces and mayors of megacities are centrally appointed (Steytler 1999*b*). Perhaps reflective of ANC thinking, the chairperson of the Municipal Demarcation Board, previously an ANC member of the KwaZulu-Natal provincial legislature, has publicly questioned the need for provinces in light of the new local government dispensation.[9] Even the ANC premier of the Eastern Cape has stated that while the "hybrid quasi-federal system" has served the country well, in the long term provincial powers must be devolved to local government "as a permanent function of cutting-edge service delivery."[10] He argues that provinces should be stripped down to mere oversight bodies and the thousands of provincial civil servants be deployed to local government.

The scepticism regarding provinces is fed by their poor performance both as legislatures and administrators. Provincial legislatures have not been very active and their administrators have not been shining examples of excellence in service delivery.[11] Provincial corruption and incompetence have been recurring themes in the media. They are perceived mainly as agents implementing national policy, the product of an extreme case of vertical fiscal imbalance (see Abedian, Ajam and Walker 1997; Ajam 1998). For the fiscal year 1999–2000, 96 percent of the revenues of the provinces came from the central fiscus.[12] Although the intergovernmental transfer was 58 percent of the national budget (excluding the 22 percent for debt-servicing), provinces have little discretion as to how to divide the "cake." The bulk of revenue goes to education, health, and welfare, and the expenditures on these items are predetermined by national standards. The end result is that 85 percent of all the funds a province receives have already been pre-allocated by the national government. In addition, the Treasury exerts considerable financial control by closely monitoring provincial expenditure. A casualty of weak provinces has been the NCOP (Levy *et al.* 1999; Murray and Simeon 1999). Not only is it dominated by one party, but the provinces that must breathe life into the institution, have failed to do so.

In contrast to its ambivalence toward strong provinces, the ANC has favoured strong local government (South Africa. Ministry of Provincial Affairs and Constitutional Development 1998). The December 2000 elections drastically reduced 842 local authorities to six metropolitan, 47 district, and 232 local municipalities that will enjoy limited self-rule (Mastenbroek and Steytler 1998). Unlike the provinces, local government has a secure and constitutionally protected tax base which presently provides over 92 percent of income. The six metropolitan municipalities, in particular, will compete with the provinces for political and economic dominance. The mega-cities in Gauteng (three), Durban, Port Elizabeth, and Cape Town, not only contain a significant proportion of the provincial populations, but form the industrial base of South Africa. The new City of Cape Town, for example, includes 75 percent of the Western Cape's population and economic output and its budget of R9 billion equals that of the province, but without the latter's limitations.

In sum, South Africa's federal system is dominated by a party that is ambivalent about the need for provinces. The provinces are not performing well and national control over their expenditure is increasing. About to emerge and compete with them is strong local government led by six mega-cities. This may prefigure an hourglass scenario with a thin provincial waist in the middle. The extent and direction of South Africa's global and regional integration will not leave the process and direction of decentralization unaffected.

GLOBAL AND REGIONAL INTEGRATION

After the years of apartheid isolation, the democratic South Africa entered the world arena with vigour, although not always with a consistent policy. An early promise of charting its foreign policy along a human rights and democracy track, foundered upon the harsh realities of the *real politik* of its economic interests and strategic partners (see Mills 2000*a*; Mawby 2000). Its foreign relations initiatives are, however, firmly embedded in the globalization discourse. As Foreign Minister Dlamini-Zuma recently told ministers of the NAM: "Globalization means that none of us is able to stand alone politically, economically, scientifically or otherwise. We have to work to ensure that our continent does not continue to be marginalized."[13] Mills contends that South Africa assumed, consciously or not, "the role of a middleman between the North and the South in attempting to change the rules of the global economy and establish the necessary political architecture and institutions" (Mills 2000*a*, p. 279). This role is played out in both political and economic relations.

Political Relations

The South African government has set as its priority the creation of a rules-based system which levels the playing field between states where "the weak have the same voice as the powerful."[14] Returning as a member of the United Nations, South Africa has been advocating the reform of the institution which would include a permanent seat on the Security Council for an African country.

Given its apartheid history, South Africa has sought to internalize the rules of the international community, particularly as far as human rights norms are concerned. It has acceded to most UN human rights instruments and in the writing of the 1996 constitution in particular, there was a conscious and deliberate attempt to harmonize the domestic Bill of Rights with international norms. In addition to enshrining one of the most extensive Bills of Rights worldwide, the constitution also compels courts, when interpreting the Bill of Rights, to consider international law. Both the High and Constitutional Courts have complied with this injunction and in a number of cases international norms were determinative of the issue. In law-reform projects, international law has also been influential. For example, in the drafting of a new juvenile justice bill, the South African Law Commission consciously sought to implement the Convention on the Rights of the Child (Sloth-Nielsen 2001). Because the legal protection provided by the domestic Bill of Rights far exceeds that of international instruments, and with an active Constitutional Court implementing the rights effectively, the UN monitoring committees policing the human rights instruments have not, to date, been significant for domestic policy. This is in sharp contrast to Australia, where the absence of a domestic Bill of Rights has forced complainants of human rights violations to invoke the support of UN institutions.

Other multinational organizations in which South Africa participates have not progressed to the level of governance. The Commonwealth, a "loose trans-global organization" of 54 nations mainly from the old British Empire, which includes the world's richest and poorest economies and a quarter of the world's population, is an odd organization as it is not built around security, geopolitical or economic interests (Burford 1999, p. 86). This club of nations had, with apartheid South Africa as a focus, a sense of mission, but has since then found it difficult to exert much pressure on member states that abandon democratic rule or violate human rights. An exception could be the suspension of Nigeria's membership and the imposition of sanctions against the military dictatorship of Abacha; it may have played a part in encouraging the restoration of democracy in 1998 (ibid., p. 88).

With the prominence of its newly won democracy, South Africa assumed a level of influence in NAM. This conglomeration of developing countries, born out of the Cold War divide, is seeking to reinvent itself as the organized south. As chairperson and host of the last four yearly conferences, South Africa sought to direct NAM toward development and globalization issues (Mills 2000*a*, p. 78).

South Africa's leadership is perforce more pronounced in Africa where there is both the external expectation and the internal capacity to play such a role (ibid., p. 303). The Organisation of African Unity (OAU) has proved to be a weak group for promoting democracy and human rights effectively.[15] Perhaps due to its poor functioning, new initiatives are afoot for more effective continentwide political integration. In 1999 Colonel Gaddafi from Libya proposed a grandiose United States of Africa. This proposal was watered down at the extraordinary meeting of the OAU in Sirte, Libya, to an African Union based on the European Union concept.[16] This organization, which is to replace the OAU, will have a Pan-African Parliament that can take binding decisions. At a meeting of 200 parliamentarians in Pretoria in November 2000, a concept document outlining the Parliament was signed and was to be submitted to the OAU summit meeting in July 2001 (*Beeld*, 7 November 2000; 11 November 2000). It is envisaged that this Parliament would at first have only consultative and advisory powers, but that within five years it would be able to pass laws. The aim, phased in over 25 years, is to give the people of Africa a direct say in the affairs of their continent, promoting good governance and democracy and protecting human rights. Already South Africa is promoting the idea that it would be a suitable host (*Beeld*, 11 November 2000).

The principle of a pan-African court has already been accepted. In 1998, a treaty was concluded to establish the African Court of Human and People's Rights, operating under the auspices of the OAU and enforcing the provisions of the African Charter on Human and People's Rights. The aim of the court is, as in the case of the European Court of Human Rights, to be a powerful guardian of human rights on the continent. The treaty comes into operation when 15 countries have ratified it, but to date only four have done so. South Africa, which drove the initiative and hosted the conference that concluded the treaty, has not yet ratified it because of the concern that this continental court will trump its own Constitutional Court. South Africans are, however, already lobbying for the court to be located in South Africa.[17]

African ambitions also cover continental economic integration. Under the auspices of the OAU, the African Economic Community treaty was signed in 1991 by 49 of the 51 members of the OAU. The main objective of the treaty is to promote economic, social, and cultural development; the integration of African economies in order to increase self-reliance; and indigenous and self-sustained development (Peter 1997, p. 361). The community will be established in six stages over a period not exceeding 34 years. With the required ratification of two-thirds of the OAU members for establishment far from reach, it is still viewed as "an institution of the future" (ibid., p. 362). With a poor record of effective pan-African organizations, the focus shifts inevitably to the southern African region.

South African Development Community

In response to the dominance of apartheid South Africa, the neighbouring southern African countries founded in the late 1970s the Southern African Development community (SADC) with the aim of not only reducing their dependence on racist South Africa but also of promoting equitable regional integration (Peter 1997, p. 365; Heiman 1997, p. 649). By 1992, the organization was replaced by the Southern African Development Community, and a democratic South Africa joined in 1995.[18] The treaty calls for basic regional cooperation, relying on separate protocols to add the meat. For example, provision is made for a tribunal to adjudicate disputes relating to the treaty, but the composition, powers, functions, and procedures are to be provided for in a protocol. To date, 14 protocols have been signed, of which seven have entered into force (Pahad 2000, p. 49).

South Africa has sought to play a leading role in giving content to the SADC structures. However, sensitivities about its hegemonic role abound, and South Africa has to proceed cautiously so as not to alienate members (Mills 2000a, p. 337). The failure and resultant need for restructuring of the Protocol on the Organ of Security, Defence and Politics, controlled by President Robert Mugabe of Zimbabwe, was high on the South African list for reform (Breytenbach 2000; Chigara 2000). Its efforts were rebuffed by the other members and political progress has been slow. However, at the extraordinary summit in Windhoek, Namibia, in March 2001, the SADC leaders not only agreed on restructuring proposals to merge the organization's 21 sectors into four directorates, but also that the powers of the security organ would be whittled down.[19] The summit also revealed the fragile unity of the group. It was reported that Lesotho, Swaziland, and Botswana threatened to withdraw from SADC if the larger nations imposed their candidate for secretary-general.

One area where the political borders have come down in southern Africa is the establishment of the Transfrontier Parks that straddle international borders, allowing the free movement of animals and tourists. The first Transfrontier Park was established in 2000 by combining two game reserves along South African and Botswana borders in the Kalahari desert. A second Transfrontier Park, agreed upon in November 2000, will link the Kruger Park with reserves in Mozambique and Zimbabwe, creating one of the largest wildlife areas in the world.[20]

While border controls remain in place, regulating the annual three million visitors from Africa to South Africa, there is an equal number of unofficial migrants that cross South African borders in search of economic survival. Along with the informal network of migration comes gun-running and other criminal networks. What is clear is that "South Africa cannot exist as an island of prosperity in a sea of poverty" (Pahad 2000, p. 48). The problem of economic migration can only be solved with a more balanced economic development of the entire region, a reality that emphasizes the important role of SADC.[21]

Economic Relations

After the years of apartheid isolation and protectionism, the stated goal of the new government was the reintegration of the South African economy into the global economy. The process has been painful and job losses have spiralled. Speaking to the left-wing trade union, NUMSA, of which he was a leading activist and theorist before 1994, the minister of trade and industry, Alec Erwin, noted that globalization had widened the gap between the rich and the poor, and said that "our response is not to say we are not going to be part of globalization, we have to have a clear strategic response to it."[22] The government's strategic response included promoting trade through participation in formal institutional mechanisms and aligning domestic macroeconomic policies to attract foreign investment.

The return to the international fold has not led to a dramatic increase in foreign trade. Over the last ten years the share of exports in goods and services of the gross domestic product (GDP) has remained constant at 25 percent[23] while the share of imports is around 22 percent.[24]

After reaching a peak in 1995, the percentage annual growth in trade has been declining, with exports showing no growth in 1999 and imports a negative rate of 7 percent (World Bank 2000*a*; South Africa. Department of Finance 2000, Table 2.3).

South Africa's trade partners have not changed much since 1994. In 1998, 48 percent of South Africa's imports were from Europe, 29 percent from Asia, 18 percent from the America, 3 percent from Oceania, and 2.5 percent from Africa. Of its exports, 31 percent went to Europe, 17 percent to Asia, 14 percent to Africa, 10 percent to the Americas and 1 percent to Oceania (South Africa 2000, p. 432). The major trading countries were the United States (ranked first for the first time in 1998); Germany (2); United Kingdom (3) Japan (4); China/Hong Kong (5); Netherlands (6); Italy (7); France (8); Belgium (9); and Taiwan (10) (ibid.). Trade with SADC is limited, imports from SADC totalled 2 percent of the country's imports while exports to SADC were 11 percent of the country's exports, giving a trade ratio of one to six (Thomas 1999, p. 117).

Foreign direct investment (FDI) in South Africa after 1994 did not materialize in the volumes hoped for and has proved to be inconsistent. Reaching the $1 billion mark in 1999, there has been a rapid decline in 2000, recording a 52 percent drop to $492 million FDI (*Business Report*, 23 January 2001, BusinessMap survey).

To advance its trade relations, South Africa has participated in a number of institutionalized forums on bilateral, regional, and global levels.

SA-EU Trade and Cooperation Agreement

With the EU, South Africa's major trading partner, and political sentiment on its side, a free trade agreement was an important objective. With negotiations dragging on for years, marred by petty protectionist demands from some EU member states on the use of the terms "port," "sherry," "grappa," and "ouzo," agreement was eventually reached in January 2000. It rests on three pillars: the three agreements on cooperation in the areas of science and technology, wine and spirits, and fisheries; South Africa's partial accession to the Lome Convention (Bertelsmann-Scott 2000); and a Trade and Cooperation Agreement to cover all aspects not addressed in the Lome Convention. The latter is most important as it includes a free trade agreement. The EU will fully exempt 95 percent of South African imports from tariffs within ten years, while South Africa need only liberalize

86 percent of the European imports within a 12-year period (ibid.; Stahl 2000). Reflecting the aid component of the agreement is the so-called "political dialogue" clause. At the commencement of the negotiations, the EU insisted on a discontinuation provision if South Africa violates respect for democratic principles, fundamental human rights, the rule of law, and good governance. South Africa resisted this clause as it feared a unilateral EU definition of its content. It was, however, included in the agreement subject to consultation before suspension of the agreement.

Southern African Customs Union (SACU)

South Africa's longest multilateral financial agreement is the Southern African Customs Union, dating from 1910, which includes the small states surrounding South Africa: Lesotho, Swaziland, Botswana, and Namibia. These countries' economies are both minute and extensively reliant on its larger neighbour. Until recently South Africa set the tariff rates for the union. The new democratic government committed itself to a more equitable dispensation and a deal recently struck gives its neighbours a greater say in running the affairs of the union (*Business Day*, 13 September 2000).

Southern African Development Community Free Trade Protocol

A larger market is the SADC region and a trade protocol, agreed upon in 1996, came into force in January 2000 with an implementation date of 1 September 2000. The protocol calls for a regional free trade area by 2008 (with 85 percent of all trade to be undertaken at zero tariffs) and total liberalization by 2012. The protocol deals with tariff schedules, rules of origin, dispute settlement and the elimination of non-tariff barriers. A protocol is being finalized to set up a tribunal. Again, as with other SADC initiatives, there is a gap between the paper protocol and national implementation measures. When the protocol became operational, only South Africa and Mauritius, an export driven island economy, had legislated the new tariffs and rules (Editorial, *Business Day*, 6 September 2000).

The intra-SADC trade is limited and currently stands at 10 percent of the total exports (as compared to 24 percent of Mercosur, 55 percent of the EU and 52 percent of NAFTA) (Pahad 2000, p. 52). The problem with trade within SADC is not so much tariff barriers but other factors, such as low incomes, long distances between markets, weak transport infrastructure and political instability.[25] There is also no complementarity of products and it is feared that South Africa's dominance, with trade six to one in its favour, could end up impoverishing its neighbours (Thomas 1999, p. 117). To address this problem the agreement establishes an asymmetrical regime whereby South Africa would meet 97.6 percent of its obligations within four years, while other members have eight years grace (Pahad 2000, p. 52). The role of the protocol has thus been described as primarily being a mechanism to liberalize the other SADC countries' access to the South African market (Stahl 2000, p. 85).

Overlapping and competing with the SADC protocol, is the Common Market for Eastern and Southern Africa (COMESA), stretching from Egypt in the north to Swaziland in the south (Peter 1997, p. 366). Rivalling the SADC protocol, nine of the 20 members of COMESA (Djibouti, Egypt, Kenya, Madagascar, Malawi, Mauritius, Sudan, Zambia, and Zimbabwe) agreed in November 2000 to launch their own free trade area, guaranteeing the immediate free movement of goods and services and the removal of tariff and non-tariff barriers (Games 2000). More ambitious plans are also in store. By 2025 a full monetary union is possible, including the use of one common currency issued by a common central bank.[26] The secretary-general of COMESA ascribed South Africa's abstention from this organization to its hegemonic role: "They are very protective. They want to control regional integration and development" (ibid.). Whatever the current political differences, it is foreseen that the overlapping jurisdictions will eventually lead to the amalgamation of COMESA and SADC (Mills 2000c).

South Africa Trading as an African Country

Although located in Africa, South Africa's advanced economy has disqualified it from benefiting from development trade packages. Full membership was refused to the Lome Convention (now the Cotonou Agreement) between the EU and the ACP (African, Carribean, and Pacific) countries (Phillipe 1997). This distinction is not made in the recent US law — the *African Growth and Opportunity Act* — which came into operation on 1 October 2000. The Act allows duty-free US market access to African-assembled clothing. Conditions of access relate primarily to matters political and economic. The benefits are only available to African countries declared by the US administration to have met broad political and economic conditions. These include "making progress" toward establishing market-oriented, trade- and investment-friendly economies in which the rule of law, property and labour rights are respected (Barber 2000*a*). These conditions include African governments taking steps that are consistent with the WTO agreement on clothing and textiles (Barber 2000*b*).

Indian Ocean Rim Association for Regional Cooperation

Looking east, a more recent venture has been the first tentative step toward cooperation with countries joined by the Indian Ocean Rim. In March 1997, 14 countries — Australia, Indonesia, Malaysia, Singapore, India, Sri Lanka, Oman, Yemen, Mauritius, Madagascar, Kenya, Tanzania, Mozambique and South Africa — established the Indian Ocean Rim Association for Regional Cooperation. The charter of this organization lists its purpose as promoting trade, facilitating investment, and advancing institutional and human development. It has been described as a case of "open" regionalism of a functionalist kind (Breytenbach 1999). The openness of the design, it has been argued, allows for the possibility that with the creation of free trade areas both in Africa (SADC and COMESA) and Asia (ASEAN) within the next ten years, there will be a changeover from regional cooperation to regional economic integration (ibid.). This possibility is not too remote given the growth in trade along the Indian Ocean Rim (Holden and Isemonger 1999).

Looking west, linkages across the south Atlantic are also in the offing in a concerted south-south bonding. The first stages of formal linkages between southern Africa and Mercado Comun del Sur (Mercosur) of South America are taking place. In December 2000 President Mbeki participated in the summit of presidents of Mercosur, while his trade and industry minister signed a framework agreement to launch negotiations on a South Atlantic FTA which could bring together Mercosur and the Southern African Customs Union (SACU), in time extending to SADC (*Business Report*, 24 January 2001).

World Trade Organization

Since the signing of the Marrakech Agreement in April 1994, establishing the WTO, South Africa has been an enthusiastic participant in its activities.

At the failed Seattle Round of talks, its mission was the restructuring of the international trade regime. While reform is still only an item on the agenda, the bite of the trade regime has been felt in an area critical to the health and well-being of many South Africans — the provision of afford-able anti-retroviral drugs for AIDS suffers. The *Medicines and Related Substances Control Amendment Act* of 1997 empowers the minister of health to procure cheaper drugs through compulsory licensing, which allows companies other than the patent holder to produce or import drugs (Du Plessis 1999, p. 63). The Pharmaceutical Manufacturers' Association of South Africa, consisting mainly of foreign drug companies, has waged a protracted three-year battle against the legislation. It is challenging the legislation on the grounds that it gives the government excessive ability to issue compulsory licences in violation of, *inter alia*, South Africa's inter-national obligations in terms of the TRIPS Agreement (ibid.). In the wake of adverse publicity (putting profits before lives), the court challenge was eventually dropped (*Cape Times*, 20 April 2001). The battle continues, however, and the Pharmaceutical Research and Manufacturers of America (PhRMA) have requested that South Africa be put on a United States watch list for possible trade sanctions (*Mail & Guardian*, 9–15 March 2001).

The reform of the international trade regime is also pursued in other less formal settings. In February 1998 South Africa was admitted to the Cairns Group, an association of agricultural exporting countries[27] whose objective is to strive for fair and free trade in global agricultural markets (South Africa 1999, p. 286). South Africa has also joined the "middle-class" G20 group of nations aimed at reforming the institutions of global governance, including the Bretton Woods institutions (Mills 2000*a*, p. 353).

Bretton Woods Institutions

The International Monetary Fund (IMF) and the World Bank loom large on the South African horizon, although South Africa has thus far resisted the temptation to become a major client of these institutions. It has borrowed US$67 million from the World Bank for small-scale develop-ment projects, but is considering a $200 million loan to revamp public hospitals which, it is said, will be the first of a series of World Bank in-volvements in this sector. Significantly, the loan includes both finance as well as assistance in economic and financial analyses in hospital management (*Business Day*, 30 August 2000).

Despite recent protest worldwide, the government remains committed to these institutions. At the meeting of the IMF and World Bank in Prague in September 2000, the minister of finance, Trevor Manuel, chairing the board of governors, said that he did not believe, like the protestors outside the convention centre, that the institutions should be abolished. But they must be reformed in a fundamental way. The task ahead was to ensure that the benefits of globalization are spread equally. First, the 4.38 percent voting right of the 43 African countries should be increased because they are the largest borrowers. Second, the manner in which the institutions implement lending programs in the developing world should be reformed. While there is resignation to the fact that structural and economic reform will come with loans, it was, however, objectionable to "micromanage the economies of sovereign states" through detailed conditionalities attached to loans.[28] Too often their country representatives are seen as "latter day colonial administrators" (Katzenellenbogen 2000).

The message from the IMF and the World Bank has been to shrink the state, cut social spending and drop trade protection and exchange controls.[29] More specifically, they have been urging the South African government for some time to reform the labour laws to ensure greater flexibility. The feeling is that the cost of labour is too high.[30]

While the first wave of global governance was concerned with macroeconomic policy, a second wave is concerned with efficient government structures and good governance. The international development agencies and the donor community are increasingly positing that decentralization can be beneficial for economic development. Although much of the decentralization in the past decade, the World Bank notes, has been motivated by political concerns, it may be a case "where good politics and good economics serve the same end. The political objectives of increased responsiveness and participation at the local level can coincide with the economic objective of better decisions about the use of public resources and increased willingness to pay for local services" (World Bank 2000*b*). As part of the good governance ethic, decentralization thus becomes a means of improving public sector efficiency (World Bank 2000*c*, ch. 6; Dentier 2000).

While the formal linkages between South Africa and the IMF and the World Bank remain limited in the absence of any structural adjustment programs, the informal network and buy-in are increasing. South Africa has already internalized the basic principles of structural adjustment programs in its growth, employment and redistribution policy of 1997, the objectives of which are the reduction of the budget deficit, privatization of state assets, restraint on wage increases, downsizing the public service and economic growth through greater private sector investment.

Despite having these macroeconomic policies in place, the South African economy is not achieving the 6 percent growth necessary to meet its unemployment challenge of absorbing the daily 1,000 new entrants into the labour market. In new initiatives to prompt growth, major players in the global marketplace are asked for advice.

President Mbeki first established an International Investment Council, consisting of leading international businessmen, including Jurgen Schrempp of Daimler-Chrysler and George Soros, to advise him on ways to improve the investment climate in South Africa. More recently, at a closed meeting called by Mbeki to devise strategies for economic growth, the guests included James Wolfenson, president of the World Bank and the deputy managing director of the IMF.[31] In formulating policy responses to globalization, Mbeki noted after the meeting that one of the key issues was the relative cost of labour to the cost of capital, yet another way of saying that labour costs are too high.[32]

The impact of global integration on domestic economic policy is intensifying, reducing the government's policy options (Abedian 1998, p. 510). The governor of the SA Reserve Bank, Tito Mboweni, a former minister of labour in the first ANC government and a former trade unionist, describes the impact in the following terms:

> Globalization ... concerns the worldwide integration of financial markets. Therefore active participation in this integration process implies that [domestic] monetary and fiscal policies have to be subjected to the disciplines of the international market. Globalization mercilessly exposes the shortcomings in national economic policies in countries that do not apply the universal "laws" for prudent macroeconomic management (Mboweni 2000).

These "laws," Mboweni said, include "rigour and transparency in overall economic management; banking and financial sector soundness; reform of the institutions of the state in terms of seeking public sector efficiency; appropriate regulation; emphasis on the rule of law; independence of the judiciary and central banks; anti-corruption measures; and growth that is centred on human development" (ibid.). For the Reserve Bank, it required the framework and banking structure of the country to be adapted "to comply with the international best practice as understood by international investors and regulators" (ibid.). It has thus far resulted in a convertible currency and the progressive reduction of the exchange control. More recently, the government has allowed the major industrial giants to move their primary listing from the Johannesburg Stock Exchange to foreign bourses such as London and New York.

In sum, the impact of global and regional integration on South Africa has been varied. While regional integration in both political and economic fields has been rudimentary, integration in the global economy has been profound. At a formal level, South Africa has bound itself to the WTO trade regime and sought bilateral free trade agreements. Perhaps more significant have been the economic "laws" of the global economy which have been incorporated into domestic policy. The net result has been that government's policy options have shrunk considerably. The question is now how these realities impact on the emerging decentralized system described earlier.

EXTENT AND IMPACT OF GLOBAL AND REGIONAL INTEGRATION ON INTERGOVERNMENTAL RELATIONS

South Africa's integration into the global economy is increasingly impacting on how the three spheres relate to each other and how they interact collectively and separately with the international community. With regard to international trade, the national government is covering the terrain shared with the provinces. As compensation there are some initiatives to draw the provinces into these trade relations. Provinces and cities are becoming increasingly aware of globalization and are both reaching out to the international stage and preparing for participation in the global economy. The most important impact of globalization may be the fiscal squeeze and the demand for good and efficient governance that the national government is applying to the other spheres of government.

Given the reach and effect of national commitments to the WTO, the national government will increasingly dominate the competencies shared with the provinces. Areas that provinces exercise concurrently with the national government include trade, industrial promotion, provincial public enterprises, and agriculture. While provinces are constitutionally barred from imposing customs duties, conflicts may arise in the area of non-tariff barriers. Should this occur, national legislation will readily override provincial measures on the constitutional grounds that it is in "the economic interest of the country as a whole" or for protecting national economic policy (Steytler 1999a). Given the impact that national trade commitments have on provincial interests, the focus has shifted toward intergovernmental relations both at legislative and executive levels.

Sitting mostly in joint committee with the National Assembly, NCOP has become part of a more inclusive treaty-making process. Parliament has in the past been confronted with an all-or-nothing choice; it must either approve or disapprove an extensive international agreement. Because of this impossible choice imposed on it, Parliament has insisted on being informed earlier in the negotiation process. In 1998, the parliamentary Portfolio Committee on Trade and Industry played an active role in respect of bilateral agreements. During the negotiations of the South Africa-European Union Free Trade Agreement the Portfolio Committee made a number of submissions to the trade negotiations. In respect of the WTO, the Department of Trade and Industry (DTI) has also brought offers to the attention of the Portfolio Committee on Trade and Industry and sought a mandate for its negotiating position (ibid.).

With its power to veto the ratification of international treaties, NCOP can play an independent role in the ratification process. No evidence has yet emerged that NCOP has played such an assertive role. This is symptomatic of the overall marginal role that NCOP plays in Parliament. There are both institutional and political reasons for this role. First, provinces that must drive the NCOP process are lacking in the skills and knowledge to participate in debates on complex international trade relations. Second, the centralization of political power within the ANC hierarchy is not conducive to a more independent role for provinces (Steytler 1999b). With the premiers of the ANC-run provinces appointed by the central party structure, it makes it unlikely that they, as leaders of their provincial delegations to the NCOP, will publicly challenge government trade policy in that forum.

At the executive level, the Department of Trade and Industry (DTI) has also sought consultation with the provinces. This process takes place through regular meetings between the minister of trade and industry and the provincial members of the executive councils (MECs) responsible for Economic Affairs, the so-called MINMEC (minister-MECs) meetings. These meetings serve as a forum for both information distribution and consultation. The DTI has also included provincial representatives in a number of their delegations to WTO trade negotiations (Steytler 1999a, p. 100).

On the whole, the provinces and local government have played a limited role in articulating provincial interests in trade relations. Not even the province with an extensive wine industry, the Western Cape, participated in the debate about the renaming of "port" and "sherry" during the EU free trade negotiations. Again, when the SADC trade protocol came into force, it was not the subnational units that raised concerns, but the trade unions and the textile industry. Their low-key position is attributed, again, to the current lack of maturity of the provincial system.

The discourse on globalization and its impact on subnational entities have not, however, passed provinces and cities by altogether and conferences on this theme have been convened.[33] In all provinces there has been a concerted effort to connect with the outside world. Twinning agreements with German länder and Canadian provinces has been popular. Although provinces do not have the constitutional power to conclude international treaties (that is the reserve of the national government), they have concluded "cooperation agreements" with other subnational entities (Berg 2000). The Western Cape has such agreements with the Free Province of Bavaria (Germany), Upper Austria (Austria), Tunis (Tunisia), Shandang (China), Madeira (Portugal), and Pusang (Korea). These agreements are aimed at joint projects that benefit communities within the provinces, strengthen cooperation and exchange of expertise and personnel (ibid.). In 1999 the Western Cape, along with Quebec, was admitted as the only non-European members to the Assembly of European Regions.

Although there is considerable potential, there is scant evidence of provinces and municipalities engaging in transnational enterprises. As part of SADC's development program, spatial development initiatives (SDI) have been initiated by the region's governments and some of these SDIs provide considerable opportunities for provinces to engage in cross-border transactions. The best known SDI is the Maputo Development Corridor which links Gauteng and Mpumalanga with the Mozambican port of Maputo (Pahad 2000, p. 51), an opportunity the Mpumalanga government is apparently not exploiting.[34] A further SDI with transnational possibilities for KwaZulu-Natal is the Lubombo SDI, linking Southern Mozambique, Eastern Swaziland, and Northern KwaZulu-Natal in a large eco-tourism area (SADC 2000, p. 76). Metropolitan Cape Town is negotiating with Namibian authorities to pipe natural gas from that country to fire the city's power station.

There appears to be a realization in some provinces and cities that the national government will not necessarily be able to mediate the adverse effects of globalization and that they should engage actively with the issue. The more important response to globalization has therefore been the shaping of domestic policy to cope with the dangers of growing poverty, inequality, and marginalization that globalization may bring and to utilize the opportunities that it may also present (Western Cape 2000, p. 1). This has occurred both at the provincial and local levels.

The Western Cape provincial administration published in May 2000 a Green Paper entitled *Preparing the Western Cape for the Knowledge Economy of the 21st Century*. The premise of engagement is that globally particular regions (rather than countries) have been successful in promoting economic development, noting Bavaria and Upper Austria as examples. It argues that with increasing global governance, national borders have become less important, while "regional characteristics [subnational and transnational] are becoming increasingly significant in location decisions made by firms." For a region to succeed in an increasing international competitiveness, its advantage can come from either of two sources: low-cost leadership (particular low, but skilled wages) or product differentiation (through innovation, quality, and the development of a distinctive brand image). With regard to both sources, the province sees itself playing a facilitative role. The report is, however, fully aware of the underlying tension that the new knowledge-based economy inevitably entails; the employment and income gap will increase between skilled and unskilled labour. The province is further alive to the fact that the Cape Town metropolitan authority, with 75 percent of the population and gross geographical product within its area, will be the key engine driving development in the region (ibid., p. 26).

The Metropolitan Council, too, has engaged in this type of exercise. Again the strategy is, as a title of its 1999 policy document suggests, *Going Global, Working Local: A Strategy for [Cape Metropolitan Area] Cooperation to Reduce Poverty and Build Global Competitiveness in the 21st Century*. The dilemma is familiar: while globalization with knowledge-based business as the primary engine of economic growth is seen to increase inequality between the skilled and the unskilled, the challenge for local government is to make Cape Town a globally competitive city and, at the same time, reduce levels of poverty. As with the Western Cape, it realizes the growing importance of regions and cities, rather than nations, as the centres of economic activities and that the future of the country depends on South African cities becoming globally competitive. However, with rapid urbanization, cities are also increasingly the centres of poverty. To take advantage of the knowledge-driven economy will prove difficult, as there is a critical skills gap between demand and supply; only 15 percent of the people in Cape Town between 18 and 65 have a postsecondary education (Unicity Commission 2000). The understanding is emerging that the new metropolitan city of Cape Town would have to move beyond the current emphasis on service provision, to one of facilitating development and providing civic leadership in the race to become globally competitive and to reduce poverty.

Arguably the most significant impact of globalization has been the way the national government relates to the provinces. Driven by the global "laws" of fiscal discipline and efficient government, the relations between national government and the provinces are increasingly being dominated by the national Treasury. Without taxing powers, provinces are held captive by the Treasury in an extensive system of financial supervision. While the provinces in 1996 received their equitable share of the revenue raised nationally in two trances, currently it is done on a monthly basis. This is accompanied by extensive monthly reporting duties (*National Treasury's Intergovernmental Fiscal Review*, October 2000). An early warning system has been implemented which requires that provincial departments report monthly to the provincial Treasury which, in turn, does the same to the national Treasury. Where provinces have exceeded their budgets, they have been bailed out under strenuous conditions. In two provinces, the national government has intervened by issuing detailed directives on financial matters (Levy *et al.* 1999, p. 86). The overall effect of the fiscal discipline imposed by the national Treasury has been the shrinking of the provinces' room for manoeuvre.

Within the framework of good governance, the priority will be the reform of institutions of the state in terms of seeking public sector efficiency. In particular, the political ambiguity about the need for provinces will be fuelled by concerns about their inefficiency and poor management. With democracy not enhanced, and little evidence of innovation and efficiency in the provinces, the drive toward good governance may well mean greater reliance being placed on local government as the engine for growth and the locus of subnational democratic accountability.

The global demands of fiscal discipline, efficient government and development through decentralization, may give additional impetus and direction to the debate around the future of the provinces. The "laws" of the new global economy may result in the hour-glass configuration where provinces are reduced beyond recognition by the pressures of national and local government. Much depends, though, on the form and direction that globalization takes over the next 15 years.

FUTURE SCENARIOS

The four global scenarios developed for this project — shared govern-ance, global club, regional dominators, and cyberwave — are by nature speculative, representing accentuated models and discounting combina-tions of elements of the various scenarios. Whatever elements emerge dominant, South Africa's place and role in these scenarios will certainly be reflected also in the way decentralization evolves in South Africa.

Shared Governance

The *shared governance* scenario posits a world order where the equality and responsibility of states are recognized. It is a rule-based governance that accommodates the developing world, giving an egalitarian slant to trade relations and providing for extension of aid and the transfer of in-formation technology. It is also a milieu for the environment and the preservation of cultural differences. It is a scenario in which South Africa played its bit part in creating.

South Africa's voice, speaking for the Southern African region and increasingly on behalf of Africa and the south, was heard in international forums. Advocating the principles of equality and global solidarity, the reform of the UN Security Council, giving a permanent seat to Africa, was the first milestone. Other international organizations followed and in the wake of the international protest, the reform of the IMF and the World Bank was swift, increasing the voting power of the borrowing countries considerably. The WTO implemented the principle of limited reciprocity and made the dispute-settlement procedures more accessible to developing countries. The Cairns Group proved its worth and succeeded in persuading the remaining developed countries to abolish their protectionist agricultural policies.

With poverty alleviation an international concern, international assistance benefits both South Africa and Africa. The Millennium Africa Plan, presented by South Africa, Nigeria, and Algeria to the World Economic Forum in Davos in 2001, bore fruit.[35] Under the leadership of Mbeki, and with the backing of the US, EU, and Japan, efforts to promote foreign investment, trade concessions and flows of aid to Africa were coordinated. The major achievement of the African Renaissance, Mbeki noted in 2009, his last year in office, was that the conditionality to the plan — support for peace and democracy and the fight against corruption — was imposed and executed by African leaders and not the IMF and the World Bank. With South Africa's well-being intertwined with that of the region, equitable economic development is engineered through a highly developed SADC.

With increased access to the North American and European markets, the South African economy maintained a growth rate of 6 percent. Despite political opposition from the left, the ANC government was vindicated in that their conservative macroeconomic policy was the only correct route to follow. South Africa benefits significantly from the rise of the "green" ideology. Not only did "emissions trading" result in increased foreign direct investment in South Africa, but eco-tourism in and around the major "transfrontier parks" kick-started the economic development in previously underdeveloped rural areas. Southern Africa has become a prime tourist destination.

With a strong economic growth the pressure of fiscal discipline abates somewhat. Nevertheless, the government, moving under the banner of good governance, targets the provinces, claiming that their functions have been effectively usurped by efficient mega-cities and district municipalities. The latter have shown their mettle with necessary leadership becoming engines of economic development and poverty alleviation. However, efforts to reduce provinces to administrative agencies met fierce local as well as international opposition. The party discipline in the ANC mellowed and elites in some provinces couched their provincial interests in terms of the rising tide of indigenous peoples to self-determination. Ethnicity in the globalized world has become a commodity that in the face of uniformity is treasured. With corruption under control and greater efficiency in place, provinces withstood the onslaught with ease. Other beneficiaries of the movement were traditional leaders and isolated pockets of Afrikaner "volkstaters" who were accommodated in local government structures. In terms of the shared governance scenario multi-level government is likely to be bolstered by this direction of globalization.

Global Club Scenario

In terms of the *global club* scenario — an extension and accentuation of the present — the outcome changes. Wealth and power are concentrated in few countries and multinational companies and they, forming a "club," come to dominate global affairs. No country in Africa becomes a member. Equality and solidarity are not guiding principles and the governance of the IMF and World Bank and the rules of the WTO remained unchanged. The prosperity that effective global governance brings, trickles down to developing countries, but the gap between rich and poor widens.

South Africa is not a club member and sees the riches in which it cannot partake. It voices the discontent of Africa, but the discordant notes are discounted by the club. The marginalization of South Africa caused it to turn increasingly toward Africa both as a market and a political terrain. The grandiose schemes of the OAU such as an African Parliament, an African Court of Human Rights, have come to naught. However, regional integration in southern and east Africa has deepened because South Africa, after a number of regional crises, plays a hegemonic role in the regional institutions to secure stability in the region. A free market of southern Africa is functioning, although the trade is still heavily weighted in favour of South Africa. The free movement of people is not formally allowed but the illegal migration continues unabated as the economic decline of its neighbours continues. As Africa has become difficult to police, the club has abandoned a direct policing role in the ever-increasing social turmoil and internal conflicts. Instead, the club assists South Africa and Nigeria to play the international policeman under the banner of promoting the African renaissance.

South Africa's economic growth strategy battles against the odds. Labour costs remain high and the AIDS pandemic causes the loss of 25 percent of the workforce. After a long fruitless battle to get "the balance between labour and capital" right, the ANC lost the election to a populist party, dominated by organized labour. A skills and capital drain coupled with the inability to turn around the education system, did not produce an innovative and entrepreneurial culture. The technological gap between South Africa and its preferred markets of the club members has increased and the skewedness of the WTO trading rules has driven local businesses out of the market.

The lack of sustained growth has led to South Africa's increasing indebtedness to the IMF and the World Bank. Although the required macroeconomic policy was in place by 2000, the failure to implement it effectively resulted in the "micro-management" of policy and practice through a number of structural adjustment programs. One of the casualties was the political structure of the provinces. The ANC's ambivalence toward the provinces coincided with the demands for lean and mean government. The corrupt and inefficient provinces whose political elites showed increasingly independent tendencies, were sacrificed in the name of good government. The savings effected in eliminating 423 MPLs and the entourages of the provincial executives was acclaimed internationally as prudent housekeeping. Provincial appeals to the federal sentiments of club members, notably the United States and the European Union, did not receive a favourable hearing. The national government successfully argued that local government would more than adequately provide political accountability. Provincial claims, backed-up by threatened ethnic conflict, are met with increased powers to municipalities in the area of education, health, and welfare.

By 2015 more than 60 percent of the population will live in metropolitan areas. With 80 percent of all economic activity located in the mega-cities, they manage a level of financial viability. Within an overall national policy of fiscal restraint, the gap between the rural poor and the urban social net of services will increase.

Regional Dominators Scenario

In the *regional dominators* scenario, major geopolitical blocs, showing a high degree of internal integration, confront one another in a new struggle for economic and political advantage. International organizations, depending on cooperation, are increasingly irrelevant. With economic growth low, the inequality between the developed and developing worlds increases. The neo-conservative agenda also means less government. In Africa the developed worlds showed little interest in supporting economic development or intervening in local conflicts.

After years of lobbying, negotiating, and uniting African countries behind its efforts to reform the UN, South Africa took its permanent seat on the Security Council. However, the reform of the Security Council was symptomatic of its irrelevance and ineffectiveness, and it could do little to prevent the increasing tensions between the dominant blocs and aggressive competition. A similar fate befell developing countries' efforts at reforming the WTO rules making the international trade regime more equitable to the marginalized economies of the developing world.

Faced with two regional blocs showing only limited interest in the African market and raw materials, South Africa, and the regional formations it leads, faced a difficult choice: to choose between the spheres of influence of the North American or the European bloc. The advantages are limited. From the European bloc, development programs in the form of the Cotonou Conventions have long lapsed. Bilateral agreements in the style of the South African-EU free trade agreement are the order of the day. The North American bloc is less charitable. In developing its North American bloc, the US focused on South America and the black congressional lobby is only able to offer the *African Growth and Opportunity Act* of 2000 which, due to administrative manipulation and red tape, is a dead letter. In the end, the only choice South Africa could make was to opt for the European bloc.

With market access to the major economic blocs more and more difficult because of the breakdown of the WTO's rule-based system, South Africa turned inevitably to the African market, driving both the full implementation of the SADC free trade protocol, as well as its amalgamation with COMESA. With nearly half of the sub-Saharan countries in a free trade zone, the African Economic Union is slowly becoming a more realistic goal.

Riding on the back of the successful implementation of the Southern and Eastern African Free Trade Agreement, SADC has been reformed politically and South Africa plays a leading role in maintaining stability within the community. With the developed world showing little interest in local conflicts, South Africa is called upon to intervene, but act only in cases of direct strategic interest. Africa's other pet projects of continental integration have, however, fallen on hard times. The African Parliament, thought to be an attainable ambition 15 years ago, has been reduced to a "chat room" on the Internet.

The regional trade advances that South Africa achieved have displayed a poor return. African markets remain small and the growth rate seldom exceeds the population growth. The number of African countries on the UN list of heavy indebted countries has increased, since the debt relief efforts of the early 2000s withered away. Foreign aid has also declined.

South Africa's economic performance is no exception. Foreign direct investment did not materialize. The labour costs remained high and the AIDS pandemic has reduced life expectancy to 46 years and increased the cost of production by 25 percent. The only interest that multinational corporations show is in the traditional areas of raw materials. With poor growth, access to state machinery becomes an important resource for income and corruption is rampant. To control the burgeoning national debt, government cuts back on social spending. Following the example of the successful economies of the regional dominators, smaller government is the new mantra. The first and obvious target is the provinces. A costly echelon of politicians and senior officials has added little value to service delivery. The rampant corruption in the areas of social security results in little opposition from the public. Their death knell has long been rung by metropolitan and district municipalities which have politically eclipsed their provincial competitors.

The social unrest that has followed the increased disparities in income and the cutbacks in social spending has been primarily an urban phenomenon. Ethnic demands for greater provincial autonomy are muted and effectively deflected by granting greater powers to local authorities. To cope with the crime wave, security is taken over by public-private partnerships managed by municipalities. The metropolitan municipalities brace themselves as they become home for millions of illegal immigrants — economic refugees of the neighbouring countries. They deal directly with the countries of origin in futile attempts at repatriation. In rural areas the land-grabs of farms owned by white farmers are rife and ethnic tensions are defused by granting traditional leaders effective local government powers.

Cyberwave Scenario

The *cyberwave* is "characterized by rapid, unpredictable and continuous technological change that drives business and stimulates growth, but frequently outstrips the ability of public institutions to stay abreast of change and respond effectively." A key feature is that rapid growth is skewed both within developed countries and between developed and developing countries. Both domestic and international political institutions weaken. The benefits of the cyberwave bypass the African continent altogether and the rapid and continuous technological change has left Africa further behind. With less financial aid from international organizations and market access to the West less secure, Africa struggles.

South Africa's desperate attempts to gain some advantage in the slip stream of the wave are met with limited success. It has not become a participant in the "new technology economy"; the human capital that drives the new technological economy is absent as the educational system fails to retool itself for the hi-tech knowledge industry. The cyberwave has, however, noticeable ripple effects on the country. One of the early bio-technological products is a vaccine for HIV. The price is, however, exorbitant in a free-falling exchange rate. The absence of IMF balance-of-payment loans places the cure beyond the open market. The parallel importation of a generic vaccine from southeast Asia, which has the capacity to copy the technological advances of the West at a fraction of the price, saves the day. North American companies are frustrated by the weakness of the WTO to protect their patents and police licensing agreements. Lacking support and financing by the leading capitalist democracies, the WTO has been unable to deal effectively with patent piracy on any significant scale. The decline in IMF lifelines compelled the South African government to ignore the remaining WTO-sponsored sanctions for its violation of the TRIPS agreement.

Given the public rejoicing in the HIV vaccine — the products of the new technological economy — the ideology that follows in the cyberwave wake finds receptive ground in South Africa. Political elites transpose the philosophy of the new entrepreneurial class to politics. Small government is best as innovation and experimentation are only possible in small units. Local communities have the best answers to social challenges. The national government was helpless in the face of the HIV/AIDS pandemic and it had no answer to the question of how to engineer economic growth. The government's view of smaller government — the elimination of provincial government — elicits the opposite response. Small government means less central government and its efforts to abolish the provinces falter before political opposition. The rigid and

hierarchical political structure of the ANC finally cracks, not on traditional ideological lines of the past, but on the basis of new regional interests.
The newly formed regional splinter parties contest the future election and
the ANC loses control. The glue of the new coalition government is the
common belief in a weak centre and strong and autonomous provinces.
Provincial individualism is encouraged and celebrated. Provincial powers
are increased and provinces form alliances with the mega-cities, placing
their faith in local entrepreneurs to provide practical answers.

The best future scenario, and the one South Africa is working toward,
is shared governance. Growth and global interest and concern for ethnicity
may save the day for the provinces. Under the cyberwave, the result is the
same. Common to both scenarios is a weakened national government — in
the case of shared governance because of the strength of global governance,
while in the other, by its absence. The future of the provinces looks less rosy
where global forces lead to strong central governments as in the case of the
global club and regional dominators scenarios. In all the scenarios, the new
mega-cities will emerge as key players on the domestic scene.

CONCLUSION

The constitutional compact of 1993 gave South Africa the rudiments of a
federal system. The 1996 constitution entrenched decentralization and
with the full implementation of the local government provisions in December 2000, which included the establishment of strong mega-cities,
the legal architecture is largely in place. The present system can best be
described as an emerging system of decentralized government the contours of which will evolve in the near future.

Although the system is a highly centralized form of federalism, provinces have not yet fully explored the constitutional space that is available
to them. Within the present confines of the constitutional framework,
the full exploitation of the current federal features can deepen the process
of decentralization. For example, NCOP could become a powerful forum
where provinces play a meaningful role in the legislative field and assert
their weight in foreign policy through NCOP's power to co-determine
international treaties. National legislation regulating the provinces' con-
stitutionally-protected taxing powers could lead to more accountable and
innovative provincial governance. Whether this would happen depends
on a change in political circumstances.

The experience in India was that a quasi-federation, which lay dormant for several decades, underwent a dramatic process of federalization over the last decade. This occurred when the centralizing force of the Congress Party dissipated and a federal political culture emerged. Ironically, central party control undermined the popular structures of the Congress Party. The decline in the autonomy of the party organization in the states led to a weak and attenuated party and lack of stable loyalty structures (Hargraves 1975, p. 165). Could the same happen in South Africa?

The longer the South African system continues in its present form, the more likely it is that the federal elements would take root and deepen. Over time a federal political culture may well emerge within the current centralist ANC. It has been suggested that greater centralization, which is in evidence in the party today, would be at the cost of increasing organizational decay (Giliomee and Simkins 1999, p. 345). If there is little political reward for provincial and local leadership, it may impact adversely on the political organization at branch and grassroots levels (Steytler 1999b). The emergence of a federalizing process in South Africa similar to that in India, may, however, be pre-empted by both domestic and international developments.

The dominant ethos within the ANC leans at the moment toward the scaling down of the provinces. They were regarded as a necessary compromise in the early 1990s, but they have not excelled in clean and efficient government for service delivery. At a party political level, factionalism has thrived in some provinces. Given the state and role of provinces, it has been suggested that the newly established metropolitan and district councils could readily step into the provincial shoes.

Political opposition to the eclipse of provinces will come mainly from the IFP where the withering away of provincial political structures would relegate the party to the rural backwaters of KwaZulu-Natal. While the ANC could manage IFP opposition by drawing it into a closer alliance at the national level, the opposition from the Democratic Alliance (DA), drawing support mainly from white, coloured, and Indian communities, would be discounted. In any event, the resultant strengthening of local government would also benefit the DA which seeks to make the metropolitan city of Cape Town its showcase for good government and economic development.

Coinciding with the process of decentralization has been South Africa's enthusiastic participation in the international community. Because the process is unsettled, global integration may exert significant influence indirectly on the direction that this process takes. The argument of this chapter has been that the pre-existing tendency toward centralization and localization in South Africa may be reinforced by the pressures of global integration.

In the short term, South Africa's commitment to abide by the "universal 'laws' for prudent macroeconomic management" has resulted in domestic policies that entailed, among other things, fiscal discipline, downsizing of the public sector, and public sector efficiency. As a direct consequence, intergovernmental relations are dominated by the national Treasury; and provincial spending is carefully monitored and supervised, shrinking provincial space considerably.

In the long term, the ANC's ambiguity toward the provinces is reinforced by the very same economic laws. Lean and mean government does not require provinces since the service-delivery function could be done more effectively either by national or local government. Moreover, strong local government dovetails well with the second wave of global good governance which posits localization of government functions as an effective and efficient vehicle for development and accountability. The result will then be an hourglass federation — squeezed between the national and local governments, provinces lose many of their powers to the other two spheres of government.

The impact of globalization on the evolving process of decentralization is not, however, unilinear; globalization will not inevitably contribute to the decline of the provinces. The different routes that globalization may take, as described in the various scenarios, may have different outcomes. While the global governance scenario favours the position of provinces, as does the cyberwave scenario, they will do less well if the global club or regional dominators scenarios eventuate.

At present, the external influences on domestic policy flow from global integration. Because regional integration is currently so shallow it has had no impact on the process of decentralization. This may change, however. The pressures of global economic integration will certainly propel the regional integration process forward. In the past, the process of integration in southern Africa was largely driven by politics and not economics as is the case in other regional integration projects. The impact of global economic integration may change this fundamentally. The establishment of the SADC free trade protocol signals a change in approach. When integration makes economic sense, political integration becomes more feasible. Regional integration may, then, bring to bear its own dynamic on South Africa's decentralized system.

Notes

1. Eastern Cape (iziXhosa 82.3 percent); KwaZulu-Natal (isiZulu 79.3 percent); Northern Cape (Afrikaans 66 percent); Western Cape (Afrikaans 62.2 percent); North West (Setswana 59 percent); Free State (Sesotho 57.4 percent) Northern Province (Sepedi 56.7 percent). RSA *Statistics in Brief* (1997, Table 3.9).

2. "Rich Are Getting Richer, the Poor Are Getting Poorer," *Business Day*, 9 November 2000.

3. Dr. Malegapuru Makgoba, president of SA Medical Research Council, quoted in "SA Could Face AIDS Holocaust — Makgoba," *Business Day*, 22 November 2000.

4. Countries with a GNP per capita of between $2,996 and $9,265 are classified by the World Bank as upper-middle income countries. These include Argentina, Brazil, Malaysia, Hungary, Poland, and Saudi Arabia. World Bank. *Data & Maps*. At <http:/www.worldbank.org/databytopic/class.htm>.

5. For 1996 and 1997 the GDP growth rate was 3.1 percent, dropping in 1998 to 0.6 and rising in 1999 to 1.2 percent. World Bank. *South Africa Data Profile* at <http:/devdata.worldbank.org/external/.htm>. The predicted growth rate for 2000 is 3 percent.

6. "FDI Plummets 43% in 2000, Survey Shows," *Business Report*, 23 January 2001.

7. This section is drawn from Steytler (2000*a*).

8. For a discussion on the classification of the interim constitution of 1993, see Elazar (1994, p. 29); Watts (1994, p. 75).

9. "Provinces could go, says Sutcliffe," *Independent*, 14 October 2000.

10. "Strip down provinces, says premier," *Sunday Times*, 18 March 2001.

11. For the first six years (1994–99) the average number of laws passed annually was 6.7 (excluding appropriation bills).

12. National Treasury's Intergovernmental Fiscal Review 2000, quoted in *Sunday Times*, 22 October 2000.

13. The Non-Aligned Movement Ministerial Conference at the 8th summit of the Inter-Governmental Authority on Development, reported in the *Cape Times*, 24 November 2000.

14. Jackie Selebi, Director General of Foreign Affairs, quoted in Mills (2000*a*, p. 329).

15. See John Dludlu, "A weak OAU exposed by Cote d'Ivoire farce," *Business Day*, 6 Novemer 2000.

16. The African Union (AU) was established in July 2002 at a heads of government meeting in Durban, South Africa. The AU replaced the OAU.

17. "SA bid to host human rights court," *Sunday Times*, 5 November 2000.

18. The 14 countries are: Angola, Botswana, Namibia, Lesotho, Swaziland, Zimbabwe, Mozambique, Tanzania, Zambia, Malawi, South Africa, Mautirius, Seychelles, and the Democratic Republic of Congo. Uganda is considering applying for membership.

19. John Dludlu and Christof Maletsky, "SADC unity put to tough test," *Business Day*, 12 March 2001.

20. "Big plans for mega park," *Mail & Guardian*, 24 to 30 November 2000.

21. "SA must pave the way for regional trade development," *Business Day*, 8 September 2000.

22. "Globalisation needs union movement, says Erwin," *Business Day*, 23 August 2000.

23. It was 26.2 percent in 1989, 23 percent in 1995, 25.7 percent in 1998, and 25.4 percent in 1999.

24. Imports were 21.2 percent of the GDP in 1989, 22.1 percent in 1995, 24.4 percent in 1998 and 22.9 percent in 1999.

25. Thomas (1999, p. 113). See also African Development Bank report, quoted by Parsons "SA must pave the way for regional trade development," *Business Day*, 8 September 2000.

26. "Southern and eastern African states set 2025 as target date for monetary union," *Sunday Times*, 22 Octobeer 2000.

27. Argentina, Australia, Brazil, Canada, Chile, Colombia, Fiji, Indonesia, Malaysia, New Zealand, Paraguay, the Philippines, Thailand and Uruguay.

28. "Manuel to seek reforms in Prague," *Business Day*, 12 September 2000.

29. Patrick Bond in *Reconstruct*, 17 September 2000; IMF, *World Economic Outlook* 2000 first half, reported in *Business Day*, 20 September 2000.

30. Eduardo Aninat, deputy managing director of the IMF, reported in editorial *Beeld*, 7 November 2000; El Tigani Ibrahim, IMF's South African country representative, reported in *Business Day*, 7 November 2000.

31. "Wolfenson at SA workshop," *Business Day*, 3 November 2000.

32. "Mbeki in fresh bid to boost economy," *Business Day*, 6 November 2000.

33. See, for example, the Western Cape: from 5–7 June 2000 there was a conference in Bavaria on the theme of Consequences of Globalization and

Localization for Germany and South Africa, for Bavaria and the Western Cape. Three months later the Western Cape government hosted its own conference on the theme, "Globalization and International Relations: Challenges and Opportunities for the Provinces" 31 August–1 September 2000, Stellenbosch.

34. "ANC lambasts 'rudderless' Mpuma premier," *Mail & Guardian*, 17–23 November 2000.

35. "Leaders have plan for African poverty," *Business Day*, 27 November 2000; "Mbeki's grand plan for Africa's recovery," *Cape Times*, 29 January 2001. The New Partnership for African Development (NEPAD) was established in 2002, forming the basis for an economic recovery plan for Africa.

References

Abedian, I. 1998. "Economic Globalization: The Consequences for Fiscal Management," in *Economic Globalization and Fiscal Policy*, ed. I. Abedian and M. Biggs. Cape Town: Oxford University Press.

Abedian, I., T. Ajam and L. Walker. 1997. *Promises, Plans and Priorities: South Africa's Emerging Fiscal Structures*. Cape Town: IDASA.

Ajam, T. 1998. "The Evolution and Devolution of Fiscal Decentralization in South Africa," in *Economic Globalization and Fiscal Policy*, ed. I. Abedian and M. Biggs. Cape Town: Oxford University Press.

Barber, S. 2000*a*. "US Officials at Odds on Growth Act," *Business Day*, 18 September.

—— 2000*b*. "Clinton Eases Africa's Trade Terms," *Business Day*, 2 October.

Berg, R. 2000. "Provincial Autonomy, the South African Constitution, and Globalisation: A Consideration of Provincial Powers in the Context of the Increasing Integration of the World." Paper presented at conference on Consequences of Globalization and Localization for Germany and South Africa, for Bavaria and the Western Cape, 5–7 June, Evangelische Akademie, Tutzing, Germany.

Bertelsmann-Scott, T. 2000. "The SA-EU TDCA and its Impact on South African Provinces." Paper presented at conference on Globalization and International Relations: Challenges and Opportunities for the Provinces, Western Cape Provincial Administration, Stellenbosch, 31 August.

Boulle, L., B. Harris and C. Hoexter. 1988. *Constitutional and Administrative Law*. Cape Town: Juba & Co.

Breytenbach, W. 1999. "Indian Ocean Rim: Assessing the Prospects for Cooperation and Integration," *Development Southern Africa* 16:69.

—— 2000. "Failure of Security Co-operation in SADC: The Suspension of the Organ for Politics, Defence and Security," *South African Journal of International Affairs* 7:85.

Burford, G. 1999. "Dinosaur or Dynamic Organisation? The Future of the Commonwealth," *Indicator South Africa* 16(3):86.

Cape Metropolitan Council. 1999. *Going Global, Working Local: A Strategy for CMA Co-operation to Reduce Poverty and Build Global Competitiveness in the 21st Century.* Cape Town: The Council.

Chigara, B. 2000. "Operation of the SADC Protocol on Politics, Defence and Security in the Democratic Republic of Congo," *African Journal of International and Comparative Law* 12:58.

Dentier, J. 2000. "Some Remarks of Fiscal Decentralisation." At <http://www.imf.org/external/pubs/ft/seminar/sppp/idn/dethier>.

Du Plessis, E.D. 1999. "The TRIPS Agreement and South African Legislation: The Case of the Parallel Importation of Medicines," *Law, Democracy and Development* 3:55.

Elazar, D.E. 1994. "Form of State: Federal, Unitary, or ..." in *Birth of a Constitution*, ed. B. de Villiers. Cape Town: Juba & Co.

Ellman, S. 1993. "Federalism Gone Awry: The Structure of Government in the KwaZulu-Natal Constitution," *South African Journal of Human Rights* 9:165.

Games, D. 2000. "Free Trade Area Launch a Big Step for Africa," *Business Day*, 7 November 2000.

Giliomee, H. and C. Simkins. 1999. "Conclusion," in *The Awkward Embrace: One Party Domination and Democracy*, ed. H. Giliomee and C. Simkins. Cape Town: Tafelberg.

Hargraves, R.L. 1975. *India: Government and Politics in a Developing Nation*, 2d ed. New York: Harcourt Brace Jovanovich.

Heiman, M.R.A. 1997. "The Drive Towards Regionalisation in Southern Africa: Fictional Reality," *African Journal of International and Comparative Law* 9:639.

Holden, M.G. and A.G. Isemonger. 1999. "A Review of Trade Trends: South Africa and Indian Ocean Rim," *Development Southern Africa* 16:89.

Karrim, Q.A. 2000. "Trends in HIV/AIDS Infection: Beyond Current Statistics," *South African Journal of International Affairs* 7(2):1.

Katzenellenbogen, J. 2000. "Representative in SA Reflects New Face of IMF," *Business Day*, 7 November.

Levy, N. *et al.* 1999. *The Intergovernmental Relations Audit: Towards a Culture of Co-operative Government.* Report to the Department of Provincial and Local Government, Pretoria.

Mastenbroek, R. and N. Steytler. 1997. "Local Government: The New Constitutional Enterprise," *Law, Democracy and Development* 1:233.

Mawby, B. 2000. "Human Rights and South Africa's Foreign Policy: A Guiding Light or a Flickering Candle?" *South African Journal on Human Rights* 16:372.

Mboweni, T. 2000. Speech given at the Diplomatic Forum, Rand Afrikaans University, 25 October 2000. *Business Day*, 1 November.

Mills, G. 2000*a*. *The Wired Model: South Africa, Foreign Policy and Globalisation.* Cape Town: Tafelberg.

—— 2000*b*. "AIDS and the South African Military: Timeworn Cliche or Timebomb?" in *HIV/AIDS: A Threat to the African Renaissance?* Occasional Papers. Johannesburg: Konrad Adenauer Stiftung.

—— 2000*c*. "COMESA and SADC Should Combine into One Coherent Unit," *Business Report*, 31 October.

Murray, C. and R. Simeon. 1999. "From Paper to Practice: The National Council of Provinces After its First Year," *South Africa Public Law* 14:96.

Pahad, A. 2000. "Regional Integration, Globalisation and Democratic Stability: A South-South Perspective," in *Southern Africa and Mercosur/I: Reviewing the Relationship and Seeking Opportunities*, Report of Conference held in Sao Paulo, Brazil. Johannesburg: Konrad Adenauer-Stiftung.

Peter, C.M. 1997. "Regional Integration in Africa in the 1990s: The Impact of South Africa Within the Region," in *Democracy, Human Rights and Development in Southern Africa*, ed. N. Steytler. Johannesburg: Lex Patria.

Phillipe, X. 1997. "The Lome Convention and Trade Between Europe and South Africa," in *Democracy, Human Rights and Development in Southern Africa*, ed. N. Steytler. Johannesburg: Lex Patria.

Quattek, K. 2000. "The Economic Impact of AIDS in South Africa: A Dark Cloud on the Horizon," in *HIV/AIDS: A Threat to the African Renaissance?* Occasional Papers. Johannesburg: Konrad Adenauer Stiftung.

Schonteich, M. 2000. "Age and AIDS: A Lethal Mix for South Africa's Crime Rate" in *HIV/AIDS: A Threat to the African Renaissance?* Occasional Papers. Johannesburg: Konrad Adenauer Stiftung.

Shell, R. 2000. "Halfway to the Holocaust: The Economic, Demographic and Social Implications of the AIDs Pandemic to the Year 2010 in the Southern African Region," in *HIV/AIDS: A Threat to the African Renaissance?* Occasional Papers. Johannesburg: Konrad Adenauer Stiftung.

Simeon, R. 1998. "Considerations on the Design of Federations: The South African Constitution in Comparative Perspective," *SA Public Law* 13:42.

Sloth-Nielsen, J. 2001. *The Impact of International Law on the Juvenile Justice Reform in South Africa.* LL D thesis, University of the Western Cape.

South Africa. 1999. *South African Yearbook 1999.* Pretoria: Government Printers.

—— 2000. *South African Survey 1999/2000.* Pretoria: Government Printers.

—— Department of Finance. 2000. *Medium Term Budget Policy Statement.* Pretoria: Department of Finance.

—— Ministry of Provincial Affairs and Constitutional Development. 1998. *White Paper on Local Government.* Pretoria: Government Printers.

Southern Africa Development Community (SADC). 2000. Southern Africa Economic Summit 2000 prepared by SADC Finance and Investment

Coordinating Unit, Department of Finance, South Africa, for SADC and the World Economic Forum.

Stahl, H.-M. 2000. "Towards a South Atlantic Free Trade Area? The Business, Trade and Investment Dimensions," in *Southern Africa and Mercosur/I: Reviewing the Relationship and Seeking Opportunities.* Johannesburg: Konrad Adenauer-Stiftung.

Steytler, N. 1995. "Constitution-Making: In Search of a Democratic South Africa," in *Negotiating Justice: A New Constitution for South Africa*, ed. M. Bennun and M.D.D. Newitt. Exeter: University of Exeter Press.

—— 1999*a*. "Global Governance and National Sovereignty: The World Trade Organisation and South Africa's New Constitutional Framework," *Law, Democracy and Development* 3:89.

—— 1999*b*. "One Party Dominance and the Functioning of South Africa's Decentralised System of Government." Unpublished paper.

—— 2000*a*. "Sudafrika — Eine foderale Verfassungsordnung in Werden," in Europaishe Zentrum fur Foderalismus-Forschung Tubingen *Jahrbuch des Foderalismus 2000.* Baden-Baden: Nomos Verlagsgesellschaft.

—— 2000*b*. "Concurrency and Cooperative Government: A South African Case Study." Paper for the Conference "Reform of German Federalism: An International Comparative Approach" Bertelsmann Stiftung, Berlin.

Steytler, N. and J. Mettler. 1998. "Federalism and Peacemaking: The South African Experience." IACFS conference, Jerusalem. Unpublished paper.

Thomas, R.H. 1999. "The World Trade Organisation and Southern African Trade Relations," *Law, Democracy and Development* 3:105.

Unicity Commission. 2000. *Discussion Document: Developing the Future City of Cape Town.* Cape Town: Unicity Commission.

United Nations Development Programme (UNDP). 1999. *Human Development Report.* New York: United Nations.

—— 2000. *Transformation for Human Development: South Africa.* Pretoria: UNDP.

Watts, R.L. 1994. "Is the New Constitution Federal or Unitary?" in *Birth of a Constitution*, ed. B. de Villiers. Cape Town: Juba & Co.

Welsh, D. 1994. "Federalism and the Divided Society: A South African Perspective," in *Evaluating Federal Systems*, ed. B. de Villiers. Cape Town: Juba & Co.

Western Cape. Department of Economic Affairs, Agriculture and Tourism. 2000. *Green Paper: Preparing the Western Cape for the Knowledge Economy of the 21st Century.* Cape Town: Provincial Administration of the Western Cape.

World Bank. 2000*a*. *South Africa at a Glance.* New York: World Bank.

—— 2000*b*. Web site at <http:/www.worldbank.org/publicsector/decentralization/rationale.htm>.

—— 2000*c*. *World Development Report 2000.* New York: Oxford University Press.

TRANSFORMING SYSTEMS

Globalization and the European Union: Shared Governance on a Regional Scale

Liesbet Hooghe

INTRODUCTION

Globalization, as this chapter understands it, refers to processes — economic, military, environmental, and social — that thicken interdependence among individuals across different countries (Keohane and Nye 2000). Globalization undercuts the normal patterns of interaction in Europe, which, for much of the twentieth century, had been confined within the boundaries of the nation-state and regulated by sovereign national governments. Globalization, then, can be expected to create conflict since private actions and government measures often adversely affect neighbours.

A functional response to these externalities would be to internalize them in a global political unit, or more precisely, a multitude of political jurisdictions where, for each policy problem, the optimal territorial scope of government would be determined in light of externalities (Alesina and Spolaore 1997; Casella and Weingast 1995; Frey and Eichenberger 1999; for a critique of this neoclassical theory of authority, see Marks and Hooghe 2000). For example, one would want a global government to address global warming, a US-EU government to solve trade-related issues that affect both regional economies, and localized cooperative arrangements between subregional or local governments to deal with, say, externalities from waste disposal or urban planning.

Of course, reality is more complex. Actual responses to globalization differ from the ones predicted by functional imperatives. A major
reason is that individuals do not agree on what is efficient or functional.
Which solution is considered "efficient" or "functional" is the outcome of
political struggle, not of value-free analysis. That leads us to examine the
coalitional politics that underlies particular institutional responses to
globalization.

In Western Europe, European integration has been the chief retort
of national governments, political parties, and private actors to globalization. European integration accelerated in the mid-1980s, and again in the
mid-1990s, and this acceleration was a direct response to problems attributed to globalization — augmented national vulnerability to trade and
financial flows, eroding competitiveness for European firms, structural
unemployment and labour market rigidities, and increasing immigration
from its poorer eastern and southern Mediterranean neighbours into the
European Union (EU). I do not mean to say that globalization determined how Europe's institutions, policies, and politics changed. "Domestic
politics" — national and European leaders' preferences, and societal interests as expressed by producer groups and political parties — has mediated
these changes. Yet I will show that the European Union has become a
battleground for opponents and proponents of globalization. Some want
the EU to be a bulwark against global pressures, and others want it to
accelerate the pace of increasing *global*, as opposed to national or European, interdependence.

A CAUTIONARY NOTE

The European Union is different from the other political systems examined in this book. It is not a state because it is not ruled by a single regime.
It is certainly not an established federation like the United States, Canada,
Australia, or even South Africa or India. The European Union does not
have a constitution; it is based on treaties.

There is more that distinguishes the EU from the other cases in this
book. The EU was born out of the ashes of war. In technical terms, one
could say it was a direct response to a security dilemma, military interdependence, in Western Europe 50 years ago. These links of interdependence
have broadened into the economic and social sphere. At one level, therefore, the EU is not only at the receiving end of globalization but it is itself

an agent of globalization in Europe. Yet it is not a mere muscular brother of the North American Free Trade Agreement (NAFTA), or the World Trade Organization (WTO). That would miss the point about the European Union. Over the past 50 years of its existence, it has been transformed from a security and trade organization into a polity in which nation-states as large and as powerful as Germany, France, and the United Kingdom have ceded national sovereignty, the ultimate authority, over virtually all policy areas, and decision-making looks and feels very much like the kind of politics one finds in democratic federal states such as the US, Canada, or Germany. That transformation has happened at break-neck speed.

I find myself chasing independent variables. Is it European integration — the process by which interdependence between societies and groups in Europe is promoted and regulated through EU membership? Am I seeking to understand, in other words, how the European Union, as the specific embodiment of globalization in Europe, affects interstate and intersociety relations in Europe? Or is the independent variable the amalgam of global and regional economic, social, cultural, and other pressures that are pounding on the EU's institutions, policies, and politics as they are pounding on the Canadian or the German federation? This makes the European Union the dependent variable. I feel I need to address both, and that explains the somewhat different structure of this chapter.

I begin by positing the European Union as the dependent variable. In the next section, I will briefly sketch the history and institutions of the EU, and I go on to examine whether global pressures or domestic factors influenced the acceleration of European integration over the past 15 years. I then shift European integration to the independent variable side of the equation, and I examine how global and EU pressures have affected key dimensions of politics in Europe.

SITUATIONAL CONTEXT

The European Union was created in 1957, when six countries signed the *Treaty of Rome* that set out to establish a customs union by 1970. From the start, the European Union (then still called the European Economic Community) had greater ambitions than NAFTA, which is a free trade area only. France, Germany, Italy, and the Benelux (Belgium, the Netherlands, Luxembourg) completed the customs union two years ahead of time in 1968. The next boost to European integration came with the accession of Britain, Ireland, and Denmark in 1973. Norway had negotiated accession as well, but a public referendum in Norway struck that down. It was not until the mid-1980s that European integration really took off, with three major treaty revisions in a row: the *Single European Act* (SEA) of 1987, which committed member states to the creation of a single market by 1992, the Treaty of European Union (*Maastricht Treaty*) of 1993, which paved the way for Economic and Monetary Union (EMU) — that is, a single currency — by 1999, and the *Amsterdam Treaty* of 1999, which shifted power in a range of non-economic policies, strengthened the institutions, and laid the foundation for a common foreign policy.[1] The European Union now resembles more a political federation than an international organization for economic cooperation.

Deepening of European integration went together with widening membership. In 1981, Greece became the tenth member, and in 1986 Spain and Portugal followed. In 1995, Sweden, Austria, and Finland left the European Free Trade Association to join the European Union, while the Norwegian people, for the second time, voted against. Ten more countries are set to join in 2004: the Czech Republic, Estonia, Hungary, Latvia, Lithuania, Poland, Slovakia, Slovenia, as well as Cyprus and Malta. By 2010, more countries may come in: Bulgaria, Romania, the newly created republics from ex-Yugoslavia, perhaps also Albania, and Turkey.

After the accession of the first ten countries, the population of the European Union will have grown from 374 million in 2000 to almost half a billion people. Its gross domestic product (GDP) per capita — now at over US$22,300 per head — will decline by 18 percent; the average GDP per capita of the incoming countries is just below US$3,300. The economic and socio-political differences between the current EU and the prospective members are unparalleled in EU history.

In the remainder of this section I highlight the changing division of authority between national and European institutions, and I introduce the EU's main decision-making institutions.

The Shift of Authority from the National to the European

Figure 1 and Table 1 provide a bird's eye view of how authority has been reallocated between the nation-state and the European Union since 1950. The bars in Figure 1 indicate, for each of five time points, what proportion

FIGURE 1
National and EU Power, 1950–2000

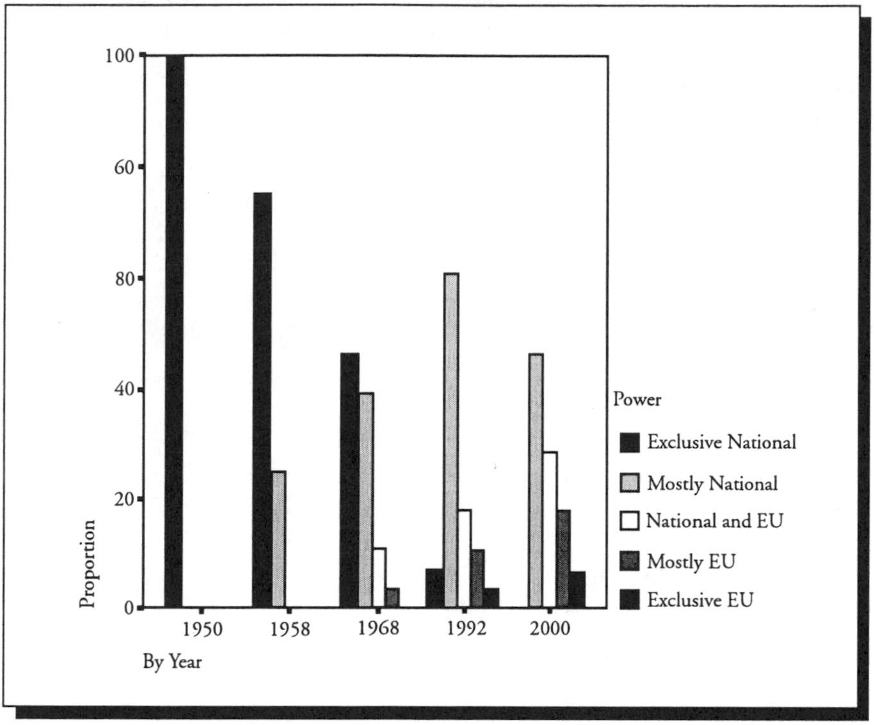

Source: Based on Hooghe and Marks (2001, Appendix 1).

of policy areas is exclusively national (score 1), mostly national (score 2), shared EU-national competence (score 3), mostly EU (score 4), or exclusively EU (score 5). Table 1 provides details on these shifts by policy area.[2]

In 1950, policy-making in all 28 areas was determined exclusively in territorial states. The state reigned supreme. This was the outcome of a process of state-building in Europe that lasted centuries, and that involved the creation of national legal systems, national armies, national systems of taxation, national parliaments, and over the past century, national welfare, national health, national education, and national industrial-relations systems. This changed to some extent when the Treaty of Rome was signed in 1957, which created the European Economic Community (EEC). Some areas in the economic field — regulation of goods and services, industry,

TABLE 1
Supranational Power, 1950–2000

	1950	1957	1968	1992	2000
ECONOMIC POLICY					
Goods/services	1	2	3	4	4
Agriculture	1	1	4	4	4
Capital flows	1	1	1	4	4
Persons/workers	1	1	2	3	4
Transportation	1	2	2	2	2
Energy	1	2	1	2	2
Communications	1	1	1	2	2
Environment	1	2	2	3	3
Regional policy	1	1	1	3	3
Competition	1	2	3	3	3
Industry	1	2	2	2	2
Money/credit	1	1	2	2	5
Foreign exchange	1	1	2	2	4
Revenue/taxes	1	1	2	2	2
Macroeconomic	1	1	2	2	3
SOCIAL/INDUSTRIAL POLICY					
Work conditions	1	1	2	2	3
Health	1	1	1	2	2
Social welfare	1	2	2	2	2
Education and research	1	1	2	2	2
Labour relations	1	1	1	1	2
LEGAL/CONSTITUTIONAL POLICY					
Justice	1	1	1	3	3
Citizenship	1	1	1	2	3
Participation	1	1	1	2	2
Police and order	1	1	1	1	2
INTERNATIONAL RELATIONS/SECURITY					
Trade negotiations	1	1	3	5	5
Economic-military aid	1	1	1	2	2
Diplomacy	1	1	1	2	3
Defence and war	1	1	1	2	2

Notes: 1 = All policy decisions at national level;
2 = Only some policy decisions at EC level;
3 = Policy decisions at both national and EC level;
4 = Mostly policy decisions at EC level;
5 = All policy decisions at EC level

Source: Hooghe and Marks (2001, Appendix 1).

transport, energy, competition — shifted from exclusively national to mainly national with some European Community (EC) competence.

In 1968, the EC completed the customs union, and this is reflected in the rising bar for shared EU/national competence. In three areas — competition policy, trade negotiations, and internal market regulation (to ensure free movement of goods and services) — the European Commission began to play a major role: it was building up precedent in competition policy, it began negotiating on behalf of member states in trade negotiations on goods, and it drafted proposals for harmonizing product regulation across the European Community. In addition, agriculture became primarily a European competence in the 1960s. Until the 1980s, the common agricultural policy (CAP) took up between 60 and 80 percent of the European Community's budget.

By 1992, national sovereignty, exclusive and ultimate authority to bind one's citizens, had virtually disappeared. The European Community, renamed as the European Union, was now involved in all but a handful of policy areas. The exceptions were some aspects of social policy, such as industrial relations, and some areas in the legal-institutional domain, such as police, law, and order. The acceleration of European integration was set in motion by the SEA, which came into force in 1987. The central objective was to realize full free movement of goods, services, capital, and labour (or persons) — a single market — by the end of 1992, by abolishing non-tariff barriers. But the expansion of EU involvement reached well beyond the internal market into environmental regulation, industrial policy, research and development, and a new ambitious regional policy (EU cohesion policy) to reduce regional and social disparities through the Union. This policy constituted by 1992 the second-largest item on the EU budget (after agriculture), representing one-third of EU funding, or 0.4 percent of EU GDP. Figure 1 also reflects the fact that the EU obtained exclusive power in trade negotiations.[3] This means that the European Commission, not the French or German governments, negotiates on behalf of the European Union in the General Agreement on Tariffs and Trade (GATT) or WTO negotiations. This also entails that member states cannot unilaterally impose or lift trade sanctions against third parties. The Greek government experienced this when it tried to impose a trade embargo on newly independent Macedonia in 1995, but was barred from doing so by the European Court of Justice.

By 2000, the European Union had become an encompassing political system involved in all areas of life that governments usually care to regulate. From agriculture to capital flows, to transportation, to education, defence, regional policy, energy, or environment, national governments share authority with the European Union. In 1999, monetary policy was added to the exclusive EU list for the 12 members of the Euro-zone.[4] On 1 January 1999, national authority over monetary policy was ceded to an independent European Central Bank, and in conjunction with that, joint macroeconomic policy-making was strengthened. Members of the Euro-zone are legally bound to run balanced budgets over the economic cycle, and to incur no more than a 3 percent budget deficit in any year. Violators can be fined an amount up to 0.5 percent of GDP per year. The Treaty of Amsterdam, which came into force in 1999, shifted parts of asylum and immigration policy to the EU level, and it strengthened EU capacity in foreign and defence policy. In the second half of 2000, the European Union announced the creation of a rapid reaction force, a 60,000-person strong "European army," designed to take on peacekeeping and peacemaking missions independent from the North Atlantic Treaty Organization (NATO). While it remains to be seen whether this plan will succeed (at the time of writing, Turkey has lifted its veto of essential NATO assent), this completes the process of sharing authority in areas traditionally seen at the heart of national sovereignty: border controls, currency, diplomacy, and an army.

Institutions and Decision-Making Rules

Decision-making in the European Union evolves around five institutions: the European Council, the Council of Ministers, the European Commission, the European Parliament, and the European Court of Justice. The last four were created with the Treaty of Rome; the European Council was only formally added in the 1986 *Single European Act*, though it existed informally.[5]

The *European Council* is the summit of the government leaders of the member states (plus the president of the European Commission), which is held three or four times a year. The European Council has immense prestige and quasi-legal status as the body that defines "general political guidelines" (title 1, article 4 TEU, ex-D). This is the body where major deals are clinched and treaty changes are negotiated. But outside these roles, its control of the European agenda is limited. It meets only intermittently, and it provides the European Commission with general policy mandates, and seldom with specific policy proposals. European Council mandates have proven to be a flexible basis for the Commission to build legislative programs.

The *European Commission* is the executive-bureaucratic body of the European Union. It consists of a political and bureaucratic layer. The College of Commissioners, one commissioner per member state and two for the five largest countries, is appointed every five years by the European Council and requires majority support in the European Parliament. The 4,000 plus policy-making bureaucracy consists of permanent officials who are recruited through a central exam. The Commission has the formal, and exclusive, power to initiate and draft legislation, which includes the right to amend or withdraw its proposal at any stage in the process.[6] It is also the think-tank for new policies (article 221 TEC, ex-155). In this capacity it annually produces two to three hundred reports, white papers, green papers, and other studies and communications (Ludlow 1991). Some are highly technical studies about, say, the administration of milk surpluses. Others are influential policy programs such as the 1985 White Paper on the internal market; the 1990 reform proposals for the common agricultural policy, which laid the basis for the European position in the GATT negotiations; the 1993 White Paper on *Growth, Competitiveness and Employment*, which argued for labour market flexibility; or the 1997 *Agenda 2000*, which shaped the debate on enlargement to central and eastern Europe.

The Commission has significant autonomous executive powers in competition policy; it vets mergers of a certain economic size in the internal market, and it scrutinizes whether state aid — national, regional or local — is compatible with EU competition law. As mentioned above, it is the Commission that negotiates trade disputes and agreements with third parties on behalf of the Union, and this includes enlargement negotiations. The Commission reports back on progress to a committee of member-state representatives, as well as to the European Parliament. Complicated rules govern whether and to what extent the Commission needs approval for its actions, but the bottom line is that the Commission is an executive body without legislative power. So it does not vote on the final WTO agreement, or on enlargement, that is the task of the Council of Ministers and the European Parliament.

According to the original treaties, the Commission was not expected to perform ground-level implementation, which was left to the member states, except in unusual circumstances (such as competition policy, fraud, etc.). Yet, in some areas this has changed. The most prominent example is cohesion policy, which was significantly expanded in the 1980s and again in the 1990s to counter the effect of the internal market program (and later EMU) on regional and social disparities. Policy-making involves regional and local governments as well as social actors in all stages of the policy process in "partnership arrangements" — the selection of priorities, choice of programs, allocation of funding, monitoring of operations, and evaluation and adjustment of programs. Each region or country receiving funding is required to set up monitoring committees with a general committee on top, and a cascade of subcommittees focused on particular programs. Commission officials can and do participate at each level of this tree-like structure (Bache 1998; Hooghe 1996).

According to the EU treaties, the main legislative body is the *Council of Ministers*, which is composed of national ministers. The actual composition varies depending on the topic; so there is a council for ministers of agriculture, an economic and financial affairs council, an environment council, etc. Member states have votes roughly proportionate to their population, though small countries are over-represented, and Germany is considerably under-represented.

Participation in the Council of Ministers no longer guarantees individual national sovereignty. The proportion of rules stipulating unanimity in the Council has steadily declined. Qualified majority voting, that is 70 percent of the votes, is now the rule for 80 percent of decisions. That includes the single market, competition policy, economic and monetary union, regional policy, trade, environment, research and development, transport, employment, immigration and visa policy, social policy, and education. Qualified majority voting also applies to some provisions of foreign and defence policy, and some issues on policy cooperation, justice, and immigration. The decision rules are complex, but the bottom line is clear: over broad areas of EU competencies, individual governments may be outvoted. The weekly *European Voice* estimated that between January 1995 and January 1998, Germany was outvoted most often in the Council, followed by Britain and, at some distance, Italy (*European Voice*, 15–21 October 1998, p. 4).

There are ways for national governments to defend national interests, but they depend on the consent of the other governments. For example, governments can build special safeguards into the treaties, a practice that has proliferated since the 1993 Maastricht Treaty. Particular states have been granted derogations, or special exemptions. The United Kingdom and Denmark each have derogation from the European monetary union. Some countries achieved derogations in the areas of state aid, environmental policy, and energy policy. Sometimes derogations are written into special protocols, such as those attached to the Amsterdam Treaty that meet concerns of Denmark, Ireland, and the UK on border controls, and EU immigration and visa policy. The Amsterdam Treaty also inserted a new decision rule, constructive abstention, which allows a member state to abstain from voting on an issue and to formally declare that it will not implement a decision that commits other EU member states. Constructive abstention is, however, restricted to certain foreign policy and defence issues (Stubbs 1999). In addition, the treaties preserve unanimity for the most sensitive and contested policy areas, particularly major foreign policy decisions, nearly all decisions on justice and home affairs, and much of fiscal policy.

From the 1980s the Council of Ministers and individual governments became intimately involved in the executive powers of the Commission. The term for this is comitology, which refers to the practice of having a committee of national representatives assist the Commission in its executive work. Many EU regulations have their own committee. National governments often select people outside the central executive to represent them in comitology. Most participants are not national civil servants, but subnational officials, interest group representatives (particularly from farming, union, and employer organizations), technical experts, scientists, or academics. Though these representatives are selected by their national government, they have particular territorial or group interests, as well as the national interest, to defend. Comitology was designed to allow national governments to monitor the Commission, but it has unintentionally led to deeper subnational and group participation in the European political process.

The Council of Ministers shares legislative authority with the *European Parliament*, which has been transformed from a decorative institution to a directly elected co-legislator. The first direct elections took place in 1979. The European Parliament has three major powers. First of all, it can fire the European Commission, which almost happened in 1999. (The Commission pre-empted a vote of no confidence by resigning voluntarily.) Second, its assent, an up or down vote, is required over enlargement of the EU and over most association agreements and treaties between the

European Union and third parties (Falkner and Nentwich 1999, p. 26). And third, since 1993, under the co-decision procedure the European Parliament co-legislates with the Council of Ministers on single market issues, and most other policy measures; the main exceptions are fiscal policy, foreign and defence policy, police and justice cooperation, and monetary policy. The co-decision procedure gives the European Parliament the power to amend and veto Council legislative proposals. If Parliament and Council are deadlocked, a conciliation committee, consisting of representatives from both institutions, with a representative of the Commission as broker, hammers out a compromise. To become EU law, a compromise needs to be approved by a majority in the Parliament and a qualified majority in the Council. So the co-decision procedure comes close to putting the European Parliament "on an essentially equal footing with the Council" (ibid.). The Council of Ministers is still the stronger legislative chamber as it votes on all EU issues. But the trend is clear: the European Parliament has become a force to be reckoned with.

The final EU body is the *European Court of Justice* (ECJ). It may be argued that an impartial dispute-settlement arrangement is necessary to solve problems of incomplete contracting in international agreements. But the European Court of Justice is more than that (Alter 1998; Burley-Slaughter and Mattli 1993; Dehousse 1998; Mattli and Slaughter 1995; Stone Sweet and Brunell 1998; Weiler 1991). With the help of the Commission, and in collaboration with national courts, the ECJ has transformed the European legal order in a quasi-federal order.

ECJ case law has established the treaties as documents creating legal obligations directly binding on national governments and individual citizens. These obligations have legal priority over laws made by member states. Directly binding legal authority and supremacy are core attributes of sovereignty, and their application by the ECJ suggests that the EU is becoming a constitutional regime.

The Court has been able to get away with this expansive interpretation for several reasons. First, the failure of the treaties to delineate national and EU competencies has provided the Court with substantive reasons for expanding treaty law. The treaties set out "tasks" or "purposes" for European cooperation, such as the custom union (Treaty of Rome), the completion of the internal market (*Single European Act*), or economic and monetary union (Maastricht Treaty). The Court has constitutionalized European law and European authority in other policy areas by stating that these were *necessary* to achieve these functional goals (Weiler 1991). Furthermore, article 234 (ex-177) of the Treaty of Rome stipulates that national and lower courts may seek "authoritative guidance" from the ECJ in cases involving EU law. In such instances, the ECJ provides a preliminary ruling that specifies how EU law should be properly applied to the issue at hand. The court that made the referral cannot be forced to follow the ECJ's interpretation, but if it does, other national courts will usually accept the decision as a precedent. Preliminary rulings expand ECJ influence, and judges at lower levels gain a *de facto* power of judicial review, which was usually reserved for the highest national court (Burley-Slaughter and Mattli 1993). Article 234 gives lower national courts strong incentives to circumvent their own national judicial hierarchy, and they have done so with gusto.

The substantive extension of European integration into all policy areas has gone hand in hand with an institutional transformation from a limited, primarily intergovernmental form of international cooperation to a system of multi-level governance, where autonomous supranational institutions — Commission, European Parliament, European Central Bank, and European Court of Justice — and institutions representing national governments — European Council and Council of Ministers — share authority. The result is a malleable and open system that is accessible to diverse actors. It is true that decision-making rules are biased in favour of governments. But in federalist fashion, the rules favour governments of smaller states more than those of larger countries. Decision-making rules also allow for other actors — political parties, subnational authorities, and national and European interest groups — to influence EU decisions. Politics in the European Union looks remarkably like domestic politics.

CRISIS, CHOICE, AND CHANGE: THE RELAUNCH OF EUROPEAN INTEGRATION

To what extent has the acceleration of European integration in the 1980s and 1990s been a response to globalization?[7] And to what extent has it been driven by "domestic," that is, internal-European, developments? I will show that the push for European integration was motivated by a perceived inability of Europe's economies to compete with the US and Japan at a time when financial and trade flows were rapidly thickening. But to understand why this integration took the form it took — not only market integration (internal market), but also political integration in non-market areas — one must take into account domestic developments.

Economic Recovery: A National, Global or Regional Strategy?

The two global oil crises of the 1970s precipitated a period of long-term sluggish economic performance in western Europe. Industrial productivity lagged US and Japanese figures. Europe was particularly uncompetitive in technology-intensive sectors. In 1981, the 12 largest European electronics firms issued a communiqué in which they highlighted Europe's paltry 10 percent share of global markets for information technology (IT) and its declining 40 percent share of its own markets (Peterson and Bomberg 1999, pp. 205-06). Europe's economies seemed to lack competitiveness, and this while several European economies, including the German and British economies, were more exposed to the world economy than the Canadian economy.[8] Unemployment leapt to the high single digits or, in some countries, double digits for the first time since the 1930s. The social consensus of the 1960s and 1970s was under duress, and social unrest was on the rise. The world had changed, and Europe was not adjusting well.

The search for economic recovery led European governments to consider three strategies for reviving economic growth: a national, a global, and a regional path. First, several countries attempted to bolster national capacity for Keynesian economic management by tightening restrictions on trade and financial flows. They wanted to shut globalization out. Nowhere was this national option pursued as enthusiastically as in France, and its defeat there in the early 1980s pushed it off the table in the rest of Europe. After the socialist victory in the presidential elections of 1981 and parliamentary elections of 1982, the French government attempted to build "socialism in one country," which involved the nationalization of a dozen industrial groups and 36 banks; a Keynesian policy of demand stimulation through wage increases, enlarged social security benefits, increased government spending, and higher taxation of wealth and profit; and stronger capital exchange controls. But the policy failed. By the fall of 1982, unemployment was rapidly rising as more and more firms filed for bankruptcy, inflation was still 14 percent, and the deficits in both the national budget and the trade balance were increasing at alarming rates. The socialist party split over the appropriate reaction to the crisis, with the left-wing wanting to radicalize economic policy behind protectionist walls, and the right-wing arguing for a reversal to a supply-side policy emphasizing budget austerity, low inflation, and industrial restructuring to encourage export-led growth. While the former wanted to insulate the French economy from global pressures — including potential withdrawal from the European Union, the latter maintained that French industry should become more competitive abroad — first and foremost by facilitating trade in the European Union. By early 1983, the latter had won the argument.

The failure of Keynesian economic policy was not simply the failure of a particular set of macroeconomic policies, but of a mode of policy-making that was distinctly national (Hooghe and Marks 1999). With trade and financial interdependence at such high levels in Europe, many believed that the cost of national regulation was too high. The search for alternative policies went in several directions, but common among them was a belief that the nation-state could no longer serve as the privileged architect of economic prosperity. There were two broad streams of innovation. One championed a general global shift toward neo-*laissez-faire*, and this faction was strongest in the UK and Anglo-American democracies. It also influenced to some extent societies where neo-corporatism was entrenched, such as Germany, where the Free Democrats and the pro-business wing of the Christian Democrats argued for neo-liberalism. The other stream wanted to open up national economies within the European region, and this group proposed the internal market project. In the end, the regional strategy won. The reasons for this are multiple.

Reasons for the Single Market

One reason concerns the density of *economic transactions*. By the mid-1980s, European economies had become open economies. Trade openness, measured in Table 2 by exports as a percentage of GDP, varied between well above 70 percent for Belgium and just below 20 percent for Greece and Spain, but the average for the EU was 39 percent, against 11.4 percent for Japan and 7.4 percent for the United States. The more export-dependent an economy, the more dependent it is on growth in demand, and access to that demand, in foreign markets (McKeown 1999). Economic rationality induced European governments to prefer trade openness to protectionism. This is a fundamental reason for why the national strategy was not a viable option. But it does not explain why the regional path was preferred to the global path.

Aggregate trade and financial patterns suggest some functional reasons why European governments chose the regional strategy, but neither is conclusive. The simplest story concerns trade. More than half of a typical European country's trade was with other members of the European Community/Union, and this proportion was growing. Note the contrast with Canada, where, as Richard Simeon points out in his chapter, interprovincial trade was declining as a proportion of overall provincial trade. In contrast, European governments could expect an integrated European market to further boost this high intra-European interdependence. Still, that left a sizeable proportion of trade with the outside world, and this might have been enough to tip the balance in favour of a global strategy (see Table 3). In 1991, extra-regional trade (exports plus imports) represented almost 14 percent of EU GDP, against 11 percent for the US and 15.5 percent for Asia-Pacific. World trade is as important to the countries in the European Union as it is for the United States or Japan (Wolf 1994, pp. 13-16).

While trade patterns were first and foremost intra-European, financial flows were primarily transcontinental. European economies were critically dependent on foreign direct investment (FDI) from the United States, and to a lesser extent Japan. By the mid-1980s, 40 percent of US investment was directed to Europe, and between 20 and 30 percent of Japanese investment. At first blush, then, one might expect governments to prefer a global strategy to buttress these sizeable FDI flows. Yet, historical experience tells us that European integration is good for FDI in Europe. The two periods of rapid growth in the European share of total US direct investment — the main source of FDI in Europe — coincided with the two phases of most intensive integration among European economies: the early 1960s after the signing of the Treaty of Rome, and 1973–80 after the accession of the UK, Ireland, and Denmark. European governments could reasonably expect further European integration to give another boost to US and Japanese FDI. And they were right: as a response to the launch of the internal market program, US firms rushed into Europe, so that by 1990 the European share of US FDI abroad had risen from 40 to 50 percent. The European share of Japanese investment rose to 30 per-

	TABLE 2 Trade Dependence 1958–1995				TABLE 3 Trade Concentration 1958–1995			
	Exports as Percentage of GDP				Percentage of Exports to other EU States			
	1958	1973	1986	1995	1958	1973	1986	1995
Belgium	31.9	55.6	70.5	72.6	45.1	73.1	73.2	71.6
Luxembourg	77.3	88.1	98.3	91.8				
Netherlands	48.3	46.0	50.7	53.3	41.6	72.6	74.9	75.7
France	12.3	17.6	21.2	23.5	22.2	54.7	55.3	62.8
Germany	22.1	21.8	30.2	23.6	27.3	47.1	50.8	57.0
Italy	12.5	17.4	20.2	27.6	23.6	50.1	53.7	56.8
United Kingdom		23.7	25.7	28.4		31.8	48.0	53.9
Ireland		36.2	52.7	74.6		76.0	72.0	72.2
Denmark		28.5	32.0	34.5		45.3	47.0	61.6
Greece			17.0	16.5			63.7	55.5
Spain			19.9	23.7			60.3	72.3
Portugal			29.5	33.3			68.3	80.3
Austria				37.7				59.3
Sweden				40.9				56.9
Finland				38.0				56.7
EU[a]	34.1	37.2	39.0	41.3				
Japan	11.0	10.0	11.4	9.4				
United States	5.0	6.9	7.4	11.4				

Note: [a]Average of ratios for EU member states.

Source: Cameron (1998, pp. 193, 194) based on OECD statistics.

cent (Thomsen 2000). Financial investors want to place their money in vibrant, growing markets, and whether such growth is produced by national, regional or global trade liberalization does not seem terribly important.

In some respects, a European strategy of trade liberalization was not well-suited to problems at hand. Market competition in technology-intensive sectors and in financial services, the engines of the third industrial revolution, was more global than European. Many influential European multinational companies believed that it made more sense to pursue a global strategy encompassing the US and Japan than a European one.[9] The benefits of specialization through free trade were potentially greater between European and non-European firms than within Europe (Sandholtz and Zysman 1989). For these companies, the European strategy was second best.

All this suggests that, on purely functional grounds, governments could have gone either way — the regional course or the global path — though the balance was slightly tipped to the former.

A more compelling reason why governments preferred the regional to the global path is that they had at their disposal *ideas that could serve as focal points* for clinching credible regional commitments. A rich stock of ideas underpinned the European market project. Economic studies of the benefits of deeper market integration in Europe had been floating around in the Commission for years. By 1985 more than half of the internal market legislation was already in draft form (Cameron 1992; Ross 1995). Various economic studies were eventually bundled, updated, and coordinated in three famous reports: the Padoa-Schioppa Report of 1987, the Cecchini Report of 1988, and the Emerson report of the same year, all of which suggested that economies of scale and competition in an integrated European market would yield a cumulative benefit of between 4.3 to 6.4 percent of aggregate GDP (see Padoa-Schioppa 1987; Cecchini 1988; and Emerson 1988). There were also ideas about how to lower non-tariff barriers. Most important was the principle of mutual recognition formulated in 1979 by the European Court of Justice in the Cassis de Dijon case (Alter and Meunier-Aitsahalia 1994).[10] This happened while, at the global level, the Uruguay Round had reached the impasse due to a dearth of ideas (as well as deep conflicts of interests between Europeans and the US, Canada or Australia on issues ranging from agriculture to intellectual property rights to services). At the level of ideas, plausible solutions to coordination problems, regional integration had a clear edge over global integration.

Furthermore, strong *pre-existing institutions at the European level* made it likely that agreements would be implemented. As we saw above, the European Commission's empowerment as competition authority and the European Court of Justice's jurisprudence establishing the supremacy of EU law preceded the internal market program. By the mid-1980s, these supranational institutions had the authority and the muscle to sanction free riders (Garrett 1992; Pierson 1996). Equivalent global institutions for monitoring national commitments were lacking, or, in the case of GATT, far less authoritative than EU institutions. Even the WTO does not require a *de jure* surrender of national sovereignty because a member state can always refuse to comply with a ruling (though *de facto*, smaller or economically more dependent countries may find it difficult to exercise that sovereign right). In contrast, EU Commission fines and ECJ rules are *de jure* and *de facto* binding — for Luxembourg and Germany alike.

To say that the functional, ideational, and institutional conditions for a new policy are favourable is not to say that the policy will be pursued. A decisive source of the EU's market project was the *breadth of its support* among diverse constituencies: supranational actors, business community, national governments, and, with some delay, organized labour. In contrast, support for a global strategy was much weaker, and opposition was more organized. The character of this "domestic" coalition, more than functional pressures, explains why regional integration won out over global free trade.

One group of this coalition consisted of long-time proponents of a federal Europe, and this group was particularly strong in the European Parliament and the Commission. For them, the single market project was merely the first, but essential, step in a larger venture. Activists in the Commission were led to the market project because they thought that economic integration would lead to political integration. When Jacques Delors assumed the presidency of the European Commission in January 1985, he saw the market project as just the first of four major initiatives to deepen political integration; the three others were a European cohesion policy for the regions, the development of a citizens' Europe based on a stronger European Parliament and extensive social policy, and economic and monetary union. He achieved much of this agenda, except for an extensive social policy (Ross 1995; Grant 1994).

Business was interested in the single market project in and of itself because it had much to gain from lowering market barriers in Europe (Sandholtz and Zysman 1989). The core of this support was among multinational corporations. They had organized themselves into the European Round Table, which had among its membership giants such as Philips, Siemens, Volvo, ICL, Thomson, Olivetti, etc. This was a heterogeneous group: some firms conceived of the market project as a means to neoliberal deregulation in Europe and, in a next step, the globe, while others wanted a single market with a European-wide capacity for industrial policy (Ross 1995; Sandholtz and Zysman 1989; Cameron 1992; Cowles 1995). But all supported the internal market project, and the European Round Table became a highly effective lobbyist for the program. Support reached beyond these major multinational firms into the wider European business community. Virtually every member state had a large and growing constituency in favour of fewer national trade barriers, especially within Europe. While the United States has remained, in John Kincaid's terms, a 90 percent domestic economy, the European economies had become less-than-50 percent domestic economies, and much of this external trade was intra-European. The voice of mobile capital sounded all the louder because many sectors dominated by national capital did not expect to be affected by the internal market project, and so they had little incentive to mobilize against the project (Smith and Wanke 1993). The asymmetry in gains/losses between mobile capital on the one hand and national capital on the other helped proponents of liberalization to make a case for regional integration.

EU treaties are negotiated by national governments, and so one must ask oneself why they accepted to cede sovereignty on a vast range of policy areas. Ideological consistency provides a major part of the answer. In the mid-1980s, nine of the then-twelve member states — Germany, Britain, Italy, the Netherlands, Belgium, Denmark, Portugal, Ireland, and Luxembourg — were governed by right or centre-right parties which were favourably oriented to mobile capital and market competition. The one major exception was France, but by the mid-1980s the modernist wing of the socialist party had asserted control in the Mitterrand government.

Would history have played out differently if socialists or social democrats had been in power in the mid-1980s? The French government's position suggests that the internal market could also gain support left of centre. After all, Commission president Jacques Delors, who placed the plan on the EU agenda and lobbied hard for its acceptance, was a social democrat. Throughout Europe, traditional social democracy was in disarray in the 1980s, because its preferred strategy to deal with globalization, national Keynesianism, had proved ineffective. By the end of the decade, most social democratic parties had given up on demand-oriented Keynesianism and supported supply-side policies prescribing an altogether humbler role for government in facilitating market competition (Kitschelt

1994). Yet social democrats did not endorse the single market with the same enthusiasm as the right. For them, it was the second-best option after national Keynesianism. They liked it to the extent that it promised to strengthen EU regulatory capacity against globalization. They hoped to use these bolder EU institutions to entrench some social democratic priorities, perhaps Euro-Keynesianism, at the European level.[11] With social democrats dominant in the European Council, the internal market program might have stayed on the shelf a few more years, so the timing might have been different. More importantly, if social democrats had held the pen, they would have complemented economic market integration with more qualified majority voting on EU industrial policy, EU social policy, and EU environmental regulation. Social democrats wrote the 1999 Amsterdam Treaty, which helps explain why it is the first EU Treaty that talks little about market liberalization and a great deal more about employment, solidarity, citizenship, democracy, and human rights.

This unwieldy coalition of European, national, and transnational actors differed greatly in their ultimate goals: from British Prime Minister Thatcher's desire to extend neo-liberal policies across Europe, over the left's hope to replace ineffective national regulation by EU regulation, and European multinationals' desire to catch up with American and Japanese competitors by exploiting economies of scale in the European home market, to Jacques Delors' and the European Parliament's ambition to build a political union. Yet for each of them, the creation of the internal market was the necessary first step to more distant goals.

The creation of the internal market was sold as Europe's response to globalization, but the form it took owes much to "domestic" economic and political concerns. As far as hard figures go, the single market was more a response to Europeanization than to globalization: the economic or social transactions between, say, Germans and French have increased much faster than those between Germans and non-Europeans — globalization in Europe has been regional. Furthermore, while it is well-established that national Keynesianism becomes increasingly ineffective in open economies, there is less evidence that trade openness rules out public choice in size and role of government. As Fritz Scharpf and others have shown, different types of welfare states have proven relatively resilient in the face of "globalization," though there may be economic costs to maintaining particular programs or social priorities (Scharpf 1999; Huber and Stephens

2001). So when governments downsize social programs, it is usually not because they are pulled by global forces but because they are pushed by certain political coalitions at home. Similarly, European governments decided to cede sovereignty in a range of policy areas that went far beyond what functionality called for. They did so because they thought it would help them achieve specific political goals; by shifting authority to Brussels, they could divert blame for unpopular measures, or tie the hands of their successors (Marks 1996).

The key to the political success of the internal market program was its ambiguity; it was all things to all actors. The market program, a goal shared by many in 1985, became a point of departure for contending political agendas. For parties or interest groups with a neo-liberal outlook, market liberalization was a necessary step in limiting European integration to an economic enterprise administered by insulated government elites. But other parties conceived of the SEA as a jumping-off point for regulating capital at the European level in line with European social democratic and Christian democratic traditions.

Economic and monetary union, decided at Maastricht in 1991, was a replay of the politics of the internal market program. Neo-liberals perceive EMU as the crown on their project to insulate economic activity from political regulation. With monetary policy securely hived off to an independent central bank, national governments will be induced to compete for investment by reducing the overall tax burden and shifting its incidence from mobile capital to less mobile factors of production. Opponents of neo-liberalism, on the other hand, believe that EMU will trigger deeper political regulation at the European level. They expect that asymmetrical economic shocks will press national governments toward ad hoc redistributive measures and, eventually, to some form of European fiscal policy. The implications of EMU are no less ambiguous than those of the internal market program, which is why EMU has been able to attract support on the left as on the right.

What began as a reaction to globalization has become an authoritative structure with the capacity to deepen ties of economic, social, and cultural interdependence in Europe. Hence, in an unconventional way, one could conceive of the European Union as Europe's local producer *and* regulator of globalization.

THE EFFECT OF GLOBALIZATION AND EUROPEAN INTEGRATION ON EUROPE'S POLITICS AND SOCIETY

How have the twin forces of globalization and European integration influenced Europe's politics and society over the past decades? I organize my thoughts around four basic questions.

Has Globalization/European Integration Decreased or Increased Regional Conflict?

Perhaps the greatest achievement of European integration is its pacifying impact on centuries-old warring relations in Europe. Jean Monnet, Robert Schuman, Konrad Adenauer, Paul-Henri Spaak, and Alcide de Gasperi conceived the European Union as a response to the horrors of war in Europe, as a means to tame destructive nationalism. The founders hoped to weaken national animosities by establishing an international legal order that would constrain realist anarchy. They wanted to domesticate international tensions within stable supranational institutions. Fifty years after the Schuman Declaration, skirmishes between Germany and France are as inconceivable as a war between Ontario and Quebec. In the 1980s, EU membership was critical in consolidating democracy in the former authoritarian regimes of Greece, Portugal, and Spain, and now hopes are high that the European Union may pull off the same in completing the transition in central and eastern Europe.

That does not mean that conflict between nation-states — particularly national governments, but sometimes also national firms, national interest groups, or national electorates — is nonexistent. Territorial difference, and particularly national difference, is still a major cleavage in EU politics. Yet, while some states are more likely to form alliances than others, so far no permanent blocs of countries have emerged. On trade issues, an Atlanticist bloc comprising the UK, the Netherlands, and often Germany and the Scandinavian countries, tends to vie with a Europeanist bloc around France, Italy, and often Belgium and Spain. On environmental issues, countries tend to align differently, with the Scandinavians and Germany in the pro-environmentalist camp, France and Belgium in the middle, and the UK with Spain, Portugal, and Greece in the environmentally laggard camp. On social and employment policy, Scandinavian countries sometimes join forces with southern countries. Moreover, these policy blocs change with the colour of governments or the changing political landscape. For example, the German government, red or black, was always a fervent supporter of the common agricultural policy, but it made a u-turn in the fall of 2000, pushed by the political fallout of mad cow disease, hoof and mouth disease, and other food scandals attributed to the industrialization of agriculture promoted by CAP.

Third countries sometimes manage to exploit divisions among EU members. For example, in trade negotiations the United States has repeatedly tried to drive a rift between the Atlanticist bloc led by the UK and the Europeanist bloc led by France. However, the fact that the European Union has exclusive authority over trade, and that the Commission is the sole negotiator, makes that a difficult and politically delicate exercise. On the whole, EU member states have learned that they tend to be better off when they stick together.

In conclusion, European integration has effectively defused interstate conflicts in Europe. Moreover, it has, so far, not led to the emergence of quasi-permanent regional blocs. This may be because the EU deals with a vast range of issues. While it is possible to frame some issues in terms of national interest, most issues are divisive within societies, and this ideological contestation is likely to undermine efforts to forge a "national position." Instead, groups are tempted to take their ideological positions from the national to the EU arena where they can find like-minded allies from other countries.

Has Globalization/European Integration Fuelled or Diffused Ideological Conflict?

Most political economists agree that increased economic globalization, or more specifically, market liberalization and trade, increases aggregate economic growth, but it also intensifies economic uncertainty, income inequality, and it creates economic winners and losers (Rodrik 1997; Garrett 1998).[12] Winners want to deepen market liberalization, while losers, or defenders of those who suffer, want regulation of global market vagaries. This contestation is often characterized as one between right, those in favour of market liberalization, and left, those in favour of more government regulation of markets. For simplicity's sake, I adopt this convention here.

The challenge for proponents of political regulation is that there is generally a mismatch between the territorial scope of the market and government authority. In a world where markets are increasingly transnational or global, international institutions with real authoritative capacity are generally weak or nonexistent. Absent international regulation, proponents of regulation can push for national regulation, but that risks being ineffective, or it may only be possible if one is willing to sacrifice growth. It is rational, then, for the left to be wary of globalization. That is why organized labour in the US and in Canada tends to be suspicious of NAFTA or the WTO (Marks and Down forthcoming).

The European Union is an exception. It is the one supranational institution with considerable capacity to regulate market forces beyond the national state. So the question then becomes how the existence of the European Union affects left/right politics in Europe? European integration encompasses a variety of particular policies and reforms with very different implications for left and right (Marks and Wilson 2000). Parties on the economic right should be in favour of market integration in the European Union, and policies that constrain government spending, but they should be wary of political integration that may strengthen re-regulation at the European level. Parties on the left and centre-left too should be weighing conflicting considerations. On the one hand, market integration threatens left achievements at the national level because it intensifies international competition while undermining Keynesian responses to it. On the other hand, deeper political integration may enhance the possibilities for social democracy by creating democratic authoritative institutions capable of pursuing employment, environmental, or cohesion policy at the European level: regulated capitalism. As a Flemish socialist exclaimed during a parliamentary debate on Belgian participation in EMU in 1996: "Why do you think that the German labour unions hope that the third stage of EMU will succeed? ... They know that EMU will create the foundations for a Rhine-land model on a European scale, for a project that will meet the needs of all Belgians and Europeans. That model will preserve our social welfare in a globalizing economy" (quoted in Beyers and Kerremans 2001, p. 144).

Because of these complex expectations among right and left parties one would not expect to see a clear relationship between left/right placement and support for European integration. And indeed, the overall association between left/right and European integration is non-linear and weak.[13] But this result conceals two divergent dynamics.

On the one hand, Euro-scepticism among radical left-wing parties pulls down the curve on the left side of the dimension. Opposition to European integration is deeply entrenched among the radical left. It is rooted in the perception that the institutions of the European Union have been irreparably co-opted by mobile capital. According to the radical left, the European Union is biased beyond repair, and so one should stay out of the European Union. For example, at the same time that the Swedish social democrats applied for Sweden to join the European Union, their main competitor to the left, Venstre, rejected such efforts on the grounds that "the message in the Maastricht Treaty was the construction of a capitalist block" (Christensen 1996, p. 534). The electoral significance of the extreme left is still considerable in Europe: 7.2 percent in 1999 (of which 85 percent is Euro-sceptical).

On the other hand stands an opposite dynamic among major parties, which represent approximately 80 percent of Europe's voters. Figure 2 displays the relationship between left/right positioning and European integration for parties in the major party families — social democrats, Christian democrats, liberals, and conservatives. When one simply asks whether these parties support or oppose European integration, there is a gentle slope from left down to right. The association of −0.20 just fails significance at the 0.10 level. Moderate left *and* right are broadly in favour.

The picture changes markedly when one examines particular EU policies. Support for EU employment policy and EU cohesion policy is powerfully associated with left/right positioning (R=−0.67 and −0.52, respectively). EU environmental policy is also strongly associated with left/right (R=−0.45). So the moderate left in Europe wants to strengthen EU regulation of market forces: they support the internal market and EMU, but they also want more EU powers in employment policy, cohesion policy, and environment policy. The reverse logic is at work among parties on the economic right. As Figure 2 shows, the strongest opponents of EU employment policy tend to be parties with the highest value on the left/right scale, that is, the most neo-liberal parties. Parties on the economic right want to limit EU political regulation: they like the internal market and EMU, but they dislike EU capacity to re-regulate this freshly liberalized market.

FIGURE 2

Positioning on Selected EU Policies by Left/Right
Dimension for Mainstream Parties

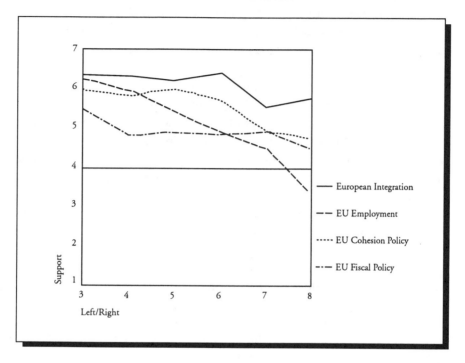

Social democratic parties are not monolithically in favour of deeper integration. Minorities in some parties, particularly in Sweden, Denmark, and Germany, remain doubtful about the potential for a European social model, and argue that while European legislation may ratchet up social democracy in poorer countries, it stands in the way of higher standards in the social democratic heartland of Europe. But this is a minority view. Majorities in one social democratic party after another have come to perceive European integration as a means for projecting social democratic goals in a liberalizing world economy (Hooghe and Marks 1999; Ladrech 1997; Katz and Wessels 1999).

A broader point deserves to be emphasized here. Moderate left and right hold contending conceptions of what kind of political economy should be created in the European Union: a "social model" built on European regulated capitalism versus a neo-liberal Europe based on market competition. These are not fluid disagreements on specific issues, but contrasting worldviews that motivate groups to form coalitions.

The neo-liberal coalition attempts to insulate markets from political interference by combining European-wide market integration with minimal European regulation. They reject democratic institutions at the European level capable of regulating the market, and seek instead to generate competition among national governments in providing regulatory climates that mobile factors of production find attractive. Neo-liberals want to import globalization into Europe. Proponents of regulated capitalism, on the other hand, propose a variety of market-enhancing and market-supporting legislation to create a social democratic dimension to European governance. This coalition seeks to increase the European Union's capacity for regulation, by among other things, upgrading the European Parliament, promoting the mobilization of a wide range of social groups, and reforming institutions to make legislation easier (e.g., by introducing qualified majority rule in the Council of Ministers). They want to regulate globalization in Europe.

The division between neo-liberalism and regulated capitalism has been alternatively described as one between a neo-American model and social democracy (Wilks 1996), between unfettered and institutional capitalism (Crouch and Streeck 1997), liberal market economies and coordinated market economies (Soskice 1992, 1999), or between the Anglo-Saxon model and the Rhine social market economy (Rhodes and Van Apeldoorn 1997). This is a fundamental division, yet if one compares it with historical divisions between left and right in Europe during much of the twentieth century, it takes place within relatively narrow parameters. European integration has altered left/right politics in Europe. It has highlighted, and hastened, the declining feasibility of national social democracy, but at the same time it has drawn attention to the capacity for regulation at a level beyond the national state. Loss has been sweetened by anticipation of future gains. This has resonated best with Europe's socialist and social democratic parties, which rely on the prospect of stronger regulatory capacities for the European Union to offset the electoral fallout of the breakdown of national Keynesianism. And here globalization and European integration differ profoundly. While globalization unmediated by international regulation has become the number one enemy of the left outside Europe, for *Europe's* left, European integration has become a source of hope.

Has Globalization/ European Integration Hardened or Eroded National Identities?

The tension between the economic right and economic left has old roots. In contrast, the new politics cleavage is, as its name suggests, more recent. Since the 1970s, a set of broadly cultural issues has become salient in many advanced industrial societies: lifestyle, policies toward "others" (gays, women, minority cultures, immigrants) and cultural diversity, national sovereignty and patriotism, and ecology. A variety of labels have been attached to this phenomenon, including post-materialism/materialism (Inglehart 1990), new politics/old politics (Müller-Rommel 1989), green/traditionalist, left-libertarian/authoritarian (Kitschelt 1994). At one pole, this dimension is described by some combination of ecology (or greenness), alternative politics (including participatory democracy), and libertarianism. One may conceive of this as the Green/Alternative/Libertarian or GAL pole. The opposite pole is characterized by some combination of support for traditional values, opposition to immigration, and defence of the national community. This is the Traditional/Authoritarian/Nationalism or TAN pole. Although this type of new politics is more salient in Europe than in North America, Japan or the Antipodes, it is present in all advanced economies.

Scholars of this cultural cleavage, such as Ronald Inglehart and Herbert Kitschelt, link its existence to the emergence of a category of people with considerable economic security. Affluence and education — the main resources for economic security in a modern world — breed tolerance for the other, adherence to freedom and individual rights, and quality of life. Affluent and educated people demand policies that address these issues: equal opportunities for women, minorities and gays; tolerance to immigrants and asylum-seekers; privacy and expanded personal freedoms; and greater democratic participation. Conversely, people who are economically insecure are likely to reject these values and want regulation to sustain their familiar homogeneous communities.

How does globalization play into this? Globalization produces economic insecurity, and at the same time, it brings about increased cultural and social transactions that make it more difficult to insulate one's own community from interference. Small, formerly homogenous cultures, are drawn into the global trading place. The law of the numbers predicts that, in a situation where two or more cultures interact, there is a good chance for the smaller culture to be ultimately assimilated by the larger one (Axelrod 1997). In Europe, as in Canada, the larger culture is Anglo-American. And so one may expect globalization to intensify cultural conflict between the GAL and TAN, and to strengthen particularly the TAN side.

For many EU citizens, European integration signifies increased economic, cultural and social interactions that cut across traditional communal identities. Yet, European integration also refers to a set of tangible institutions with the capacity to actively enact policies that sustain or undermine GAL or TAN values. For people and parties with TAN values, European integration exacerbates the disruptive effects of globalization. They perceive European integration, like globalization, as a threat, because it limits national culture, national community, and national sovereignty. The French anti-globalization hero José Bové, who became known for his attacks on McDonalds in France, is also an opponent of the European Union. The defence of "the national," conceived as a distinguishing, exclusive set of deeply rooted cultural and institutional characteristics that bind a national community, is the core of party ideology at the TAN pole. The empowerment of authoritative supranational institutions, and EU policies that weaken national control, challenge them directly. Extreme right parties — on average 6.1 percent of the national vote in 1999 — are deeply opposed to European integration: the French National Front, the Flemish Vlaams Blok, the Austrian FPÖ, the Italian Northern League, etc. In 1992, the then-leader of the French National Front, Jean-Marie Le Pen, described the Maastricht Treaty as "suicide national," "une entité supranationale qui passe par l'éclatement de la nation." The Euro-scepticism of these parties is linked to their opposition to immigration. They see themselves as defending the national community and culture against foreigners, and this leads them to oppose the free movement of people in the single market, a concern that has intensified with prospective enlargement to the east. Jörg Haider, leader of the Austrian Freedom Party, has opposed enlargement to the countries on Austria's eastern border: "From the moment we open our borders, 200,000 people will come here, settle, and look for jobs" (*The Economist*, 11 July 1998, p. 55).

But the effect of TAN reaches beyond the radical right. Among mainstream parties, the higher their score on TAN, the more Euro-sceptical they are. These include, for example, the British Conservatives, the Italian Forza Italia of Berlusconi, the Portuguese Partido Popular, and the French Gaullists. While they are not so extreme as radical right parties, these conservative parties defend national culture, national community, and national sovereignty against the influx of immigrants, against competing sources of identity within the state, and against external pressures from other countries and international organizations (Betz and Immerfall 1998; Kitschelt 1995). The French conservative right has gone furthest in emphasizing the alleged deficiencies of the European Union in relation to immigration and asylum. But other parties have also spoken in explicit language. In the spring of 2000, Forza Italia published proposals for highly restrictive legislation. In the ideological preamble to the document, Forza Italia made an explicit commitment to a "Christian" model of society based on the "primacy of the nation understood in the romantic sense, as a nucleus and base of values, religion, culture, language, dress and tradition." The document rejects "a universal, multi-racial society that is rooted in the markets" (Quoted in the *Financial Times*, 1 April 2000). And in the spring of 2001, the British Conservative leader, William Hague, made anti-immigrant statements that, according to *The Economist*, had a suspiciously ethnicist undertone.

The national orientation of these parties has an unambiguous bottom line for their position on European integration: the nation-state should be extremely wary in weakening its legitimate sovereign right to govern persons living in its territory. Euro-sceptical voices in conservative parties rarely seek withdrawal from the European Union, but they typically argue for a looser confederation. The Portuguese Partido Popular, for example, opposes the Europe of Maastricht and the EMU, which it labels the "federal peril," and argues for a Europe "respectful of the diversity and the Will of the nations of which it is constituted." The resurgence of nationalism, and the ensuing connection between the TAN and Euro-scepticism, is a major new development in the European Union.

The impact of European integration on GAL values is less clearcut (Bomberg 1998). This is because each one of the three constituent elements — greenness, alternative politics and participatory democracy, and personal liberty with respect to lifestyle — is two-sided. The *ecological* implications of European integration depend on where one sits. Countries with advanced environmental regulations (i.e., the richer countries, in which green parties are strongest) may extend their own standards to less-developed countries with the help of supranational legislation, but their own standards are unlikely to be raised. Many ecological issues demand transnational cooperation, and the European Union is a more effective arena for dealing with them than either global or national arenas. The *democratic* consequences of European integration have been mostly negative for those who care about participation. The European Union stands for much that parties toward the GAL pole instinctively oppose: technocratic policy-making; secretive decision-making; distant institutions; and the dominance of intergovernmental bargaining (Bomberg 1998). Yet, democratic control over EU policies has been buttressed with the Maastricht and Amsterdam Treaties. Though far from perfect, the opportunities for a variety of actors to influence and co-decide are far greater in the European Union than they are likely to become in the foreseeable future in other regional or global regimes. Finally, from a *libertarian* standpoint, European integration is both liberating, in that national restrictions on freedom of movement are eased, and restrictive, in that it creates an additional layer of authority removed from individual control. So one would expect mixed support for European integration among green parties.

This ambivalence is reflected in green parties' stances on European integration — the more extreme parties on the GAL side. Green parties clearly support European integration in environmental policy and they favour EU-asylum policy as well as a strengthening of the European Parliament, but they are wary to wholeheartedly support an international organization that is democratically non-transparent. As Elizabeth Bomberg observes: "Greens in Europe ... face a strategic paradox: the incentives to work through the EU are great, yet how can they work through institutions that inherently violate green principles?" (Bomberg 1998, p. 4; Rüdig 1996, p. 268). The paradox of green opposition is that democratizing EU institutions demands a stronger European Parliament, in other words, more, not less, integration.

A major determinant of green party positioning on European integration is the relative weight of pragmatic ("realo") versus principled ("fundi") tendencies. A second, related, influence is whether the party is purely environmentalist or combines green and radical-left views

(Christensen 1996; Bomberg 1998). The more reformist and environ-mentalist the party is, the more likely it is to support European integration. In recent years, reformism has been ascendant in the larger green parties, including the influential German Greens. Back in 1984, the German Greens condemned European integration in sweeping terms as an attempt to create a European superpower. By the early 1990s, they had become supportive. In their 1992 policy reversal, they stated that, "especially in view of increasing nationalistic and racist opinions and attacks in Ger-many and elsewhere, the Greens emphasize the importance and necessity of European integration" (Policy statement of the Land Council, October 1992, quoted in Rüdig 1996, p. 263). Increasing support for European integration has been most pronounced in the larger green parties, par-ticularly the Austrian, Belgian, Dutch, Finnish, French, and German greens. Green parties represented only 4.3 percent on average of the na-tional vote in 1999, but their strength varies considerably from country to country. They are politically influential in Germany, France, and the Benelux countries. Moreover, most social-democratic parties also strongly support GAL values.

There is no simple answer to the question of whether national iden-tity politics has been mitigated or hardened as a result of European integration. The empirical evidence suggests that it has been a bit of both. For radical right parties, nationalism and Euro-scepticism have come to fit snugly with anti-immigrant policies, alongside cultural traditionalism and authoritarianism. And this has carried over to mainstream parties on the conservative right. But at the same time, parties that espouse libertar-ian, alternative, pro-immigration and pro-cultural diversity views have come to embrace European integration, albeit with misgivings, as a bullwark against exclusive nationalism. So European integration seems to contribute to the polarization of identity politics in Europe.

Has Globalization/ European Integration Spurred Centralization or Decentralization of Authority?

The deepening of European integration represents an unprecedented cen-tralization of authority in Europe. Yet it would be wrong to argue that a European superstate has replaced national states. The system that has emerged in Europe is one where national states still play a major role —

in terms of Figure 1, a predominant role — in most policy areas. But they have lost the capacity to make *sovereign* decisions on policies. They share decision-making with one another in the context of the EU, and with autonomous EU institutions.

European politics, however, has been characterized by a second major development that further qualifies the impression of a European superstate. This concerns the empowerment of regions inside nation-states between 1950 and 2000. Figure 3 illustrates how much regions have gained in power within states since 1950. It is based on an index developed by Gary Marks and myself, in which we use four indicators to capture the extent of regional self-rule and regional shared rule in national decision-making (Hooghe and Marks 2001, Appendix 2). In 1950, six of the now 14 EU countries (15 minus Luxembourg) were purely unitary, four were quasi-unitary, three were regional, and only two (Germany and Austria) were federal. By 2000, only two (Sweden and Ireland) were purely unitary, four

FIGURE 3
National and Regional Power, 1950–2000

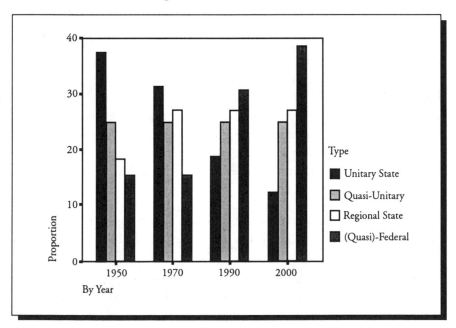

Source: Hooghe and Marks (2001, based on Appendix 2).

were quasi-unitary, three were regional, and five were federal or quasi-federal (Germany, Austria, Belgium, Spain, and Italy). The greatest changes have taken place in the larger countries — Spain, France, Italy, and Spain — as well as in Belgium. Except for periods of home rule in Northern Ireland, the United Kingdom remained the odd unitary state in one of the most populous and ethnically diverse countries in the EU. However, that was before the reforms of the past five years, which led to the creation of a Scottish Parliament and Welsh Assembly, and with assemblies for English regions on the agenda.

It would be wrong to contribute this regional empowerment directly to globalization or European integration. The main impetus has been domestic. Strong bottom-up regionalism and nationalism are far more important causes for regional empowerment in Belgium, Spain, and in the United Kingdom. Regionalization has also been pushed from the centre. There are several reasons why national politicians may want to shift power downwards (Marks 1996). They may do so to modernize policy-making, to shed unpopular or expensive policy tasks, or to increase democratic participation.

The direct effect of European integration on regional empowerment has been limited, although real. The most tangible impact has been through EU cohesion policy. The 1988 reform of this policy instituted "partnership" among the Commission, national authorities, and regional/local governments in designing, running, and monitoring economic development programs. Partnership became a powerful tool for the Commission to break open its two-level, dyadic relations with each national government into multi-level relations among supranational, national, and subnational governments (Hooghe 1996; Hooghe and Marks 2001). In some cases, such as Ireland, Greece, and to some extent Portugal, the European Commission has made EU funding conditional upon the creation of regional administrations. In other cases, such as in the UK, the Commission has built alliances with regional and local authorities, and by doing so strengthened their hand vis-à-vis their national governments. The Commission is following a similar strategy in the prospective member states of central and eastern Europe, where it is pushing reluctant national governments to put in place effective regional governance structures.

Yet the most important impact of European integration on regional empowerment has been indirect. European integration lowers the threshold for regions to demand power from their national governments because they do not risk losing market access. While an independent Quebec would have to renegotiate NAFTA membership with the United States, Mexico and Canada, an independent Scotland or Flanders could simply accede to the EU *acquis communautaire* — the cumulative body of EU law. Membership of an economic and monetary union is qualitatively different from membership of a free trade association. National leaders, from their side, may find it attractive to devolve authority to the extent that, by doing so, they can shed responsibility for the implementation of unpopular EU regulation. European integration takes economic risk out of the equation, and it provides national politicians with opportunities to reduce electoral risk. The European Union sets the economic and political parameters within which diffusion of authority takes place.

THE FUTURE OF "SHARED GOVERNANCE" IN EUROPE AND BEYOND

European integration is both a dependent variable, influenced by globalization, and an independent variable, a specific embodiment of globalization. As an independent variable, it resembles most closely the model of shared governance set out in the scenarios in chapter 1. It is a mode of governance that transcends traditional interstate relations. Authority is diffused across national, subnational, and supranational actors. EU policy-making is decided primarily through negotiations between supranational and national institutions. And shared governance also includes subnational governments and domestic interest groups; this is more likely to happen in some policy areas (e.g., regional policy, environment, social policy, and industrial relations) than others (foreign policy, trade policy, competition policy), in certain policy stages (implementation stage) than in others (legislative process), or by actors other than national governments of some member states (federal countries, i.e., Austria, Belgium, Germany, and quasi-federal or regional countries such as Spain, Italy, and to a lesser extent France and the UK) than others (unitary states). National governments are still the most powerful players, but their exclusive control over EU decision-making, both individual and collective, has slipped away.

Shared governance in the European Union has helped a budding European public space, where basic options for European societies can be and are contested. The public space is still largely segmented into national public spaces, but political parties have begun to formulate explicit connections between domestic contestation and European integration. European integration has heightened unease with the erosion of national identity, and this has benefited the radical right. But it has also renewed hope (or tempered despair) for social democratic values beyond the nation-state, and this has benefited the centre-left.

The European Union will be, with the United States, the major player in shaping global governance. But it has an edge over the US, in that it is also the first serious form of governance beyond the nation-state. It is a laboratory for global governance. The kind of governance that prevails in the European Union may influence disproportionately the future of global governance.

So how stable, then, is the current EU model of shared governance? The model faces two major challenges over the next decades. First, it needs to deal with emerging global regimes such as the WTO, which may develop rules that constrain EU capacity to regulate markets. And second, as of 2004, another ten countries are virtually certain to become member states, with several other applications, from the Balkans, eastern Europe and Turkey, still pending. Taking account of these two challenges, what might be the affect of the governance scenarios, as laid out in chapter 1, on the structure and processes of the EU?

Global regulation of regime competition is bound to be less encompassing, less binding, and less specific than EU regulation. It would be confined primarily to negative integration: trade liberalization, while it would not create much in terms of political regulation of markets, and certainly not a level of environmental and social standards that is equivalent to the EU level. However, a *global club* scenario, with a WTO that has significant authority to regulate economic but not social matters, might constrain the EU from enacting positive regulation. That would almost certainly create major tensions within the Union. It might even paralyze decision-making, which rests on a delicate bargain between supporters of global markets, one the one hand, and of European solidarity on the other. In effect, this scenario could weaken the authority of Brussels in the EU and stall or even reverse the trend toward a more federalized EU. And there would be strong resistance in the European Union against this kind of outcome. The main purpose of proponents of regulated capitalism is precisely to strengthen EU capacity for authoritative regulation to avoid such entropic processes. A much weakened deregulated EU, however, fits with the neo-liberal project. And neo-liberalism enjoys some support among liberal and conservative parties, among parts of the corporate sector and financial services, as well as some public opinion leaders.

In this sense, the global club scenario, in an EU context, could lead to results that are similar in direction, if not degree, to the *cyberwave* scenario. In both cases, the social contract (regulation of capital) of the EU would be undermined although, in the case of cyberwave, the effect for the EU would be even more fragmenting. In contrast, the shared governance global scenario would reinforce the shared governance that now characterizes the EU and thus reinforce the federalizing process within the EU.

Enlargement to the east is the more immediate challenge, and it may induce current "insiders" to reduce positive integration. This particular enlargement differs in two respects from previous rounds. First of all, the administrative and legal systems of the prospective members are less developed than those of any previous round, while the EU *acquis communautaire* — the accumulated body of EU law — is much more encompassing and constraining than at any other stage in EU history. And second, the ten newly entering members are economically and culturally more unlike the current EU members than prospective members have been in the past. For one thing, GDP per capita of these prospective new members is less than one-third of the average GDP per capita of the European Union. An extrapolation of current EU policies to these members would therefore necessitate a doubling of the EU budget, and this is not on the agenda. Instead, the European Union has chosen a mishmash of internal reshuffling of resources, policy reforms, and phasing-in of policy programs, all of which is aimed at controlling costs. To ease accession, prospective members have negotiated long transition periods in which they phase in compliance with current EU legislation in competition policy, environmental standards, and social policy, but they have also had to accept temporary exemptions from the EU's generous regional policy and common agricultural policy. The two policies are currently under review with an eye to reducing the overall bill. At the time of writing (August 2003), it is still unclear whether the current 15 will succeed in their efforts to rewrite the rules before the ten new countries become full voting members in January 2004. If they do, the enlarged European Union will be less attractive to the new members on the inside than it looked from the outside when they applied for membership.

The future shape of the European Union will influence global governance, though one can only speculate how. If shared governance prevails in the European Union, it would certainly help to bring about global shared governance. If it gives way to a deregulated authoritatively weak EU, as described above, this is likely to reinforce market pressures for a global cyberwave. But, given the existence of extensive authoritative institutions at the EU level and the electoral strength of political parties opposed to a cyberwave model, this may be the least likely outcome. Of course, as Sam Goldwyn once uttered, predictions are always difficult — particularly of the future.

Notes

1. The latest is the Nice Treaty, which comes into force in 2003. It changes decision rules to prepare the European Union for the accession of ten new countries in 2004. For example, it reweights voting in the Council of Ministers, and redistributes seats in the European Parliament. In 2001, many political leaders, from federalist German Foreign Minister Joschka Fischer to Euro-sceptical French President Jacques Chirac, began to campaign for a wide-ranging *constitutional* debate to perhaps lead to a European constitution (instead of a treaty). In February 2002, a "convention on Europe" began work on a blueprint for a European constitution. The composition of the convention is unusually open. There is an equal balance between governmental and parliamentary representatives: the European Parliament, the European Commission, and the national governments and national parliaments, not only from the 15 existing member states, but also from the accession countries (which have full participation and voting rights). The convention also sets up hearings for organized civil society. If the convention agrees on a blueprint by mid-2003, it will be submitted to an intergovernmental conference. In the end, then, national governments have the last word over the draft, before it is sent out for ratification by the national parliaments, or in some countries, by citizens through a referendum.
2. The scores in Table 1 are drawn from Lindberg and Scheingold's book *Europe's Would-Be Polity* (1970), from an expert survey conducted by Schmitter (1996), and from evaluations by Marks and Hooghe in 2000 (Hooghe and Marks 2001).
3. This exclusive competence was initially limited to goods and capital, while the status of services was unclear. But in 2000, the member states agreed

to give the Commission full competence to negotiate on their behalf in services as well.

4. Eleven countries joined in 1999, and Greece joined as from 1 January 2001. At the time of writing, Denmark, Sweden, and the UK are not part of the Euro-zone.

5. This section is based on Hooghe and Marks (2001, ch. 1).

6. Except for foreign and defence policy, immigration, and justice, where it shares this power with the Council of Ministers.

7. This section borrows its title from the classic: *Crisis, Choice, and Change. Historical Studies of Political Development* (Almond, Flanagan and Mundt 1973).

8. By one generally used measure of trade openness: imports and exports as percentage of GDP, the evolution for key countries was the following (McKeown 1999, p. 13):

	1960–73	1974–79	1980–89
Sweden	45	58	63
Denmark	60	61	69
Netherlands	92	96	110
Germany	39	51	61
France	26	39	45
Italy	31	41	42
United Kingdom	41	55	53
Canada	39	48	52
United States	10	17	18
Australia	30	31	33
Switzerland	61	66	73

9. In the strategic areas of electronics and telecommunications, many of Europe's largest firms, such as Bull, Thomson, Siemens, Philips, Olivetti, and ICL were more interested in alliances or mergers with US or Japanese firms than with European firms (Cawson *et* al. 1990; Sandholtz 1992).

10. Member states were compelled to recognize each other's standards as equivalent. The expectation was that market competition would ultimately make standards converge to the most efficient level. So *ex ante* politically negotiated harmonization would be replaced by *ex post* market-driven harmonization (Majone 1996). The Commission stated in a communication in 1980 that it would use the idea as the foundation for a new approach to harmonization (Alter and Meunier-Aitsahalia 1994).

11. The main exception was British Labour, which was still staunchly socialist and by implication, against European integration in the mid-1980s.

12. This and the following section are largely based on Hooghe, Marks and Wilson (2002).

13.   This is based on data on party positions of 142 national political parties, which were collected through an expert survey conducted in 1999/2000 by Gary Marks, David Scott, Marco Steenbergen and Carole Wilson. The survey asks country experts for all EU member states (except Luxembourg) to evaluate political parties on where they stand on a new politics dimension as well as on an economic left-right dimension (ten-point scales, ranging from one to ten), and to place these parties on a seven-point scale with the lowest score representing strong opposition to European integration and the highest score representing strong support for European integration, and to do this as well for seven policy areas tapping into aspects of political and economic integration (Hooghe, Marks and Wilson 2002). The 1999 expert survey is an extension of a survey conducted by Leonard Ray, who gathered data on party orientations to European integration (but not on seven policy areas, nor on the economic left/right and new politics dimension) for four time points: 1984, 1988, 1992, and 1996 (Ray 2000).

References

Alesina, A. and E. Spolaore. 1997. "On the Number and Size of Nations," *Quarterly Journal of Economics* 112:1027-56.

Almond, G., S. Flanagan and R. Mundt, eds. 1973. *Crisis, Choice and Change: Historical Studies of Political Development.* Boston, MA: Little, Brown.

Alter, K. 1998. "Who are 'the Masters of the Treaty'? European Governments and the European Court of Justice," *International Organization* 52(1):121-47.

Alter, K. and S. Meunier-Aitsahalia. 1994. "Judicial Politics in the European Community: European Integration and the Pathbreaking Cassis de Dijon Decision," *Comparative Political Studies* 26(4):535-61.

Axelrod, R. 1997. "The Dissemination of Culture: A Model with Local Convergence and Global Polarization," *Journal of Conflict Resolution* 41(2):203-26.

Bache, I. 1998. *The Politics of European Union Regional Policy.* Sheffield: Sheffield Academic Press.

Betz, H.-G. and S. Immerfall, eds. 1998. *The New Politics of the Right: Neopopulist Parties and Movements in Established Democracies.* New York: St. Martin's Press.

Beyers, J. and B. Kerremans. 2001. "Diverging Images of Consensus: Belgium and its Views on European Integration," in *Nationality versus Europeanisation. The National View of the Nation in Four EU Countries*, ed. K. Goldmann and K. Gilland. Stockholm: Department of Political Science, Stockholm University, pp. 126-65.

Bomberg, E. 1998. *Green Parties and Politics in the European Union.* London: Routledge.

Burley-Slaughter, A.-M. and W. Mattli. 1993. "Europe before the Court: A Political Theory of Legal Integration." *International Organization* 47:41-76.

Cameron, D. 1992. "The 1992 Initiative: Causes and Consequences," in *Europolitics: Institutions and Policymaking in the "New" European Community*, ed. A. Sbragia. Washington, DC: The Brookings Institution, pp. 23-74.

—— 1998. "Creating Supranational Authority in Monetary and Exchange Rate Policy: The Sources and Effects of EMU," in *European Integration and Supranational Governance*, ed. W. Sandholtz and A. Stone Sweet. Oxford: Oxford University Press, pp. 188-216.

Casella, A. and B.R. Weingast. 1995. "Elements of a Theory of Jurisdictional Change," in *Politics and Institutions in an Integrated Europe*, ed. B. Eichengreen, J. Frieden and J. von Hagen. New York/ Heidelberg: Springer Verlag, pp. 11-41.

Cawson, A. *et al.* 1990. *Hostile Brothers: Competition and Closure in the European Electronics industry.* Oxford: Clarendon Press.

Cecchini, P. 1988. *The European Challenge 1992: The Benefits of a Single Market.* Aldershot: Wildwood House.

Christensen, D.A. 1996. "The Left-Wing Opposition in Denmark, Norway, and Sweden: Cases of Europhobia?" *West European Politics* 19(3):526-46.

Cowles, M.G. 1995. "Setting the Agenda for a New Europe: The ERT and 1992," *Journal of Common Market Studies* 33(4):501-26.

Crouch, C. and W. Streeck. 1997. "Institutional Capitalism: Diversity and Performance," in *Political Economy of Modern Capitalism: Mapping Convergence and Diversity*, ed. by C. Crouch and W. Streeck. Thousand Oaks, CA.: Sage.

Dehousse, R. 1998. *The European Court of Justice.* Basingstoke: MacMillan.

Emerson, M. *et al.* 1988. *The Economics of 1992: The EC Commission's Assessment of the Economic Effects of Completing the Internal Market.* Oxford: Oxford University Press.

Falkner, G and M. Nentwich. 1999. "The Amsterdam Treaty: The Blueprint for the Future Institutional Balance?" in *European Integration after Amsterdam. Institutional Dynamics and Prospects for Democracy*, ed. K. Neunreither and A. Wiener. Oxford: Oxford University Press, pp. 15-35.

Frey, B. and R. Eichenberger. 1999. *The New Democratic Federalism for Europe. Functional, Overlapping and Competing Jurisdictions.* Cheltenham: Edward Elgar.

Garrett, G. 1992. "International Cooperation and Institutional Choice: The European Community's Internal Market," *International Organization* 46(2):533-60.

—— 1995. "The Politics of Legal Integration in the European Union," *International Organization* 49:171-81.

—— 1998. *Partisan Politics in the Global Economy.* Cambridge: Cambridge University Press.

Grant, C. 1994. *Inside the House that Jacques Built*. London: Nicholas Brealey.

Hooghe, L., ed. 1996. *Cohesion Policy and European Integration: Building Multi-level Governance*. Oxford: Oxford University Press/Clarendon Press.

Hooghe, L. and G. Marks. 1999. "The Making of a Polity: The Struggle over European Integration," in *Continuity and Change in Contemporary Capitalism*, ed. H. Kitschelt *et al*. Cambridge: Cambridge University Press, pp. 70-97.

—— 2001. *European Integration and Multi-level Governance*. Boulder: Rowman & Littlefield.

Hooghe, L., G. Marks and C. Wilson. 2002. "Does Left/Right Structure Party Positions on European Integration?" *Comparative Political Studies* 35(8):965-89.

Huber, E. and J.D. Stephens. 2001. *Political Choice in Global Markets: Development and Crisis of Advanced Welfare States*. Chicago: Chicago University Press.

Inglehart, R. 1990. *Cultural Shift in Advanced Industrial Society*. Princeton, NJ: Princeton University Press.

Katz, R. and B. Wessels, eds. 1999. *The European Parliament, the National Parliaments, and European Integration*. Oxford: Oxford University Press.

Keohane, R. and J. Nye. 2000. "The Club Model of Multilateral Cooperation and Problems of Democratic Legitimacy." Paper prepared for the annual conference for the American Political Science Association, Washington DC.

Kitschelt, H. 1994. *The Transformation of European Social Democracy*. New York: Cambridge University Press.

—— with A.J. McGann. 1995. *The Radical Right in Western Europe*. Ann Arbor: University of Michigan Press.

Kitschelt, H., P. Lange, G. Marks and J. Stephens, eds. 1999. *Continuity and Change in Contemporary Capitalism*. Cambridge: Cambridge University Press.

Ladrech, R. 1997. "Partisanship and Party Formation in European Union Politics." *Comparative Politics* 29(2):167-85.

Lindberg, L. and S. Scheingold. 1970. *Europe's Would-Be Polity: Patterns of Change in the European Community*. Englewood Cliffs, NJ: Prentice-Hall.

Ludlow, P. 1991. "The European Commission," in *The New European Community*, ed. R.O. Keohane and S. Hoffmann. Boulder, CO: Westview Press, pp. 85-132.

Majone, G. 1996. *Regulating Europe*. London: Routledge.

Marks, G. 1996. "An Actor-Centered Approach to Multi-Level Governance," in *The Regional Dimension of the European Union: Towards a Third Level in Europe?* ed. C. Jeffrey. London: Frank Cass, pp. 20-40.

Marks, G. and C. Wilson. 2000. "The Past in the Present: A Cleavage Theory of Party Positions on European Integration," *British Journal of Political Science* 30:433-59.

Marks, G. and I. Down. Forthcoming. "Regional Regimes and the Left: NAFTA and the European Union Compared," in *Rebundling Territoriality*, ed. G. Di Palma and C. Ansell. Oxford: Oxford University Press.

Marks, G. and L. Hooghe. 2000. "Optimality and Authority. A Critique of Neo-Classical Theory," *Journal of Common Market Studies* 38(5):795-816.

Mattli, W. and A.-M. Slaughter. 1995. "Law and Politics in the European Union: A Reply to Garrett," *International Organization* 49(1):183-90.

McKeown, Timothy. 1999. "The Global Economy, Post-Fordism, and Trade Policy in Advanced Capitalist States," *Continuity and Change in Contemporary Capitalism*, ed. Kitschelt *et al.*, pp. 11-35.

Müller-Rommel, F., ed. 1989. *New Politics in Western Europe: The Rise and Success of Green Parties and Alternative Lists*. Boulder, CO: Westview Press.

Padoa-Schioppa, T. 1987. *Efficiency, Stability and Equity*. Oxford: Oxford University Press.

Peterson, J. and E. Bomberg. 1999. *Decision Making in the European Union*. New York: St. Martin's Press.

Pierson, P. 1996. "The Path to European Integration: A Historical Institutionalist Analysis," *Comparative Political Studies* 29(2):123-62.

Ray, L. 2000. "Measuring Party Orientations Towards European Integration: Results from an Expert Survey," *European Journal of Political Research* 36:283-306.

Rhodes, M. and B. Van Apeldoorn. 1997. "Capitalism versus Capitalism in Western Europe," in *Developments in West European Politics,* ed. M. Rhodes, P. Heywood and V. Wright. New York: St. Martin's Press, pp. 171-89.

Rodrik, D. 1997. *Has Globalization Gone too Far?* Washington, DC: Institute for International Economics.

Ross, G. 1995. *Jacques Delors and European Integration*. Oxford: Oxford University Press.

Rüdig, W. 1996. "Green Parties and the European Union," in *Political Parties and the European Union,* ed. J. Gaffney. London: Routledge, pp. 254-72.

Sandholtz, W. 1992. "Esprit and the Politics of International Collective Action," *Journal of Common Market Studies* 30:1-22.

Sandholtz , W. and J. Zysman. 1989. "1992: Recasting the European Bargain," *World Politics* 42(1):95-128.

Scharpf, F. 1999. "The Viability of Advanced Welfare States in the International Economy: Vulnerabilities and Options," Max-Planck-Institut Paper No. 99/9. Saarbrücken: The Max-Planch-Institut für Informatik, Universität des Saarlandes.

Schmitter, P. 1996. "Examining the Present Euro-Polity with the Help of Past Theories," in *Governance in the European Union*, ed. G. Marks, F. Scharpf, P. Schmitter and W. Streeck. London: Thousand Oaks: Sage, pp. 121-50.

Smith, D.L. and J. Wanke. 1993. "1992: Who Wins? Who Loses?" in *The State of the European Community.* Vol. *2. The Maastricht Debates and Beyond,* ed. A.W. Cafruny and G.G. Rosenthal. Boulder: Lynne Rienner, pp. 353-72.

Soskice, D. 1992. "Productive Constraints: On the Institutional Conditions of Diversified Quality Production," in *Social Institutions and Economic Performance,* ed. W. Streeck. London: Sage.

—— 1999. "Co-ordinated and Unco-ordinated Capitalism," in *Continuity and Change in Contemporary Capitalism,* ed. Kitschelt *et al.,* pp. 101-34.

Stone Sweet, A. and T. Brunell. 1998. "Constructing a Supranational Constitution: Dispute Resolution and Governance in the European Community," *American Political Science Review* 92:63-81.

Stubbs, A. C-G. 1999. "Negotiating Flexible Integration in the Amsterdam Treaty," in *European Integration after Amsterdam: Institutional Dynamics and Prospects for Democracy,* ed. K. Neunreither and A. Wiener. Oxford: Oxford University Press, pp. 153-74.

Thomsen, S. 2000. *Investment Patterns in a Longer-Term Perspective.* OECD Working Paper on International Investment 2000/2. Paris: OECD.

Weiler, J. 1991. "The Transformation of Europe," *Yale Law Review* 100:2403-83.

Wilks, S. 1996. "Regulatory Compliance and Capitalist Diversity in Europe," *Journal of European Public Policy* 3(4):536-59.

Wolf, M. 1994. *The Resistible Appeal of Fortress Europe.* London/Washington: Centre for Policy Studies/American Enterprise Institute for Public Policy Research.

The Effects of Global and Continental Integration on Cooperation and Competition in German Federalism

Rudolf Hrbek

INTRODUCTION

When it was created in 1948–49, the West German state adopted a federal political system. Since then, federalism and its concomitant features have significantly influenced the West German polity and its political process. Moreover, federalism as a basic constitutional principle has acquired wide recognition and acceptance in Germany. At the same time, certain features of German federalism have attracted the attention of other countries, both federal and non-federal, that have been searching for solutions to the territorial dimensions of their politics (e.g., Spain after the Franco regime). On the whole, the dynamics of the way the German federal system has developed make it an interesting case for research and analysis among federalism scholars.

The Federal Republic of Germany (FRG) is one of the six founding members of the European integration project, which started in 1951 with the establishment of the European Coal and Steel Community. The pact continued with the Treaties of Rome in 1957, which established the European Economic Community (better known as the Common Market), and EURATOM. These three communities formed the basis for the dynamic and relatively fast-paced development toward what is now the

European Union. Without doubt, the EU is the most highly developed model of regional integration in the world. For the FRG, membership in the EC/EU, and engagement in the deepening and widening process of continued integration has always been an important part of Germany's *Staatsräson*. That is to say: as a modern nation-state, belonging to the larger framework of the EU was regarded as crucially important to the continued existence and development of the West German state (and after reunification, for reunified Germany as well).

With its export-oriented economy, the FRG has always been involved in the global economic system, and, as a consequence, it continues to depend on globalization processes. Although membership in the EU is important for Germany's foreign economic relations (exchange of goods and services and foreign investment) there are also valuable economic partners among non-EU member countries as well. These include: the United States, Japan, Canada, China, and South East Asian countries. Additionally, the countries in central and eastern Europe that will soon become EU-members also have a role to play in the FRG's foreign economic relations.

As mentioned already, German federalism has undergone a dynamic transformation; it has adapted itself in response to both internal and external challenges. Unitarian tendencies, "cooperative federalism" and *Politikverflechtung* (Joint Tasks) are features of the adaptation to internal challenges. With respect to external challenges, the German federal system has had to cope, first, with the consequences of reunification, and thus integrate the five new Länder into its framework; and second, with the implications of European integration, adapt its structures to this new context.

This chapter is devoted to assessing the impact of global and regional integration on Germany and German federalism. Regional integration, for our purposes, is identical to the European integration project (or, EU-integration). The EU represents a treaty-based legal community, and from a political science point of view, it has also been perceived as a political system with good reason (see Hix 1999; Lindberg and Scheingold 1970). Since Germany forms one component part of the EU-system, both the EU-system and the integration process have influenced German federalism. In other words, EU-governance (Kohler-Koch and

Eising 1999; Hooghe and Marks 2001), which has emerged as a new framework, has been accompanied by adaptations and adjustments ("Europeanization") of the German polity within its federal system (Sturm and Pehle 2001). With respect to the impact of global integration and the various possible meanings of globalization, this chapter will concentrate on *economic* globalization, which can be defined as the "integration of financial markets and integration of product markets" (Deeg 1996). The following section will address, in more detail, both global and regional integration as it has influenced the German federal system.

It is the thesis of this contribution that both forms of integration, as phenomena of "de-bordering," have had a strong impact on German federalism (Albert and Brock 1996; Börzel 2002; Kohler-Koch 1998). The effects can be observed from the 1980s onward. During this period, globalization became more visible, while the European integration process accelerated and deepened simultaneously.

Unitarian tendencies and the emergence of "cooperative federalism" (vertical as well as horizontal) culminated in the 1970s in a pattern labelled as *Politikverflechtung* and are major features of German federalism (Scharpf, Reissert and Schnabel 1976; Scharpf 1985). These features are criticized by academic observers. In the past ten to fifteen years, political actors, most of them from the stronger Länder, have become visibly uncomfortable with these developments, and have begun making demands for substantial reform of German federalism (see Lehmbruch 2000; Große Hüttmann 2002). Their objective has been to encourage the growth of "competitive federalism," or at least the inclusion of competitive aspects in the German federal system. Here, I argue that the German Länder have been remarkably successful in strengthening their position by developing autonomous activities, especially in the field of economic policy; and furthermore, that they could enhance their participation in decision-making on European Union matters at both the domestic and EU-level. As a result, German federalism adopted some features of competitive federalism, but has not replaced the structures and practices of cooperative federalism. German federalism, therefore, is characterized by some tension between these two tendencies and structures, but neither of them prevails; instead they coexist, nourish the dynamics of the federal system, and have, on the whole, arrived at a fair balance between these two forms.

SITUATIONAL CONTEXT

Germany is geographically situated in the centre of Europe. During the Cold War, the dividing line (iron curtain) separated the two sections of Germany which became integrated into the Western and Eastern blocs respectively. The decision to establish the Federal Republic of Germany as a democratic political system also implied a decision to become an integral part of the West. This fundamental decision was implemented during the first few years of the development of the FRG within its political, economic, and military integration via membership in the Council of Europe (1950), the European Coal and Steel Community (1951), the Western European Union (WEU) and the North Atlantic Treaty Organization (NATO) (1955), and the EEC and EURATOM (1957). The eastern border of the FRG was also the Soviet bloc border. Eastern territories of the FRG situated on that border line were marginalized by their locale, and thus became dependent on special support for their development.

The commitment for the European integration project was linked with the development of the FRG from the beginning (Hrbek and Wessels 1984). The integration project was perceived as establishing a values-based community; a peace and security community; a larger economic area, where economic recovery and growth could be achieved more easily; and a framework that would contribute to problem-solving, since the nation-state was no longer capable of performing this task autonomously. Belonging to this overall framework, therefore, was regarded as the *Staatsräson* of the FRG. Since the second half of the 1950s, there has been no dispute on this general orientation among major political parties and forces. As a consequence, Germany has always been engaged in attempts toward the deepening and widening of the European Community and could rely on what has been correctly described as the "permissive consensus" of the population (Lindberg and Scheingold 1970).

As an export-oriented economy, dependent on external markets, the FRG made successful efforts to become integrated into the world market, and has continuously advocated an open, anti-protectionist,and liberal international economic system. With its strong economic weight, the FRG belongs to the founding nations of the G7. Another factor affecting Germany's international position is the fact that after the end of World War I, Germany no longer had the status of a colonial power.

Since the demographic development in the FRG was characterized by stagnation and a growing proportion of elderly people, the country has been dependent on migrant workers. From the early 1960s to 2000, the number of migrant workers has increased to approximately two million; the total number of non-Germans is 7.3 million (which makes up 9 percent of the whole population).

The reunification of Germany, as a consequence of the collapse of the Soviet empire, brought with it a series of changes. The centrality of Germany in the heart of Europe was again put into effect. Open borders offer opportunities (e.g., to be close to new markets and resources) and imply risks (e.g., transnational crime, migration flows); and they require efforts to manage new neighbourhoods. Accordingly, special bilateral and multilateral relations at the subnational level (cross-border regional cooperation) needed to be set up. In this context, economic and social disparities and historic legacies have to be faced as special problems. It is important to note that, due to geographic centrality, Germany has become a transit country.

German reunification has been a challenge in further respects. There is a dividing line between the old and the new Länder, which is due not only to economic disparities but to the differences in attitudes and political culture between the old and new Länder. Furthermore, there has been a continuous migration from the former GDR to the western Länder (approximately 2.5 million from 1989 to 2000), negatively affecting the chances of the new Länder to recover and catch up economically.

CONSTITUTIONAL/FEDERAL FRAMEWORK

Germany has a parliamentary system of government with a strong chancellor. The pattern, however, is far different from an "elected dictatorship." Consider the following points: first, there have always been coalition governments and the chancellor, as the political leader of the dominant governing party, has to take into account interests and concerns of the smaller partner (who will try to make its own indistinguishable profile visible).[1] A second factor reducing the power of the chancellor (and the federal government) stems from Germany's federal system. Federal governments have always had to take into account the interests of the Länder or a majority of the Länder, especially if the majority in the Bundesrat — in political party terms — is not identical to the political majority in the Bundestag.[2]

Negotiations between different political actors and forces, therefore, play an important role and give the political process in Germany a special character. The emergence of neo-corporatist patterns and arrangements also fit into this context. In many respects, one can argue about whether the FRG does not belong to concordance-type political systems (with consensus orientation of major political actors) (Scharpf 1997).

The federal system is characterized by the "state" quality of the constituent entities — the Länder (Jeffery 1999; Kilper and Lhotta 1996; Laufer and Münch 1998). Only some of the Länder can claim to represent "historic" subnational entities, since most of them were created after World War II as more or less "artificial" entities; in the meantime, nevertheless, they have developed what can be considered "regional identities." The Länder have their own constitutions (these, however, must be in accordance with basic features laid down in article 28 of the Basic Law) and their own system of government (with some differences in aspects of the parliamentary system of government).

Federalism was introduced to the Federal Republic of Germany in 1948–49 primarily because of the "checks-and-balances" effect expected from and attributed to a federal structure. There was no fragmented or heterogeneous society in ethnic, religious or linguistic terms; and the millions of refugees from former German territories in the east have spread throughout the Federal Republic and become fully integrated.

With regard to the allocation of competences that the constitution provides, besides those that are concurrent, it also allows for exclusive competences for both the federation and the Länder. From the beginning, however, the development tended toward unitarian (not centralist) solutions and features. This was due, first, to vertical links between the federation and the constituent units (the Länder); and second, to horizontal arrangements (between the Länder). An additional feature that distinguishes German federalism from other federal systems is that, whereas the federation has legislative authority, it is the Länder that have the responsibility for administrative and executive implementation.

The fact that German federalism has never adopted the quality of "dual federalism" is due to a series of factors:

- The unique postwar situation, with sharp economic disparities among the constituent units and a general trend toward improving the living conditions on as high a level as possible, favoured unitarian solutions.

- With respect to the distribution of competences, there was, besides exclusive competences for the federation and the Länder, the area of concurrent competences. And the criteria within the area of concurrent competences allowed the federation to take action without being confronted with protests from the Länder (whose authorities had to take into account expectations and demands from the citizens for uniform and high standard solutions).
- Shared resources characterize the financial system as far as major tax revenues are concerned. In addition, a very comprehensive equalization mechanism emerged, which distributed funds from the federation to the Länder as a whole, to individual Länder, and among the Länder themselves (horizontal equalization), which became split between net-payers and net-receivers. This pattern has been a source of permanent dissatisfaction and conflict.
- The participation of the Länder in decisions at the federal level via the Bundesrat (a special type of second chamber containing representatives of Länder governments as members)[3] contributed to the trend toward unitarian solutions. Since part of federal legislation requires the explicit assent of the Bundesrat, consensual solutions on the basis of a common denominator (frequently a compromise) have become the rule.

The pattern that emerged was not only one of cooperative federalism, but it was characterized by a high degree of interpenetration of the two levels, especially with the introduction (from the late 1960s) of the so-called "joint tasks," which prompted some observers to speak of "a unitary state in (federal) disguise." Scharpf coined the term *Politikverflechtung*, which may be translated as "interlocking federalism" (Scharpf, Reissert and Schnabel 1976).

The governments in the Länder vary greatly in terms of their political party composition. There have been one-party governments and coalition governments, but only some of them resemble the coalition pattern at the federal level. Party competition, therefore, coexists with consensus orientation, since agreement is necessary in many cases in order to arrive at a solution. Another feature of the German polity is that the local level is given some autonomy; but there are, with respect to competences and financial resources, severe restrictions. It has always been a major concern for municipalities that they have been charged with special tasks, especially by the federation, which often does not supply the necessary financial resources.

There are no referendums at the federal level; several attempts to amend the Basic Law, in this respect, have failed. At the Länder and local levels, however, referendums are constitutionally possible. In practice, though, referendums have rarely been used. A last noteworthy feature of the German polity is the existence of the Federal Constitutional Court, which may be called upon during federal conflicts, in addition to the adjudication of other types of constitutional issues.

THE IMPACT OF GLOBAL AND REGIONAL INTEGRATION ON GERMANY

As shown earlier, the FRG has devoted itself from the beginning to the European integration process, which implies a reduction of autonomy, combined with and compensated by, an increase in the capacity to solve problems and fulfil tasks. Therefore, the integration process has been accompanied by a gradual transformation of the nation-state: it has not disappeared or faded away, but is losing the ability to exercise national sovereignty autonomously. Instead, the nation-state belongs to a larger entity, and must share its sovereignty with other nation-states.

In an attempt to characterize the political and legal quality of the EU, and to give more substance to the often-used label "*sui generis,*" Wolfgang Wessels (1992) introduced the term "fusioning federal state" (*fusionierter Föderalstaat*), which is more precise than speaking of a "multi-level system" (Hooghe and Marks 2001). The latter term is useful to analyze the EU as a polity, the politics in this framework, and the policy dimension. "Fusion" refers to the exercise of sovereignty and a new form of governance "beyond the nation-state." The EU has already adopted the pattern of pooled and then shared sovereignties. The term "state" indicates that the institutions of the EU, the decision-making process of the EU and its policies (e.g., regulatory and redistributive policies) are similar to those we would normally associate with the nation-state. And the term "federal" refers to a structure characterized by different levels or orders of government forming one comprehensive whole. Parallel to the gradual extension of the functional scope of the EC (since the Treaty of Maastricht: the EU) over the years (and especially since the mid-1980s) the process that created that pattern has accelerated and intensified. The Federal Republic of Germany, as a component part of the EU entity, has lost its ability to exercise autonomous action in many fields, as it has participated in steps toward the pooling of national sovereignties, and as it has accepted the new rules of the game in this special "multi-level system."

As mentioned above, the FRG as an export-oriented country is integrated into the global market and is therefore dependent on the global market's dynamism and development. Along with the ongoing and intensifying European integration process, developments in the global economy have affected the EU as a whole — as a "fusioning federal state" — and its individual member states. Inevitably then, the EU has reacted to global economic developments; and there have been, and will continue to be, special impacts from globalization on individual member states. Furthermore, as a consequence, EU member states have made efforts to respond on a national basis. This is particularly true for a country like Germany, which is so intensely interwoven into the global economy. Therefore, this section will deal with the impact of regional integration in the EU and of globalization on Germany. The next section will then investigate the impact of these two processes on German federalism — the core question of the whole project.

The Impact of European Integration on Germany

Integration can be defined with respect to several different dimensions of the process, and all of them need to be taken into account in order to assess the impact of integration on Germany.

One aspect of integration is the functional scope of the EU, which has been extended gradually. Four subsequent comprehensive treaty reform processes — the *Single European Act* (SEA) of 1986; the Treaty of Maastricht, signed in 1992 and in force from November 1993, following a long and difficult ratification process; and the Treaty of Amsterdam of 1997; along with the Treaty of Nice of 2000 — have sanctioned and legitimized this extension. In the meantime, more or less all policies have adopted a European (that is to say: an EU) dimension; this, in turn, means that EU matters have become domestic concerns in all member countries. Some examples should help to illustrate what this means for Germany: first, the project to establish and realize an internal market via mutual recognition of norms and standards (liberalization) or harmonization has necessarily entailed the disappearance of the closed national market, and as such, there is no possibility for national economic policy to set rules for markets. This larger economic area without borders offers opportunities for all (goods, services, capital, enterprises, sectors, individual economic actors), which are efficient and competitive. The Internal Market program gave incentives for a large-scale privatization.

Second, the common competition policy established a strict subsidy control regime that does not allow national measures (subsidies), which are designed to support individual enterprises, in the field of structural or industrial policy. Third, the Monetary Union[4] brought an end to national autonomous monetary policy. In addition, the Stability Pact implies the obligation for all member states to make sure that their public debts do not exceed an agreed-upon mark. For a federal system such as Germany this requires cooperation and coordination amongst the different orders of government; federation, Länder, and municipalities must work together to achieve this goal.

Fourth, new provisions on employment policy, introduced with the Treaty of Amsterdam, seem to follow the pattern of "open coordination" by jointly deciding on guidelines that the member countries are expected to meet. This may lead to political party disputes at the national level, if political parties advocate clearly divergent approaches and strategies in an attempt to reach this goal. Fifth, in the field of environmental policy, the EU may decide on a directive (which is a piece of communitarian legislation setting the goal), but leave the ways and means open to implementation at the national, regional, or even local level, depending on the distribution of competences pertaining to the particular issue. And finally, in the field of structural and cohesion policy of the EU, the five new Länder belong to the group of net receivers, and consequently Germany has a vital interest in maintaining this policy.[5]

Opinion poll data show, over past decades, a positive attitude toward the integration process, interpreted as diffuse support or "permissive consensus" (Hrbek 2002). In connection with the Internal Market project in the mid-1980s, support for EC membership reached a peak of 65 percent, and in 1990 (during the euphoria in connection with the German and European reunification) support reached over 70 percent. This was followed by a sharp and significant decline to only 50 percent support in

1993, and then another drop to less than 50 percent in 1996 — in connection with the debate on the establishment of the monetary union and the introduction of the Euro to replace the Deutschmark. The figures in the new Länder were even lower. Evidently, a utilitarian evaluation of EU membership prevails; speaking directly to the evaluation of gains and losses from EU membership, there has been a remarkable decline during the 1990s, and in the five new Länder the decline has been even more dramatic.

A second dimension of integration concerns the decision-making system of the EU. The institutions — European Council (the "Summits"), Council of Ministers, Commission and European Parliament — are linked with each other in a pattern of complex relations and the decision-making system became multi-layered with numerous complicated procedures, including "comitology" (with a large number of committees composed either of national civil servants or of experts with an advisory function) (Wessels 1998).[6] There are additional actors involved in the decision-making process: political parties, interest associations, and NGOs. The emergence of a transnational infrastructure of such actors — they form Euro-organizations — is a special feature of the integration process.[7] German actors participate formally and informally in this new framework and form part of it.

A third dimension of integration should not be ignored: public awareness of all of these aspects of integration and the "Europeanization" of politics is causing the emergence of a European identity that complements national, regional, local or "group" identities. Data collected in different EU-member states and in the EU Commission-managed "Eurobarometer" (two issues per year) discuss these tendencies. The fact that a majority of people declare that the national route is no longer effective at dealing with particular problems, and that European solutions should be achieved (e.g., on environmental issues) is one indication that there is an emerging European identity. Furthermore, a slowly growing number of people admit to feeling a sense of being both German *and* European; thus, one could indeed, speak of shared identities.

A fourth aspect of the integration process has to do with the question of which nations should gain admittance to the EU. Germany and its citizens have always advocated enlargement. Certainly the most ambitious and sensitive issue on the EU agenda is the prospect of eastern enlargement; here the support for EU enlargement is shrinking. In 2002, only

43 percent of Germans were in favour of enlargement. These figures reflect uncertainties or perhaps, even fear, concerning the possible negative consequences of an enlarged EU.

The Impact of Globalization on Germany

Economic globalization is alleged to reduce substantially "the ability of national governments to pursue macroeconomic policy strategies that differ significantly from those of other major industrial economies" (Deeg 1996). Globalization, therefore, represents a severe challenge for nation-states, since they must respond to the loss of (economic) policy autonomy. There are two major aspects of economic globalization: "the integration of financial markets and the integration of product markets" (ibid.).

First, concerning the former, it means greater capital mobility. This, "in turn, weakens the effective utilization of fiscal and monetary policies to control domestic growth, inflation and investment. Consequently, macroeconomic strategies such as Keynesianism and Monetarism are undermined" (ibid.). In order to respond to this challenge and to adjust their economies, political authorities in countries hit by globalization concentrated on supply-side policies and "submitted themselves to a process of policy convergence around the promotion of market forces through privatization, deregulation and a general reduction of state economic intervention" (ibid.). This is what happened in Germany, where it was not only the federal government, but also primarily individual Länder governments, that launched such new strategies.

Second, product market integration means much more competition for goods and services at all levels: from local to international. An individual enterprise, located at the local or regional level, will therefore find itself situated in this larger (often global) context. "For Germany, this means an accelerated decline of sectors based on low-wage, low-skill production (e.g., textiles) and sectors facing global overcapacity (e.g., steel)" (ibid.). The federal government has been providing support for such troubled sectors, but it was primarily the Länder governments that launched initiatives "to generate new growth sectors" and to systematically develop strategies to adjust their economies to globalization. "Thus, ... the globalization and regionalization of economic activity are directly related processes" (ibid.). Germany clearly illustrates this point.

The focus on supply-side policies has also been a focus on structural policy. In this field, one can identify three functionally distinct policy groups: sectoral policies, regional policies and small business or *Mittelstand* policies. With respect to sectoral policy, efforts have focused on "promoting the growth of 'knowledge-intensive' industries and managing the decline of old industries" (ibid.). In the meantime, the focus is on new industries, and it is here that the Länder have acquired the role of active promoters. All Länder began with their own technology programs, and many of them have invested in education policy as a complementary component to improve and upgrade the qualifications of individuals. Additionally, efforts have been made to encourage privatization and deregulation; here the links with developments in the European Union (Internal Market) are obvious.

In the field of regional policy, the federal government and the Länder governments were confronted with the strict competition policy regime of the European Union, according to which, subsidies for individual firms are not allowed. There is, however, one important exception: the five new Länder lagging behind the Länder of the old Federal Republic fell into the category of regions that qualified for special regional support, from the European Union as well as from the federation.

The *Mittelstand* policy (a policy in favour of small and medium-sized enterprises) is considered by the Länder to be "their 'natural' area of structural policy" (ibid.).

> All Länder governments have special economic development banks that provide regional *Mittelstand* firms with loans for various purposes, such as business start-ups, firm modernizations, expansions and R&D projects. They subsidize business-consultation services for small firms, and their technology programs are overwhelmingly oriented to them…. In the 1980s, promotion of exports by *Mittelstand* firms becomes another focal point of Länder structural policy. In effect, several of the bigger Länder were aggressively pursuing their own foreign economic policy with the aim of cultivating direct economic links between their regional economies and foreign markets (ibid.).

State-visits of prime ministers of the Länder have become routine events during the past few years, and the delegation is composed primarily of representatives of businesses of the respective Länder.

In their attempt to respond to economic globalization, German Länder have developed an additional strategy: Länder governments gained the support of subnational societal organizations. Throughout Germany we observe the emergence of "regional policy networks" which

> are characterized by stable, interorganizational relationships between Länder governments and regional societal actors for the purposes of policy making within clearly defined policy sectors.... Organizations that are typically part of a regional economic policy network include business and trade associations, public banks, Chambers of Industry and Commerce, Crafts Chambers, credit-guarantee cooperatives, equity-participation corporations, and, sometimes, unions. Such networks follow the logic of an exchange of resources, such as information, legitimacy, authority and money (ibid.).

Observers also note some politization (in political party terms) of the administration of Land governments in this context.

The analysis of concrete activities of such networks show not only similarities, but some interesting differences which can be taken as an indication that there is room for developing autonomous Länder policies related to special structural needs, political preferences, and available resources. For example, Baden-Württemberg created organizations, within this emerging network, that focus on small and medium-size enterprises *(Mittelstand)*. North-Rhine-Westphalia followed a slightly different strategy by putting more emphasis (at least in the beginning) on larger corporations; it has since "discovered" the value of supporting small and medium-size enterprises. There are two other aspects that are noteworthy: North-Rhine-Westphalia (the biggest German Land) established 15 sub-regions; and some emphasis was put on the inclusion of the unions.

In the new Länder, efforts have been made to preserve "industrial cores," in order "to revitalize the most regionally significant firms" (ibid.). In Thuringia and Saxony, the establishment and promotion of industrial holdings with strong government support instead of privatization is featured. It is evident that there are disparities between the 16 German Länder. The richer and more developed Länder are more likely to maintain, or regain, some autonomy in their attempts to adjust their economies to economic globalization. There are, no doubt, two classes of Länder and this disparity has consequences for the pattern of German federalism, its dynamism and development. This dimension will be dealt with in the next section.

There are other dimensions of globalization, beyond the economic. These have, however, only little effect, if at all, on German federalism. It is, therefore, sufficient to mention them only briefly. International migration (from those seeking asylum to those who would like to immigrate and settle in Germany) has been perceived as a severe challenge. Political parties disagree on how to respond and deal with these issues: with the Christian Democrats' more restrictive attitude versus a less restrictive approach favoured by Social Democrats and Greens; this cleavage becomes visible in diverging attitudes held by the federal and Länder governments. But all agree that international migration would require an EU-wide response. Since 1999, the issue has appeared on the EU agenda under the headline "An Area of Freedom, Security and Justice." The same applies to pressures from organized international crime and global terrorism: there is consensus in Germany that transnational/international problems cannot be dealt with at the national level but that an EU-wide policy is needed.

There is a growing awareness of global environmental issues and national responses are regarded as not adequate; and the EU has already been given a co-responsibility for these questions. On the topic of activities and policies that should be pursued, opinions differ along political party lines. Effects of global cultural flows can be observed in Germany, as elsewhere. But they coexist with still existing features of national and regional cultures. As concerns the latter, one can even speak of a renaissance of regional consciousness and identity.

THE IMPACT OF EUROPEAN INTEGRATION AND GLOBALIZATION ON GERMAN FEDERALISM

Both European integration and globalization can be understood (and have been described) as processes characterized by "de-bordering." Borders of nation-states have not disappeared, but nation-states have lost momentum, related to a variety of policy fields. This provokes the question: How far will new forms of governance — "beyond the nation-state" — become necessary or have already emerged? Processes of de-bordering can be expected to have a strong impact on federalism, and Germany can be taken as an example that illustrates the consequences. And when those consequences are considered as a whole, they are ambivalent or even contra-dictory, and thus do not result in a uniform pattern. So, the major question is: Will these integration processes result in competitive or cooperative federalism, or will we be able to identify a complex blend of these two different patterns?

It is the thesis of this chapter that the change pressures on German federalism from European integration have been far more important than the change pressures coming from globalization. We argue that many problems resulting from globalization appear first (and automatically) on the EU agenda, since the functional scope of the EU has extended sub-stantially, and make the Länder concentrate on efforts to adapt German federalism to this framework.

We further argue that European integration brings with it a large number of concrete challenges which demand immediate response, so that the Länder have further strong reasons to give priority to this dimension. In addition, the bargaining power of the Länder in the EU context was much greater since the ratification of EU treaty reforms requires the as-sent of (a majority of) the Länder in the Bundesrat.

Last, but not least, in terms of the response to the challenge of Eu-ropean integration, the Länder have agreed to strengthen their position vis-à-vis the federation via new and extended rights of participation, but they did not agree on what the adequate response to the challenges of globalization should be. The demand for greater autonomy for the Länder, put forward by those that are economically stronger, was not seen as a possible solution for the weaker Länder.

Globalization and German Federalism

Globalization creates an additional incentive for national governments to transfer economic policy competences, especially in the economic area, on supranational (and international) institutions. The European Union, understood as a "fusioning federal state," is a good example. Germany was among those countries to favour such transfers (or share sovereignty) in order to improve and strengthen its problem-solving capacity.

However, as we have already seen, economic globalization also put pressure on subnational entities (the German Länder) to become more active in economic policy-making and to acquire greater autonomy. Ger-man Länder (those bigger and economically stronger) can be regarded as global market players which have increased their external activities. However, the term "paradiplomacy" (Aldecoa and Keating 1999) may be misleading since these independent activities of the Länder are not primarily political or "diplomatic" in character, but rather focus on the economic dimension; here we identify primarily efforts to support exports and to attract foreign investment.

This strategy — to make the Land an economically strong and competitive region and perform successfully as a global player — has given the Länder a stronger role as component parts of the German federal system. This is evident in economic policy and in related fields such as education. So, the pendulum has swung toward the Länder level, thus "promoting a shift from 'cooperative' to 'competitive federalism'" (Deeg 1996, p. 48). This implies vertical competition because the stronger Länder have made efforts to strengthen their position vis-à-vis the federal government (and also toward Brussels). It also implies horizontal competition, in that the individual Länder compete amongst themselves.

The reality of economic globalization, therefore, has become one core argument for those of the German Länder, demanding a thorough reform of German federalism toward competitive federalism (Große Hüttmann 2002, pp. 300-01). The points on this reform agenda include an increase in the scope of autonomous Länder legislation, including tax policies and a comprehensive reform of the system of financial equalization, especially horizontal equalization amongst the Länder.[8] One should not forget, however, that it is the stronger Länder that put forward such demands, whereas the weaker realize that such a reform would cause them to lose financial resources, and/or make them more dependent on the federation. The existence of two classes of Länder — a pattern that has heightened since reunification — is one reason for this reform debate, and at the same time, it is a barrier against greater changes, since constitutional reforms require a two-thirds majority, that is to say: consensus. And as long as there are no changes in the pattern of German federalism, the need to continue with cooperative federalism will have to be recognized, even by the stronger Länder. Moreover, there is, as before, the need to coordinate horizontally between the Länder and, vertically, with the federal government and the EU level in Brussels.

There are two additional consequences for German federalism: first, the existence of two classes of Länder prevents them from forming a unified front or bulwark against the federal government. Political party considerations also discourage the formation of a permanent front of all Länder against Berlin.

Second, Länder governments have strengthened their position vis-à-vis Länder parliaments. The decline of the parliamentary factor accelerated and intensified as a consequence of the emergence of the "regional economic policy networks."

In conclusion, economic globalization has generated more competition within German federalism, yet the competitive dimension does not dominate. There are, as we have seen, counterweights, such that cooperative behaviour continues to be a characteristic feature of German federalism.

EU-Integration and German Federalism

European integration can be understood as another "de-bordering" process. But contrary to (economic) globalization, the European integration process was launched consciously as a primarily political project designed to establish a new order for Europe. The integration process should establish, maintain, and further develop — via "deepening" and "enlargement" — a community of peace and security, and a value community (with a commitment to human rights, democracy, the rule of law, and social justice). Economic goals complemented these overall objectives and did not play an exclusive or even dominating role. The integration process established a legal entity, based on treaty provisions that have been subject to a series of amendments and reforms, especially since the mid-1980s. The EC/EU, as a result of the integration process, has rightly been conceived as a political system and we must discuss its impact on German federalism and the subsequent adjustments of the federal system that have taken place.

During the integration process, two different species of development can be discussed: economic dynamics and political dynamics. Regarding economic dynamics, we are facing a pattern similar to that of economic globalization. This is particularly true with respect to the Internal Market project. Its inherent dynamism requires greater competition. What we have said above on reactions of the German Länder applies equally here.

Since European integration has been primarily a political project, its political dynamics have to be carefully taken into account. Here political developments spurred the emergence of a new type of governance, beyond the nation-state, but, at the same time, it encompasses the member states. The challenge confronting German federalism is how to come to terms with, and adjust to, EU multi-level governance.

The following sections deal with the question of how the German federal system responded to this challenge, and therefore, what has changed in German federalism (Hrbek 1999). The federal structures have the ability to adapt and achieve their goal: to maintain a balance between different levels of government. Therefore, it might be expected that, although competitive behaviour and patterns may emerge, they do not prevail; instead, cooperative approaches remain the characteristic feature of German federalism. *"Politikverflechtung"* will not become obsolete or substantially weakened in the integration process and within "EU-governance." Rather, it will continue in a more complex pattern of "multi-level governance." And *"Beteiligungs-Föderalismus"* (participatory federalism), not "dual federalism" remains valid for the German federal system within the framework of the political system of the European Union.

The Impact of EU Integration on the German Länder

The EU has continuously extended the spectrum of its functions over the course of its development. What this extension has consisted of is not so much a schematic transfer of competences from member-states to the EU, but rather the acquisition by the EU of co-responsibility and of possibilities of co-determination with the member-states in ever more policy areas. The activities of the EU range accordingly: from establishing law through projects supported largely by the EU budget, to encouragement of more cooperation and coordination of member-state policies. Since Maastricht, there is scarcely a policy area that is not, at least in part, dealt with within the framework of the EU.

The Treaty of Amsterdam has further intensified this pattern. The treaty contains a new chapter on employment policy: a sensitive (and from a political party perspective, controversial) policy field in Germany. Furthermore, the treaty introduced provisions of the so-called Stability Pact designed to maintain economic and financial stability in the framework of the Monetary Union. These provisions will have implications not only for the federal government, but also for Länder governments and even the municipalities, insofar as they have fiscal responsibilities. In addition, key issues in the field of justice and home affairs have been transferred from the intergovernmental Third Pillar of the Treaty of Maastricht to the First Pillar where Community rules and provisions have to be observed.[9]

Under the Finnish presidency, in the second half of 1999, two ambitious projects were launched within the EU: the establishment of an Area of Freedom, Security and Justice (involving a series of detailed measures which have been compared, as far as their substance and impact are concerned, with the Internal Market program of the 1980s) and the development of a Common Security and Defence Policy. The German Länder regard this deepening of the EC/EU as a severe challenge.

The first challenge for the Länder arises from the fact that a number of these policy areas are ones reserved to the Länder in the internal allocation of competences in Germany. This applies, for example, to culture and the media, education and training, health, the environment, research and technology and, in particular, regional structural policy.[10] The activity of the EU in these fields and the constraints placed on the Länder in this wider supranational framework of political interaction have the effect of considerably limiting the autonomy of the Länder to structural politics and policy within their territories.

The second challenge has arisen from the modalities of decision-making in EU affairs. The most important decision-making and legislative body has always been, and still is, the Council of Ministers, in which the Federal Republic is represented by the federal government. Therefore, it has participated in decisions in fields which not only impinge on Länder concerns, but also, in part, on their exclusive competences. While the federal government possesses no internal decision-making competence in such fields, it has the ability and duty (externally) to participate in decision-making processes under the terms of Community law.

Here, the Länder are further affected. Within the German federal system, they have extensive powers of implementation, and their rights of participation in federal legislation give them the possibility of co-determining implementation rules. Although the Länder are also responsible for the implementation of European law, they lack the ability to participate in such legislation. Furthermore, the Länder are under a strong degree of control by the federal government, which is responsible to the EU institutions for ensuring proper implementation of European legislation.

The Reactions of the German Länder

It was recognized from the beginning, though initially only by a small group of expert observers and those directly involved, that the Federal Republic's membership in the EC would have consequences for the federal system.[11] The Länder were therefore interested from the outset, in participating in internal decision-making on EC affairs, particularly in the determination of the positions the federal government would take in the Council of Ministers (Morawitz 1981; Jaspert 1982). What the Länder initially achieved in this respect was modest, but acceptable, given that the activities of the EC were initially quite limited and had barely noticeable effects on the level of the Länder. From the middle of the 1970s onwards, the situation changed. The European Regional Development Fund was established in 1975 and marked the start of a separate EC regional policy; this was clearly expressed in the treaty changes and supplements of the SEA in 1986 and the Maastricht Treaty of 1992–93. Henceforth, the Länder found themselves affected more and more by EC policies and the possibilities of participation open to them were, in their eyes, insufficient and ultimately ineffective. The Länder reacted to this new situation in three ways.

- Through defensive protest: by criticizing the "actionism" and "flood of regulation" stemming from Brussels and by urging the European Commission, in particular, to show restraint in the introduction of Community measures. Since the end of the 1980s, the Länder have continually demanded strict observance of the principle of subsidiarity in this context.
- Through the extension and strengthening of possibilities of participation: first, by embedding formal rights of participation in the internal discussion of EC matters; and second, by taking initiatives with the aim of direct participation in the decision-making process at the Community level.
- Through the establishment and development of autonomous EC activities: by establishing and using direct contacts of various forms — as it were, in circumvention of the federal government — with institutions and actors at the supranational level. The Länder countered criticism from the federal government that such activities amounted to a legally and politically inadmissible "auxiliary foreign policy" through reference to the emergence and existence of a "European domestic policy."[12]

All of these strategies reflect the situation that emerged in an EC/EU characterized by a double *Politikverflechtung* (Hrbek 1986): the EC/EU had become a form of multi-level union with the Länder as an autonomous regional level. In such circumstances, it was necessary and legitimate for the Länder to establish themselves as players in an increasingly differentiated European decision-making apparatus. The experiences of the Länder in the day-to-day interaction of federalism within the Federal Republic proved a valuable basis for this enterprise. The different strategies are discussed and their effect assessed below.

The establishment of internal rights of participation in EU decision-making up to Maastricht. The concern of the German Länder to compensate for the (EU-caused) loss of intra-Land political autonomy and rights-of-participation in federal legislation by establishing internal rights of participation in European matters extends back to the founding treaties. As mentioned earlier, the success of the Länder was initially only modest, but over time, they managed to improve their position in the sense of a strengthening of "participatory federalism" (Morawitz 1981; Jaspert 1982; Hrbek 1992).

The Bundesrat procedure. Following the ratification of the Rome Treaties in 1957, the federal government was obliged to keep the Länder constantly informed of developments at the European level. On this basis, the Bundesrat had the opportunity to present opinions on proposed EC legislation. In the absence of any appropriate legal foundation, it was not, however, guaranteed that the federal government would take such opinions into account in discussions in EC bodies.

The Länder participation procedure. This procedure, established in an exchange of letters between the federal chancellor and the president of the Conference of Minister-Presidents in 1979, initially brought an improvement. The federal government committed itself to delivering more comprehensive information to the Länder at an earlier stage, and declared itself prepared to follow Länder views strictly if Länder competences were affected, and if no "foreign or integration policy" concerns stood in the way. In contrast to the Bundesrat procedure, however, the Länder had to establish a unanimous view, which required a considerable coordination effort. For this reason, the Bundesrat procedure proved to be the superior one, even if individual Länder could not have their views represented whenever they fell on the wrong side of a majority vote.

The establishment of rights-of-participation in the Law of Ratification of the SEA. The Länder exploited the opportunity provided by the Law of Ratification of the SEA (BGBI II 1986, p. 1104), which required Bundesrat consent to expand and legally entrench their internal rights-of-participation. Article 2 of the Law, passed on 28 February 1986, together with the supplementary Federal-Länder Agreement (1987, Sekretariat des Bundesrates 1988, pp. 428-34), extended the duty of the federal government to provide information and allowed for rights-of-participation for the Länder, graded in terms of the extent to which their responsibilities and interests were affected by proposed EU measures. The federal government was thus obliged to secure opinions of the Bundesrat before it consented to EC decisions, and to take these opinions into account in negotiations. If the federal government diverged from the Bundesrat view in any vote, it was obliged to explain and justify to the Bundesrat why it had done so.

The Law also provided for the possibility of representatives of the Länder being sent to negotiations on Commission and Council bodies, although the federal government still remained in overall control of the German negotiating position. While the Länder evaluated their experiences with the new participation procedure positively — as evidenced in the report of the Heads of the Länder Missions to the Federation of 16 May 1990 — they were still eager to strengthen their internal position (Hrbek and Weyand 1994, p. 90). The opportunity to do so came in connection with the Treaty of Maastricht, since the ratification and implementation of the treaty required internal constitutional changes.

The new Article 23 of the Basic Law (the "Europe Article"). The provisions of the new article 23 (BGBI I 1992, p. 2086), enacted as a quid pro quo for Länder ratification of Maastricht and the constitutional changes required by it, strengthened the position of the Länder, as well as the wider German federal structure in a number of ways. First, *the "structural security clause" (Struktursicherungsklausel).* The article confirms that the Federal Republic continues to be committed to the aim of furthering the integration process, that is, participating in the further development of the EU as well as remaining a member. The structural security clause establishes that the EU has to display certain structural features: democracy, the rule of law, the principles of the social state, federalism, respect for the principle of subsidiarity, and effective protection of human rights.

The federal structure of the Federal Republic is thereby implicitly confirmed.

Second, *the procedure for transferring sovereignty*. The procedural conditions for the further development of the EU were an important innovation. The basis for transfers of competence had hitherto been article 24/1 of the Basic Law ("The federation may by legislation transfer sovereign powers to intergovernmental institutions"). In 1948–49, the Parliamentary Council discussed whether constitutional (i.e., two-thirds) majority should be required for transferring sovereign powers. At the time, this was explicitly rejected with the reason given that the transfer of sovereignty should deliberately be made easy. The new Europe article reversed the situation. If certain conditions are met — namely, if transfers alter the content of the Basic Law or make alteration possible — then a constitutional, two-thirds majority in support of the measure is necessary in the Bundesrat (and the Bundestag). The simple legislative process is therefore explicitly restricted to legislation on treaty changes that do not materially alter the Basic Law. However, recent experience has shown that this provision is open to interpretation in individual cases, and can lead to conflict between the federal government (and its Bundestag majority) and the Bundesrat (Oschatz and Risse 1995).

Third, *rights-of-participation of the Länder in EU affairs*. Building on the provisions of the SEA ratification law, the new Europe article comprehensively regulates the rights-of-participation of the Länder in EU affairs. The "Law on the Cooperation of Federation and Länder in Affairs of the European Union" of 12 March 1993 (BGBI I 1993, p. 313) and the subsequently concluded agreement between the federal and Länder governments of 29 October 1993 (*Handbuch des Bundesrates 1994/95*, Bonn 1995, pp. 168-76) supplemented the constitutional provisions in the article. The federal and Länder governments attempted to find a *modus vivendi* through these comprehensive supplementary provisions, and thereby, possibly avoid future constitutional conflict. The examination of the federal-Länder agreement undertaken by the Länder in February 1997 found that "the regulations of the federal-Länder agreement have proved themselves without exception and represent a suitable framework for good and trusting cooperation." It did, however, point out that negotiations conducted with the federation on these regulations had left a number of open questions.

The regulations provide for the following: first, *the duty of information of the federal government.* Existing practice was essentially confirmed here. Cooperation between the federal economics ministry (responsible for distributing information) and the Bundesrat is described as "good" by those involved.

Second, *Bundesrat opinions.* Detailed and complex provisions set out a graded obligation on the part of the federal government to observe Bundesrat opinions. The general rule is that the federal government allows sufficient time for the Bundesrat to have the opportunity to present an opinion, within an appropriate period, on matters that touch on the interests of the Länder. Sufficient time means enough time for a Bundesrat view still to be adequately considered in further negotiations in EU bodies. If the proposed EU measure is in an area of federal competence, the federal government is required merely to take into account the Bundesrat view. By contrast, Bundesrat views must be decisively taken into account if the EU measure concerned falls within Länder competence. The federal-Länder agreement stipulates that in cases of disagreement the two sides should still seek to reach a compromise. If that fails, and the Bundesrat confirms its view by a two-thirds majority vote, then the federal government is obliged to hold to the Bundesrat view. The federal government still, however, has the final say in any cases in which decisions could lead to increased expenditure or reduced income for the federation.

Third, *the procedure with respect to the measures based on article 235 (now article 308) of the EC treaty* is especially controversial, and still needs to be clarified. Article 235, often known as the *Kompetenz-Kompetenz*, the competence to define competences, allows the European Union to take action even when it is not explicitly empowered by treaty to do so, if the member-state governments are unanimously of the view in the Council of Ministers that the measure in question should be taken to realize the aims necessary in the framework of the Common Market. In such cases, the procedure is that federal government approval on such a measure has to be backed up by the approval of the Bundesrat. There is, however, no agreement on whether Bundesrat approval is also required if the federal government abstains in a Council vote where the effect is one of not preventing the measure being taken. How this issue works out in practice will determine whether the federation and Länder find a *modus vivendi* or whether disagreement will require adjudication by the Federal Constitutional Court.

Fourth, *Länder representatives in EU bodies*. The provisions on this question are intended to allow the Länder direct participation in negotiations in EU bodies. To this end the Bundesrat nominates Länder representatives, hitherto around 400, who then, on a case-by-case basis, form part of the German delegation in the negotiations. The effectiveness of this form of participation in any particular case will depend on how well-qualified the representative is to deal with the question at hand. While such participation is non-controversial as such, the question of transferring the lead role in the negotiations to Länder representatives does raise problems. The precondition for this is specified in the federal-Länder agreement as: whenever the matter concerned "centrally affects exclusive legislative competences of the Länder." Predictably, differences of interpretations occur, and, as a consequence, conflicts may frequently arise. Similarly, the participation of Länder representatives in discussions on the determination of the German negotiating position in EU bodies is open to the same problem. Here too, there will frequently be cases in which the Länder are dissatisfied with the extent of the participatory powers allocated to them.

The establishment of the so-called Europe Chamber (*Europakammer*) of the Bundesrat is also seen in connection with the new provisions in article 23 (Oschatz and Risse 1989). The chamber is a constitutional innovation to the extent that, unlike the committees of the Bundesrat, it is not just a forum for discussion, but one with decision-making powers. Decisions of the Europe Chamber have the same status as decisions of the Bundesrat plenary. The establishment of this new institution was justified by the fact that EU legislative proposals frequently need to be dealt with quickly. Given that the Bundesrat plenary does not meet often enough to ensure this, the establishment of the Europe Chamber was intended to make possible a prompt Bundesrat response. In practice, however, the normal rhythm of Bundesrat plenary meetings has proved adequate, and the Europe Chamber has rarely been convened. A second reason for the establishment of the chamber, which does not meet in public session, was to make it possible, where necessary, for Bundesrat votes forming part of the German negotiating position to remain confidential.

Independent EU activities of the Länder. The Länder have developed independent activities, in parallel to their concern, to entrench formal rights of participation in EU affairs. These activities are diverse in form and collectively support the Länder's aim of acquiring European capacity (*Europa-Fähigkeit*) (Wessels 1986, p. 1); that is, the Länder are actively trying to establish themselves as players in the wider arena of European policy-making and thus generate a capacity to represent and carry through their concerns as effectively as possible.

Organizational measures by Länder governments. European policy sections were created throughout most of the Länder ministries during the 1980s. In the state ministries and chancelleries (the Minister-Presidents' departments) coordination centres were established with the intention of ensuring as optimal a level of agreement as possible in the European policy positions of the Land concerned. The incorporation of European policy questions into training programs was designed to improve the "Euro-qualification" of Länder civil servants. Competence in European affairs has already become a criterion in the appointment and promotion of civil servants. And the Missions of the Länder in Bonn (now in Berlin) have been explicitly allocated European affairs as a new responsibility.

Inter-Länder cooperation in European policy. The relations of the Länder to one another have an especially important role in German federalism. The Conferences of the Minister-Presidents and of ministers in particular areas (e.g., Finance, Justice, etc.) are important institutionalized forms of cooperation. They are concerned more and more with EU matters, illustrating how far Europe has permeated the most diverse policy areas. A new coordination institution focused specifically on EU policy — the Conference of European Ministers — was established in 1993 (Gerster 1993). It meets three times a year, supplemented by more intensive cooperation at the civil service level. Its agenda has consisted of questions concerning the European policy role of the Länder, debate on, and contributions to, the Maastricht Treaty revision Intergovernmental Conference of 1996–97, and selected European policy issues. The more specialized political issues are dealt with in the relevant sectoral ministerial conferences.

Information offices of the Länder in Brussels. The western Länder established information offices from 1985–87, with the eastern Länder following their example later. The offices were initially subject to federal government criticism which claimed that these offices represented instruments of "auxiliary foreign policy," but they are now perceived and treated as normal. The federal government even committed itself to supporting the work of the Länder offices, in particular through its permanent representation in Brussels in the 1993 federal-Länder agreement. The functions of the information offices are diverse: they secure and pass on information; they are involved in the economic promotion of their Land and assist firms or other bodies in the development of projects in which EU institutions play a role; they act as representatives of their Land; and they are an important forum for discussion (Hahn 1986; Jeffery 1996). The number of staff in the offices has grown as work on behalf of their Länder has intensified.

The European policy role of the Länder parliaments. The Länder parliaments have hitherto played only a minor European policy role in comparison to their executives (Straub and Hrbek 1998; Johne 2000). The Conference of Landtage Presidents has called repeatedly for the incorporation of the Landtage into the European decision-making process, arguing in particular for the right to information by the Land's government and for the possibility of having influence on the formulation of the position represented by the Land government in the Bundesrat. But the role of the Länder parliaments remains marginal even though a number of Länder governments do inform their parliaments. Still, Landtage present opinions on EU matters; and specialist European policy committees have been established in some Landtage.

Lobbying activity in the framework of the Assembly of the European Regions. The Assembly of the European Regions (AER) was founded in 1985 in order to represent specific regional interests at the European level, in particular vis-à-vis EU institutions (Hrbek and Weyand 1994, pp. 103-07). Its aim, according to its statutes, is "to strengthen the representation of regions at European institutions and to facilitate their participation in the construction of Europe and in the decision-making process at the level of the European Community in all its concerns." The Länder originally distanced themselves from the new institution, with the Land Baden-Württemberg the first to join in 1987. The reason for this circumspection was the heterogeneous composition of the AER. The Länder, with their quality of autonomous statehood, initially saw no advantages in working with territorial units of varying and, in comparison to themselves, less legal and political quality. Only when it became clear that international coalitions of interest with other subnational territorial units could be useful in securing specific Länder concerns, did they commit themselves to the AER. The AER has since clearly developed the most comprehensive European representation of regional interests. The influence of the Länder on the work of the AER has been considerable, most notably in the AER's adoption of demands formulated by the Länder in the debate surrounding the Maastricht Treaty.

Institutionalized participation at the European level. The Länder have never left any doubt about their positive commitment to the European integration process and their support for its further development toward a progressively deeper European Union. They have supplemented this general commitment with concrete views on how this union should be created and upon what structural principles it should be based. Among these have been statements about the position of territorial units below the level of the nation-state, that is, in Germany's case, the Länder, in the developing union, including the effective participation of these units in the legislative process of the Union. Their ideas on these matters have been systematically developed, in light of the deepening European integration, in the framework of the intergovernmental conferences since the SEA came into force. They have also been introduced into European-level debates, primarily via the federal government.

The starting point for this series of initiatives was the resolution of the Minister-Presidents' Conference in Munich in October 1987, where the goal of "a Europe with federal structures" was formulated (Bauer 1991). Two years later, the minister-presidents established a Working Group of the Minster-Presidents' Offices to report on the position of the Länder and regions in the further development of the EC. The comprehensive report, presented in May 1990 (ibid., Document 4), contained concrete proposals for revisions to the Community treaties which were distilled into four points: the incorporation of the subsidiarity principle; models for the participation of Länder and regions in the Council of Ministers, the creation of a "regional organ" at the supranational level; and the introduction of an independent right of appeal of the Länder and regions to the European Court of Justice. These demands were confirmed in a resolution of the minister-presidents on 7 June 1990 (ibid., Document 5) and in a Bundesrat resolution of 24 August that year (ibid., Document 6). In addition, the federal government was called upon in the Bundesrat resolution to involve the Länder in the work of the intergovernmental conference, including the preparatory discussions that would define the German negotiating position. The federal government ceded this demand,

and only in the concluding negotiations of the heads of state and government at Maastricht were the Länder excluded. In the preparation phase the relationship of the Länder to the federal government developed in an extremely cooperative way. From the Länder perspective, the results of the intergovernmental conference, as reflected in the Treaty of Maastricht, can be summarized as follows.

The subsidiarity principle. The Länder could only be satisfied, in part, with the provisions on the principle of subsidiarity in article 3 b of the Maastricht Treaty (Hrbek 1994). The "principle of limited individual empowerment" confirmed in paragraph 1 met the Länder position insofar as they had criticized initiatives of the Commission taken without a legal foundation. Moreover, if the member states wanted to make use of article 235 of the EC Treaty — a general empowerment to fill in gaps in the treaty — they would now have to justify doing so much more carefully (Beutler *et al* 1993, p. 188). The underlining in paragraph 3 of the principle of proportionality of Community measures was also in line with the Länder viewpoint.

The wording on the subsidiarity principle, in its narrow sense, in paragraph 2 was, however, unproductive for the Länder. The provision only went as far as the relationship between the community and the member states, and left out the regional level. The ambiguous legal concepts in the formulation of paragraph 2, "not sufficiently" and "better," raised doubt about whether the subsidiarity principle is usable at all in this formulation as a justiciable basis for any appeal or whether it can ultimately, if at all, develop any restraining political effect. Practice hitherto indicated that the latter function is the one that has relevance.

Direct participation of the Länder in the Council of Ministers. The revised version of article 146 of the EC Treaty, which determines the composition of the Council, has given the Länder the opportunity to represent the Federal Republic in the Council.[13] No clear view has yet emerged on how this new channel of participation has worked.

The creation of the Committee of the Regions. The demand of the Länder for a "regional organ" was only very imperfectly fulfilled with the creation of this new institution (Hrbek and Weyand 1994, pp. 125ff; Loughlin 1996). The committee is restricted to merely advisory functions. Its organizational infrastructure and its financial resources are extremely modest. But the main weakness is the wide heterogeneity in its composition. The regions represented differ considerably in terms of legal status and political quality. The committee will therefore find it hard to develop an autonomous profile and grow into the role of noteworthy player in the European decision-making process. Given these weaknesses, it quickly became clear after the committee took up its work, that the Länder had considerably downgraded their expectations of it.

In contrast to the expectations and demands of the Länder, not all of the 24 German seats on the committee were reserved for the Länder; three seats were allocated to the three highest organizations of German local government. Each Land has one representative; the five biggest Länder send, in the first period of office, a second member. The executive branch dominates these; parliamentary representatives from the Länder are found only among the alternate members and the second representatives of the bigger Länder.

The right of appeal to the European Court of Justice. Neither individual regions (or Länder), nor the Committee of the Regions were awarded an independent right of appeal to the European Court of Justice. If the Länder wish to pursue an appeal, for example, against decisions of the Commission, they have to rely on the cooperation of the federal government. The preconditions for this process were established in the Law on Cooperation and the federal-Länder agreement, although answers to procedural questions about such an appeal process remain unclear.

More Recent Developments

As we have seen, the German Länder could strengthen their position vis-à-vis the German federal structure (see Hrbek and Große Hüttmann 2002; Hrbek 2001). This is clearly true for the period around the Treaty of Maastricht. However, one could observe that during the preparation of the governmental conference in 1996 (which in 1997 brought the Treaty of Amsterdam), demands of the German Länder at the conference were formulated with much less emphasis and agreement amongst each other.

At the Conference of the Ministers for European Affairs of the Länder, four demands were approved by the prime ministers and submitted to the federal government to be put to a vote before the Bundesrat.[14] The demands were: to better operationalize the Principle of Subsidiarity; to decide on a catalogue of competences which should, as precisely as possible, allocate powers for the Community, the member states and subnational territorial entities (if these possess genuine powers); to upgrade the Committee of the Regions; and finally, to give the Länder the right to appeal directly to the European Court of Justice. Both the smaller Länder and the new Länder (except Saxony) did not put the same emphasis on these demands as the others. This can be explained by the fact that some Länder feel satisfied by what had already been achieved (article 23 of the Basic Law); and that it would require great effort for them to properly exploit the existing possibilities for participation in European Union issues.

The same pattern of lack of coherence and agreement amongst the Länder can be seen in the day-to-day business when EU-issues are on the agenda. This is partly due to political party differences, and partly due to disparities in the structure of the Länder, which results in diverging interests and priorities. Here, examples include the reaction of the Länder to the question of which steps and measures should be started as a consequence of the new treaty chapter on employment. The majority vote in the Bundesrat, supported by the Social Democratic-led Länder governments, favoured more coordination and multi-lateral supervision, whereas the minority (Länder governments led by the Christian Democrats) was opposed. Another example is illustrated by the opinion of the Länder to the Commission proposal, *Agenda 2000*. There was, at first, agreement on a key question under the federal structure: What should the role of the Länder administrations be in the implementation of structural policy measures? Then, reactions to the Commission proposals concerning reform of the Common Agricultural Policy reflected structural differences amongst the Länder.

In connection with the intergovernmental conference in 2000, which resulted in the Treaty of Nice in December, the German Länder reached agreement again on some key issues as far as the federal structure and position of the German Länder are concerned. The position of the Länder can be found in a statement of the Bundesrat (4 February 2000):

- The Committee of the Regions should be given the right to appeal directly to the European Court of Justice and the right to put questions to the European Commission. This aims to strengthen the committee's position in the inter-institutional dialogue.
- The principle of local self-administration, laid down in the German Basic Law, shall be included in the EU treaties.
- The Länder demand, again, to formulate a catalogue of competences that would allocate the competences to the EU, the member states

and territorial entities at the subnational level. The Länder seemed
to be satisfied — as most recent discussions show — provided that
their core concerns are included in this catalogue. And they do not
have an extensive, detailed catalogue in mind.

- Institutions in the field of "public services" (*Daseinsvorsorge*), which
the European Commission in Brussels has been looking at in the
context of its competition policy, are of particular concern for the
German Länder. These institutions include: savings banks, at both
the local and regional levels (Landesbanken); broadcasting companies under public law; and public welfare associations. The German
Länder perceive these institutions as belonging to their "core substance," which they are going to defend in order to avoid erosion in
these areas.

- A totally new element in the considerations of the prime ministers
of the Länder has to do with the voting procedure in the Council,
which is one of the crucial issues on the agenda of the intergovernmental conference. On the one hand, the Bundesrat advocates
majority decisions as a general rule, since this would improve the
chances that the Länder will realize their concerns at the European
level with greater efficiency. On the other, the Bundesrat under-
lines the fact that unanimous decisions, in certain cases, might be
more likely to safeguard the competences of the Länder. Therefore,
the Bundesrat has concluded that clearly defined competences, allocated to the different orders of government, are a necessary
precondition before majority decisions can be regarded as the rule.

Two representatives of the Länder (from Baden-Württemberg and
Rheinland-Pfalz) participated in the intergovernmental conference; they
were part of the German delegation. Signals from the Länder were such
that they could decide not to ratify a reformed treaty if their key concerns
were not met. It was more than doubtful that such a scenario could become a reality. In the case of a conflict, the Länder would have to examine
carefully what would follow from the principle of "federal comity"
(*Bundestreue*). Their reaction to the results of the Nice summit was positive, although not all their demands have been fulfilled. They interpreted
the decision of the summit, to continue the discussion on the future shape
of an enlarged European Union, the so-called "post-Nice-process," as their
success; since one topic that had been included on that reform agenda is

of significant concern to the German Länder: to demarcate the competences between the EU and the member states, while observing the goal of the principle of subsidiarity. Their success can be taken as an indicator of their active role as co-players in the European arena. Two German Länder, Bavaria and North-Rhine-Westphalia, were among a group of so-called "constitutional" regions (regions with genuine legislative powers in specific policy fields) which asked to be included in the current reform debate. Walloonia and Flanders had also taken this initiative, and completing this pressure group were Catalonia, Salzburg, and Scotland. The group's main concern was that their position as territorial entities with autonomous legislative powers would be taken into account in a new constitutional or treaty design for the European Union.

The EU summit in Laeken in December 2001 established a convention and gave it the mandate to prepare the next treaty reform/amendment, which would be decided formally by a governmental conference to be held in 2004. This body is composed of representatives of the governments of the member states, national parliaments, and the European Parliament. Also included as members, but in an advisory capacity only, are representatives from the Committee of the Regions and of the applicant countries from central and eastern Europe. The convention started to work (under the presidency of former French president, Giscard d'Estaing) in March 2002. From the German parliament there are two representatives: one member of the Bundestag and one member of the Bundesrat; Erwin Teufel, the prime minister of Baden-Württemberg, took this on.

The German Länder focus on the division of competences and the application of the principle of subsidiarity. Although they agree on these issues in general, their positions concerning details, differ. For example, there is no consensus on what should be included in a revised treaty: should it be a detailed catalogue with competences for the EU and the member states, plus regions, or should it identify only different categories of competences. Clearly, the German Länder have a recognized role in contributing ideas to the project of further constitutionalization of the EU. It is their goal to strengthen their position vis-à-vis the federal government and the European Union. Moreover, they view their engagement in the European reform debate as linked with their efforts toward reforming German federalism. It is, however, primarily the stronger German Länder that advocate greater autonomy. The Länder have always emphasized that the major reason for demanding a thorough reform of German federalism lies in the challenges connected with changes in the international environment: European integration and globalization. Obviously, the focus of the Länder is on responding to EU-integration, but strengthening their roles and position within the EU system would, at the same time, support their efforts to adjust successfully to the challenge of globalization.

FUTURE SCENARIOS

In the previous two sections, we have analyzed the impact of global and regional integration on Germany and German federalism. We have tried to show that both forms of international integration had a considerable impact on German federalism and to describe how the German Länder managed to respond and adjust the German federal system to this dual challenge. Against this background, we now look ahead and discuss the impact of future scenarios on German federalism.

The four scenarios that are suggested here represent accentuated models for alternative developments in the world order. It is not the task here to discuss which of them could, or should, be the most likely to happen. Or, for that matter, if a combination might not be the most probable outcome. Nevertheless, we will take the four scenarios as independent variables and analyze their probable impact on German federalism, including responses from the component parts of the German federal system.

We have argued that membership in the European Union and active involvement in the European integration process has been a priority for Germany; and this is undisputed among major political parties and actors in Germany. In addition, we have argued, in accordance with the mainstream of observers and actors, that the European Union has acquired the quality of a legal entity and can rightly be understood and analyzed as a political system. It was, therefore, our thesis that the impact of European integration on German federalism was much stronger than the impact of globalization. For our discussion of the impact of each of the four scenarios on German federalism, it follows that we must analyze how the scenarios affect Germany as an integral part of the EU-system; also, we assume that the EU-system will continue to exist in all scenarios, perhaps with the exception of the *cyberwave* scenario, and that the European Union has been evolving in a way that is similar to the *shared governance* scenario and diametrically opposite to the cyberwave scenario; these two represent the opposite alternatives, with the other two scenarios — *global club* and *regional dominators* — resting between them. Our considerations will, therefore, start with the two opposite scenarios.

Shared Governance

A major feature of this scenario is interdependence and its mutual recognition. In order to manage this complex interdependence, states and non-state actors will need to cooperate. We have already mentioned the emergence of particular types of networks that include public and private actors that are linked because they are mutually dependent on each other. This is a type of governance that we already observe in the present European Union. This scenario seems to be very close or almost identical in character to the present pattern. Therefore, the effect of this scenario on German federalism would be more or less identical to the impact of European integration on German federalism. Regional networks as aspects of a shift toward competitive federalism would continue to be given attention by individual Länder, primarily by the stronger. The Länder would continue to try to strengthen their position vis-à-vis the federal government and the European Union, but they would also be well aware that they are dependent on the federal government to bring about a formal change in constitutional rules in Germany and treaty provisions in the European Union.

Cyberwave

In this scenario, borders would continue to lose relevance; the process of de-bordering and of abolishing previous structures, rules and procedures would accelerate. This scenario seems to have as a premise the notion that an entity like the European Union would have been dissolved, or at least transformed into a very loose entity, leaving its members freedom to manoeuvre. It is not just for this reason that this scenario seems to be the most unlikely. The underlying premise of this scenario is that major changes will occur that are so fundamental that we find ourselves on uncertain ground, with the result that it will be difficult to make a forecast regarding consequences and reactions to such a new constellation. Here, there seem to be more questions then answers; that is, regarding the probable tendencies within the German federal system in such a situation.

One could, for example, argue that economically strong Länder could try to emancipate themselves further, in order to prepare for autonomous activities and form entirely new coalitions or alliances. This would also mean an end to the unitarian tendencies, which have been characteristic of German federalism in past decades. These tendencies are the starting point for demands of especially stronger Länder for a substantial reform of German federalism toward "competitive federalism." The slogan: "diversity without unity" could then become appropriate for understanding German federalism. One could, on the other hand, doubt that individual Länder would be capable of "surfing" successfully in this cyberwave world. This would then be an argument calling for the strengthening of cooperative strategies between the Länder and the federal government and among the Länder themselves.

Global Club

One major feature of this scenario is that interdependence will become recognized throughout the world and that economic interdependence would increase. It seems to be a premise of this scenario that not only Germany, but also the European Union, as a legal entity would be club members. This scenario would bring with it incentives for more autonomous activities (especially in the economic field) of the Länder; particularly, it would be the stronger Länder that would gain (achieve more autonomous activities). The well-known pattern of two classes of Länder (as one feature of present German federalism) would become strengthened. In the political dimension, however, incentives for cooperative approaches will continue. As a result, the competitive character would become, to a certain extent, strengthened, but it would not dominate; instead it would coexist with well-known practices of cooperative federalism.

Regional Dominators

This scenario emphasizes the emergence of geopolitical blocs that would compete with each other; the pattern of this world order would be highly conflictual. Germany would continue to be an integral component part of the European Union, which would in turn be a part of one of these blocs. And the European Union would be obliged to pay more attention to its external relations, as well as improve and strengthen the "domestic" basis, in order to perform in this constellation successfully.

Externally, vis-à-vis other blocs, the federal government — as a representative of Germany and, at the same time, as one of the larger EU member states — would gain and would play a more dominant role in the economic and in the political area. Germany would be one of the bloc leaders. This would encourage a trend to reduce or give up all claims toward autonomous activities of individual German Länder vis-à-vis other blocs or members of other blocs. But within the European bloc (the still existing European Union), Länder would continue the strategy we have explained in previous chapters. That is, the Länder would try to cope with the challenge by increasing their competitiveness, and thereby gain more economic autonomy.

Politically, however, the Länder would continue to follow a co-operative strategy since the European Union as a whole would need to be further deepened and strengthened in order to be better positioned in this conflict between competing blocs. This would result in a blend and co-existence of competitive and cooperative federalism, where we could identify, as before, two classes of Länder. The stronger would gain from this bloc-confrontation scenario; the majority, however, would play only a marginal role in their relation to the federal government and to the stronger Länder. The federal government would win, since weaker Länder would become more dependent.

CONCLUSION

The goal of this chapter has been to assess the impact of global and regional integration on German federalism. With respect to global integration, we focused on economic globalization, and with respect to regional integration, we dealt with the European integration process in the EC/EU. Since it is our premise that participation in European integration has always been a key concern and priority for Germany (*Staatsräson*), this chapter has put particular emphasis on the effects of European integration on German federalism and on its adjustment; the details given illustrate the ability of a federal system to adapt, as well as the richness of solutions and the new patterns found therein.

Our conclusion can be brief. A major point to be made is that both forms of international integration (as the phenomenon of de-bordering) had a strong impact on German federalism and that the German Länder managed to respond successfully and adjust the German federal system to this dual challenge.

The economic dynamics stemming from both forms of integration (economic globalization and the establishment of the internal market in the EU) have resulted in more competition and a shift toward competitive federalism. The political dynamics, on the other hand, were followed by attempts by the Länder to strengthen their position via autonomous activities. But at the same time, we observe that the pattern of cooperative federalism continues to be dominant: *Beteiligungsföderalismus* (participatory federalism), in connection with the Europeanization processes has been made more complex. This development has negative consequences for democratic legitimacy, which, in turn, means that cooperative federalism, in large measure, continues to be a characteristic feature of German federalism.

Both elements coexist, neither prevails, and thus they find themselves, on the whole, in balance. The ongoing dynamics of both forms of integration (EU development with deepening and widening, and globalization) will continue to represent challenges for German federalism. We may, given previous experience, expect that German federalism will manage to adjust in the future, as well. This applies to at least three of the scenarios discussed at the end of the chapter, since cyberwave is understood as the least probable development pattern.

Notes

This text is the enlarged and revised version of the author's contribution to the conference in December 2000. My thanks go to Harvey Lazar, Hamish Telford and Ronald L. Watts for their valuable comments on my paper and the draft of this manuscript; to other conference participants for their remarks; and to my assistant Martin Große Hüttmann for his support in preparing the paper and the manuscript.

1. This was the case with the Liberals (FDP) as the smaller partner of the Christian Democrats (CDU/CSU) 1949–65 and 1982–98, and of the Social Democrats (SPD), 1969–82; and it is now the case since 1998 with the Greens as the partner of the SPD.

2.   This is a well-known constellation since in political party terms Länder governments frequently differ from the federal government: in the Länder there have been one-party governments and coalition-governments in various compositions.

3.   The votes of each Land (from three to six according to the size of the population) have to be cast as a whole.

4.   In force since 1999 with 12 EU member countries. The UK, Denmark, and Sweden have remained apart.

5.   This policy means that Germany, as biggest net-payer in the EU, can reduce the volume of its financial contribution. There have been, recently, proposals and demands from Germany (federal and Länder governments) to renationalize structural policy which would reduce the German contribution to the EU-budget and make more money available for autonomous structural policy in Germany.

6.   In the 20-member Commission there are two German nationals, in the European Parliament there are 99 German deputies (total number: 626). In the Council there are either unanimous decisions — which give each member state the "right" to a veto — or qualified majority voting; in the latter case, 62 of the total of 87 weighted votes, depending on size, are required. Germany, one of the so-called four big member countries, has ten votes.

7.   For political parties, see Gresch (1978) dealing with the beginning of these developments; or Hix and Lord (1997), giving a more recent overview. For interest associations see Greenwood (1997).

8.   To an extent, this aspect of the reform follows the Swiss model.

9.   Issue areas include migration, asylum, and refugees.

10.   In this field the Länder have to observe the EU subsidy-control regime (articles 87–89 of the EC treaty).

11.   On the early development of the EC through to the 1980s, see Birke (1973) and Oberthür (1978).

12.   See Hahn (1986). The Rhineland-Palatinate Minister-President Bernhard Vogel dismissed the thesis of "auxiliary foreign policy" in a speech entitled "Gibt es eine Nebenaußenpolitik der Länder? Eine Klarstellung aus der Sicht eines Ministerpräsidenten," presented at the Deutsche Gesellschaft für Auswärtige Politik, 19 February 1987.

13.   "The Council shall consist of a representative of each member state at the ministerial level, authorized to take binding decisions for the government of that member state" (after the re-numbering through the Amsterdam Treaty this article is now article 203 of the EC Treaty).

14.   The demands of the Länder are formulated in a declaration of the Bundesrat of 15 December 1995 (see Bundesrat-Drucksache 667/95, Beschluss).

References

Albert, M. and L. Brock. 1996. "Debordering the World of States. New Spaces in International Relations," *New Political Science* 35:69-106.

Aldecoa, F. and M. Keating, eds. 1999. "Paradiplomacy in Action. The Foreign Relations of Subnational Governments," *Special Issue of Regional & Federal Studies* 9 (1):S1-214.

Bauer, J. ed. 1991. *Europa der Regionen. Aktuelle Dokumente zur Rolle und Zukunft der deutschen Länder im europäischen Integrationsprozeß*. Berlin.

Beutler, B., R. Bieber, J. Pipkorn and J. Streil. 1993. *Die Europäische Union. Rechtsordnung und Politik*, 4th ed. Baden-Baden: Nomos Publisher.

Birke, H.E. 1973. *Die deutschen Bundesländer in den Europäischen Gemeinschaften*. Berlin.

Börzel, T.A. 2002. "Föderative Staaten in einer entgrenzten Welt: Regionaler Standortwettbewerb oder gemeinsames Regieren jenseits des Nationalstaates?" in *Föderalismus: Analyse in entwicklungsgeschichtlicher und vergleichender Perspektive, PVS-Sonderheft 32/2001*, ed. A. Benz and G. Lehmbruch. Opladen: Westdeutscher Verlag, pp. 363-88.

Deeg, R. 1996. "Economic Globalization and the Shifting Boundaries of German Federalism," *Publius* 26 (1):27-52.

Gerster, F. 1993. "Die Europaminister-Konferenz der deutschen Länder: Aufgaben, Themen, Selbstverständnis," *Integration* 16:61-67.

Greenwood, J. 1997. *Representing Interests in the European Union*. Basingstoke: Macmillan.

Greiffenhagen, M. and S. Greiffenhagen, eds. 2002. *Handwörterbuch zur politischen Kultur der Bundesrepublik Deutschland*, 2d ed. Opladen: Westdeutscher Verlag.

Gresch, N. 1978. "Transnationale Parteienzusammenarbeit in *der EG*." Baden-Baden: Nomos Verlagsgesellschaft.

Große Hüttmann, M. 2002. "Die föderale Staatsform in der Krise? Die öffentliche Debatte um *'Cheques' and balances* im deutschen Föderalismus," in *Die deutschen Länder. Geschichte, Politik, Wirtschaft*, 2d ed., ed. H.-G. Wehling. Opladen: Leske & Budrich, pp. 289-311.

Hahn, O. 1986. "EG-Engagement der Länder: Lobbyismus oder Nebenaußenpolitik?" in *Die deutschen Länder und die Europäischen Gemeinschaften*, ed. Hrbek and Thaysen, pp. 105-10.

Hix, S. 1999. *The Political System of the European Union*. Basingstoke: Macmillan.

Hix, S. and C. Lord. 1997. *Political Parties in the European Union*. Basingstoke: Macmillan.

Hrbek, R. 1986. "Doppelte Politikverflechtung: Deutscher Föderalismus und europäische Integration. Die deutschen Länder im EG-Entscheidungsprozeß," in *Die deutschen Länder und die Europäischen Gemeinschaften*, ed. Hrbek and Thaysen, pp. 17-36.

——— 1992. "Die deutschen Länder vor den Herausforderungen der EG-Integration, " in *Föderalismus in der Bewährung*, ed. B. Vogel and G.H. Oettinger. Stuttgart: Kohlhammer Verlag, pp. 9-33.

——— 1994. "Das Subsidiaritätsprinzip in der Europäischen Union," in *Europäische Bildungspolitik und die Anforderungen des Subsidiaritätsprinzips*, ed. R. Hrbek. Baden-Baden: Nomos, pp. 9-20.

——— 1999. "The Effects of EU Integration on German Federalism," in *Recasting German Federalism*, ed. Jeffery, pp. 217-33.

——— 2001. "Die deutschen Länder und das Vertragswerk von Nizza," *Integration* 2:102-13.

——— 2002. "Europa," in *Handwörterbuch zur politischen Kultur der Bundesrepublik Deutschland*, ed. Greiffenhagen and Greiffenhagen.

Hrbek, R. and M. Große Hüttmann. 2002. "Von Nizza über Laeken zum Reform-Konvent: Die Rolle der Länder und Regionen in der Debatte zur Zukunft der Europäischen Union," in *Europäisches Zentrum für Föderalismus-Forschung*, ed. Jahrbuch des Föderalismus. Baden-Baden: Nomos, pp. 577-94.

Hrbek, R. and U. Thaysen, eds. 1986. *Die deutschen Länder und die Europäischen Gemeinschaften*, Baden-Baden: Nomos.

Hrbek, R. and S. Weyand. 1994. *Betrifft: Das Europa der Regionen*. München: Beck Verlag.

Hrbek, R. and W. Wessels, eds. 1984. *EG-Mitgliedschaft: ein vitales Interesse der Bundesrepublik Deutschland?* Bonn: Europa-Union Verlag.

Hooghe, L. and G. Marks. 2001. *Multi-Level Governance and European Integration*. Boulder: Rowman & Littlefield.

Jaspert, G. 1982. "Der Bundesrat und die europäische Integration," *Aus Politik und Zeitgeschichte* B12/82:17-32.

Jeffery, C. 1996. "Regional Information Offices in Brussels and Multi-Level Governance in the EU: UK-German Comparison," *Regional & Federal Studies* 6:183-203.

——— ed. 1999. *Recasting German Federalism*. London and New York: Pinter.

Johne, R. 2000. *Die deutschen Landtage im Entscheidungsprozeß der Europäischen Union*. Baden-Baden: Nomos.

Kilper, H. and R. Lhotta. 1996. *Föderalismus in der Bundesrepublik Deutschland*. Opladen: Leske & Budrich.

Kohler-Koch, B., ed. 1998. *Regieren in entgrenzten Räumen, PVS-Sonderheft 29/1998*. Opladen: Westdeutscher Verlag.

Kohler-Koch, B. and R. Eising, eds. 1999. *The Transformation of Governance in the European Union*. London: Routledge.

Laufer, H. and U. Münch. 1998. *Das föderative System der Bundesrepublik Deutschland*. Opladen: Leske & Budrich.

Lehmbruch, G. 2000. "Bundesstaatsreform als Sozialtechnologie? Pfadabhängigkeit und Veränderungsspielräume im deutschen Föderalismus," in *Europäisches Zentrum für Föderalismus-Forschung*, ed. Jahrbuch des Föderalismus. Baden-Baden: Nomos, pp. 71-93.

Lindberg, L.N. and St. A. Scheingold. 1970. *Europe's Would-Be Polity: Patterns of Change in the European Community*. Englewood Cliffs, NJ: Prentice-Hall.

Loughlin, J. 1996. "Representing Regions in Europe: The Committee of the Regions," *Regional & Federal Studies* 6:147-65.

Morawitz, R. 1981. *Die Zusammenarbeit von Bund und Ländern bei Vorhaben der Europäischen Gemeinschaft*. Bonn: Europa Union Verlag.

Oberthür, K. 1978. "Die Bundesländer im Entscheidungssystem der EG," *Integration* 1:58-65.

Oschatz, G.-B. and H. Risse. 1989. "Bundesrat und Europäische Gemeinschaften. Neue Verfahrensregeln der Bundesrats-Geschäftsordnung für EG-Vorlagen," *Die öffentliche Verwaltung* 42:509-19.

—— 1995. "Die Bundesregierung an der Kette der Länder? Zur europapolitischen Mitwirkung des Bundesrates," *Die öffentliche Verwaltung* 48:437-52.

Scharpf, F.W. 1985. "Die Politikverflechtungs-Falle: Europäische Integration und deutscher Föderalismus im Vergleich," *Politische Vierteljahresschrift* 4:323-56.

—— 1997. "Nötig, aber ausgeschlossen. Die Malaise der deutschen Politik," *Frankfurter Allgemeine Zeitung*. 5 June.

Scharpf, F.W., B. Reissert and F. Schnabel. 1976. *Politikverflechtung: Theorie und Empirie des kooperativen Föderalismus in der Bundesrepublik*. Kronberg/ Ts.: Scriptor Verlag.

Sekretariat des Bundesrates, ed. 1988. *Bundesrat und Europäische Gemeinschaften*. Dokumente, Bonn, pp. 428-34.

Straub, P. and R. Hrbek, eds. 1998. *Die europapolitische Rolle der Landes- und Regionalparlamente in der EU*. Baden-Baden: Nomos.

Sturm, R. and H. Pehle. 2001. *Das neue deutsche Regierungssystem. Die Europäisierung von Institutionen, Entscheidungsprozessen und Politikfeldern in der Bundesrepublik Deutschland*. Opladen: Leske & Budrich.

Thumfart, A. 2002. *Die politische Integration Ostdeutschlands*. Frankfurt am Main: Suhrkamp.

Wessels, W. 1986. "Es geht um Europafähigkeit," *Europäische Zeitung* 6:1.

—— 1992. "Staat und (westeuropäische) Integration. Die Fusionsthese," in *Die Integration Europas, PVS-Sonderheft 23/1992*, ed. M. Kreile. Opladen: Westdeutscher Verlag, pp. 36-61.

—— 1998. "Comitology: Fusion in Action. Politico-Administrative Trends in the EU System," *Journal of European Public Policy* 5(2): 209-34.

Contributors

BRIAN GALLIGAN, Professor of Political Science, University of Melbourne

LIESBET HOOGHE, Associate Professor of Political Science, University of North Carolina

RUDOLF HRBEK, Jean Monnet Chair, Institute of Political Science and European Center for Research on Federalism, University of Tübingen

JOHN KINCAID, Director, Robert B. and Helen S. Meyner Center for the Study of State and Local Government, Lafayette College

HARVEY LAZAR, Director, Institute of Intergovernmental Relations, Queen's University

RICHARD SIMEON, Professor, Department of Political Science and Faculty of Law, University of Toronto

MAHENDRA PRASAD SINGH, Professor of Political Science, University of Delhi

JÜRG STEINER, Professor of Political Science, University of Bern and University of North Carolina

NICO STEYTLER, Director, Community Law Centre, University of the Western Cape

HAMISH TELFORD, Department of Philosophy and Political Science, University College of the Fraser Valley, Abbotsford, British Columbia and Institute of Intergovernmental Relations, Queen's University

RONALD L. WATTS, Fellow, Institute of Intergovernmental Relations, Queen's University

Queen's Policy Studies
Recent Publications

The Queen's Policy Studies Series is dedicated to the exploration of major policy issues that confront governments in Canada and other western nations. McGill-Queen's University Press is the exclusive world representative and distributor of books in the series.

School of Policy Studies

Delicate Dances: Public Policy and the Nonprofit Sector, Kathy L. Brock (ed.), 2003
Paper ISBN 0-88911-953-8 Cloth ISBN 0-88911-955-4

Beyond the National Divide: Regional Dimensions of Industrial Relations, Mark Thompson, Joseph B. Rose and Anthony E. Smith (eds.), 2003
Paper ISBN 0-88911-963-5 Cloth ISBN 0-88911-965-1

The Nonprofit Sector in Interesting Times: Case Studies in a Changing Sector,
Kathy L. Brock and Keith G. Banting (eds.), 2003
Paper ISBN 0-88911-941-4 Cloth ISBN 0-88911-943-0

Clusters Old and New: The Transition to a Knowledge Economy in Canada's Regions,
David A. Wolfe (ed.), 2003   Paper ISBN 0-88911-959-7 Cloth ISBN 0-88911-961-9

Knowledge, Clusters and Regional Innovation: Economic Development in Canada, J. Adam Holbrook and David A. Wolfe (eds.), 2002
Paper ISBN 0-88911-919-8 Cloth ISBN 0-88911-917-1

Lessons of Everyday Law/Le droit du quotidien, Roderick Alexander Macdonald, 2002
Paper ISBN 0-88911-915-5 Cloth ISBN 0-88911-913-9

*Improving Connections Between Governments and Nonprofit and Voluntary Organizations:
Public Policy and the Third Sector,* Kathy L. Brock (ed.), 2002
Paper ISBN 0-88911-899-X Cloth ISBN 0-88911-907-4

Governing Food: Science, Safety and Trade, Peter W.B. Phillips and Robert Wolfe (eds.),
2001   Paper ISBN 0-88911-897-3 Cloth ISBN 0-88911-903-1

The Nonprofit Sector and Government in a New Century, Kathy L. Brock and Keith G.
Banting (eds.), 2001   Paper ISBN 0-88911-901-5 Cloth ISBN 0-88911-905-8

The Dynamics of Decentralization: Canadian Federalism and British Devolution, Trevor C.
Salmon and Michael Keating (eds.), 2001   ISBN 0-88911-895-7

Institute of Intergovernmental Relations

Canada: The State of the Federation 2001, vol. 15, *Canadian Political Culture(s) in
Transition,* Hamish Telford and Harvey Lazar (eds.), 2002
Paper ISBN 0-88911-863-9 Cloth ISBN 0-88911-851-5

Federalism, Democracy and Disability Policy in Canada, Alan Puttee (ed.), 2002
Paper ISBN 0-88911-855-8 Cloth ISBN 1-55339-001-6, ISBN 0-88911-845-0 (set)

Comparaison des régimes fédéraux, 2ᵉ éd., Ronald L. Watts, 2002
ISBN 1-55339-005-9

Health Policy and Federalism: A Comparative Perspective on Multi-Level Governance,
Keith G. Banting and Stan Corbett (eds.), 2001
Paper ISBN 0-88911-859-0 Cloth ISBN 1-55339-000-8, ISBN 0-88911-845-0 (set)

Disability and Federalism: Comparing Different Approaches to Full Participation,
David Cameron and Fraser Valentine (eds.), 2001
Paper ISBN 0-88911-857-4 Cloth ISBN 0-88911-867-1, ISBN 0-88911-845-0 (set)

Federalism, Democracy and Health Policy in Canada, Duane Adams (ed.), 2001
Paper ISBN 0-88911-853-1 Cloth ISBN 0-88911-865-5, ISBN 0-88911-845-0 (set)

John Deutsch Institute for the Study of Economic Policy

Framing Financial Structure in an Information Environment, Thomas J. Courchene and
Edwin H. Neave (eds.), Policy Forum Series no. 38, 2003
Paper ISBN 0-88911-950-3 Cloth ISBN 0-88911-948-1

*Towards Evidence-Based Policy for Canadian Education/Vers des politiques canadiennes
d'éducation fondées sur la recherche,* Patrice de Broucker and/et Arthur Sweetman (eds./dirs.),
2002 Paper ISBN 0-88911-946-5 Cloth ISBN 0-88911-944-9

*Money, Markets and Mobility: Celebrating the Ideas of Robert A. Mundell, Nobel Laureate
in Economic Sciences,* Thomas J. Courchene (ed.), 2002
Paper ISBN 0-88911-820-5 Cloth ISBN 0-88911-818-3

The State of Economics in Canada: Festschrift in Honour of David Slater,
Patrick Grady and Andrew Sharpe (eds.), 2001
Paper ISBN 0-88911-942-2 Cloth ISBN 0-88911-940-6

The 2000 Federal Budget: Retrospect and Prospect, Paul A.R. Hobson and
Thomas A. Wilson (eds.), Policy Forum Series no. 37, 2001
Paper ISBN 0-88911-816-7 Cloth ISBN 0-88911-814-0

Available from: McGill-Queen's University Press
c/o Georgetown Terminal Warehouses
34 Armstrong Avenue
Georgetown, Ontario L7G 4R9
Tel: (877) 864-8477
Fax: (877) 864-4272
E-mail: orders@gtwcanada.com

Institute of Intergovernmental Relations
Recent Publications

Political Science and Federalism: Seven Decades of Scholarly Engagement, Richard Simeon, 2000 Kenneth R. MacGregor Lecturer, 2002
ISBN 1-55339-004-0

The Spending Power in Federal Systems: A Comparative Study, Ronald L. Watts, 1999
ISBN 0-88911-829-9

Étude comparative du pouvoir de dépenser dans d'autres régimes fédéraux, Ronald L. Watts, 1999   ISBN 0-88911-831-0

Constitutional Patriation: The Lougheed-Lévesque Correspondence/Le rapatriement de la Constitution: La correspondance de Lougheed et Lévesque, with an Introduction by J. Peter Meekison/avec une introduction de J. Peter Meekison, 1999   ISBN 0-88911-833-7

Securing the Social Union: A Commentary on the Decentralized Approach, Steven A. Kennett, 1998   ISBN 0-88911-767-5

Working Paper Series

2003

1. *Too Many Cooks? Dealing with Climate Change in Canada* by Matt Jones, Bob Masterson and Doug Russell

2. *The Web of Life* by Elizabeth Dowdeswell

3. *Aboriginal Governance in the Canadian Federal State 2015* by Jay Kaufman and Florence Roberge

4. *Canada 2015: Globalization and the Future of Canada's Health and Health Care* by Michael Mendelson and Pamela Divinsky

5. *Implications for the International and Canadian Financial Services Industry and their Governance of Varying Future International Scenarios* by Edward P. Neufeld

6. *The Impact of Global and Regional Integration On Federal Systems Domestic Case Study-Agriculture and Agri-Foods* by W.M. Miner

7. *Federalism and the New Democratic Order. A Citizen and Process Perspective* by Thomas J. Courchene

8. *Understanding the impact of Intergovernmental relations on public health: Lessons from reform initiatives in the blood system and health surveillance* by Kumanan Wilson, Jennifer McCrea-Logie and Harvey Lazar

9. *Le Québec et l'intégration continentale: Les stratégies caractéristiques* by Nelson Michaud

2002

1. *Redistribution, Risk, and Incentives in Equalization: A Comparison of RTS and Macro Approaches* by Michael Smart, Department of Economics, University of Toronto

For a complete list of Working Papers, see the Institute of Intergovernmental Relations Web site at: www.iigr.ca. Working Papers can be downloaded from the Web site under the pull down menu "Research."

These publications are available from:
Institute of Intergovernmental Relations, Queen's University, Kingston, Ontario K7L 3N6
Tel: (613) 533-2080 / Fax: (613) 533-6868; E-mail: iigr@qsilver.queensu.ca